RAISING
CHICKENS

CYNTHIA HAYNES

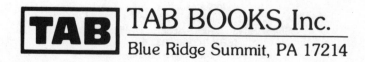
TAB BOOKS Inc.
Blue Ridge Summit, PA 17214

Debeaker, Super Debeaker, Super V Precision Debeaker, Dual Debeaker, and Beak-Heat-Treator Debeaker are registered trademarks of the Lyon Electric Company, Inc.

To my dad, who taught me to regard all Nature's creatures as essential—even daddy longlegs!

FIRST EDITION
FIRST PRINTING

Copyright © 1985 by Cynthia Haynes
Printed in the United States of America

Library of Congress Cataloging in Publication Data

Haynes, Cynthia.
Raising chickens.

Bibliography: p.
Includes index.
1. Chickens. I. Title.
SF487.H413   1985   636.5   85-17347
ISBN 0-8306-0963-6
ISBN 0-8306-1963-1 (pbk.)

Contents

Acknowledgments

Although there are many greatly appreciated companies and individuals not mentioned for the actual input they've contributed to the formation of this book, the following went beyond the call of duty—taking time from their daily routine to assist and help educate: Dr. William G. Bickert, Mr. and Mrs. Kenneth Cameron, Dean Hanke, Dr. Robert Ofoli, Dr. Allan P. Rahn, Larry W. Robinson, H.R. Schonhoff, Dr. L. Dwight Schwartz, C.B. Thayer, Dr. Robert Yeck, and Mr. and Mrs. Forrest Wilcox.

I'd also like to thank the many handlers who entrusted me with their questions. They provided me with the foundation from which this book was built.

Preface

More and more people are moving to country property with the idea of growing things to meet their own needs. While operating a small country hatchery and breeder farm for 8 years, I've found many of these people begin their country experience with chickens.

My business has enabled me to meet and talk with thousands of beginning and experienced poultry raisers. And, because we've never shipped chicks, every customer has been met face to face. This is how a hatchery operator gains insight to the many problems that plague poultry raisers. It's also a great way to acquire special tips and techniques from others in the poultry business. I also discovered that a multitude of people were in need of helpful suggestions and some were embarrassed to admit they were having poultry problems.

The homemaker who's been buying cut-up fryers at the grocery store is suddenly confronted with the need to cut up home-butchered chickens. City-bred parents might not be able to provide advice. Neighbors might not be familiar with chickens either because they own a dairy or truck farm. Newcomers might not want to seek advice for fear of looking as green as the pasture.

Raising chickens is an extension of self-sufficiency for most people. To be self-sufficient is to be proud of getting by without help. There's also a fear of ridicule when you feel you are asking a "foolish" question or a question "everybody" should know. With most people, I've found it breaks the ice when they're invited to ask questions. When raising chickens, there is no room for shame, ignorance, neglect, carelessness or supposed infallibility; these can be the first costly mistakes you can make.

I've seen experienced raisers continue to do the same wrong thing for years because they will not ask pertinent questions for fear of appearing inferior. It's a shame when beginners will not ask questions, but it's a total disgrace for experienced raisers if they're too embarrassed to ask. This is not totally the fault of the raisers. There are large agencies designed to help commercial poultry raiser. Generally, this is information smaller raisers—with 200 birds or less—can't possibly use because of economics and technicalities.

When you begin to ask questions and constantly receive information a small raiser can't use, are given the wrong information, or you are actually snickered at, frustration mounts. Soon you're not asking questions and perhaps you even give up on the venture. If you have an extension agent, university poultry specialist, or a veterinarian nearby that caters to small-scale poultry raisers, consider yourself fortunate because many small raisers are on their own.

Some of my ideas are from the old school of thought, and would be shunned by experts who have tunnel vision when it comes to small raisers. Their skills are designed to help large, modern commercial growers whose margins of profit depends on the efficiency of large, expensive equipment, machines, buildings, paid help, and supply and demand.

Because I declare no degree in modern poultry production, I need not be afraid of offending any university in what I teach. I believe experience is the best teacher. The second best source is information from an experienced person who has actually raised chickens, lost chickens, sold chickens, housed chickens, killed, and eaten chickens.

Situations arise where you need help immediately—not when "Mr. Expert" gets back from his vacation or when the office reopens on Monday. I dearly know the urgency, fear, and concern of the person who calls me at midnight because he claims his chicks "act funny."

After receiving your chicks from the hatchery, you can't always rely on obtaining information from the hatchery. Some companies are too busy to give you the run down on raising chicks. Because most hatcheries close in June, you might be unable to gain any information when you need it later.

Everyone who raises chickens is a beginner at sometime. Just as there is no formal training as to what to expect when raising children, the same is true of raising small flocks of chickens. My intention is not to make beginners look bad or for experienced raisers to look like know-it-alls, but to allow everyone to experience other's mistakes and accomplishments as a tool to be used in the learning process. It's through our own costly mistakes that we usually learn. What better and least costly method of learning could there be than to make use of this tool instead of wasting it?

Customers have frequently asked me for sources of publications that would help them throughout various phases of chicken raising. They wanted something to get them past the hobby stage and into the economics and realities of raising chickens. Embarrassed, I had to tell them there was no such book available (as if their venture was meaningless, senseless and unusual). So, I waited—along with many other handlers—for such a book, one neither too technical or too basic, to appear on the market. Feeling the needed information was long overdue, I gathered my research and ambition and took the needed time from other commitments to bring about this book.

My intention has been to make this the most completely detailed book to ever be published about chickens for small-scale raisers. You will find no information on raising other poultry in this book. This is done as a courtesy for fellow handlers who are eagerly beginning to incorporate all the details of raising chickens. My experience with beginners has shown that when brooding procedures, feeding practices, and management for various species are taught at the same time, there is sometimes much confusion and resultant losses.

All who raise chickens are chicken handlers because you must handle them physically, economically, and, above all wisely, to be successful. You're the manager of your own poultry enterprise. It's up to you to make it work. I sincerely hope this book helps all handlers to achieve this goal.

Raising chickens is a never-ending experience; there's always more you can learn. Even experienced handlers should find useful information throughout. Read it thoroughly and then keep it handy during each phase of your enterprise.

Introduction

This book is designed to bring the chicken enthusiast past the hobby stage and into the realities and economics of successfully raising chickens for food and fun. Any handler, from a 10-year-old child interested in 4-H to an old-timer raising 6 to 200 chickens, can use this information to fully understand chickens and the chicken-raising process.

Here is a complete guide to chickens with which to profitably follow through on brooding, purchasing, housing, raising, selling, butchering, selecting and using equipment, treating diseases, and producing, collecting, and storing an overabundance of eggs.

I'll further explain the "why's" behind all procedures instead of simply stating instructions and facts. Many methods are included only because they work and not because they are necessarily modern or what the industry proclaims to be ideal. New technologies and trends are included only if they are worthy for small-scale raisers to employ. Many modern methods involve using products or equipment unattainable to small-scale raisers because of large quantity packaging or quantity sales.

Explained are new technologies and trends that can be improvised to fit the small growers' needs. Most "trade secrets" are actually only helpful hints not known by all. Much such information is dispersed throughout the book under the guise of helpful suggestions that any handler can apply.

When raising chickens, there are no basics to get by on, and a beginner is not a beginner for long. After raising a brood of chicks for only a few days, basics will no longer suffice. A handler must be at least one step ahead of his chickens. He must be ready to handle any problem that arises or provide any needed change in management. If, for instance, a handler does not know the signs to look for between feather pulling and poor feathering, he cannot correctly remedy the situation. If he is unprepared to spot signs of egg eating in the flock, dozens of eggs can be lost without him knowing.

The following pages will help handlers to avoid and recognize problems and disease before they get out of hand. Handlers will be able to figure just how profitable their venture is (or isn't). You'll see how certain environments, equipment and management methods will bring rewards of better-producing chickens and savings in time and money (which are the main goals of any handler).

You'll find out why today's broilers cripple and how to eliminate the problem. Learn how to choose between watering, feeding, or warming chicks when you receive them and how to spot shipping stress and avoid losses.

All types of brooding are discussed, with a special chapter on battery brooding and what's been accomplished to date in regards to experimental solar brooding. Learn how to spot the most common ailment of chicks—coccidiosis—and how to treat it using ordinary household vinegar. Uncover the unspoken health hazards of which every handler should be aware.

In the following chapters, you'll also find many old-time methods and remedies that are still useful today and will save handlers money. You'll be informed about today's poultry equipment and discover how this contrasts with the ingenious equipment available to handlers over 60 years ago.

Small-scale raisers have been backed up against barriers, pushed into corners, and trampled on by commercialism. They often have been left with butchered dreams of profit. This book is intended to make those dreams become an economic reality.

Chapter 1

Choosing Your Chicks

You must decide on what you want out of chickens before you choose a breed. You might want just a good egg layer. Do you prefer brown eggs or white? Are you looking only for a good meat bird? Will you need to choose breeds with a quiet temperament?

Do you want something more colorful to look at than just a white chicken? For some people, the pleasure of caring for a family of chickens can be increased if there isn't monotony of color in the flock. Would you want to take care of your house if all the walls and furnishings were green?

What kind of housing do you have for your chickens? Is it ventilated, tight, roomy, or cold? Heavier breeds will do better in chillier quarters than lighter-weight breeds because of the amount of body fat they contain.

You might even decide that raising chicks is not for you. If so then subsequent chapters will help you purchase pullets and hens wisely. If after reading this book, you decide not to raise chickens, you will have saved money and headaches without the bother of experimenting with the venture.

BREEDS AND STRAINS

Chickens are usually purchased by selecting a breed of a particular strain or variety. Most beginners and experienced small poultry raisers are not concerned with the strain as long as the breed they choose fits the norm of production. It would be a rare poultry raiser who was not concerned with their chickens' production in laying eggs, rate of growth, and mortality as compared to his neighbor's chickens down the road.

Newcomers to poultry will most likely buy from a hatchery's catalog listing of available breeds using the descriptions provided as a guideline. Some large hatcheries also carry a variety and/or a strain of some breeds.

Most chicks hatcheries sell chicks that are from parent stock known to produce a good quantity of eggs or a fast rate of growth. Having a strain or tradename does not mean the birds are good. A tradename indicates only that person or company has produced a specific line within a breed or breeds. If you raised a particular breed of chicken for a few years and they reproduced chicks possessing common characteristics—good or bad— on a regular basis, you would have your own "strain" of that breed.

A good hatchery keeps itself informed as to the best strains developed. Work can be saved if you rely upon their judgement because repeated business from customers is dependent upon this.

You can check on production of various strains yourself by requesting a current copy of the *Random Sample Egg Production Tests* put out by state universities and the Agriculture of Canada, Poultry Division. See Appendix A for addresses. The publication is designed to provide poultrymen, hatcherymen, and breeders with a guide to performance of various egg production strains. It may look confusing, at first, but with careful study you'll soon learn which strains have the highest mortality, the largest eggs, and which are the most economical to raise.

Currently there is no such book available for meat-production birds because most large-scale tests were phased out about 12 years ago. There are still a few small, independent tests scattered throughout the country but information is almost unattainable. In addition, the availability of these meat strains will be limited to the types your hatchery supplies.

If all you're looking for is a good economical bird, you'll do good by simply choosing a well-known common breed or variety without knowing its strain. Dealing with a good reliable hatchery will assure you of this.

Sticking with a more common breed will assure you of finding better strains. The strain is everything. Good breeders ruthlessly cull out and dispose of chickens that just don't measure up. That makes for good strains.

Table 1-1 lists the more commonly known breeds. Any others might constitute a more hard-to-obtain breed such as show birds or birds that might not fare well. The fancy, uncommon breeds can always be tried later for fun.

One of the reasons fancy breeds cost so much is that most lay fewer eggs. Without much reproduction fewer birds are available. Hatcheries limit orders on these and call them "hard-to-find breeds."

If you want a fancy breed with a somewhat fairly good strain, your best bet would be to

Table 1-1. Breed Chart.

Breed	Mature Weight	Skin Color	Feather Color	Eggs Only	Egg Color	Meat Only	General Purpose
Bar. Plymouth Rock	7 1/2 9 1/2	yellow	bl/wh		brown		X
Black Australorp	6 1/2 8 1/2	white	black		brown		X
Buff Orpington	8 10	white	gol/buff		brown		X
New Hampshire	6 1/2 8	yellow	med/red		brown		X
Rhode Island Red	6 1/2 8 1/2	yellow	deep/red		brown		X
White Jersey Giant	10 13	yellow	white		brown		X
White Plymouth Rock	7 1/2 9 1/2	yellow	white		brown		X
Wyandotte-Silver Laced	6 1/2 8 1/2	yellow	white		brown		X
Black Minorca	7 1/2 9	white	black	X	white		
Brown Leghorn (Dark)	4 1/2 6	yellow	red/brn	X	white		
White Leghorn	4 1/2 6	yellow	white	X	white		
Broiler Strains- 8 wks.	4 1/2 5 1/2	yellow	white		brown	X	
Arbor Acres Hubbard Vantress	Can grow to 16 1/2	- - -	- - -		- - -	- - -	

purchase directly from an independent breeder who is associated with a club whose purpose is to better certain rare breeds. See Appendix A.

The size of chickens is commonly called either *standard* or *bantam* when referring to the breed. All chickens are considered to be standard size except for miniatures bred from the same breed or the miniatures that are a breed of their own (called bantams).

BROILER CROSSES

There are certain chickens grown strictly for meat purposes. They are referred to as *broiler crosses* or *broiler hybrids*. Breeders prefer to use the word *hybrids* for aesthetic reasons. These chickens will reach a weight of over 3 pounds at the end of 6 weeks growing time. An average heavy standard breed's weight will only be 1 1/2 pounds. See Fig. 1-1.

Cornish Rocks or Cornish Rock Crosses are

Fig. 1-1. From left to right, a 12-week-old White Jersey Giant cockerel, a 6-week-old Cornish Cross pullet and a 6-week-old Buff Orpington pullet.

first crosses between a Cornish rooster and a White Plymouth Rock hen; some are produced from two different strain crosses. See Fig. 1-2. The largest improvements in these birds—which changed the

Fig. 1-2. White Cornish rooster with White Plymouth Rock hen breeders (National Archives photograph).

3

Fig. 1-3. A top-notch Cornish rooster breeder (courtesy of Arbor Acres Farm, Inc.).

poultry industry—came in the mid 1960s. After years of tremendous research and work at genetically selecting and breeding for today's type of fast-growing broiler, great improvements were achieved with these birds. Independent companies and breeders continue to look for ways to improve.

Don't think you can easily breed for this type of bird. Besides years of research, every one of these companies protects the composition of their stock; some even carry patents. Only the company is entitled to know what strains make up their broiler stocks.

These top-secret holders might raise 10,000 cockerels for breeding purposes but will choose only the best 500 for actual breeding (Figs. 1-3 and 1-4). There may be 25,000 pullets raised, but only 3000 will be picked for breeding (Figs. 1-5 and 1-6) to produce hatching eggs for the creation of chicks. The results are plump, good-tasting birds that can be butchered at eight to ten weeks of age.

Contrary to what most people believe, these stock birds mate naturally and are not artificially inseminated. If you still want to try your hand at producing broiler chicks from your own stock, keep your breeding hens and roosters on a strict diet. Feed them only 70 percent of what they'll eat. Heavy breeders do not mate well.

If you're familiar with Cornish roosters, you'll know they have quite a problem breeding as it is. They are top heavy and fall off the backs of the hens quite a lot. You'll have to know what to look for in body type or you'll end up with a large amount of infertile eggs for setting.

Pure Cornish are very slow growers. I once purchased some top-priced White Cornish and Dark Cornish chicks from a well-known hatchery. The whites were butchering size by eight weeks. I knew they were growing too fast. They kept doubling the weight of the darks because they were crosses. Because of problems somewhere, the hatchery did not carry White Cornish chicks the following year.

Without getting into genetics, remember that crosses will not breed true. Once two purebreds are crossed, you should not cross these crosses because

Fig. 1-4. A selected Cornish rooster used for breeding purposes (courtesy of Hubbard Farms).

4

Fig. 1-5. Quality breeder pullets like this one are used to produce hatching eggs for fast-growing meat chicks (courtesy of Hubbard Farms).

To allow these birds to continue growing past 12 weeks of age is a waste of money because they mainly acquire fat from that point on. If allowed, they will grow past 16 pounds. The ideal dressed weight is 4 or 5 pounds at eight weeks.

The money saved raising broilers instead of another standard heavy breed for meat comes in the form of the labor saved in raising them to butchering size. Whereas broilers will eat twice as much feed as standard breeds, you'll be butchering them three months sooner than the standard heavy breed. Even if you're looking for economy, you should always figure your labor is worth something in dollars and cents.

Broilers, like other breeds, have defined characteristics and behavior patterns. They will grow faster than turkeys—which are considered fast growers—during the first twelve weeks of growing. It's been said that, "You can almost watch them grow!" They mature physically in that the rooster chicks can be heard crowing at three days of age!

the chicks produced will usually revert back and carry undesirable traits (unless you are trying for a new breed). Constant successions of breeding for so many years must produce birds that consistently are alike. Even in today's pure breeds, there are some "throwbacks" produced. Examples are a four-toed chicken when the breed should have five, a black feather here or there on a pure white breed, or long legs on a breed that should have short legs.

The traditional small cornish game hens, you see so commonly packaged in pairs in the grocery store, can be achieved by just butchering Cornish Rocks at four weeks of age (like the commercial companies do). A 2 pound live weight would give you the ideal cornish game hen dressed weight of 1 1/2 pounds.

Cornish crosses have a nice yellow skin so sought after in a broiler-roaster. When butchered, you might be surprised at the amount of fat these birds acquire around the pubic bones at eight weeks of age. That's what makes them such nice broilers; you can cook them without additional fat for basting.

Fig. 1-6. Years of careful selection are behind this pullet used on breeding farms that produce hatching eggs (courtesy of Arbor Acres Farm, Inc.).

Heat is not tolerated by the chicks as much as other breeds. Their temperature should be about five degrees lower than other chicks, which would call for a thermometer reading of 85° F. (29° C.) during the first week.

During the heat of summer, sometimes you can find broilers panting, with wings drooped, standing in their pan of drinking water. To correct this situation, you will need extra ventilation in the building (possibly a fan or shaded windows).

The hens will not lay well (if kept) unless you're able to keep them on a low-fat diet. This would be expensive because inexpensive grains produce fat. These birds are slow, clumsy, and lazy by nature, and the added fat will enhance this.

Leg problems are the main concern with broilers. As they reach a certain weight at four weeks of age, these birds will "go down on their legs" and cripple. These broilers have very fat, thick legs that are characteristic of Cornish. Their legs look as though they could support a baby elephant. Actually the unnaturally speeded growth of these birds calls for added vitamin D_3 to their diet. Vitamin D_3 is needed for absorption of calcium into the bones. With a vitamin D_3 deficiency, the leg bones will become soft and springy, unable to support the increasing body weight. This is a form of rickets. See the section on rickets in Chapter 4.

One of the broiler crosses, that doesn't seem to go down on their legs as much, has thinner, longer legs and is a bit slower growing. The desirous weight and wide breast conformation isn't there either. Most people do not want to watch these birds suffer as they hobble around to try and reach food and water.

Remedies have included using wood chips for litter, a higher ration of protein in the diet, less protein, a ration of oats, a diet of wheat, extra vitamins, and various drinking-water additives that contain medication. What is used and the results you get are what really counts when raising any fowl.

I can support no better preventative for this crippling than the *faithful* use of a good, fresh grade of cod liver oil added to the chicks' drinking water from their fifth day of life to the age of three or four weeks old. I say faithful use because people say

they are giving the oil, but they're only fooling themselves if they don't do it faithfully. Giving the oil earlier than five days of age or giving too much can result in loose droppings because it is a laxative. A good clue to the right amount to administer is to watch the droppings the first few days after it's been given. See Chapter 2.

A discarded plastic squeeze bottle makes a fine dispenser for the oil that is then squeezed in drops onto the drinking water surface daily. An amount of 4 ounces should be sufficient for 25 chicks during three to four weeks administration.

Do not place the oil in cone or jar waterers, but only on the surface of the chicks' water. Because oil floats, it will go to the top of the cone or jar's water surface and be made unavailable to the chicks. Placing the oil in feed or mash is not a good idea because the oil can turn rancid in feed that is not eaten quickly.

Although chickens will assimilate vitamin D from sunshine, the vitamin is diffused through panes of glass coming through windows. Do not count on this form of vitamin D for your chicks, but give them nature's substitute by using the oil at least to the age of three or four weeks. Going overboard and giving the oil within two weeks of butchering can lead to a fishy taste in the dressed birds.

The fantastic breeding of fast-growing Cornish Rock Cross broilers has made the caponizing cockerels economically obsolete. The practice of surgically removing the testicles from four-week-old cockerels (usually New Hampshire, Rhode Island Red, Plymouth Rock, and White Cornish) so the tender meat qualities of a broiler can be kept until the bird becomes larger at 9-12 months old (when uncaponized cockerels have toughened flesh) is just not an economical venture anymore.

EGG BREEDS

Egg breeds are usually described as being light in weight (up to 5 pounds), able to adjust to laying-cage confinement, and are suggested as laying more eggs than the heavies. Most are from the Mediterranean Class, with the White Faced Black Spanish

Fig. 1-7. Pair of White Faced Black Spanish (Artist, George E. Howard, Secretary of National Poultry and Pigeon Association, USDA circa 1896).

(Fig. 1-7) being the oldest in the class and the Black Minorca (Fig. 1-8) the largest. The Leghorn (Fig. 1-9) is the breed most commercial egg factories keep.

Light-weight egg breeds fit into the layer cages better than general-purpose breeds, but I can't say these flighty, nervous-acting birds adjust to the circumstances any better. As far as laying, heavy breeds can do just as good in egg production. Sometimes heavies, such as the Black Australorps, are crossed with Leghorns to gain production, stamina, and body type.

It's all in management. Any chicken fed a high fat, low protein diet will become fat and lazy in her endeavors to lay eggs. Furthermore, if the day comes when you decide you want to butcher lightweight hens, you'll be screaming "Where's the meat?" because there's almost as much bone as meat on these birds. Their increased activity also seems to toughen the meat. I've never found any sense in going through the trouble of butchering them. Some chickens crossed for egg production, such as Golden Comets, are heavier and can be stewed. It's the Leghorn type that cannot even be successfully stewed.

The egg breed's lighter weight also enables

Fig. 1-8. Black Minorca cockerel. (Artist, George E. Howard, Secretary of National Poultry and Pigeon Association, USDA circa 1896).

Fig. 1-9. Single-comb White Leghorn cock (Artist, George E. Howard, Secretary of National Poultry and Pigeon Association, USDA circa 1896).

Fig. 1-10. Blue Andalusian hen (Artist, George E. Howard, Secretary of National Poultry and Pigeon Association, USDA circa 1896).

GENERAL-PURPOSE BREEDS

General-purpose breeds are breeds that can be raised for both meat and eggs. They are also referred to as all-purpose and multi-purpose breeds. Such chickens are a good medium between the egg breeds and the broiler strains.

The rate of laying can be as good as the egg breeds. The most common, well-known, general-purpose breeds are brown egg layers. General purpose chicks will not grow as fast as a broiler cross. You'll have to wait 16 to 20 weeks to butcher them. Most will not have plump legs like your broilers, but rather long, meaty legs at that age.

General-purpose breeds can be used for reproduction of baby chicks whereas broilers can't. You can keep supplied with meat and egg birds for years by hatching their eggs. Broiler crosses will not breed true. The chicks from them will not be like the parent stock. Only true breeds, not crosses of breeds, will breed true to form.

General-purpose breeds can be butchered as stewing hens after their egg production declines whereas the exclusive egg breeds cannot. General-purpose breeds also tolerate heat better than broilers and cold better than egg-production chickens. There's a better array of feather colors in the general-purpose breed for a more colorful flock. Most have fairly quiet temperaments.

The more common general-purpose breeds have been around for years with time to develop

them to fly more readily than heavies. Lighter chickens create more dust (to be inhaled by you in the building) if not confined to cages. They are also more apt to fly over fences unless wings are clipped. See Chapters 2 and 7.

Lighter birds will not tolerate below-freezing temperatures. Therefore, they'll refuse to lay good and will spend most of their time on the roost trying to keep warm. Commercial egg factories keep a temperature of 40° F. (4.44° C.) or more in the building even if it is below zero outdoors (mainly through the use of the birds' heat as they're confined in the building).

The larger combs of your lightweights (Fig. 1-10) may frost, causing frozen combs in below freezing temperatures. Rose comb breeds (Fig. 1-11) do not frost as easily, but most have not been bred consistently for high production.

Egg breeds are fine if you plan on layer cage confinement or wing clipping, can tolerate their natural nervousness, can keep them in an above-freezing comfort range, and don't plan on butchering them.

Fig. 1-11. Pair of Silver Spangled Hamburgs (Artist, George E. Howard, Secretary of National Poultry and Pigeon Association, USDA circa 1896).

Fig. 1-12. White Plymouth Rock pullets (courtesy of Hubbard Farms).

better strains. These include many American Class breeds: White Plymouth Rock (Fig. 1-12), Barred Plymouth Rock (Fig. 1-13), New Hampshire, Rhode Island Red, Jersey Giant, and Wyandotte (Fig. 1-14 and Fig. 1-15).

The larger, general-purpose category includes breeds from the Asiatic Class: Cochins (Fig. 1-16), Brahmas (Fig. 1-17), and Langshans (Fig. 1-18).

Both Orpingtons and black Australorps, from the English Class, are fairly well-known, dual-

Fig. 1-13. Pair of Barred Plymouth Rocks (Artist, George E. Howard, Secretary of National Poultry and Pigeon Association, USDA circa 1896.

Fig. 1-14. Silver Laced Wyandotte cockerel (Artist, George E. Howard, Secretary of National Poultry and Pigeon Association, USDA circa 1896).

Fig. 1-15. Silver Laced Wyandotte pullet (Artist, George E. Howard, Secretary of National Poultry and Pigeon Association, USDA circa 1896).

purpose breeds. The Dorking (Fig. 1-19) is one of the lesser known but one of the most ancient of all breeds.

The Houdans (Fig. 1-20) is today considered a rare and fancy breed in the (French) Continental Class. Some 100 years ago, they were claimed to be the best for meat purposes and prolific layers of large white eggs.

If you do not care to separately purchase an egg breed for eggs and a broiler strain for meat, then the general-purpose breed is what you'll want. These are what most beginners choose. There is a large variety from which to choose.

KEEPING BANTAMS

There seems to be more good points going for Bantams than bad. Bantams take up little space, will lay eggs regularly, and require less feed and water. All this saves time and labor on your part. They brood easily, are almost always good mothers,

Fig. 1-16. Pair of Buff Cochins (Artist, George E. Howard, Secretary of National Poultry and Pigeon Association, USDA circa 1896).

Fig. 1-17. Pair of Light Brahmas (Artist, George E. Howard, Secretary of National Poultry and Pigeon Association, USDA circa 1896).

and they seem to enjoy attention and handling more than large breeds. Their friendliness makes them a delight to care for. See Fig. 1-21.

Bantams are usually about one fourth or one fifth the weight of standard breeds. Larger Bantams can be butchered if you choose. Their smallness makes them sometimes harder to work with while

dressing them out. They're usually cooked whole or in pieces as for stew.

A Bantam's egg can be as large as a graded small egg from the grocery store. It depends on the size of the breed you choose. In Bantams, the larger the bird, the larger the egg you'll get. That is not the case with standard breeds.

Bantams sometimes can seem as though they're fussy eaters when whole grain scratch feeds are fed to them. They have trouble eating some large grains and will sometimes take a preference to ground grains. There's no reason why your chicken raising should extend any further than a backyard flock of these miniatures if that's what you choose. See Fig. 1-21.

WHICH SEX?

Most chicks for practical purposes are bought as straight run (abbreviated as SR in chick catalogs). This is the same as unsexed. This means that as the chicks are hatched and placed in their box at the hatchery, you purchase *these* chicks as hatched. These will be both cockerels (males) and pullets (females). It's like grabbing a handful of candy where all the white ones would be the cockerels and all the pinks would be the pullets. Odds are that of

Fig. 1-18. Pair of Black Langshans (Artist, George E. Howard, Secretary of National Poultry and Pigeon Association, USDA circa 1896).

Fig. 1-19. Silver Gray Dorking cock (Artist, George E. Howard, Secretary of National Poultry and Pigeon Association, USDA circa 1896).

Fig. 1-20. Pair of Mottled Houdans (Artist, George E. Howard, Secretary of National Poultry and Pigeon Association, USDA circa 1896).

Fig. 1-21. About twice as many bantams can be housed and penned in the same area as for standard breeds.

the chicks hatched, half will be cockerels and half will be pullets.

You can buy straight-run chicks and keep the pullets for laying eggs and the cockerels for meat. Do this only with the heavy breeds. It's uneconomical to do this with light breeds such as Leghorns, because you can get more meat from a heavy breed than a light breed by feeding almost the same amount of feed to both. You'll have trouble finding the meat on most light breeds and the flavor won't be there because of their lack of body fat that they burn off.

Sexed chicks can also be purchased. This simply means that the chicks have been sorted out and the pullets and cockerels are separated at hatching time. You can buy either pullets or cockerels separately. These sexed pullets will cost more. The cockerels will cost less than the SR chicks, except in the case of Cornish Rock Broiler Crosses. In that case, cockerels will cost more because they are in demand for a heavy butchering bird (the cockerels get larger). The higher cost of pullets and the lower cost of cockerels will average out to the cost of SR chicks.

These chicks are sexed quickly at the hatchery by, of course, special chick sexors (most of which are Japanese). Because of the fine dexterity and feeling the Japanese are said to have in the tips of their fingers, they are employed to do delicate vent sexing at various hatcheries. Some independent sexors travel from hatchery to hatchery. It's been stated these sexors receive as much as $35 per hour. With a lighted magnifying glass strapped to their head they can sex one chick per second. A lot of egg breeds are sexed in this way, and accuracy can be 90 to 95 percent.

There are also "sex-linked" chicks whose sex can be determined by the color or rate of feathering. Genetics has enabled chickens, mainly broilers, to be feather sexed. Through special breeding there is a "criss cross inheritance" where females will show a rapid feathering in the length of the primary feathers of the wings. The parent stock must possess certain chromosomes for this to occur. This type of sexing is 99.99 percent accurate on day-old chicks and 90 accurate at the age of three

days when 10 percent of the males will begin to feather faster.

Sexing can also be accomplished when two certain breeds are crossed. The resulting chicks will hatch with cockerels of one color or defined marking and the pullets of another color or marking. Only certain breeds will produce these chicks.

If you want both meat and eggs from your birds, there are several ways you can proceed.

☐ Buy light-breed pullets bred just for their egg-laying capabilities and purchase heavy-breed cockerels for meat. This is the preferred method only if you can house the lighter-breed pullets in temperatures above freezing during winter. The light breeds don't fare well in northern winters. They become stressed from the cold and their egg production drops substantially. In this case, you're not ahead of the game.

☐ Buy straight-run chicks in the general-purpose, heavy-breed class. Just figure how many chickens you want for butchering in one year and how many you'll need for egg laying throughout the year. This is the easiest method. Add these two figures and purchase that amount (plus five extra per hundred for losses).

☐ Purchase excellent egg-laying pullets for your egg needs. Then purchase good meat birds as straight-run (either heavy general-purpose or the broiler crosses) stock.

☐ Or you obtain straight-run chicks in an excellent egg laying light breed. Sort them out later as they grow and dispose of the cockerels. It won't be worth the time and trouble butchering these cockerels but you might be able to sell them for a dollar apiece to make up for your feed cost in raising them. Keep in mind that you'll actually be raising the cockerels for nothing, but this might be the only way to purchase them. Then purchase a heavy breed straight-run for your meat. Either sex will be all right for butchering purposes in the heavy breed.

PERSONALITIES

After you've raised and tried different breeds, you'll

find personality traits vary within the breeds. Try to pick breeds with traits that will suit you. For instance, if you have a lot of noise and havoc around your place, flighty egg breeds might not do as well because they get upset easily. This affects egg-laying production or growth.

Because they are nervous acting, they can make some people nervous just caring for them. They might run and scream in front of you causing you to believe you've just stepped on one of them. They'll sometimes cluck for what seems like forever until you leave the building. It's difficult to use their clucking as a guide to imminent danger within the building. A faint breeze might have waved a cobweb above their heads. They'll also demand more attention when wintering in cold climates, and this can cause some people to feel "needed" too much by these birds.

The heavies might not be flighty but you might have to push them out of your way or step over them to avoid stepping on them. If you are lucky, you'll have just enough nervousness in your stock to cause them to jump out of your way when you enter.

Most heavies won't holler and run out of the nest—possibly breaking eggs in their excitement—when you reach under them looking for eggs. Most flighty birds will. Even the most experienced chicken raiser can be startled by the experience. It helps if you train yourself to collect the eggs in a certain fashion.

Chickens will alert each other to preying cats and hawks. The roosters will watch over their hens and sometimes attack their keeper at the slightest squawk from one of the hens. If you feel you can't handle this gallant behavior or if small children will be collecting eggs, don't keep any roosters past six months of age.

As spring approaches and love is in the air, your roosters will act "strange" as they begin their courting. With his head proudly held high, chest pushed outwards, and wings fanned toward the ground, the rooster will pursue the hen with a stomping jig. The hen will then either bob her head up and down, trying to avoid his advances, or immediately squat to the ground—spreading her wings outward. Of course she might squat as *you* approach her also. Don't worry—she has only taken a fond liking to you. Her instinct at this time is to act submissive to anybody she's acquainted with or trusts. Most of these submissive types will be the first with motherhood on their minds. Hens will act this way whether there's a rooster in the flock or not.

If you plan on floor raising the hens, expect more broodiness than with your caged layers. This you must deal with if you want a constant quantity of eggs and have not chosen breeds that are least likely to brood. Most egg breeds are fairly "non-broody."

Expect a few pecks on your hand as you reach under hens to collect eggs from floor-raised birds. Some hens do not like to be intruded upon as they are deeply occupied with the serious business of laying eggs.

Chickens have their own pecking order and will not let strange ones join their flock without getting to know them first. It's a good idea to raise all the birds you plan to keep together in a flock at one time. Otherwise you'll have to use precautions on placing them together. First the new chickens will have to be approximately the same size before you attempt to do this. Then they must be penned nearby where the new ones and first ones can see each other for a few weeks. A good idea is to let them mingle "accidentally" after the few weeks introductory period is up by leaving the pen doors open instead of placing them together on your own. If you do not take precautions, it's likely you'll find some of them pecked to death by the first residents.

"Birds of a feather flock together," as the old saying goes, is pretty much true with chickens. As you watch a flock of different breeds graze outdoors, you'll find the various breeds of one color seem to naturally hang around together. This would not be noticeable with penned birds. There's no need to be concerned with this. Birds of different colors can be kept together.

There are only two instances where there should be a concern over the color of the chickens' feathers. With a dark-feathered chicken after butchering, there will be some dark pigment oils left in the skin pores. The other factor is cannibalism by the white breeds.

It seems that the cannibalism is worse with the whites because every speck of dirt, grain, manure, or blood will show up on the white feathers much more readily than on dark-colored feathers. Because chickens peck at all small objects brought to their attention, the result is they peck at the small particles on the feathers of these white birds. Constant pecking at one area will draw blood, which in turn is also pecked at further and further. There are preventive measures for cannibalism in all colors of chickens. Don't be discouraged into not choosing white chickens at all. Cannibalism can pretty well be avoided under the right conditions. These are the main personality traits that should be thought about.

You'll find many other quirks about chickens as you raise them. Some personalities will stand out among others. The Bantam, for instance, might have you fooled into thinking he honestly won't eat unless you continue to hand feed him. Your "mean and aggressive" rooster might take off running with his tail dragging the ground if he thinks *you* might be after *him*. Chickens can be spoiled by the regular offering of treats. The flock will crowd at the pen door waiting for it. You can almost hear their command, "Give us our treat and then we'll get down to the business of laying!"

HOW MANY CHICKENS?

After choosing a breed or breeds of chickens, decide on how many and what sex you want. The amount will depend on many personal factors. Are your chickens going to be for eggs only? If so, will they be for your own use or do you plan on selling eggs for extra pocket money? Will you proudly be giving your home grown eggs away to family and friends?

A formula to use on figuring how many pullets (young female chickens) to keep is shown in Table 1-2. If there's a remainder, add one egg to your answer. In our example we'd have 11. The answer will be the average number of eggs per day you'll need for your weekly quota.

Now figure the chickens will be laying only 50 percent on their low days. This 50 percent would be a good average to figure for pullets that just start laying and older hens that are ready to peter out. With this percent figure you won't be short eggs. It's better to have too many than not enough. The extras can be kept refrigerated for up to one month, waterglassed, or scrambled and frozen. Because 50 percent means approximately half of your chickens are doing their job, you would need twice as many hens to fill your egg quota. In our example, that would be 22 pullets (11 × 2 = 22).

If you want chickens only for eggs, then purchase sexed pullets and figure 5 percent extra chicks to cover any losses you encounter. In our example, that would be 23 total pullets (22 × .05 = 1.10 extra). If you are unsure of your chick-raising abilities, you might want to include a few more. You might want 25 total pullets.

If you order straight-run (which includes pullets and cockerels), you'll have to figure on ordering twice as many chickens as the pullets you figure

Table 1-2. Pullet Formula.

	Example:
How many eggs would your family consume in one week?.	28
How many would be used in one week for cooking purposes only (pancakes, cakes, dumplings, etc.)?.	8
How many would you sell per week?.	24
How many might you give away per week?.	12
Add these figures to get total.	72
Now divide 7 days into your total. Our example: 72 ÷ 7 = 10 with remainder of 2.	

you need. That would bring our example figure up to 50 chickens total.

Figuring Cornish Rock Crosses is easy. Just order the number you plan on butchering and add 5 percent for losses. The pullets in a straight-run in these crosses will make just as good a butchering carcass as the cockerels. You can order all cockerels if you prefer, but you're not that much ahead doing it this way because the cockerels cost more to begin with in these strains and don't grow that much larger than the pullets unless you keep them past the age of eight weeks old. After that time they get more leggy than anything and just acquire more fat. Cockerels will also consume more feed, and therefore ultimately cost more to raise.

If your chicks are going to be sent to you through the mail, you'll have to order at least 20 to 25 chicks. The smallest boxes made for shipping chicks safely holds 25 average-size chicks. The 25 chicks in this size box will create enough body heat from the chicks to keep them alive and comfortable during transit. Any fewer chicks (except during extremely hot weather) would jeopardize the lives of the chicks. The amount of body heat generated by the babies would not be the needed 90 to 95 degrees Fahrenheit (32.22-35 degrees C.). They would get chilled and either die soon or will be stressed. Stressed chicks either die shortly after you receive them or they'll take longer to perk up and grow.

PURCHASE OR HATCH

It's entirely your choice to purchase or hatch chicks. I can only give the pros and cons as to the economy involved with both.

Purchasing chicks already hatched from a good company has its merits. A good, reliable hatchery sells chicks from pullorum free and tested flocks. There isn't much pullorum anymore, but if you're going to put out the money anyhow for quality chicks you might as well make sure the stock they come from has been tested.

Years ago, pullorum disease was formerly called bacillary white diarrhea. It's a very small organism that infects the ovary of the hen. It has also been found in the yolk sac and intestinal tract of chicks.

The problem begins when chicks recover from the disease and retain the organism in their bodies; the disease situates itself in the active ovary. These hens are then carriers. Ovaries of an infected hen contain yolks that are angular in shape, shrunken, hard, and discolored dark brown or greenish. Eggs laid by these hens become infected and hatch infected chicks. Infected chicks infect others and so on.

Adult hens show no external symptoms but infected chicks show symptoms four to 10 days later. Signs include drowsiness, squeaky chirps uttered, and fluffed-up down. The vent might be smeared with fecal matter.

A bleeder loop and a bottle of antigen can be purchased for testing, but I do not recommend doing it yourself unless you have over 200 birds. The smallest bottle of antigen with the purchase of a bleeder loop is for 1,000 birds. The cost will be well over $30, it's very time-consuming, and you must be experienced in bleeding the birds, handling the stained antigen mixture, and knowing what to look for when the two are mixed. Label precautions should always be followed.

If you purchase chicks, you can try various strains and breeds and get some guarantee (which varies from hatchery to hatchery) on them. Also, it's almost as exciting as getting a birthday gift when you receive your chicks in the mail or go to pick them up. You'll know what I mean if you ever went somewhere to pick out a brand new puppy.

Of course it's equally satisfying to hatch your own chicks if you can do it successfully. If none of your eggs hatch, it's also equally frustrating! A persistent and good researcher can find out what went wrong and persist until chicks are obtained from 80 percent of the set eggs. By hatching you can produce your very own strains and crosses with very mixed results. Plan on crossing purebred chickens only one time for best results. A chicken that is already a cross and is then crossed again usually produces chicks that are not any better than the parent stock—and probably less than desired.

Daughters can be bred with the father but not

sons to mother to set good traits. A new blood line introduced into the flock at least every two years would mean obtaining new roosters. New hens could be purchased but this would not be very economical. You can hatch your own chicks for years if you like and never have to purchase more than a few new roosters.

Prue breeds are kept for hatching. You can cross two different breeds, but be prepared to also keep a supply of purebred chicks on hand so they can be crossed again two years later when you renew your flock. Only a few purebred chickens are necessary in order to accomplish this. Because your hatching eggs can be stored for up to two weeks in a 50-degree Fahrenheit (10 degree C.) temperature (a damp, cool basement is great) you can use Table 1-2 to figure the amount of hens to keep to set so many eggs.

For instance, if you can expect an 80 percent hatch and want 100 chicks from one setting, you'll need 18 hens in order for you to collect the 125 needed eggs in two weeks time. If you make two settings, you'll only need nine hens; three settings will require six hens, etc.

If different hatches will be brooded together, take this into consideration because it will be harder to introduce day-old chicks into a brooder that contains three week old chicks. As long as there's only two weeks difference in age, there is no need for extra worry. They can be put together.

It's surprising but each egg you collect is worth at least 25 cents if you're looking at the money side of hatching your own. You'll soon be screaming at the kids each time they accidentally break one. Of course, if you break one make sure nobody knows.

To purchase a new incubator is unwise if you don't plan on hatching many chicks because its resale price would drastically drop once purchased. You'd have to hatch at least 300 chicks in a $100 incubator to honestly be able to say you're producing the chicks less expensively than if you bought them. By taking the price of a certain quantity of chicks you'd normally buy, continue to add this figure until it equals that of the purchase price of the incubator and operation costs. You'll soon find how many chicks would have to be

hatched for the incubator to pay for itself.

It's generally less expensive and makes better sense to look for a second-hand incubator. Most are easy to fix if broke. Forced air fan types have motors that can cost a lot if they need to be replaced. But wafers, snap switches, and heating coils on smaller incubators are easy and inexpensive to repair.

The use of broody hens for hatching is fine if there are enough broodies to keep you in chicks. This can't always be determined. There might be only two brood hens (clucks) out of a flock of 100. It's interesting but small flocks generally have more broody hens because they're cared for slightly different. At times, broodiness seems to be catchy. If you continue to keep the clucks for a couple of years then there might be enough to hatch a large number of chicks in one season. Give each one a dozen eggs to sit on and expect eight to 10 to hatch from good, fertile eggs. If 100 chicks are needed, you'll have to have nine hens for this method because the hens will not hatch over and over again in one season. A hen will only raise one brood per season.

Muscovey hens make very good setters too, but care will have to be taken near pans of drinking water because the chicks will follow close to their mother and get wet or drown as she drinks. The problem can't be solved with a chick waterer because the mother will be unable to rinse out her nostrils (as ducks should and must do) to keep them free of mud and debris.

It's really best to take these duck-hatched chicks away from their mother and brood them yourself. The fascination you can get from watching chicks as they peep and peck their way out of their shell can be a joy. See Fig. 1-22.

HOW TO PURCHASE CHICKS

Be wary and wise about hatcheries that advertise: Surplus Cockerels for Fryers, Assorted Surplus Chicks, Super Cockerel Specials, Fryer Specials, Barbecue Specials, Early Season Bargains, Super Cross Fryers, Assorted Chick Bargain, etc. These could turn out to be culls or light-breed cockerels

Fig. 1-22. The chicks in the upper hatching trays of this older type of Jamesway incubator are fairly dry, and most can now be placed in a brooder.

that will never grow beyond 2 1/2 pounds. Read between the lines. If they specifically say you'll receive heavy breeds in these specials, then it's fair to say the deal is a good one. If not you'll be disappointed.

Some people fall for these ads because the price is so appealing. There are no deals in the chick business. These surplus chicks, if not bought by unwary consumers, get ground up into fertilizer or livestock feed as a source of protein.

The same goes for "Free Chicks" given out as promotional devices to get consumers to buy livestock feed at feed stores and grain elevators. When "Free Chicks" are advertised and the advertisement does not specify heavy breed chicks, telephone the store making the offer and ask what breed chicks are being given out whether they're heavy or light breed, and the total number to be given out. They will truthfully tell you if they want your future business.

There is definitely a season to buy chicks and for good reason. Early hatched chicks grow faster, mature sooner, and get larger. Late-hatched chicks

of July, August, or September will grow slow, mature slower, and be slightly undersized. The weather, being cooler and damper in early spring, will bring the chicks into better and faster feathering so brooders may be eliminated sooner. As it gets cooler towards the end of summer, late-hatched chicks usually require extra brooding.

Because you'll want the chicks to be at least three months of age by the time night temperatures drop below 50 degrees (10 degrees C.) in colder climates, this would mean obtaining the chicks no later than the middle of June.

Most people want to butcher before winter or want winter-laid eggs when egg prices are high in the stores. This, too, would require spring-hatched chicks. There's a saying: "April chicks, September eggs." If you want egg production by fall, you'll have to start spring chicks.

Although I believe the best layers are produced in the very, very early hatches and very late hatches, for brooding economy and efficiency they should be started just as soon as the weather settles down and is mild.

18

FINDING CHICK SOURCES

Sometimes finding chicks can seem to be a problem all its own. It's just a matter of knowing where and when to look. You can check your local newspaper or one published further out in the country. Area hatcheries sometimes advertise in local papers with a block ad or in the classifieds under a livestock type of listing.

Feed stores or grain elevators can be a source for chicks, but remember they are middlemen and usually charge a higher price. They can be fine if you only plan on obtaining a few chicks. Don't be afraid to inquire as to where the chicks came from, if they're guaranteed, are from pullorum-free stock, and what the breed or breeds they carry are good for.

There are some poultry magazines, gardening and health magazines plus miscellaneous periodicals that sometimes have advertisements by hatcheries. The United States Department of Agriculture publishes a directory of participants belonging to the National Poultry Improvement Plan (NPIP). Participants are listed and meet the specific requirements for a "U.S. Pullorum-Typhoid Clean" classification. Some of the listed hatcheries only sell wholesale to companies (usually by contract). With the directory, you can check on further testing a hatchery engages in, their hatching egg capacity (if you want to know just how large or small the company is), and what breeds and strains they hatch that are pullorum-clean. The NPIP began operating in 1935 in an effort to improve poultry, poultry products, and hatcheries. Just because a hatchery is not listed in the directory does not mean the hatchery is not tested. They might be listed under another name or in cooperation with another. To find out for sure if the hatchery sells retail, contact the representative of the individual state listings.

Word of mouth might also provide you a source of chicks. Ask around. Feed stores, neighbors, farmers, service stations, phone books, newspaper offices, and farm equipment sales are all likely places to try. If you're a newcomer to the area, you might not know there is a hatchery just 10 miles away.

SIGHT SEXING

I call the following my own special way of sexing.

Fig. 1-23. The chick pointed out on the left is a pullet. The one on the right is a cockerel.

Because I never was concerned about selling sexed chicks at our small country hatchery—we'd be left with a bunch of cockerels that are harder to dispose of—I never got that enthused about learning how to vent sex. There are books available to show you how and explain the differences to look for between the sexes. I've found an easier way which works fine for me and with a little practice should work for you too.

You would think after hatching hundreds or thousands of baby chicks that they would all begin to look the same after a while. The opposite is true. Instead, you begin to *really* start looking at them. You start to think there just has to be something different behind that red, black, yellow, white, or gold puffball of down. Begin to look at them individually, instead of as a whole, the way you look at one single flower instead of the whole bouquet. You'll soon spot differences in the head shape and expression on your chicks.

First hold up a chick in each hand with the side of their heads facing you. Making sure their eyes stay open by gently shaking them, first look for differences in the shape of the top of the heads. A cockerel chick will have a deeper forehead with the very top of his head looking rounder and larger.

Looking at his eye, he'll have a "mean" look about him. Pullets will have a lower, sleeker looking head on top with a much "sweeter" look to their face. If you can't see a difference, hold up a different chick because you might be holding two of the same sex. This sight sexing must be done within two days of age, and the sooner the better. After that time they all mysteriously begin to look the same. This is a fairly accurate method once you get the hang of it.

I'm constantly laughed at about using this method of sexing. "You've got to be kidding! You actually think the roosters look mean and the hens look sweet, huh? Let me take a look."

What is used and the results you get are what really counts when raising any fowl. You've probably heard of the ball and string method. It's the same one used on pregnant women. Then there's the wing flapping method I came across down South. A bit cruel but they swear it works. By holding the chick's head only, watch for the wings to flap. If the wings don't flap it's a pullet—or was it a rooster? Anyway, I can only relate my experiences in handling so many chicks with a personal, noncommercial touch. The method I employ works. Try it!

Chapter 2

Management

My research has found that today's concepts of chicken raising are similar to those practiced over a half a century ago. The chickens' basic needs were known even then. Far more attention was aimed at the profitable aspects of poultry keeping. Commercial flocks, farm flocks, and backyard flocks were all treated equally when the economics of successfully raising chickens was analyzed.

Long ago there were many companies interested in helping small flock owners. Poultry-equipment companies were springing up all over the country. Since then many companies have gone by the wayside or have diversified by manufacturing other types of agricultural equipment. Very few of these original companies exist today, and even fewer are beginning new operations.

By taking a nostalgic look back in time, a small scale raiser will find many great and imaginative ideas still available.

One company still going strong is the Warner Corporation in North Manchester, Indiana. The president of The Warner Corporation is Hank R. Schonhoff. Previously employed as general sales manager at the Brower Company for 30 years, Schonhoff has experienced many years of changes in the poultry equipment industry.

Mr. Schonhoff says, "Mr. Boyd Warner started the Warner Brooder Company in a little office building in North Manchester in 1936. He started making brooders similar to the ones shown. The business grew until World War II when a lot of production was turned over to the war effort."

"After the war," says Schonhoff, "Warner branched out from poultry into hog and turkey equipment. A rectangular turkey feeder was a take off of the rectangular hog feeders. These were sold a few years and than a round hog feeder and round turkey feeder was developed. At one time, Warner was the largest manufacturer of round turkey feeders in the industry. When I traveled Missouri, for the Brower Manufacturing Company in the late '40s, '50s, and '60s, Warner was my biggest competition on turkey feeders."

"Mr. Boyd Warner had two other partners," says Schonhoff. "They conducted a very successful business until the mid '60s when they got up to retirement age. In 1966, they sold the Warner Brooder Company to S & T Industries of Louisville, Kentucky. Since 1983, the Warner Corporation has been owned by C & H Capital Corporation, also of Louisville. C & H owns about eleven different companies."

Schonhoff further explains: "In the ag industry, since the depressions in the mid '30s, there has always been peaks and valleys depending on supply and demand. Warner has diversified, and in addition to making agricultural equipment also makes some jobbed items for specialized customers and fireplace accessory items for one of our sister companies."

In the mid '50s Warner had one of the only battery brooders that contained the heating unit in the center of the brooder, leaving 4 sides from which chicks could have access to feed and water.

The James Manufacturing Company, makers of Jamesway products, had their beginning in 1905 on the dairy farm of D. D. James, near Wales, Wisconsin. Here, a new kind of patented cow stanchion was made in a small blacksmith shop. It was the start of a large livestock equipment business that included many innovated ideas in poultry equipment.

On November 6, the following year, D. D. James, his son W.D. James, and John Olson, set up a small shop in Fort Atkinson, Wisconsin. The company was headed by W. D. James from 1921 until his death in 1948.

1922. Poultrymen saw for the first time a line of mature flock equipment made of metal such as feeders, waterers and nests introduced by Jamesway.

1923. Another first for Jamesway was the introduction of commercial poultry house ventilation. This included the use of insulation in properly designed houses.

1925. Jamesway brought out a line of coal-burning brooder stoves, following through in the next 3 years with batteries for all ages of poultry. Included also at this time was a round prefab brooder house for 200 to 500 baby chicks or 40 hens. It weighed 1060 pounds without floor and was shipped "ready cut" to be erected with four six-light, steel-sash, transom-ventilating windows for sunlight. The walls were made of insulation board and damp proofed with gray enamel. The inside diameter was 11 feet 5 inches (104 sq. ft.).

1927. After experimental work on an "arch type" poultry house, Jamesway manufactured arches, windows, ventilation, and heating systems that could be installed in arch buildings according to Jamesway building plans. The development of this building was so new and promising, 125 representatives from leading farm publications from all over the nation met together for the first time at the unveiling of the first structure of this kind.

During the depression years of the early '30s, the Iron Clad line of metal barns, silos, hay keepers, corn cribs, grain bins, hog and poultry houses, and electric fan ventilation were developed.

The next few years brought brooder stoves heated with wood, oil, electricity, and gas. World War II drastically reduced farm equipment factory production. Like other industries, Jamesway turned to building war goods.

The war also brought limitations on raw materials that forced the company to drop the Iron Clad Line except for grain bins used for government storage.

1948. Jamesway acquired the Reliable Poultry Company's line of poultry equipment manufactured in Los Angeles, California.

1950. The first Jamesway Mechanical Poultry Feeder was put on the market at a time when farm labor became short.

Butler Manufacturing, founded in 1901, began with the manufacture of steel livestock watering tanks. In 1964, the company purchased operating assets of James Manufacturing Company, which then became a subsidiary of Butler. Today the company's main interest is in the manufacture of dairy equipment.

Most companies were sold and resold throughout the years. The largest "family owned" poultry equipment business in the United States is the Kuhl (pronounced cool) Corporation, Flemington, New Jersey. In 1907, Paul H. Kuhl started selling poultry equipment as a winter sideline from farming.

Most handlers, today, are familiar with the "Mother Hen Brooder" that the Brower Manufacturing Company, Inc. of Quincy, Illinois has manufactured to keep in line with other equipment for small-scale raisers.

W. J. Brower started the one-man, one-item business in a small rented area in Quincy in 1922. Factory operations began in 1933. Brower catered to small flocks. His sons, B. J. and Leonard, later followed in his footsteps.

With the acquisition of the H. M. Sheer Company in 1939, and the Mit-Shell Company in 1940, the company now has worldwide distribution, with warehouses throughout the United States and in many foreign countries.

In 1981, the company and it's name were sold to a venture capitalist group out of Chicago.

As you can see, the poultry equipment industry has changed considerably. Where small-scale equipment was the mainstay of these companies years ago, the commercialization of chickens has led these companies to follow the path of progress and economics.

While this progress has been a boon to commercial raisers, the small-scale raiser has been left with a choice of only the bare essentials of equipment from a past era. Poultry equipment was actively and creatively displayed so handlers could see a company's wares. Gone are the feed hoppers with feed-saver pans. The space-saver wall feeders complete with roosts. It's been years since a covered chick feeder has been made that definately keeps feed from being walked upon by chicks.

How about the self-cleaning nests or the trap nests inserts? Trap nest inserts are available today, but I find it amazing how culling was promoted back in 1922 to separate "the producers from the boarders, the earners from the eaters," as Jamesway put it.

Warner's Colony Nest of the '50s was a popular item. Many handlers found these dark nests to be ideal in preventing egg eating.

The Jamesway Poultry Dusting Box of 1922 contained a glass top that allowed chickens access to a sunny location outside their house in which to dust away parasites.

How about the ingenious 8-gallon Jamesway waterer heated by a kerosene container below. One was equipped with a top that could be inverted and used as a funnel for water filling. An insulated 2-gallon waterer, shaped like a drum, was easy to fill.

A steel, 3-bushel feed bin that hung on the wall was said by Jamesway to be "good insurance against the depredations of rats and mice."

Jamesway also claimed "green sprouts were necessary for big winter egg production, being easily digested and containing an abundance of the vital elements called *vitamines.*" The Jamesway Grain Sprouter Trays and Cabinets, either open or enclosed, had a kerosene lamp to provide warmth for sprouting.

An Oats Germinator consisted of five 2-foot-long cans that were rotated by a crank.

Many small handlers still prefer to use dropping boards, but what do we use to scrape them with? Usually a homemade scraper is rigged up. In 1922 a specially designed scraper was available through Jamesway.

Jamesway designed complete poultry houses for customers and even manufactured some of the materials. Sheets of insulation and steel columns made of seamless, high-pressure boiler tubes were "straight and clean as a new gun barrel," said the company. They were available for all poultry-men and made specifically for chicken houses.

Jamesway galvanized ventilated Brood Coops allowed chicks access outdoor greens, yet confined mother hen inside so she could not take chicks wandering.

There were trough and round automatic waterers as early as 1932. Designed to stand high off the ground, the surrounding perches kept hens "at the proper distance from drinking pans, overcoming much billing of water and wet, dripping wattles" and contamination of water as a result of hens scratching litter into them.

Let's face it, chickens are energetic in their

scratching for feed. It can be a challenge just to try to keep litter out of water pans. Today's raisers would benefit from watering systems such as these.

Feeder perches were built 20 inches high to prevent vent picking while birds were busy eating.

Chickens love variety in their food. The Jamesway Cafeteria Feeder gave handlers the privilege of providing the variety. The large feeder held 100 pounds of dry mash, 15 pounds of grit, 5 pounds of charcoal, 99 pounds of scrap, and 15 pounds of oyster shells—all in one compartmented unit. It provided teeter-totter perches that would joggle the fresh feed down as the bird jumped upon the perch to feed. Now that's really self-feeding!

Did you ever wonder what trouble you'd have to go through if nests couldn't be attached to your building walls? Suppose a handler wanted the nests hung in the middle of the poultry house or perhaps where open-backed nests could not be hung over bare studded walls because eggs would roll from them. Jamesway took care of that in 1932 with Metal Backs and Standards.

Metal nests were manufactured for *every* size flock and designed for any size or shape building. There were nests only 25 1/2 inches wide (3 holes high and only 2 wide). A complete nest could be had with only 3 holes for very small flocks to as many as 15 holes for a large flock.

Jamesway's wood-heated brooder provided an "Air-Moistener Pan" along with an ash pan so chicks would not be subjected to the hot, parched, air that dries up lung tissues and membranes. By removing the brooder's hover top, it could be placed down inside the Warm Air Circulator for winter use to keep hens warm (thereby obtaining more winter eggs).

There were canopy brooders only 21 inches wide for as small a capacity as 10 to 50 chicks.

Mite Proof Roost Supports, made by Jamesway, consisted for cast-iron oil cups attached between walls and roosts. The cups, when filled with coal tar, kerosene or oil, were said by Jamesway to prevent mites from reaching roosts. This would seem to work for the red chicken mite, bed bugs, and fowl ticks because they are only on the birds feeding at night.

Also used were 3-quart, glazed stoneware buttermilk feeders. Because buttermilk contains acid, these acid-proof containers were a must. Buttermilk was said by many poultrymen to increase the broilers' appetites and was used for growth and fattening.

Before the 1900s, market birds were fattened with milk products. These birds were called "milk-fed" chickens. This industry brought large numbers of young chickens to special fattening farms where they were held in crates and fed skim milk beef fat, various grains, and coarse sand for digestion. The chickens were kept for 8 to 10 days on this high-fat diet that supposedly increased their weight by about 25 percent. They were immediately dressed and sold after this confinement. There were few problems encountered keeping these older birds confined for this short period.

The problem began when the brooding of chicks was attempted. The birds would become crippled if left in this type of confinement longer than three weeks. Because the cause was not known at that time, battery brooding for chicks was not used much at first. About 1930, the cause of the crippling was found to be Vitamin D and calcium deficiencies, which induce rickets.

Vitamin D was found to be abundant in cod liver oil. With this fact at hand, about 30 firms began to manufacturer battery brooders. Hatcheries began to purchase battery brooders to hold and sell surplus chicks. Growers began using the brooders to raise chicks.

Although battery brooding really became the vogue in the 1930s, ideas were patented as far back as the 1900s. These early brooders were oddities compared to today's manufactured brooders. Not all had heat; they were simply placed in warm rooms. Some were heated by hot water pipes or forced, heated air and some contained their own humidifier.

There were some that were so self-contained that they had a door the handler walked through, which led to a small isle between rows of stacked brooders. They were not made for small-scale raisers but mainly for the commercial industry as most were monstrosities constructed of heavy wood and metal.

There were brooders measuring 19 feet by almost 11 feet with a capacity for 9000 chicks. The smallest brooders were 25 inches by 45 inches. They were compartments set into a frame that held 10 brooders of this size. Each of these smaller brooders could be operated independently of each other.

Probably the most decorative looking brooder was one made by the American Incubator Manufacturing Company. Constructed of wood with metal pans and wire floors, it resembled wooden spindled chicken crates stacked one on top of each other. The heat was supplied by hot water pipes running through the brooders, which were heated by a hot water tank.

As with every new innovation, manufacturers tried to outdo each other and incorporated all kinds of ideas into their systems. The main ideas behind these brooders—wire floors, removable dropping pans, attached feeders, and waterers and heat source be provided—always remained.

Battery brooding has always been an expensive system to set up commercially, and this has curbed it's use for many growers. On a small-scale, these brooders can pay for themselves quickly.

The battery brooders manufactured long ago would not operate properly in a room having a temperature of less than 60 or 70 degrees F. Fahrenheit (15.55 or 21.11 degrees C.). The same is true of battery brooders manufactured today.

If it weren't for Vitamin D and a chicken contest promoted by a well known chain store during the late 1940s to the mid 1950s, we might still be without Cornish Rock Cross broilers. But I would venture a guess that the small-scale poultry raisers today might be more pampered with information and ingenious ideas for equipment.

Once you get your chicks home you're on your own. You are responsible for their life, living conditions, and death. Without you to provide for their needs and to do a great deal of thinking for them, the chicks would soon perish. They feel only what nature has allowed them to sense during the early days of their life: heat, cold, pain, hunger, and fright. You must know what chicks need for comfort, how to furnish these needs, and when.

Chicks are *brooded* until they no longer require artificial heat.

☐ Keep chicks at the right temperature.
☐ Make sure bedding is dry.
☐ Keep them from drafts.
☐ Provide adequate ventilation.
☐ Teach them to roost early.
☐ Furnish the right feed, water, and equipment.

A successful poultry raiser must think like a chick and constantly ask himself questions. Are there holes in that wire brooder floor the chicks can get their legs caught in? Is there a hole in that screen where a chick might get his head caught poking it through? Can those chicks drown in that new water? Are they able to reach their feed? Why aren't they touching their water? Why are they drinking so much water? Can the chicks squeeze out or fly over their pen? Can cats or rats squeeze into the pen?

SHIPPING PROCEDURES

It's a good idea to know what goes on from the time chicks hatch at the hatchery until the time they reach their destination. The information will help you determine whether your chicks have been stressed. If they have, you'll want to take certain measures to help them recover.

Steps can be saved at hatcheries by taking newly hatched chicks right from the hatching trays and placing them into their shipping boxes. If the chicks must be sexed, vaccinated, or debeaked, they are usually taken from this first shipping box, worked on, and then placed into a second shipping box.

The necessary handling of the chicks is by no means a gentle procedure. This is a production line. Chicks are quickly grabbed and dropped into the next box. This in no way hurts them, but it's quite an experience for such a small creature. If the chicks were ordered to be sexed, vaccinated, plus debeaked, they will have been handled twice as much as straight-run chicks where no extra procedures were ordered.

Chick shipping boxes have ventilation holes that are pushed out at the hatchery according to varying climatic conditions the chicks might encounter enroute. Manufacturers of chick boxes provide estimation charts of ventilation requirements for various climatic conditions. For example, 0 to 20 degrees Fahrenheit might require only two holes in each section of the box to be punched open, whereas temperatures of over 70 degrees Fahrenheit might require all ventilation holes to be opened. Experienced hatcheries use common sense in determining the amount of ventilation required. Variances can occur. For instance, if chicks are to be flown, the airplane compartment they ride in might be very cold. Hatcheries will usually account for this.

If chicks are to be shipped long distances, this only adds to the odds of varying temperatures and amount of handling the chicks will have to endure. There are unexpected weather conditions, delays in shipping, and rough handling—all which can add to stressing your chicks.

Back at the hatchery the chicks usually remain in their chick boxes to "harden them off" before shipping. This is exactly what gardeners do to their young plants before setting them permanently into the ground. Up until hatching, the chicks were accustomed to a 100-degree Fahrenheit (37.77 degree C.) world. They now must adjust to surviving at 90 degrees Fahrenheit (32.22 degrees C.). The chicks will remain in the chick boxes for a few hours or sometimes overnight, before actually being shipped, without the addition of artificial heat. This is possible because of the built-up body heat from the chicks.*

The pad inserts placed beneath the chicks in the shipping boxes serve to prevent spraddle legs in the baby chicks that would otherwise be caused by slipping on the smooth cardboard bottom of the box. It takes a few days for the chicks cartilage to harden enough to gain sure footing in the tops of their thighs. Usually the chicks are already a few days old by the time you receive them and you would not notice this weakness in the legs.

Because it takes three days for all chicks to hatch from one setting, do not assume all your chicks are just one day old. The youngest chicks will be the ones that still have their egg tooth, seem to want to set around, and appear to walk low to the ground. If you have many such chicks and the shipping distance was short, the chicks might be young enough yet where they haven't gained their footing. It might be wise to keep them on top of bunched-up rags for a few days.

Have the chicks' quarters ready beforehand because you never know when there might be a delay in shipment or in getting them home. A matter of minutes might be crucial in getting them drinking water and under heat and light. By knowing what the chicks might have gone through and looking for symptoms of stress, setbacks in your chicks' growth and livability can be avoided.

BOX AND BROODER RAISING

The chicks' first early home can be a cardboard box, a large crate, a large discarded drawer, a cage, or, a brooder designed for chicks that sets on the floor, hangs, or is held on a rack. Almost anything will do the first couple weeks if it's kept draft free, cleaned often, and protected from pets, wild animals, livestock, and inquisitive young children.

Children and pets can do unbelievable things to baby chicks in the short time it can take you to get your daily mail or answer your telephone. Children sometimes wonder if the chicks can fly and try to prove so by tossing them in the air. They wonder if chicks can swim and place them in toilets and sinks. They've been known to flush the toilet to see if the chicks can swim back up. And trusty old Rover sometimes isn't as trusty as you think

---

*Current recommended practices for transport of baby chicks are: Temperature within ventilated carton 89° F. (32° C.) provided by chicks when standard chick cartons are used within a van at 60° F. (16° C.). (Reprinted with permission of the American Society of Heating, Refrigerating and Air-Conditioning Engineers ASHRAE), Inc., Atlanta, Ga.)

Fig. 2-1. This type of setup will do for about two weeks.

he is. It's better to protect the chicks from the start. I've seen too many unnecessary chick losses resulting from trusting children and animals.

Chicks can get wiggly and some children squeeze them too hard. Some children are afraid to grasp them securely and drop them to the floor when the chicks wiggle. Have the child sit on the floor while getting use to handling the chicks. Handling can be good in bringing both children and chicks closer.

Whenever you place your brooder or box of chicks, make sure that there is no outside door opening near them that would cause the temperature to fluctuate (chilling the chicks off and on). I've seen people wonder why their chicks were dying in spite of the "perfect" brooder set up for them. The culprit? It was an outside door, 5 feet from the chicks, that was constantly used during that cold spring month. Every time the door was opened, the inevitable draft created would whisk the accumulated heat away from beneath the brooder lamp. The problem was solved when the top of the box containing the chicks was covered so that only a small area remained open for air.

Most people raising less than 100 chicks like to keep the baby chicks somewhere in their house but confined to their own quarters for the first few weeks. This is highly advisable because you can keep a good watch over them and you won't miss out on the funny antics your chicks will display. Chicks raised in your home in the beginning weeks usually turn out to be more friendly and less nervous with people. There is less chick mortality too because a more constant watch can be kept on them in case something goes wrong. Chicks will cry when in trouble. Also, there won't be the problem with predators as there is outdoors. Most predators, such as rats, dogs, cats, owls, weasels, mink, skunk, fox, etc., love baby chicks.

The size container to begin housing your chicks should be at least four times the space the chicks take up if they were standing side by side. I say at least, for this will do only in the first week or two. The chicks should have one whole area where you'll keep their feed and water to one side. Keep the heat to the other side of the container (Fig. 2-1). The chicks must have access to a cooler part of the box to escape the heat should it become too warm for them. This also helps harden them off and feather out faster so that they can go outdoors later.

27

Two to three feet is the recommended height of the container. Day-old chicks are pretty well behaved. They will stay in a box only 6 inches tall for a few days until their curiosity increases. Then they will want to know what's on the other side of that mammoth wall. A short wall will not keep out drafts. A few brave chicks will start to fly up to the top of a 2 foot tall box at one week of age. Rig up a metal screen to cover the top of their container.

Line the container floor with something that is not slippery (to prevent spraddle legs). Shredded newsprint is fine if you are careful not to use color-printed newspaper because it can be poisonous to chicks if ingested. Newspapers are usually economical and handy to use. Shredding it by tearing in strips and ruffling it up in the box is better than laying down flat, folded paper because it's too slippery and the droppings aren't absorbed as easily. You can still use some extra paper folded underneath the shredded paper.

Straw would seem to be the ideal litter material, but sometimes, depending on the straw type, it can become slippery under the feet of chicks when it gets damp from droppings or water. The bright, clean, lightweight, wide-diameter types of straw, which are usually the better grades, are the worse for very small chicks. The coarse type is better but make sure it's not musty or it'll cause respiratory problems.

Wood shavings are good if they are not too fine. Chicks have been known to pick these up and choke. Measure the size of the shavings to the chick's mouth. If the shavings look too big to fit into a chick's mouth, it should work out fine. Fine shavings or sawdust can be a problem. Wood chips are great provided you know they haven't been treated with any chemicals.

Old, coarse, clean rags can be used in the beginning. These can be shaken out and rewashed, if you like, but make sure they're rinsed clear of chlorine bleach that can be reactivated when it comes in contact with the ammonia in the birds' droppings. The resulting fumes can kill the chicks and harm you also.

One woman I know uses peat under the feet of her chicks. It's the same type used for potting plants. It seems to function well as litter because it gives the chicks something to do as they enjoy scratching in it. I would remove any small pieces of bark or twigs the chicks might lodge in their throats.

Change the type of bedding used on the floor according to the chicks' age. For instance:

☐ 1-7 days old. Use coarse rags to prevent spraddle legs until the chicks obtain even footing. They need something coarse to grab hold of while they walk.

☐ 1-4 weeks old. Use shredded newspapers. You can mix this with wood shavings or short strands of straw.

☐ By 4 weeks of age, usually they can be put outside in a building on a good bed of straw of any type.

Consideration should also be given to litter types used under hover type brooders during the first week. Enclosed brooders with racks and dropping trays should have the racks covered with towels or rags in the area where the chicks sleep under the heat source for the first few days. Chicks sometimes get their legs caught down through the wires.

WATERING ON ARRIVAL

When you get your chicks home, first place them in their new quarters near their water source. The chicks will be very thirsty if they've been in transit for long. Use water that's room temperature so their systems aren't shocked, causing stomach upsets. If they don't eagerly drink, take a few of the unwilling chicks and dip their beaks into the water. Make sure you see them swallow the water. This should get them started.

Water is more important than the feed or heat at this point. Chicks can dehydrate without their share of water. The chick's feed isn't important for up to 48 hours from hatching time (which should be stamped on the chick's shipping box). The chicks contain their own nourishment from the egg yolk which, during hatching time, is absorbed into the intestinal tract and releases needed nourishment automatically throughout their system.

Chicks aren't usually hungry during the early hours of life and won't eat anyway. So don't worry if they're not eating right away. I've heard it said, "Never force a chick to eat for it will interfere with the normal absorption of the yolk within the chick's body." I've never seen a chick you could force feed. Either they're ready to eat or not. Just have the feed available to them where they can get to it when they are ready.

If chicks look stressed from shipping (if they're not too perky), place their water and feed under their heat source and a small 7 1/2-watt light bulb so they can find the food. If they are stressed, they'll be too weak to find their way from the water container to the heat source and back again. Leave the water and feed under the heat for a day or two. Remember that the extra heat will cause the water to evaporate so you will need to refill waterers more frequently.

It's a good idea to place small rocks or marbles in the chicks' water dish. This helps keep the chicks from falling into the water or getting knocked into the water by other eager, thirsty chicks. This would be an especially safe way to water bantams. They need only to be able to get their tiny beaks into the water. The shining marbles will also help the uneager chicks to take more notice of the water. They peck at the marbles and are soon drinking.

Continue using the marbles for about one week with standard breeds or until bantams are too large to fall in.

BROODING TEMPERATURES

Artificial heat must be supplied to chicks to imitate heat from a mother hen. The entire period for which heat is supplied is called brooding. The source for the heat is the brooder. Chicks are brooded until body feathers grow in.

The heat seems more of a problem than any other thing to most people. See Table 2-1 for current recommended practices for broilers. Egg breeds, general purpose, fancy, and bantams should be brooded at about 90° when day old.

If you have 25 to 50 chicks and they're kept in a box in your household, you can use a 40- to 75-watt light bulb for their heat. The wattage will depend on the temperature in the room or basement they are in. Warmer rooms can use bulbs with less wattage because they throw off less heat.

For 75 or more chicks, you'll need to use a brooder lamp. These are also called reflector lamps, and are made to withstand the heat from a 250 watt bulb. Usually one brooder lamp is needed for every 100 chicks. Again, this will depend on the temperature of the room or building in which the chicks are being housed. Cold rooms might require two lamps.

Table 2-1. Current Recommended Practices for Broiler Houses.

Room temperature: 59 to 64.4° F. (15 to 18° C.).
Temperature under brooder hover: 84.2 to 89.6° F. (29 to 32° C.), reducing 5.4° F (3° C.) per week until room temperature is reached.
Relative humidity: 50 to 80%.
Ventilation rate: 0.5 to 1 λ/s per kg of live weight in winter, 2 λ/s per kg of live weight in summer. The cubic feet per minute conversion would be: 1.06 to 2.12 cfm per 2.2 pounds of live weight in winter, 4.24 cfm per 2.2 pounds of live weight in summer.
Space: 0.06 to 0.09 m^2/bird (about 3/5 to 1 square feet per bird). Chicks under brooder should have 4515 to 5805 mm^2/chick (or about 7-9 square inches of space per chick).
Light: 20 lux (.03 watts per square foot) to 28 days of age.*

Reprinted with permission of the American Society of Heating, Refrigerating and Air-Conditioning Engineers (ASHRAE), Inc., Atlanta, Ga.
*Author's note: This means a 7 1/2 watt nightlight would be plenty in a 10- x -24 foot brooding and growing room.

The following precedures to adjust heat can be used for any type of brooder setup. Take a regular oral thermometer—these are more accurate than store-bought brooder thermometers—and place it in the middle of the chicks' sleeping quarters. Most homes have one of these thermometers in their medicine chest. Be sure to shake the mercury down past 90 degrees first. Now place something 2 inches high under the thermometer to raise it up. You'll get a reading that will be at the level of the chicks' heads. Either raise or lower the bulb height, change to a higher- or lower-watt bulb, or adjust the temperature control knob on gas or electric brooders. Adjust until the thermometer reads about 90 degrees Fahrenheit (32.22 degrees C.). Remember to shake the mercury down each time you take a new reading, and then let it rise again to get an accurate reading.

Keep in mind you do not want to start a fire by having the bulb too close to the chicks' flammable bedding material. Place your hand 2 inches above the bedding material under the heat. If it's uncomfortably hot, it's definitely too close to the litter, too high a wattage, or the control is set too high. Adjust accordingly.

Each week lower the temperature 5 degrees using the same procedure. This will help to harden the chicks off so that their bodies will not notice a drastic drop in temperature when the heat is finally turned off. Make sure there are no outside doors or drafts nearby that will whisk away the artificial heat.

Do not completely cover containers housing chicks with anything that will not allow the heat to escape. The built-up heat could cause a fire or kill the chicks.

Some people have set their container of chicks near woodstoves or over home heating registers to keep them warm. These methods will not concentrate the right amount of heat in one area. Chicks will become too cold, too hot, or there will be too many fluctuations in temperature. A small light bulb is too easy and inexpensive *not* to use.

Then there's "Mr. Thermometer" who definitely knows it's warm enough because "it feels comfortable to him." People perceive temperatures differently. What's comfortable to most people is not comfortable to chicks. Use the thermometer first and then use the chicks as your guide. Watch how they distribute themselves under the heat.

When the chicks are in the setup container or brooder, you might notice them sleeping out away from the light or brooder heater. This means it's too warm directly under the heat. Either raise the heat lamp up, replace it with a lower-watt bulb, or turn the brooder temperature control down. After giving the temperature a few minutes to readjust, watch where they sleep. This adjustment should only be done in the coolest part of the evening because adjusting the temperature during the day when it's warm will require doing it all over again when temperatures cool.

The chicks will give off body heat on their own, but the amount will vary as to how many chicks are being brooded and where. To allow for this body heat, make sure the chicks have ample space to move and get away from the heat section if it gets too warm. You can't adjust brooder lights or controls while you are gone or sleeping. Chicks will pant if they're overheated and can't escape the heat. If you see this adjust accordingly. Too much heat can be as bad as not enough.

If chicks are cold, they will huddle right under the heat source. They also will be peeping constantly and trying to huddle under one another. Don't confuse this peeping with that of chicks that have just arrived through the mail. The first day when these chicks arrive they are scared from all the handling and bouncing around they've experienced. They will peep like crazy, sometimes for hours, until they settle down. By nightfall they should all be calmed and quiet. If in doubt, just get out your thermometer and check the temperature again.

Once you've gained experience, you'll be able to use the chicks as your only guide in figuring the right temperature. It's a comforting feeling to know all the babies are warm enough and comfortable when you look and see them spread out evenly like a plush carpet under the heat.

EFFECTS OF CHILLING

A box of chicks that have been shipped with too much ventilation, or held in very cold storage rooms will show visual signs of chilling when received. The chicks will huddle in the boxes and perhaps some will have been smothered. Scared chicks will peep a lot. The surest sign is when the chicks seem to want to crowd under the heat, when placed in their quarters, instead of going for their water. Let them get warm first, but encourage them to drink warm water in which a teaspoon of sugar (for warmth and energy) has been added. Place the waterers under the heat. At the end of the day, or about 6 hours later, gradually move the waterers further out into the feed area by a few inches. By the third day, the waterers can be set in the original positions out near the feed area.

If the heat goes off accidentally while being brooded later on, the chicks will act the same way. The same basic procedures would be used to revitalize the chicks but the feed would also have to be put under the heat. Older chicks must have feed.

Prolonged chilling will bring on respiratory distress, smothering from crowding to try to keep warm, a diarrhea condition, higher mortality from stress, and long wing feathers. The wing feathers will develop abnormally large in proportion to the size of the chick's body. Chilled chicks are stressed chicks and they will not want to eat as much. Therefore, they are doomed from the start unless measures to remedy the situation are taken at once.

Most chicks that are shipped and chilled will revive with these measures without much mortality. If the chicks were chilled to a point where half are received dead, refuse shipment at the post office and fill out the appropriate forms. This must be done when received so check the chicks right at the post office. Once you leave with them the chicks are yours. The act of taking them home means shipment was accepted.

If the chicks were not insured, you will have to take the remaining chicks home, sort them out, and clean up the mess. Then you will have to contact the hatchery and tell them what happened.

They should make it good by sending out another shipment. If the remaining chicks look bad, tell them you will be disposing of them also because the stress factor will cause more mortality than you can handle.

Be honest with them. If the chicks remaining look as though they'll pull through within 24 hours, give the hatchery the benefit of the doubt. If the chicks aren't doing well in 24 hours, dispose of them because they will not be worth the time and money. It will be better to start with a fresh batch of chicks all the same age. This rarely happens, but you should be prepared for such mishaps.

Pasted vents are rarely seen in hatched chicks. If chicks shipped were chilled, they might experience pasted vents after a couple of days. This is manure stuck to the vent. The manure will soon harden, obstructing the vent and preventing further defecation. Waste matter will eventually kill the chick. Hold the chick hind end under warm, running water while gently working loose the mass of dried manure with your finger. It helps if the manure is squeezed to help break it up. The mass will then pull away along with the down around the vent, but this prevents further pasting. The wet vent area must be completely dried before placing the chick in with the others. A blow drier for hair works fine for this. If there is slight bleeding where the down was pulled out, spray the area with an antiseptic such as blue Wound-Cote.

EFFECTS OF OVERHEATING

Overheating during brooding will cause dehydration, which will be noticed primarily in the shanks. The shanks will look like dried-up toothpicks. There will be crowding in the brooder corners, piling, smothering, possible pneumonia, and panting from attempting to escape the high heat. It will cause uneven growth, a lack of vigor and slow feathering.

Chicks overheated during shipping will be found panting when the lid is removed. This overheating will be due to the temperature of the room or delivery truck the chicks were in last.

Overheated chicks need water immediately. Do not let them gulp down very cold water, but make sure it's warm. Use plenty of waterers, filled with warm water, the first few days.

DISCONTINUING ARTIFICIAL HEAT

The total time of brooding will depend on:

☐ How well feathered the chicks are.
☐ The indoor temperature of room or building they're in.
☐ How much changes in outdoor temperatures will affect the temperature indoors.
☐ How many chicks are being brooded together.
☐ The size of the brooding area.

Because these conditions will vary at individual farms and ranches, your best guide is common sense. Chicks should be completely feathered out to discontinue heat. Chick down only accepts heat. Feathers hold the body heat in.

If you've started the chicks at 90 degrees Fahrenheit and lowered the temperature 5 degrees weekly, this means at 6 weeks of age the chicks can tolerate 60 to 70 degrees Fahrenheit (15.55-21.11 degrees C.). It won't be an actual 5 degrees lower each week because the birds will grow larger each week and therefore throw off more body heat within their environment.

If nightly outdoor temperatures have been between 50 to 60 degrees Fahrenheit (10-15.55 degrees C.) it should be safe to turn heat completely off (provided chicks are completely feathered out). This is usually between 6 to 8 weeks of age.

Begin the process two or three weeks ahead by providing small roosts for the chicks. The earlier they learn to roost, the less they will sleep on the cold damp ground or floor. By the time they are feathered out, they can fluff up their feathers while roosting, allowing air to circulate for their own built-in air conditioner. The air cannot circulate when they sleep on the floor. The litter has a better chance to dry and the chicks will be healthier.

When you're ready to turn the heat completely off, do it during late morning or early afternoon when outdoor temperatures are the warmest so the chicks can adjust. Check on them often.

Place a very small light overhead so chicks can eat through the night. Brooder-lamp-raised chicks consider the light to be the source of warmth. Even if the heat is there, they'll feel cold and scared if the light is gone. Chicks use to light will crowd, pile and smother each other within minutes because of the absence of light.

During the first and second night the heat has been turned off, check to see how they are doing. If you've correctly figured feathering and outdoor temperatures, you'll find the chicks roosting, scampering about, eating, and drinking without being wise to the fact the extra heat has been turned off.

FEATHERNG PROCEDURE

Preparations for good feather growth should be made the day the chicks are received. Not much can be done when the chicks are several weeks old and it's discovered they are not feathering properly. Chicks should feather fast and good for looks, butchering quality, and so they can acclimate their bodies to various fluctuations in temperatures that might occur unexpectedly.

It's difficult to sell naked-backed started birds or fryers. Most people believe if birds are not fully feathered and that if the feathers are not clean and attractive, the birds are sick. The poor feathering will result in pin feathers at butchering time.

Most poor feathering today is the result of poor management of the growing chicks. Good feathering requires ventilation, humidity, temperature control, noncrowded conditions, and a nutritionally balanced feed ration. It's rare to receive a whole flock of chicks that are from a poor feathering strain as most breeders are careful in breeding this trait out of their birds.

If you come across "barebacks," first judge whether or not the birds are developing a habit of feather pulling by examining their backs. If they are, there will be little holes in the skin where the feathers have been removed. Birds with dark-colored feathers will have a small quantity of pigment in each hole. If the chicks are *not* pulling feathers you can almost assume something is wrong in their environment.

It's easy to produce feathers on the egg breeds because they mature faster. Of the heavy breeds, one of the easiest to feather is the Rhode Island Red. The Barred Rock is one of the hardest to feather at an early age.

The effect ventilation has on good feathering can clearly be seen in battery-brooded chicks. Chicks in the top levels are better feathered because the air circulation is better there. That's why fans are sometimes needed to move stale air near the floor. Chicks raised by hens outdoors are always feathered out sooner because of natural air movement outdoors. Ventilation must be provided near floors without creating drafts.

When hatched, a chick contains about 75 percent moisture. Most starter rooms and brooders do not have a relative humidity quite that high. Moisture will be lost naturally within the chick's body through the normal process of elimination and growth. When the humidity of the air is low, the chick's beginning pin feathers will become dry, brittle, and lack luster. In this condition, the feathers are easily broken off as the birds sweep against each other. Brooders and heat lamps dry up most moisture. That's why ventilation and humidity go hand in hand. Air movement will also bring moisture to the level of the chicks.

The needed humidity can't be had without odor. Only very dry conditions will prevent odor from being formed. Odorless conditions, although less offensive to us, does not necessarily mean conditions are the best for the chicks. This does not mean bedding material saturated with droppings should not be changed often. If it's changed often and there's still an odor, this only indicates there is humidity in the air. This is fine. If there's never an odor there's no humidity available. Mist the air if necessary. Very dry conditions not only produce bad feathers but can bring on lung problems too.

High temperatures will work against efforts to ventilate and humidify as it will dry up moisture faster than it can be supplied through ventilation.

Crowding chicks into confined areas will create extra humidity through the evaporation of the extra droppings but there will be a restriction in air movement between the birds.

Most feed rations provide nutrients that help produce nice feathers. The addition of cod liver oil to the drinking water (one teaspoon to a gallon) periodically will help produce good feather qualities. The first four weeks is the most important time to insure chicks have the right conditions available to grow feathers. If these needs have been ignored and the chicks have not feathered very well, it will be hard to feather them later.

Chicks grow feathers on their wings first. Tail and breast feathers usually begin to grow next. Then the back will feather. The neck and head will be the last area to feather out. By six weeks of age, all body feathers should be in and neck and head feathers follow during the next two weeks. As long as body feathers are attained and outdoor temperatures are mild, discontinuation of brooding can be attempted.

During the first six weeks, you'll notice dusty conditions from the loss of the chicks' down. Brooder trays will clearly contain down that has been shed.

Protect your lungs from "chick dust" produced from shedded down, droppings, and chick feed. Wear a mask when cleaning bedding or dropping pans. The disposable and filtered masks can be purchased where paint supplies are sold. If a mask is not available, a cloth tied around your head will serve to protect your nose and mouth from these minute particles.

Many bird and poultry farmers unfortunately have contacted hypersensitivity pneumonitis (extrinsic allergic alveolitis), which is the medical term for what is also called bird fancier's, breeder's, handler's, or pigeon breeder's lung disease. Small traces of bird protein are constantly lost from the bowel of birds. These are passed in the droppings that then dry and powder. These dried protein particles, along with shedded down and feed dust, will induce a hypersensitivity reaction in the lungs of sensitive individuals. After inhaling the allergic dust, the allergen goes through the air passages where it reaches the lungs. The most severe reactions take place within the walls of the small air passage. You can research the disease further at most hospital staff libraries.

The use of masks, filters, and the awareness of the disease helps in it's prevention. Children should also be taught to use these masks if they help tend the chickens or chicks.

SPACE REQUIREMENTS FOR CHICKS

For chicks from day old to 11 weeks, a separate brooder house is sometimes a good idea so that chicks will not have to be brooded while confined with older birds already on the premises. Various floor and hanging brooders are designed for a specified amount of chicks. Most are extremely overrated as to the capacity of chicks the brooders will accommodate. Heat lamps, one for every 50 to 100 chicks, can be used during the full brooding period. When used in a large area, any brooder or lamp will require brooder guards to keep chicks from straying too far from the heat source, feed, and water.

A hundred day-old chicks will take up approximately the size of the chick box in which they were shipped (about 1 1/2 × 2 feet). To calculate their floor area, figure 16 times this area. This would be 3 × 16 feet (or 48 square feet) of needed brooder floor space, providing 1/2 square foot per chick. The 48 square feet of space will suffice for the 100 chicks on up to two weeks of age.

After the second week, feeders and waterers are moved outward from the heat and brooder. This extra space should be taken into consideration when you first set up brooder. During this time, all the chicks will not sleep under the brooder constantly unless it's extremely cold. They need space to walk about, exercise, and condition themselves to cooler areas. This will require an additional foot of space around the entire brooder. Either enlarge the brooder guard or, if extra space is available, simply place all guards in tall corners to prevent chicks from piling.

Chicks are attracted to open square corners. Finding it's cold there, they will climb on top and under each other to find warmth and will suffocate because the air is restricted by the two corner walls.

Guards are described in the following section on equipment.

If brooder lamps are used, figure three-fourths of a square foot per chick and hang lamps 3 feet apart. Use brooder or corner guards as above.

Beginning at 5 weeks of age on up to 11 weeks, floor space can be calculated by using the following method. Take the chicks' age in weeks and consider the body size to be the exact same in inches. For instance, a 7-week-old chick's body would be 7 inches long, a 10-week-old chick's body would be 10 inches long, and so on. Then calculate this body and age number in the following manner:

☐ Multiply to find the square inches. Example: a 7-week-old chick 7 × 7 = 49 square inches.

☐ Multiply this answer by total number of chicks being raised. Example: 100 being raised would be 100 × 49 = 4900 square inches.

☐ Divide this answer by 144 square inches to get the square feet the chicks take up. Example: 4900 sq. in. ÷ 144 sq. in. = 34 sq. ft.

☐ Multiply the square foot answer by 4 to get total square footage needed for amount of chicks being raised. Example: 34 sq. ft. × 4 = 136 square feet required.

This method of calculating space will only work from age 5 weeks to 11 weeks. For easy reference use the guide below to figure the space required per chick.

☐ Day old to 2 wks. = 1/2 sq. ft.
☐ 3, 4, 5 wks. = 3/4 sq. ft.
☐ 6 wks. = 1 sq. ft.
☐ 7 wks. = 1 1/2 sq. ft.
☐ 8 wks. = 1 3/4 sq. ft.
☐ 9 wks. = 2 1/4 sq. ft.
☐ 10 wks. = 2 3/4 sq. ft.
☐ 11 wks. = 3 1/3 sq. ft.
☐ 12 and over = up to 4 sq. ft.

All figures for floor space are for heavy breeds that are fully confined. There is no access to an outdoor pen or yard. Chicks will spend more time indoors than out. Because of weather conditions, chickens sometimes will have to remain constantly indoors for a few days at a time. If you use a lighting system for older pullets in preparation to produce eggs, this will require the birds to be awake and confined for hours each day until it's light enough to venture outdoors.

Slightly less space can be figured for light breeds and bantams.

EQUIPMENT

Equipment for chicks appears simple and inexpensive. In reality, the wrong type of equipment can be costly. Because of the need for large quantities of small equipment, the cost can be similar to that of the larger equipment needs of older birds. Some handlers can get by with a homemade feeder and one waterer (Fig. 2-2) if a hen is raising the chicks.

If money never was a problem I'd simply recommend having an equipment dealer come out to design and install all automatic feeders, waterers, and brooding systems in your brand new, well-ventilated poultry house. This is the poultry handlers' dream. Unfortunately large systems are uneconomical for small growers.

The type of equipment you select will depend not only on your finances but on how many years you plan to raise poultry. Better, more costly equipment is less expensive than paying for constant replacements.

Bands. Bands are made of aluminum or plastic and are used to mark chicks for purposes of culling and breeding. Depending on the type used, bands are attached around the leg or pierced into the webbed part of the wing.

One type of aluminum leg band is sealed around the bird's leg with special pliers. Another has a tongue and slot fastener. Others made of plastic spirals are simply twisted on like a round key ring. These plastic bands are available in colors. The aluminum has numbers or letters stamped on them for identifying birds. Your name and address can be stamped for an extra charge, but I can see no useful purpose in this. All these types of bands can be removed without a trace they were ever on the birds. The sealed types can work their way loose and fall off no matter how carefully they are applied.

The best lifetime identification applied to chicks, with specially designed pliers is the wing band. It stays in place better, does not bother the bird much, and can be located easier while birds are quietly roosting. Only one size is needed, and if removed, small marks will be noticeable if your purpose of identification is for proof of ownership should your birds be stolen.

Brooders. There are four main types of brooding equipment that operate by using gas or

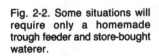
Fig. 2-2. Some situations will require only a homemade trough feeder and store-bought waterer.

Fig. 2-3. Single lamp reflectors like this one are commonly used by small-scale handlers for brooding chicks (courtesy of Brower Manufacturing Company, Inc.).

350. Naturally the larger lamps are more expensive. One with four red bulbs will cost over $60. Four single lamps with bulbs can cost almost the same. Do some figuring on what's available and the prices.

Floor brooders set on legs and can be raised as chicks grow. They can be round, square, gable, or octagon with flat or raised tops (Fig. 2-5). The open sides should contain curtains to help keep heat from escaping yet allow the chicks to walk under when they feel a need for heat. Floor brooders use natural or bottled gas or electricity.

Today, most floor brooders are electric; gas is used mainly for the hanging type. They all have thermostat controls. The electric brooders are rated at 110 to 120 volt and 250 to 1000 watt. Most four-foot floor brooders are rated for a 400-chick capacity. Consider raising only 200 under these. There are 2-foot square electric floor brooders available to accommodate 100 chicks. The main

electric. The simple and least expensive are the single-lamp reflectors (Fig. 2-3) that are hung over the chicks. Some have guards (Fig. 2-4). The temperature is controlled by lowering or raising the lamp. The metal reflector cover serves a dual purpose: protecting the glass bulbs from moisture that might drip from ceilings, and reflecting bulb heat toward the chicks.

A 250-watt red or white glass bulb is used. The red bulb gives maximum heat with a minimum of light to help prevent cannibalism. White bulbs are usually less expensive, but a closer eye must be kept on chicks because cannibalism is more prevalent under bright lights. If cannibalism does start, a switch to red bulbs will be in order. Use one single lamp for every 50 to 100 chicks. There are four-lamp brooders with flat-formed guards attached so lamps can be hung or set squarely on the floor. These four-lamp brooders have a thermostat that controls one bulb (and thereby total heat). Capacity for four-lamp brooders is rated for

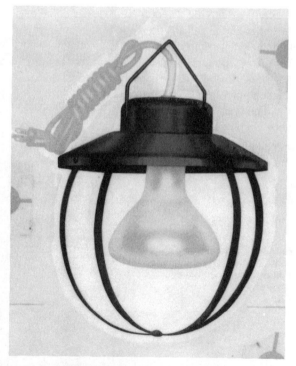

Fig. 2-4. Lamp reflectors with guards may help prevent a fire should the lamp be knocked down onto litter material (courtesy of Brower Manufacturing Company, Inc.)

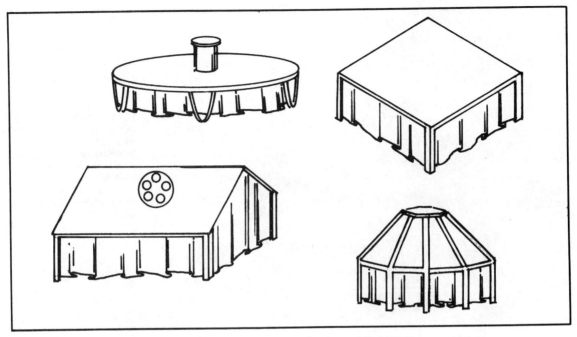

Fig. 2-5. Three electric floor brooders and one octagon type that heats with bottle gas.

problem with floor brooders is the corrosion of the legs. It's almost unavoidable that the legs come in contact with damp litter. Any adjustment slots in the legs for raising the height of the brooder usually become corroded, too. So plan on replacing legs, as they wear out, with angle iron and using bricks under legs to raise the brooder height. Prices begin at $40 for small floor brooders.

Hanging brooders are operated on natural and bottle gas or with electricity, and are usually shaped like an upside down saucer (Fig. 2-6 and Fig. 2-7). Most hanging brooders are designed for over 400 chicks, but they do come in handy for warming other farm animals such as lambs and baby pigs. One hanging gas canopy model maintains a temperature in a 12-foot diameter area. It's rated

Fig. 2-6. This 47-inch gas hanging brooder will brood from 750 to 1,000 chicks with an even temperature in a 12-foot brooding area (Courtesy of Brower Manufacturing Company, Inc.).

to brood 1000 chicks. Because most chicks would be using these brooders throughout the entire brooding period, the capacities should only be considered to be half the amount of chicks as rated by the companies.

There are some gas run models that are small and square without a canopy and throw off enough direct infrared rays to cover a brooding area for 750 chicks. The infrared rays are projected in a fashion similar to that of the sun. These are even better than saucer type hanging brooders for other baby animals because the heat can be directed to any area by simply adjusting and aiming the brooder's rays.

The gas brooders will cost more because there is more involved in their manufacture. Figure prices at just over $100.

Battery stack brooders are commonly used today. They are called stack brooders because they can be placed one on top of each other by using a rack. Older types were heavy and contained several stationary compartments in one frame that were very cumbersome for small growers (Fig. 2-8). Some single types were manufactured but not in great quantities. The new single compartment

brooders are rated for 125 day-old chicks, 100 one-week-olds, 75 two-week-olds, 55 three-week-olds, and 40 four-week-olds. These types of brooders can be purchased and placed into an available rack that will hold five brooders (Fig. 2-9). To raise 200 birds to four weeks of age would require all five brooders (which will cost over $600). Unless you plan to raise successive broods regularly, the cost does not warrant having this type of brooding system (unless a used model can be found inexpensively).

The cost of feeders and waterers will be saved with battery brooding during the first four weeks, It would cost between $50 to $60 to brood 100 chicks using two brooder lamps, six feeders, six waterers, and brooder guards and litter up to the age of four weeks old. You could raise 200 chicks this way for the same price one battery brooder would cost or you would have to brood 5 lots of 40 chicks to the age of 4 weeks old for the battery brooder to pay for itself. After 4 weeks of age, larger feeders and waterers will have to be obtained for the chicks either way they're brooded.

These brooders will not operate properly in temperatures below 50 degrees. Don't plan on operating them in an outdoor building during cold

Fig. 2-8. Although almost 50 years old, this heavy Oakes brooder might suit some small-scale raisers because of lower secondhand costs.

spring months. Most people set them up in a basement in their home. There is a curtain in front of the heating element to help hold heat in the back section. Temperature is controlled by a thermostat and regulated with a setscrew.

Cages. Cages aren't usually thought about much when a person begins raising chicks. Soon the chicks must usually be moved from a box or brooder to the brooder house, from the brooder house to permanent quarters, perhaps sorted from pen to pen, moved to butchering headquarters, or taken to market. A variety of sizes come in handy. Just make sure they're lightweight. If made of any wood they'll be heavy. The types made of welded wire mesh like rabbit cages and layer cages are made of are the lightest and easiest to handle. Some of us forget that a dozen 12-week-olds can weigh 50 pounds, but you are sure to be reminded when the time comes to move them! So remember to keep lightweight cages. A wooden cage that's been out in the rain can weigh as much as the birds it contains.

Lightweight plastic chicken crates will contain large chicks but are awkward to handle by yourself. These crates have wire floors inserted so the birds are not walking on top of droppings. Even if left outdoors to the weather, they hold up very well. The older style wooden crates break easier, warp, and are heavier.

A small, 2-×-1-foot lightweight cage is extremely useful for do-it-yourselfers. If you have trouble finding the right size wire cage, these can

Fig. 2-9. Single compartment brooders, such as these "mother hens," can be purchased separately and placed into the available rack (courtesy of Brower Manufacturing Company, Inc.).

be made yourself with supplies usually sold to rabitries.

Prepare to have small, medium, and large cages available. Don't be caught without cages when you need them.

Debeaker and Dubbing Shears. Electric debeakers (Fig. 2-10) shorten the upper beaks of chicks by cutting and heat cauterizing the cut. Careful use of nail clippers can also be used but clotting the end of the beak must be done. Electrically clipped beaks will last longer than nail-clipped beaks. All must have the operation performed sooner or later because beak grows out again.

The cost of a new electric debeaking device is usually unprofitable for small-scale raisers unless handlers want continuous accuracy throughout the procedure. Because only a certain amount of the beak is removed, depending on the type blade used, a handler can be assured of removing the right amount each time quickly.

Nail clippers are only as accurate as the

handler, but with practice 100 chicks can be done safely and quickly within 15 minutes.

Dubbing shears are used to remove combs and wattles. Usually only the males' combs stay erect and are subject to freezing. Hens with large combs usually have no problems because their comb folds over their head. This helps heat the comb to prevent freezing.

The type shears you should use depends on the age of the bird. Ordinary sharp scissors are used to decomb baby chicks while dull scissors, tin snips, or special rounded dubbing shears are used for older birds when dubbing.

Feeders. In the beginning, the chicks' feeder can be as simple as an egg carton. The carton must be one not used to hold your home grown eggs. Otherwise you may unintentionally transmit lice to the chicks. Lice can kill baby chicks. Styrofoam cartons can be immersed in bleach water and rinsed to take care of any lice they might contain.

The egg cartons can be thrown away and replaced when soiled; this saves some time. The

Fig. 2-10. The Super Debeaker debeaks and cauterizes in a single operation (courtesy of Lyon Electric Company, Inc.).

Fig. 2-11. This simple galvanized chick feeder would be sufficient for about a dozen chicks for a few weeks (courtesy of Brower Manufacturing Company, Inc.).

Fig. 2-13. Reel feeders like this one are manufactured in 18-inch, and 24-inch lengths, holding 5 1/2 and 7 pounds of feed for 20-25 chicks (courtesy of Brower Manufacturing Company, Inc.).

chicks will walk over the top of the filled cartons to peck at the feed. This is all right in the beginning week. Later you should have feeders that keep the chicks from walking into the feed because they will soil it with their droppings. The beginning feeder is only to be used while the chicks eagerly learn to eat.

Very small quantities of chicks can use a simple round nine-hole feeder (Fig. 2-11). For large amounts of chicks being brooded in a large area with hanging or floor brooders, "feeder lids" are used. These are plastic trays about 22 × 14 inches wide and 2 inches high with ribbed bottoms. The ribbed bottoms give the chicks traction as they get in the tray and peck around at the feed. The trays are very inexpensive and can be washed, stacked, and reused. They are only used for about one week.

There really aren't any feeders made for older chicks that will definitely keep them from walking on the feed. It is hard to construct a safe, clean

chick feeder for chicks because they can maneuver in, under, and around things. Making a more sanitary feeder might mean a more dangerous one for the chicks to get caught in.

With some ingenuity a handler might be able to construct a clean safe feeder that will surpass the store-bought ones. Most store bought chick feeders are long, narrow pans with a three-sided pole that runs down the middle (Figs. 2-12 and 2-13). The pole should be adjusted so it is loose enough to twirl. As chicks jump on top of this pole, the chicks cannot maintain their balance as the pole begins to twirl. They must jump back down or get knocked off.

There are long, narrow feeders with sliding lids that have holes in the top (Fig. 2-14). The holes are still big enough to allow chicks to get inside and walk over the feed. Sometimes chicks will go through the feed holes and get caught underneath. This can be a bit dangerous. There also are long, narrow feeders with wire spacers where chicks still can wiggle through, sometimes getting caught.

Whatever feeder you choose, make sure the chicks each have at least 1 inch of space around the

Fig. 2-12. A 36-inch feeder will hold 13 pounds of feed for about 50 chicks (courtesy of Brower Manufacturing Company, Inc.).

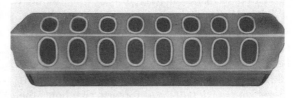

Fig. 2-14. Slide-top troughs can be purchased in 12-, 18-, and 24-inch sizes holding 4, 6, and 8 pounds of feed for 14 to 25 chicks, but should be used with a bit of caution (courtesy of Brower Manufacturing Company, Inc.).

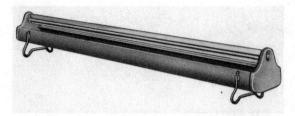

Fig. 2-15. A 36-inch trough feeder will hold 9 pounds of feed for 75 chicks (courtesy of Brower Manufacturing Company, Inc.).

sides of the feeder. For instance, a 12-inch-long feeder will be sufficient for 24 chicks. A 36-inch-feeder will suffice for 72 chicks, and so on.

These small feeders will do until the chicks are about three weeks old. Then they will need larger trough types that hold more feed.

About the time brooding is discontinued, around 7 weeks of age, the growing chicks can graduate to an extra-large, trough type of feeder or a tube feeder. There are 25-to-40-pound-capacity tubes that can be purchased with a 2-inch-deep pan on the bottom for chicks. A 12-quart tube is also available for chicks up to 12 weeks of age.

Broiler chicks will graduate to tube feeders as young as 4 weeks of age because of their extra large size as compared to an egg breed or general-purpose breed. Because they will be eating twice as much also, the extra-capacity tubes will really come in handy for use until the broilers are butchered.

Any metal feeder used should be kept off damp litter or you'll be constantly replacing them. Some have legs for this purpose (Fig. 2-15 and Fig. 2-16). All feeders should hold at least a day's supply of feed for the amount of chicks being cared for.

Feed Scoops. It pays to buy well rounded stainless steel scoops at a restaurant supply house. A good scoop will last a lifetime. Scoops get a lot of use and unintentional abuse. Try out your scoop before you purchase it by taking your other hand and applying pressure on the end of the scoop. If there's too much pull in the forearm that holds the scoop, the scoop is too long and you'll have an aching arm after scooping a hundred pounds of feed. Long scoops will require two hands to dig into the feed and lift out.

Purchase a short, fat rounded scoop. There's a lot of pressure and force in the act of scooping feed that isn't noticed until your plastic scoop breaks or your arm aches. A scoop will be used from the time your chicks arrive—right through their entire life.

Feed Storage Containers. If you're not using self-feeders or if amount of feed purchased must set around for more than a week, feed should be stored in a rodent-proof container within easy access to the chicks.

Fifty-five gallon metal drums with tight fitting lids will hold 300 pounds of feed. Feed can then be scooped out into 5-gallon buckets and carried to the chicks' feeders for filling. These drums can be moved about more easily than a metal-lined box. Lids must fit snug. If outdoors, prop the bottom of one side so rain will immediately roll off the top. A rock or other weight will keep severe winds from blowing off lids.

Rats are destructive and will eat through thin metal and thick wood containers. Metal garbage cans work well and so do 50-pound lard tins. The lard tins can be purchased at a butcher supply store.

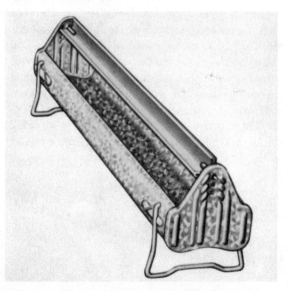

Fig. 2-16. Like most such equipment, this 36-inch trough feeder has legs that can be removed for use when chicks are too small to reach into the trough (courtesy of the Warner Corporation).

Both will cost a bit more than a drum but they are good for holding small quantities of feed and grit.

Fencing. Any fencing for chicks in indoor and outdoor pens must have small 1-inch spacings to keep chicks from going through. A good grade of chick fencing will last approximately 5 years outdoors, depending on how humid a climate you're in. Indoors, any fencing in contact with manure and damp straw will last only a couple years.

To guard against constant replacements indoors, thick-treated wood between floor and fence will save on the repairing of the bottoms of fencing. Plan this in advance of constructing your pens. It won't cost much more than the constant replacement of these fence bottoms. Plan on 2 feet of wood from floor to fence bottom. The wood barriers will also serve to protect chicks from drafts. This can be done outdoors too because it's the bottoms that rust out first. Outdoors, the wood will help keep predators out and chicks in.

Welded wire allows chicks to escape until they are about 8 weeks old (egg breeds or general purpose). Welded wire should only be used indoors because the welds break easily after quickly rusting. Most welded wire is fairly inexpensive.

Woven wire last longer but is made for larger birds and livestock. Chicks can slip through the large spacings. Most handlers will have to use good 1-inch chicken wire for either indoor or outdoor use to confine small chicks. For multipurpose pens, a 1 to 2 foot high strip of 1-inch chicken wire can be strung around the bottom of larger fencing to contain the chicks.

Fount Heaters. During most freezing weather conditions, if you're raising a late hatch during freezing weather and if chicks aren't housed using body heat for building comfort, water heaters should be used for a constant supply of water.

Round base heaters are made for both cone shaped and metal or rubber water pans.

The rod heaters are made for single open water pans or troughs without lids (Fig. 2-17). This type is more commonly used for older birds that have graduated to open pans with no fear of them drowning. Unless the electrical cords of these heaters are secured to the pan, the chickens occasionally stumble over the cord and pull the heater out of the water.

Guards. Guards are simply anything that can extend around a hanging or floor brooder in a continuous circle to keep very small chicks confined near the heat so they do not wander off. It should be at least 5 inches tall. Guards made especially for chicks are difficult to find, but plastic or aluminum lawn edgings can sometimes be found to fit the purpose. They're usually only used for a few weeks until the chicks become accustomed to finding the heat, feed, and water sources.

Corners guards are for large pen corners to keep chicks from crowding into corners to huddle and sleep. Chicks seem to be attracted to open corners. Guards can be used throughout the brooding period and sometimes afterward if chicks are not yet roosting.

The corner guards must be at least 2 feet tall and should have straw packed in behind so that the chicks do not jump over and become trapped in the corner between the guard and the wall corners.

Pilot Bulbs. Pilot bulbs used on brooders will light up only when the thermostat has turned the heating element on. As soon as the set temperature is reached, the element and the bulb will turn off.

Pilot bulbs should not be depended upon for the chicks' light source for eating and drinking. There must be another light in the building or room that

Fig. 2-17. Eight-inch long rod water heaters have a fixed temperature of 50 degrees Fahrenheit. (Courtesy of Brower Manufacturing Company, Inc.).

is on constantly or set with a timer to light the room every 2 hours.

Always check the brooder's heat if the pilot bulb is not on. This indicates the heater is not going or the bulb is burned out. A brooder will still heat correctly even if the pilot bulb burns out.

Roosts. Chicks should be given roosts as soon as possible. Even chicks in battery brooders can learn to roost early by the placement of long rods or thin perches through the sides.

In a building, chicks should be given low perches so that they learn to roost early. This gets chicks off the floor sooner. Old wooden ladders can be hung at low levels to encourage chicks to roosting before they graduate to adult-size roosts. Low, portable perches can be made out of 1-×-3-inch furring strips on the order of a sawhorse only 1 foot tall.

Thermometers. Beginners should always use thermometers to check the temperature of heat under brooders until experience is gained in adjusting temperatures only by looking at where the chicks sleep. Most thermometers will vary in the degrees they read. Some cheap thermometers might vary as much as 20 degrees Fahrenheit. When purchasing a regular thermometer at a store, look at the pile of them in the display to see if the same thermometers vary.

The most accurate type of thermometer is an oral one. This is the type most medicine cabinets contain. They read slow though.

A small, dial type of meat thermometer used for testing smoked meats reads fairly accurate and is fast, but it will cost around $15. Because it can be used for incubating, cooking, baking, smoking meats, checking room temperatures, and water temperatures for scalding during butchering, the extra cost of the thermometer will be paid off quickly with the multiple uses it has. These are purchased at butcher supply houses and restaurant supply stores.

Toe Punch. A toe punch is used to mark chicks by piercing a hole in the web between toes.

Wafers. Wafers (usually two) form a 3-inch "double" disk. Fig. 2-18. They are constructed of tempered brass and are filled with ether. Because

the ether is heated by the brooder's heating element, it expands—causing the disk to enlarge. When the disk enlarges, it touches the micro switch that then turns the heating element off in order to maintain a certain set temperature. The temperature is dependent upon how far or close the wafer disk is screwed next to the micro switch. As the ether cools, it contracts and causes the switch to turn the element on again.

There are only a few manufacturers of wafers in the United States. It will be difficult to distinguish what brand a store carries because the wafers are not marked. Brower wafers are usually sold in a marked box. Other brands might be sold alone without packaging.

A Brower wafer should be purchased by wafer numbers because some are slightly thicker or thinner and contain more or less ether for various degrees of heat. If, for instance, an incubator wafer is used for a brooder, there will be problems with the temperature staying too high. Accordingly, a brooder wafer will prevent an incubator from reaching the desired temperature and maintaining it.

The following wafer numbers are standard Brower wafers:

31-W. These are for temperatures up to 100 degrees Fahrenheit (37.77 degrees C.). They are for most electric, gas, coal, and oil brooders. They are also considered by many to be "universal" although the company says this is untrue and they should only be used for the specified type brooders.

1-WB. These are for temperatures up to 110

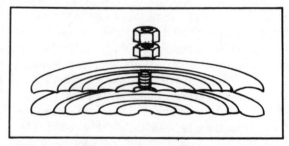

Fig. 2-18. A cutaway view of a double wafer used as a thermostat in incubators and brooders to control the temperature (courtesy of Brower Manufacturing Company, Inc.).

degrees. They are for electric and gas floor and battery brooders.

4-W. These are similar to the 31-W's but the adaptor is slightly larger for use with four-lamp type brooders.

2-W. These are for temperatures up to 120 degrees Fahrenheit (48.88 degrees C.). They are made specifically for incubators.

Other companies, such as Beacon, manufacture wafers called "universal" with a temperature range of 70 to 110 degrees Fahrenheit. These can be used in both incubators and brooders and they come with a removable adapter nut. Dealers need only carry one type of wafer for inventory simplification.

A handler should be careful about the brand because, if it's a Brower wafer, the correct number should be purchased. If the dealer says the wafer is not a Brower but claims it is universal, then it's safe to assume the wafer will be all right for both incubators and brooders. In order to check a wafer to see if it's still good, place it in a bowl of warm water to see if the disk still expands. If it doesn't it's time to replace the wafer.

Waterers. The correct waterer for chicks is one that does not allow chicks to get into it and drown. Very small chicks should be started with the metal (Fig. 2-19) or plastic (Fig. 2-20) Mason Jar founts because the dish is smaller than large double-walled founts. Some very small chicks will need stones or marbles placed in the dish to further prevent them from getting pushed into the water.

There are quail-size founts such as these that can be used for bantams, but they are harder to

Fig. 2-20. The plastic type of mason jar fount is economical to purchase and requires only to be laid over the mouth of the filled jar and inverted (courtesy of Brower Manufacturing Company, Inc.).

clean unless a brush is used. They also cost a slight bit more to purchase because they are not a standard item.

With any of these waterers, make sure the plastic ones are a rubberized plastic so cracking does not occur. The old-type glass ones are excellent because they clean easily and are heavy enough to prevent tipping. Any of these founts will only be used for a couple of weeks.

There are plastic 1-gallon founts (Figs. 2-21 and 2-22) for small chicks but they do not last as long as the small fount bases. Most are not made of rubberized plastic and they crack easily. They can be a nuisance to fill and put back together unless the locking type, other than the screw on type, is used. It's actually better to have more smaller founts situated in and around the chicks than a couple of larger founts during the first week or two anyways.

When birds are larger, bowl fountains and double-walled fountains can be used. Most bowl fountains are made of plastic. They operate automatically as they are hooked up to a water supply. Some are for low-pressure water systems only. Fairly easy to maintain and clean, they cost more than most other watering devices but last fairly long. They are used after a few weeks when chicks are accustomed to drinking from the smaller founts.

Double-wall fountains are made of metal. They hold 2, 3, 5, or 8 gallons of drinking water. The

Fig. 2-19. The only flaw in using this type of galvanized mason jar fount is that they do eventually rust, and this causes difficulty in screwing the jar in place (courtesy of Brower Manufacturing Company, Inc.).

Fig. 2-21. This plastic 1-gallon fount screws onto a 9-inch -diameter base (courtesy of The Warner Corporation).

Heat dissipates quickly through the metal sides. There is nothing in the brooder to hold the heat as there is with floor brooding. Under canopies, litter material and wood and dirt floors will absorb heat put out by the heating element. The accumulated heat in these materials, in turn helps warm the chicks.

The ultimate amount of heat from a battery brooder element is much less than a canopy brooder because it is made to heat an area of only 2 or 3 cubic feet, as compared to the average 12 cubic feet of a canopy floor brooder. Trying to cover the brooder with newspaper or blankets, without restricting needed ventilation, is dangerous and does little to hold the heat in.

Most handlers set up a battery brooder in a heated basement at 60 to 70 degrees Fahrenheit (15.55-21.11 degrees C.). Unheated basements will usually be about 50 degrees Fahrenheit (10 degrees C.). Because the temperature does not fluctuate as it does in an unheated outdoor building, covering one or two of the open sides with folded newspapers is safe, and should keep the temperature at 85 degrees Fahrenheit (29.44 degrees C.) for new chicks. Battery brooders can only be used where the room temperature stays at 50 degrees or above.

A lot depends on the amount of chicks in the

bottom is filled with water and then the top is placed down over forming the "double wall." A vacuum is created inside to control the water level in the attached pan. These will last a few years if kept free of damp litter. Small pin holes can be repaired with liquid compounds that harden. Chicks graduate to these at around four weeks of age. These waterers can be used right up until laying begins. See Fig. 2-23.

BATTERY BROODER RAISING DETAILS

The success of using battery brooders depends solely on management because they are not the ultimate trouble-free system of brooding most people believe. Do not expect to place battery brooders in an unheated outdoor building in cold weather. It simply won't work. The thermostat will constantly command the heating element to come on. You would think, because of the enclosed nature of a battery brooder, heat would stay confined. It doesn't even though some have insulation board under the top lid.

Fig. 2-22. This is a locking type of 1-gallon plastic fount (courtesy of Brower Manufacturing Company, Inc.).

46

brooder because body heat plays a big part in keeping the chicks warm. It would be unwise and uneconomical to house only a dozen chicks in a battery brooder in an unheated basement. The heating element would run constantly and probably never hold at 85 degrees. At least 50 chicks would be needed under these conditions.

While the brooder is heating, place rough rags over the wire floor in the heated area the first few days so day-old chicks can sleep comfortably. Bantams might need the rags for two weeks. The rags also prevent the chicks' legs from slipping down into the holes of the wire floor. It takes a couple days for new chicks to learn to walk on these wire floors. Rags also help to keep the heat from leaving the area through the wire floor when it's most needed.

Make sure the rags used are clean, dust free, and without loose threads. Loose threads can become entangled around chicks, killing or crippling them by cutting off circulation around neck and limbs.

A thermometer should be used at first. This is especially important if you are unsure of the room temperature in combination with the amount of chicks being brooded. Lay the thermometer on top of the rags under the heat. With the top lids in place, wait for the pilot light to switch off and then check the temperature.

Usually if the brooder can be kept at about 75 degrees Fahrenheit (23.88 degrees C.) before the chicks are put in. Having 50 or more chicks placed in the brooder will bring the temperature up to 85 to 90 degrees Fahrenheit (29.44-32.22 degrees C.).

If thermometer reads below 75 degrees Fahrenheit (23.88 degrees C.) when checked three times at 15 minute intervals, turn the setscrew just until the pilot light comes on. Then check again in same manner. When the correct temperature is reached at three readings, tighten the setscrew with a wing nut.

Watch the chicks closely the first day to see where they sleep. Wait a couple of hours because chicks that are shipped will not necessarily go under the heat right away unless they are stressed. They might stay out front to eat and drink before going

under the heat to sleep.

When most chicks are under the heating element, peek under the curtain to see if they are laying evenly—spread out like a plush carpet. If the majority are panting, lower the temperature by turning the setscrew slightly backwards. Recheck the thermometer 15 minutes later. Repeat until the desired temperature is reached.

If the chicks are standing and huddling directly under the heating element, it's too cold. Check the thermometer and turn the setscrew until the pilot light comes on. Wait 15 minutes and check the temperature again.

Some of these brooders do not indicate which direction is high or low. For convenience, you might want to mark it yourself. Although the pilot light goes on when raising the temperature, sometimes, in haste to adjust the temperature, the setscrew is turned in the wrong direction at a time when the pilot bulb burns out or the heating element goes bad.

Fill the two feed trays with feed and the one

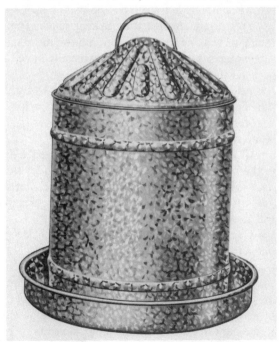

Fig. 2-23. A galvanized, 3-gallon, double-wall fount made especially for chicks because the pan depth is only 1 1/2 inches (courtesy of The Warner Corporation).

water tray with fresh water.

In the beginning, it doesn't make much difference what position the adjustable wire grids are at over the feed trays, but the grids should be at the first and smallest position over the water tray. Otherwise chicks will fall into the water and drown. Bantams can usually wiggle through the grids. A good tape can be stretched across the bottom of the feed grids so they can't escape. The water trays must be completely removed with the remaining grid taped at the bottom. Use pint jars for their water with bantam bases or fill the base with rocks or marbles.

Extremely thirsty chicks must not have access to the water tray at all because they will get wet and fall in while pushing and shoving their way to the water. Instead, place pint-size waterers with the fount area filled with marbles or rocks on the wire floor in various sections of the brooder, including one or two under the heat. After a week, the water tray can be introduced at the same time the pint jars are still in place. Use the smallest setting.

Most watering trays have too wide a space—even on the smallest—setting to keep chicks from falling or walking into the water. The small, separate water bases and pint jars will usually have to be used the first week or so.

Another plus in using the small water bases in the beginning is the ability for chicks to spot these waterers much faster than the outside water tray. They will begin drinking sooner.

Chicks that have just hatched should be placed in the rear of the brooder, on the rags, under the heat. These chicks do not require feed and water yet, but they do need the heat to fully dry and fluff them.

Chicks that were shipped should first be placed out in front so they can drink water. If they are cold, they will find their way under the curtain and under the heat.

A light must be kept on constantly in the room in which the brooder is kept as chicks cannot see in the dark to eat and drink. Nighttime can represent 8 hours or more of darkness. This amount of time without access to feed and water will cause mortality.

The pilot light does not stay on and so cannot be used as a constant source of light. The light used does not need to be very bright if you're concerned about costs. Even a nightlight will do as long as the feed and water can be seen at night and there is plenty of natural light during daylight hours.

Extra vitamin D must be given to battery-raised birds more so than others. Because they are in a box they have less access to sunlight, and therefore less of an opportunity to absorb vitamin D than chicks raised on an open building floor.

Battery chicks exercise less so they eat less feed, which is their main source of vitamin D. Because many commercially prepared medicated feeds contain less vitamin D than these chicks require, the vitamin must be supplemented. Without supplements rickets most likely will develop, especially in fast growers such as broilers.

One form of vitamin D is fresh cod-liver oil given in the drinking water until the battery chicks are out into the sun. For health reasons, all breeds of battery raised chicks should be given extra vitamin D.

The brooder's dropping pans can be lined with newspapers for easy dropping removal and to absorb moisture. Cedar shavings, moss, or sand can be sprinkled on the tray and scraped off when soiled. Some powered lime can be sprinkled on the litter or newspapers to sweeten the odor. Be sure to check daily for dead chicks back in dark corners of the brooder.

The wet, soiled newspapers and dead chicks should be incinerated or buried so as not to attract flys. It's not wise to put the papers in a compost pile because the paper takes a long time to disintegrate. A wide drywall patching knife or drywall taping knife works good for scraping the trays.

Hang fly catchers in brooder room to help prevent flys from gaining access to brooder trays. Flys can lay eggs in between daily tray clean up, resulting in a most unpleasant task of removal. Insecticide sprays should not be used because they will kill the chicks.

Disinfectant and fragrance sprays should be used with caution. Although not stated on the precautions on the cans, some brands will kill chicks. If the chick smell bothers you, either use another brooding system outdoors or place moth balls or crystals in glass containers in various parts of the room, out of the reach of children and pets. Humidity plays a large part in producing odors.

A few times a week the watering trays should be scrubbed and disinfected.

By making sure chicks cannot walk over the top of their feed during the entire brooding period, the feeders do not usually have to be changed and washed. Just run your finger through the feed to the bottom of the tray occasionally to check for hardened feed. This indicates moisture in the feed that will mold and can kill the chicks if eaten.

If feed trays must be washed, completely air dry them so no moisture remains in crevices to cause feed to mold.

Further remaining brooding care consists of lowering the temperature weekly about 5 degrees. Get in the habit of using the chicks as your guide to temperature settings. Beginners should use a thermometer until they acquire the knack of knowing how warm or cool the chicks are by watching where they sleep and whether they huddle or pant.

SOLAR BROODING

More than any other livestock, chicks depend upon fuel sources to keep them warm. When full-scale brooding of chicks began in the early 1900s, energy was inexpensive and abundant. Now there must be an alternative. Because solar heating performs better in a mild climate, the fact that most of the poultry industry is located mainly in the Sun Belt states seems to be a promising plus.

The high cost involved in equipment used for solar heating has curtailed wide scale use of the systems. As with any innovation, until mass produced, solar brooding will be expensive to install on a small-scale. For commercial growers, the initial cost of the system would pay for itself fast. Ingenious individuals who can recycle components for a small system would find the savings in fuel cost beneficial. For most small-scale raisers, there will most likely be a good many years ahead before small, solar-brooding systems are mass produced for economical purchase and use.

Following are some excerpts on solar brooding trials performed within the last few years. They have been summarized by some of the most respected names in the field of solar research engineering in the U.S. Department of Agriculture, Agricultural Research, Science and Education Administration.

[*]A solar poultry brooding research facility has been designed, built equipped, and instrumented at the Southeast Poultry Research Laboratory. The facility consists of three adjacent buildings (a solar building and two 87-m^2 broiler houses), two similar water-based systems for collecting, storing, and using solar energy, and a data acquisition system.

The goals of our research in this area are to determine the functional requirements of and establish design criteria for practical solar brooding systems. This research is supported, in part, by funds from the U.S. Department of Energy.

Six chick brooding trials, in which three types of solar brooding equipment were used, have been completed. The data from four of these trials have been analyzed and are presented and discussed in this report. The overall solar fraction of the total brooder heat was about 65%, the overall collector efficiency was about 33%, and the average utilization factor for the solar energy collected within a brooding trial was about 75%.

Brooding chicks with a solar-heated, water-to-air coil, in only the cooler months of the year, we were able to substitute solar energy for about three-fourths of the total brooder energy used in a well insulated, well stocked broiler house, using 26 m^2 of solar collector area and 2250 kg of water storage per 1000-chick brooding capacity. A 16.25-m^2 collector area, which was used in only one trial, was satisfactory in moderate weather. Water quantities

---

[*]L.N. Drury, B.W. Mitchell, and C.W. Beard, U.S. Department of Agriculture, Science and Education Administration, Agricultural Research, Southeast Poultry Research Laboratory, Athens, Georgia, *Agricultural Energy Vol 1,* reprinted with permission from the American Society of Agricultural Engineers, St. Joseph, Michigan, p. 228, p. 234.

less than 2250 kg were not used. The average insulation was less than the norm for 12 of the 14 weeks for which the brooder performance data are reported.

The overall efficiency of the solar collectors was about 33%, and the highest weekly efficiency was 50%. The overall COP of the collector circuits was only 16.5, and the highest weekly value only 26, partly because the pumps were oversized.

Eighty-seven percent of the solar heat pumped to the broiler house was "indirect," i.e., it could not have been supplied without energy storage.

Of the three types of solar brooder, the coil required less heat energy than did either the floor or the convector. The coil required more pump energy than did the floor and about the same as did the convector. The floor was able to extract heat from water of lower temperatures than those required by the coil. Comparisons of floor with coil and floor with convector suggest that the floor would probably require more heat energy than the convector would.

In these well-insulated brooder pens, the lamps plus the primary fan provided about 25% of the total supplemental heat required, leaving only 75% to be provided by the brooder.

The type of brooder used had no measurable effect on chick performance. Ventilation, at approximately the energy conserving rates recommended by Collins and Walpole (1979), did not prevent extensive pasting of the litter surface, regardless of brooder type (one of which was a conventional gas hover).

The long-term utilization of solar energy by an adequately sized solar poultry brooding system will probably be low unless progress is made toward leveling the heating demand within broods and among seasons, or other uses are found for the solar energy that can often be collected in excess of that required to heat the poultry house.

The solar brooding systems described in this report were designed to be versatile research tools and, as such, are probably not practical without considerable modification. No attempt was made to optimize these systems nor to determine their economics.

Trials were also conducted at the South Central Poultry Research Laboratory at Mississippi State University, Mississippi through the U.S. Department of Agriculture, Agricultural Research, Science and Education Administration.

Here, three trials were conducted during

Fig. 2-24. A practical approach for collectors is to face them to the south and mount them at an angle from the horizon equal to the local latitude, plus 10 to 15 degrees (courtesy of USDA, ARS, South Central Poultry Research Laboratory).

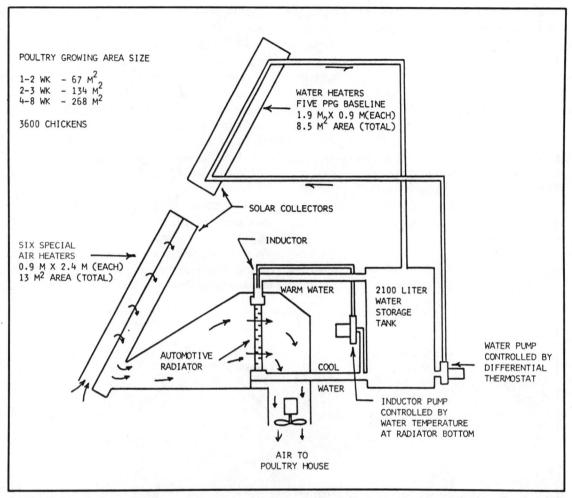

POULTRY GROWING AREA SIZE

1-2 WK – 67 M^2
2-3 WK – 134 M^2
4-8 WK – 268 M^2

3600 CHICKENS

WATER HEATERS
FIVE PPG BASELINE
1.9 M$_2$X 0.9 M(EACH)
8.5 M^2 AREA (TOTAL)

SOLAR COLLECTORS

INDUCTOR

SIX SPECIAL
AIR HEATERS
0.9 M X 2.4 M (EACH)
13 M^2 AREA (TOTAL)

WARM WATER

2100 LITER
WATER
STORAGE
TANK

AUTOMOTIVE
RADIATOR

COOL

WATER

WATER PUMP
CONTROLLED BY
DIFFERENTIAL
THERMOSTAT

INDUCTOR PUMP
CONTROLLED BY
WATER TEMPERATURE
AT RADIATOR BOTTOM

AIR TO
POULTRY HOUSE

Fig. 2-25. The first solar heating system designed and used during the first three brooding trials (courtesy of USDA, ARS, South Central Poultry Research Laboratory).

varying outdoor temperatures from 1975-1977 (with the type solar heating panels shown in Fig. 2-24).

*During the three trials using the solar heating system described, (and shown in Fig. 2-25) several operation problems were encountered. The major ones were:

1). When outside temperature was below – 6 C., ice collected in balancing valves and other plumbing associated with water-heating collectors,

which prevented prompt start-up of the system the following day.

2). The water storage tank appeared to be too small.

3). It was found that the optimum flow rate through the air heaters was about 900 liters/(min) (m^2). However, the ventilation rate required in the house during the first two weeks would permit only 300 to 600 liter/(min) (m^2). This resulted in

*F.N. Reece, U.S. Department of Agriculture, Agricultural Research, Science and Education Administration, South Central Poultry Research Laboratory, Mississippi State, Mississippi, *Use of Solar Energy in Poultry Production* (Vol. 60, No. 5; Poultry Science, May 1981), pgs. 914-916, U.S.D.A. reprint.

reduced collector efficiency when maximum heat was needed in the poultry house.

4). The ratio of water-heating collector areas to air-heating collector area was too small as a result of the fact that the water heaters were less efficient than expected, and the air heaters were more efficient than expected.

As a result of this experience, a new system was designed (as shown in Fig. 2-56). A prototype of this system was fabricated and tested at South Central Poultry Research Laboratory during the Period January 19 to March 19, 1978. In order to correct the problems encountered with the original system, the following features were incorporated in the new system:

1). The water tank is close-coupled to the water-heating collectors, with all associated plumbing and pumps contained within the water tank.

2). Water storage capacity was increased from 2100 liters to 3000 liters.

3). Provision was made to recirculate air through the air-heating collectors when ventilation requirements in the poultry house were low. The heat gained in the recirculated air is transferred to the water storage via automotive radiator.

4). The water-heating collector area was increased from 8.5 m^2 to 11 m^2.

The initial trial of the modified system indicated that the problems associated with the original design were eliminated. However, abnormally cold, cloudy weather that occurred during the test, especially during the first week, increased supplemental heat required to maintain

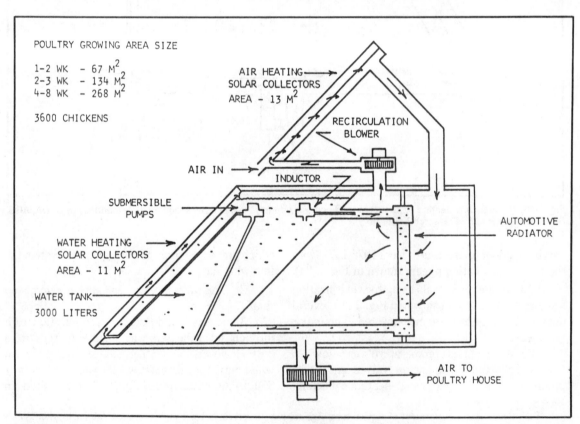

POULTRY GROWING AREA SIZE

1-2 WK - 67 M^2
2-3 WK - 134 M^2
4-8 WK - 268 M^2

3600 CHICKENS

AIR HEATING
SOLAR COLLECTORS
AREA - 13 M^2

RECIRCULATION BLOWER

AIR IN

INDUCTOR

SUBMERSIBLE PUMPS

AUTOMOTIVE RADIATOR

WATER HEATING
SOLAR COLLECTORS
AREA - 11 M^2

WATER TANK
3000 LITERS

AIR TO POULTRY HOUSE

Fig. 2-26. The second solar heating system designed and tested (courtesy of USDA, ARS, South Central Poultry Research Laboratory).

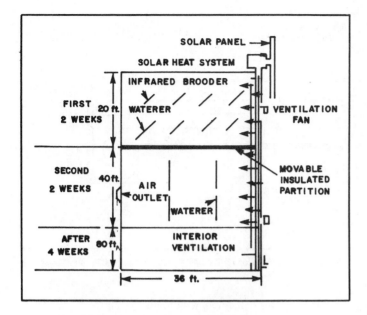

FIRST 2 WEEKS | 20 ft.

SECOND 2 WEEKS | 40 ft.

AFTER 4 WEEKS | 80 ft.

SOLAR PANEL
SOLAR HEAT SYSTEM
INFRARED BROODER
WATERER
VENTILATION FAN
MOVABLE INSULATED PARTITION
AIR OUTLET
WATERER
INTERIOR VENTILATION
36 ft.

Fig. 2-27. Floor plan of brooder house showing arrangements for one-fourth of the house for the first two weeks of rearing chicks and one-half during the next two weeks.

the desired house temperature. A total of 38 liters of LPG/1000 chickens (energy equivalent) was required to supplement the solar energy to brood and grow the chickens. Sixty-six percent of this supplemental energy was used during the first week of the 8-week growing period.

Reece further writes, in another USDA publication, the brooding area in this experiment was restricted to 25 percent of the total floor space of the poultry house for the first two weeks and to 50 percent for the second two weeks. After four weeks, the entire house was used. Dimensions of the poultry house were 36 by 80 feet (11 by 24 meters). See Fig. 2-27.

Early in the experiment, the brooding area was partitioned with polyethlene curtains. Rigid-foam insulation board later proved to be more efficient. A strip of fiberboard or cardboard can be added across the bottom to prevent chicks from pecking holes in the foam.

Continuous ventilation was provided and the relative humidity was kept to less than 70 percent. Polyvinyl ducts carried heated air to the growing area where small vents in the ducts provided even distribution of the airflow.

Thermostatically controlled electric fans were used for additional ventilation when temperatures

in the growing area exceeded 85 degrees Fahrenheit (29 degrees C.) in the first week, 80 degrees Fahrenheit (27 degrees C.) in the second week, and 70 degrees Fahrenheit (21 degrees C.) after the third week.

Figure 2-28 shows a side view of the air collector that was designed and built for the experimental broiler house. For each 1000 chickens, an area of 73 square feet (6.9 m^3) of collector surface was used. Initially, 40 percent of the collectors used water as the heat transfer medium, and 60 percent used air. Later, because efficiencies were different than anticipated, a higher percentage of water-type collectors were used.

For collector systems using water as the transfer medium, a well-insulated water tank is recommended for storage. For air-type collectors, a large, insulated area filled with small rocks or crushed stone is recommended (Fig. 2-29)

In conjunction with partial-house brooding, precision ventilation control, and improved insulation, the solar heating system in this experiment reduced the amount of energy needed to operate a brooder house by about 90 percent, and consumption of fossil fuel was negligible.

With a solar heating system, the fuel is free, but the equipment needed to collect and store solar

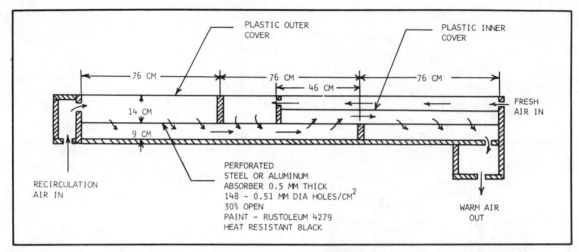

Fig. 2-28. Side view of a high-efficiency solar heat collector (courtesy of USDA, ARS, South Central Poultry Research Laboratory).

energy is large and expensive. For example, in Mississippi in 1979, replacing the full heating capacity of a $40 LPG brooder with solar energy equipment required 320 square feet (30 m²) of solar energy flat-plate collectors. The initial cost

of the collectors was about $3,200.

How Solar Heating Systems Work. Solar heating systems are designed to exploit some well-known characteristics of light. Solar energy collectors work because of a natural phenomenon

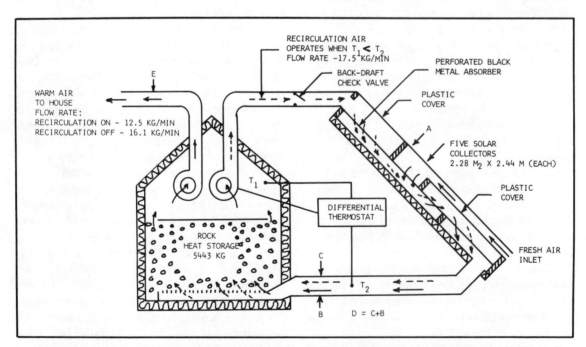

Fig. 2-29. Tanks to store heated air must be larger than tanks used to store heated water when air is the transfer medium (courtesy of USDA, ARS, South Central Poultry Research Laboratory).

54

known as the "greenhouse effect." Sunlight enters through the clear cover of an energy collector and is trapped when it changes to a longer wave length as it strikes the dark surface of an absorber. Then, a heat transfer medium, such as air or water, passes through the collector to absorb the heat energy and to move the energy to a point of use or to storage for later use.

Collectors generally work most efficiently when they are positioned perpendicularly to the angle of incoming solar radiation. A practical approach for collectors is to face them to the south and mount them at an angle from the horizon equal to the local latitude plus 10 to 15 degrees.

A good flat-plate collector will have an efficiency of 40 to 60 percent; that is, it will convert into usable heat about half of the radiation that strikes it. This type of collector will function to some extent even on cloudy or overcast days.

Auxiliary electric or fuel-fired heaters are usually needed to supplement solar systems, and they were used in the experimental system described here. They avoid the expense of building an extra-large solar heating system that would otherwise be needed to meet all contingencies.

Sound planning and careful selection of materials, preferably materials guaranteed or tested by reputable firms, are essential in building a solar-heating system. Information on adapting solar energy technology to poultry farming can be obtained from state land-grant universities or from the National Solar Heating and Cooling Information Center, P.O. Box 1607, Rockville, MD 20850.

OUTDOOR RAISING

Outdoor raising consists of using small box-like houses with attached pens (Fig. 2-30). These are good for raisers that do not have other facilities for brooding. It's a type of miniature brooder house.

The boxes can be designed to set directly on the ground or raised on legs with the pen becoming a sun deck (Fig. 2-31) where droppings are allowed to fall through the wire floor. Ground pens should only be set on grass or sand in order to prevent disease and to prevent the chicks from becoming muddy and wet and tracking it in onto their litter.

The box size is measured for space the same as for any other brooding method. Take into consideration how long the chicks will remain in

Fig. 2-30. Outdoor brooding and growing boxes with attached pens can allow chickens access to green grasses.

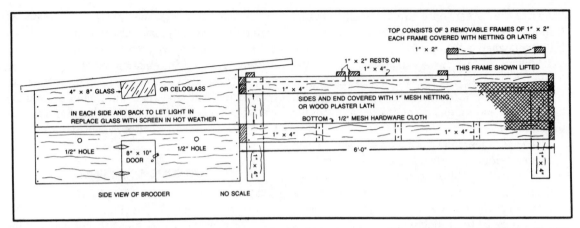

Fig. 2-31. Outdoor brooder and sun deck to construct for 60 chicks (courtesy of Texas Agricultural Extension Service, Texas A&M University System).

these boxes. Smaller amounts of chicks raised in more than one box is much better than containing a large amount of chicks in one large box because smaller boxes are easier to move, and there is less mortality when housing small lots of chicks. If predator problems do occur, the loss should not be as great because most predators will not bother to visit each box. You can gradually separate culls, cockerels, and any sick birds as spotted. Cannibalism, usually started by only a few, can be spotted more easily before it gets out of hand, and the main culprits can then be removed.

The boxes are constructed of wood. If the boxes are only going to be turned at 90 degree angles with pens, the boxes do not need to be lightweight. If the plan is to move them any great distance, because of, perhaps, a coccidiosis outbreak on that part of ground, then construct the boxes of lightweight but weatherproof materials.

The boxes should be made with a wood or tin floor to keep the soil's dampness from the chicks and to keep predators from burrowing under (Fig. 2-32). Install one 12-inch square door for chick entry, or a door on each of the four side walls that will make it unnecessary to continually move the entire box with each 90 degree turn of the pens. For convenience, the door should slide down into a track because hinged doors can be obstructed by anything in the pens, including long blades of grass.

At least two observation windows should be made on two opposite walls to check temperature and view the chicks without startling them.

One-half inch ventilation holes must be drilled on each side near the top of the box walls so built-up heat and moisture can escape and allow some fresh air to enter.

There should be a removable roof on the box that either slides off or is hinged so the chicks can be tended to easily by you. It's no fun getting down on your hands and knees or belly to reach to the other side while pulling dead chicks out or trying to retrieve live ones—they're always one step ahead of your hand.

To keep chicks busy and teach them to roost, provide small roosting bars in the cooler part of box. Attach them from wall to wall in the corner. Place the feed and waterers further down the wall so they will not be contaminated by droppings as the birds roost.

The outside pens must be constructed of small wire mesh that chicks cannot wiggle through and predators cannot wiggle into. Welded rabbit cage wire, though costly, is small diameter and will withstand years of weather. Make sure the pen contains a top to protect chicks from swooping hawks, owls, and other animals.

This system calls for a heat lamp to be hung inside the box. The trickiest part is determining what size bulb to use (Fig. 2-33). Because the box is out in the open, the sun will help heat the interior.

And, because the chicks are confined, their body heat will add to the artificial and sun-heated environment. Because outdoor temperatures cannot be controlled, the heat lamp must be positioned in one corner of the box so chicks can get away from too much heat should it become especially warm outdoors before you've had a chance to check on them.

Usually the large 250-watt lamps are too much heat during late spring and summer for this type of confinement. Before your chicks arrive, hang a large, easily readable outdoor thermometer on the

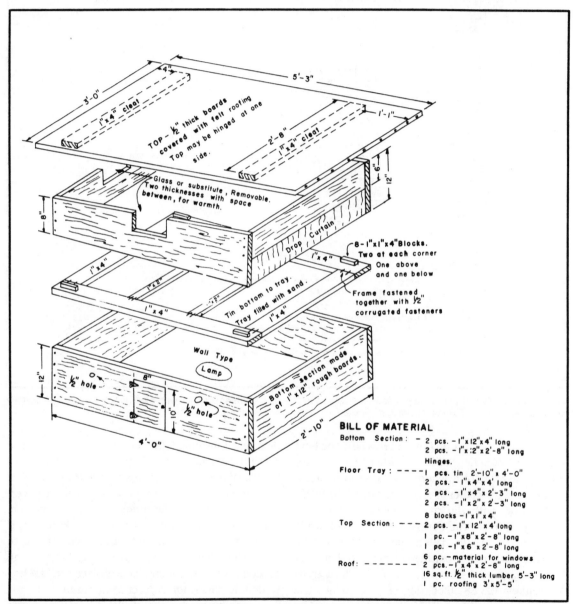

Fig. 2-32. Inside sections of the 60-chick outdoor brooder (courtesy of Texas Agricultural Extension Service, Texas A&M University System).

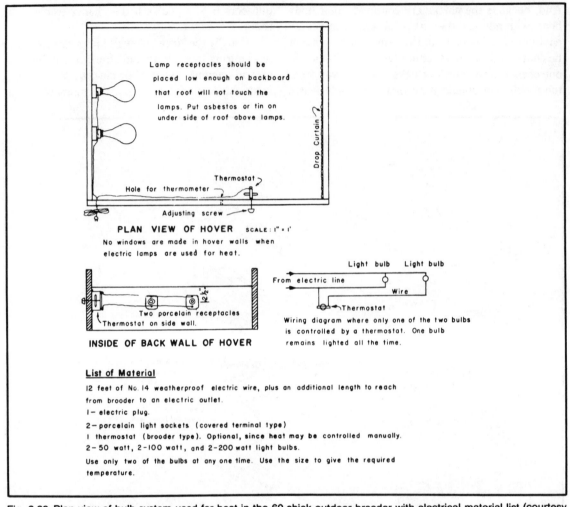

Figure content (as labeled):

Lamp receptacles should be placed low enough on backboard that roof will not touch the lamps. Put asbestos or tin on under side of roof above lamps.

Drop Curtain

Thermostat

Hole for thermometer

Adjusting screw

PLAN VIEW OF HOVER SCALE: 1" = 1'

No windows are made in hover walls when electric lamps are used for heat.

Two porcelain receptacles

Thermostat on side wall.

INSIDE OF BACK WALL OF HOVER

Light bulb   Light bulb

From electric line

Wire

Thermostat

Wiring diagram where only one of the two bulbs is controlled by a thermostat. One bulb remains lighted all the time.

List of Material

12 feet of No. 14 weatherproof electric wire, plus an additional length to reach from brooder to an electric outlet.

1 — electric plug.

2 — porcelain light sockets (covered terminal type)

1 thermostat (brooder type). Optional, since heat may be controlled manually.

2 — 50 watt, 2 — 100 watt, and 2 — 200 watt light bulbs.

Use only two of the bulbs at any one time. Use the size to give the required temperature.

Fig. 2-33. Plan view of bulb system used for heat in the 60-chick outdoor brooder with electrical material list (courtesy of Texas Agricultural Extension Service, Texas A&M University System).

inside wall of the box (in the corner where the heat lamp is near the floor). Place another thermometer directly across from where the lamp is to get a reading for the cooler area. Begin with a 100-watt bulb. Now, with the roof in place, check both readings through the observation windows while it's cool outdoors (perhaps at night or after a rain), and again when the weather is warmest. The heat lamp area should vary between 75 to 80 degrees Fahrenheit (23.88-26.66 degrees C.) while the cooler area should be 10-15 degrees cooler. The temperature is not adjusted to the needed 85 degrees Fahrenheit (29.44 degrees C.), because when the chicks are finally placed in the box, their body heat will raise the temperature. Raise or lower the lamp or replace it with a higher-watt or lower-watt bulb to adjust the temperature. Always give the box interior sufficient time to build up heat, if the roof cover is removed, before attempting to read the thermometer again. Do this same procedure when the chicks are placed in the box to double check for correct temperatures.

Begin to harden the chicks off on very warm days, when they're about three weeks old, by raising their sliding entry door a few inches every other day. The chicks will gradually venture out into the open pen, happily flapping their wings and running about. Don't worry about shooing all the chicks back in the box for the night (unless you'll be gone) because they'll go in on their own where the heat and light is. Because of their new found freedom, some will stay out to enjoy the last minute of daylight. Check on them as soon as it's totally dark outdoors. Make sure none are huddled together in the outside pen's corners. Slide the door shut so predators aren't tempted.

The pen is moved to clean ground as needed by simply moving the pen on each side of the box as soon as the grass begins to show wear. If the chicks are allowed to totally destroy and trample the grass because the pen is left in one position too long, the grass will take quite some time to revive. It's a good idea to keep chicks locked in during very wet weather for their health and the longevity of the grass.

Many chickens can be raised this way on a small amount of land. Friends of mine have used this same outdoor pen system for growing chicks and laying hens for a number of years with very good results.

OUTDOOR CHICK SHELTER

Years ago, when chickens were one of the mainstays of many farms around the country, more effort and elaborate means of housing them were employed. Remnants of this fact remain as we can still see "colony brooder houses," two-story laying houses, and long, low poultry buildings dotting the countryside. Some of these buildings are still used for chickens.

In the 1860s, chicks were brooded in the same building as the layers because the replacement chicks were hatched and brooded by hens (Fig. 2-34). The picture 50 years ago was a separate brooder house for raising chicks, with a larger laying house where the grown chicks were then transferred. The majority of cockerels were marketed and butchered.

During the 1940s, World War II brought shortages of many raw materials. Poultry raisers became more conservative in housing their chickens. Many farm flocks were brooded in the basement or garage for the first three to four weeks and then finished in a garage or shed. Material cost and labor force many small-scale raisers to brood in this fashion today.

Modern commercial broiler and pullet production today might consist of from one to ten narrow, 500-foot houses. One-hundred feet in one end of the house is closed off with a plastic curtain to hold the accumulated heat produced by the chicks' bodies and the brooders. This closed-off area is where the chicks are brooded, usually with gas hanging brooders hung in the middle of the room. At five to six weeks of age, the plastic curtain is removed to allow the chicks more space to grow another couple weeks, as in the case of broilers, or another 10 or more weeks for ready to lay pullets (Fig. 2-35).

This same system can be arranged on a small scale (Fig. 2-36) for raising family flocks. It's a good method if you raise all your chicks at one time because the brooder should be left on for a couple weeks for most breeds. The main advantage to this system is the labor saved in handling the birds. They won't have to be picked up and carted from a brooder area to growing quarters. Plus, there need be only one area for feed storage and one lighting and electrical system.

Single, small brooder houses are versatile. They can be converted into layer or bantam houses or storage.

It's entirely up to you if outdoor runs are made for the growing chicks. Grass will not grow continuously in the runs unless rotated in use. The birds will surely benefit from the sun.

If you want your chicks to feed on free greens, occasionally let the chicks out one door about one hour before it's dark outside. Make sure there is nothing that will frighten them from the building. If they're frightened, you may find yourself looking for them with a flashlight in one hand and in the other hand swatting mosquitoes.

The first few times the chicks are allowed out, they may not even leave the inside of the building because of fear of what's out there. Once they get the idea they'll be waiting at the door for you daily. Don't overdo it. If the chicks are let out daily, they'll gain too much independence, stray further away, and not want to go in with the others even when darkness comes.

If they're lightbreeds, wings should be clipped to prevent flying into tree tops out of your reach. A long-handled smelt net can be used to retrieve some of these flyers if you're not worried about the net being torn. Otherwise a rope, weighted on one

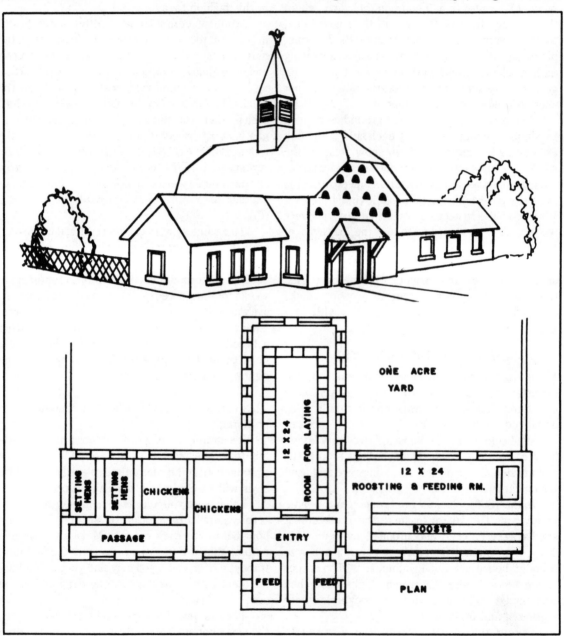

Fig. 2-34. A perspective view and plan of a poultry house of the 1860s where chicks were brooded with hens.

Fig. 2-35. Looking down one-half of a commercial broiler house in Mississippi (USDA photo by George A. Robinson).

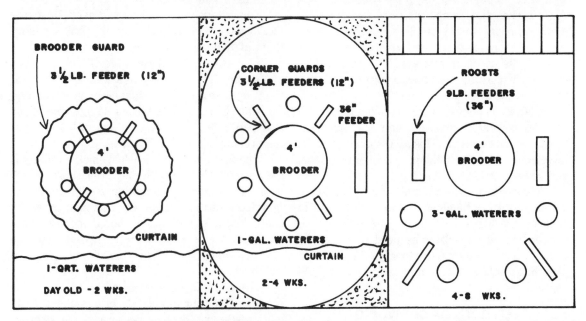

Fig. 2-36. In a small building, a curtain can be hung across the room to help conserve heat and later removed when the extra floor space is needed to finish growing the chicks.

end, can be flung over tree branches to shake the birds down. There should be no worry about the birds being hurt as they fall from the trees because they usually flap their wings on the way down and land on their feet.

Flying onto rooftops creates even more of a problem. It's better just to clip wings ahead before the problem arises. The chicks will still be able to roost indoors.

If possible, the building should be sheltered somewhat from the weather by providing windbreaks in the form of trees or larger buildings. Do not have these right up next to the chicks' house because they provide a hiding place for predators. Keep the surrounding areas at least 5 feet clear of debris, cages, feed storage containers, weed overgrowth, etc., to discourage predators.

The building should not set on low ground, which naturally stays damper, even if it sets up off the ground on blocks or piers and chicks will remain inside. Upon tending to the chicks' needs, you'll more than likely track damp matter into the building yourself.

Buildings which house chicks must be ventilated to replenish oxygen. Ventilation will dilute carbon dioxide and moisture and therefore minimize odors. In any building enough fresh air is drawn in through cracks and crevices for the very small chicks' needs. If there are 100 or more chicks or if they're cornish rock crosses, extra ventilation will be needed in a few weeks.

A large amount of 6-week-and-older chicks will give off several gallons of water through their breathing and excretion. This excess moisture must be removed from the building to keep litter, walls, and ceilings dry.

A wooden enclosure can also be built into the corner of a large building. Equip it with a lid to conserve heat and help keep predators out. A plywood board must later be used to corral the chicks when it's time to move them to new quarters. The chicks will quickly run from end to end to avoid capture.

EFFECTS OF CROWDING

Some forethought is needed with the brooding layout to avoid problems with crowding. If the day-old chicks will be kept in one particular area for four weeks, make sure the brooding area is large enough for the amount of chicks which will remain there for the entire four weeks.

This all seems very obvious, but it's easy to forget about the future environment when there's so much planning going on for the chicks' immediate needs. Sometimes we're inclined to think we can make do until the time comes when larger quarters are needed. Because the chicks make the largest leaps in growth during the early weeks, they thereby become crowded sooner than when placed in sufficiently large enough quarters after 6 weeks of age when their growth isn't as rapid.

If the plan is to move the chicks at a "predetermined" age to larger accommodations, this is fine if the maneuver is made when planned. If not, the chicks growth will be set back by them being crowded for just one or two weeks. Situations do arise when a handler just cannot move the birds as scheduled. Be safe by allowing one or two weeks of extra space by using the space reference guide listed earlier in this chapter.

For instance, 100 chicks will need 75 square feet to carry them through when the plan is to move them at five weeks of age. Two weeks later, at seven weeks of age, these same 100 chicks need 150 square feet. It's easy to see how 100 chicks, if left until seven weeks of age—in space allotted for 100 chicks at five weeks of age—would be cramped. They'd be living in one-half the space they require.

The first two weeks is when chick mortality is the greatest. Crowding chicks during this time will definitely cause needless mortality, with slower and retarded growth in others. With not much room for exercise, chicks will become bored because of the lack of activity and revert to feather and toe picking, which will draw blood and bring on cannibalism.

Crowding also interferes with the feathering process. Good air circulation brings about good, quick feathering. Further, because the chicks brush against each other more often when closely confined, new feathers are rubbed off, broken, and split. This can be the cause of some "barebacks," although quite a few would indicate bad breeding.

Less air circulation and too many birds in one area will cause the litter to stay damp under canopy brooders. Canopy brooding will require the total size of the pen or building to be governed by the amount of chicks raised during the entire period they will be housed in that area. Given this amount of space, and, because most canopy brooders are designed for more than 200 birds, this type of brooding seems to keep small-scale producers from crowding the chicks.

Battery brooders are usually crowded unintentionally because inexperienced handlers are only aware of the avoidance of problems that can immediately be seen. They know there is no need to worry about wet litter from crowding because the chicks will be up on wire floors. They will see how the confinement of the chicks might produce body heat to help keep them warm. What they won't see, until it's too late, is the retarded growth and bad feathering.

It's also almost impossible to see into every corner of a battery brooder when it's crowded. If a chick is caught in the wire or has had others begin to pick at him, the handler can miss these chicks when routinely checking the brooders. The result is the death of these chicks.

LIGHTING NEEDS

To demonstrate the importance of providing a light near the chicks' feed and water throughout the night, consider the following common occurrence: A handler purchases a battery brooder because he believes he'll be able to raise his chicks better than the brooder lamp system he previously used. The handler then sets up his battery brooder in the basement, fills the feeders and waterers, check the temperature again, and places the day old chicks inside. He cleans the brooder in the mornings and replenishes the chicks' supply of feed and water in the afternoons and evenings.

Without thinking much about it, he does notice the chicks come out from under the heating element

and curtain to greet him during every evening brooder check. What he should have noticed at the morning check was that the feeders and waterers always contained the same amount of feed and water as was left the night before.

At one week of age he experiences quite a few unexplained losses. At two, three, and four weeks of age he feels the chicks are not doing as well as they should. There seem to be quite a few more runts than usual. The chicks just aren't gaining weight as they should.

The problem? After the evening brooder check, the handler would leave the chicks for the night and turn off all basement lights before retiring. Without a source of light, the chicks were unable to find their feed and water. The pilot light does not stay on long enough to be relied upon for a source of light to eat and drink by. In fact, with no outer light, the chicks will stay under the heating element and sleep. In this case, the heater will not run as much, and, in turn, the pilot light will not be on as much either.

Chicks must be allowed to eat and drink as they desire for proper and even growth, and to prevent dehydration. The dehydration of chicks held in a battery brooder will surely develop if they must sleep under the dry heat constantly every night. Chicks cannot see in the dark and will not venture out to the feeders and waterers for any length of time with the absence of light. This seems very obvious, but it's this type of oversight that can be disastrous when raising chicks.

On occasion, handlers will try to use battery brooders in an outdoor building or barn, sometimes covering the whole brooder with a blanket to keep heat in. This also keeps light out and the chicks cannot easily find their feed and water.

Some raisers have good intentions when raising chicks without a thorough knowledge of what chicks are able to accomplish. One woman created a brooder in her garage by taking a cardboard box, turning it upside down, and hanging a lamp inside for heat. She cut out several small doors in the box near the floor for the chicks to come and go as they pleased. Feeders and waterers were placed around the outside of the houselike brooder box.

It only took a few days of finding dead chicks under the box when she realized something must be wrong. She immediately checked the temperature under the box and found it to be perfect. A bit too warm during the day, but fine at night. She thought that the chicks need only to go out through their little cut-out doors to get away from any built up heat.

In the first place, it took those chicks a few days just to find out where their feed and water was placed. They did not know enough to venture out through their little cut-out doors in order to find their feed and water. Second, it wouldn't have mattered anyway because the feed and water were kept in the dark most of the time, relying only on the sunlight coming through the window.

Chicks brooded with a mother hen do not eat while it's totally dark, but they are not subjected to such drying conditions as the heating element brings on in the brooder either. Respiration among a brood of chicks under a hen creates a humid condition that prevents the chick's body and system from drying out. This, in turn, helps the chicks to feather out faster and allows them to stay out from under their mother longer in order for them to eat what they require and drink what they need.

By about eight weeks, if the chicks are doing well, have learned how to roost, are of a good weight and no longer need brooder heat, the light can then be discontinued. Constant lighting must be taken from the chicks with caution to avoid piling and smothering problems. The sudden absence of constant light can cause the chicks to feel their heat source is gone.

Some commercial U.S. broiler growers use a timer to turn lights on and off every two hours with the thought that this stimulates the chicks' appetites. Other reasoning considers the dangers involved should a power failure abruptly turn lights off while using the constant lighting system. In Canada, most broiler growers use constant lighting, turning lights off one hour each day until market age.

The dangers of birds piling, should a power failure suddenly turn constant lighting off, cannot logically hold true for all brooding systems. If there is a power failure, an electrically supplied brooder will turn off right along with the extra lighting. If not tended to quickly, birds will therefore pile because of the lack of heat in combination with a lack of light.

Gas brooding can be considered to be safer because a power failure will not affect the chicks' heat source. If a power failure should turn lights off, the infrared rays emitted while the burner is on, will provide enough light for such emergencies. This is not enough light for growing birds during the whole brooding period.

When older chicks are accustomed to this timed lighting, which was begun when they were just day olds, the problem of piling when removing the lights is much avoided. The lights are simply left off when they are no longer needed.

ENTERTAINMENT NEEDS

Very young chicks appear to only be interested in eating, drinking, and sleeping. If watched for any length of time, the close observation will show chicks actually play. Chicks in battery brooders or on sand litter cannot grab bits of straw. Loose threads on curtains can be dangerous fun because chicks easily can get wrapped up in them. Usually the thread ends up around the neck or around their leg causing choking or lameness from the restrained circulation of the blood.

I've even seen a few chicks manage to somehow get the thread twisted tightly around their tongue. After a piece of thread has been wound tightly around the neck, leg, toe, wing, or tongue for any length of time, the part involved swells substantially. This makes removal of the thread almost impossible.

In a brooding area, there might be no place a chick can jump up to or down from—no place to test his wings. There may not be enough feeder or waterer space to keep chicks busy or a good tasting variety of feed to sustain interest in eating.

When the only form of amusement available is each other, the chicks quickly become bored. There are many ways a handler can keep his chicks busy, occupied and entertained. Just visiting the chicks breaks up the monotony in their environment.

Chicks know their caretaker. They also can be frightened by strangers.

Providing plenty of feeders and waterers well spaced among the chicks will keep them busy. Do not allow these to become empty. Check the supply frequently.

Varying the texture and taste of feed will spark an interest among the feeding trays. Occasionally treat growing chicks of over two weeks of age to some cracked grains. Feed can also be varied by using crumbles sprinkled over mash or mash over crumble type feed. Sprinkle a few handfuls over the top of their regular feed a few times a week.

Offer fine grit or sand beginning at one week of age and every day after. Chicks find grit a new and fascinating substance. Grit not only keeps the chicks occupied by pecking at it, the chicks' will use it with their gizzards to grind the feed.

Bits of grass clippings can be given to chicks after one week of age when their bodies' systems can begin to assimilate this type of roughage. Don't overdo the greens. A handful three times a week is plenty for 100 chicks at this age. Anymore can cause loose droppings. It's not meant to supplement the diet but only to keep chicks interested in what's going on around them and to keep them busy. Greens can be used to supplement a two-month old's diet. Always be certain any greens given are free of sprayed poisons.

Torn pieces of paper are a joy to chicks. I've never seen harm in giving them bits of paper to grab, run with, and chase after. Color printed papers are usually toxic so use just plain white papers. Tear a few small pieces, lay them on top of their feed, and then watch the fun.

Live insects aren't usually played with well by very young chicks. The insect usually gets away from them. Dead insects always work better for the inexperienced chicks.

Supplying small roosts from sticks or bird perches provides a form of recreation for chicks. If perches aren't provided, chicks will try to find their own by jumping on top of equipment in their brooding area. It's better to supply perches than have to clean droppings off of feeders and waterers.

For small raisers, providing entertainment should not present a problem. It should be included as part of a handler's management practices. It will pay off in bettering the health of the chicks and in warding off cannibalism losses.

When a handler is producing chickens for food, it's hard to think chicks need anything else but good feed, water, and the right temperature. If a handler claims to have never provided entertainment for his chicks before, he's either had good luck with them because his method of raising inadvertently supplied the entertainment, or he has experienced cannibalism among his chicks.

WATCH DROPPINGS

As repulsive as it may sound to some, a handler must continually check the conditions of his chicks' droppings to prevent serious disease conditions from developing and to be assured their intestinal tracts are assimilating the feed satisfactorily.

There should be more of a concern over the texture of the chicks' droppings than the coloration. The coloration will vary with the type of feed eaten. It does not include the pink or red droppings, which contain blood.

The first few days of life, chicks will excrete a normal greenish-yellow watery substance. From this point on up to two weeks of age, the chicks' droppings should be checked every few days for looseness that might indicate a digestive upset. A digestive upset at this age means any irritation of the young chicks' tender digestive lining. Problems can be caused by acids, chemicals, medications, administering too much cod liver oil, chilling, and bacteria from filthy equipment or dirty drinking water. These are the causes of loose droppings during this period. The remedy is to correct the cause by reviewing which of the circumstances prevail and to eliminate the offender.

The most important period to check droppings frequently is from the beginning of two weeks of age. This is when most outbreaks of coccidiosis begin to occur.

Because the majority of diseases and dietary deficiencies do not affect or begin to exhibit symptoms in very young chicks, the handler should concern himself with the most common disease of chicks—that of coccidiosis and it's first symptom. I make this statement because some handlers worry unduly over other less common diseases without first considering the most common.

Coccidiosis will be seen first as looseness of the droppings. As it progresses, the droppings will be watery, pink, or contain bright red spots of blood.

It's easy to check the droppings of battery-brooder-raised birds as the droppings are clearly visible as excreted on the dropping pans. The wire floors the chicks walk on can serve as a source of coccidiosis infection unless wires are removed, scrubbed, and disinfected regularly along with feeders and waterers. After a couple weeks of use, these wire floors hold manure in the crevices. Many people believe the use of battery brooders will eliminate the disease entirely because coccidiosis is spread by access to infected droppings. Their belief is that batteries keep the chicks from these droppings. Actually, there is no brooding method that will keep chicks entirely from each other's droppings.

The droppings of floor-raised or box-raised chicks is altered because the chicks walk over them constantly, making the droppings' original form and color almost impossible to distinguish. To keep abreast of the condition of the droppings of floor-raised chicks, simply lay a folded newspaper under them for a few minutes. Then remove the newspaper and do your checking.

If the droppings are checked often, the handler should not be faced with the later, more critical symptoms of coccidiosis that cannot be tended to as easily. These first symptoms can be remedied with barely any loss of chicks. Further, if coccidiosis gets a start, it will be spread rapidly from these droppings.

If frequent checks of the droppings have not been made and chicks exhibit symptoms of drowsiness, ruffled feathers, or increased water intake, the first thing a handler should do is check the droppings to affirm an intestinal upset so the condition can be remedied immediately.

Results from the constant use of irritating chemicals, acids, and medications can also be seen in the droppings. An irritating substance can cause the walls of the intestinal tract to hemorrhage. This blood will be seen in the droppings. If these substances can be ruled out, then a more positive diagnosis can be made.

Acquainting yourself with the normal odor of droppings can also help in detecting problems. There is a characteristic sour odor that experienced handlers will notice of loose droppings. With experience, a handler will be able to "smell" something is wrong upon entering the room or building in which his chicks are housed.

The feed ingested by chicks should cause normal droppings to be shapely yet crumble. If hard and small, this will suggest a lack of fiber in the feed or a highly concentrated ration, neither of which are good for proper assimilation of nutrients and digestion.

Droppings should not be too dry or too moist. Experience in checking the droppings will prove to be a very reliable method of checking your chicks' health and feed composition.

HOW TO DISINFECT EQUIPMENT

Disinfecting any equipment that comes in contact with the chicks is the main prevention of many diseases. You also must keep the litter clean and dry.

Disinfecting does not have to be a chore unless the handler enjoys scrubbing feed and water pans daily. Most handlers have other chores and jobs to tend to. They cannot possibly allot enough time and energy into a daily scrubbing routine. For them, the simplest and quickest method to aid in the prevention of coccidiosis is immersing waterers in a large bucket of chlorinated water.

Chlorine bleach contains sodium hypochlorite (5.25 percent by weight per 1 gallon bottle purchased for household use). Because this is an acid, the small amount that is left on the waterers, by using the following method, will help prevent coccidial development. Further, bacteria-holding slime and algae growths that accumulate on the interior of waterers will be kept from forming if the following method is used in order to guard against bacterial infections.

Before the daily refilling of waterers, rinse the entire jar, fount, tray, or water base free of loose debris. Have a scrub brush handy to remove any stuck-on manure. After this clear water rinse, submerge utensils and it's parts in a large bucket containing water and chlorine bleach. A 5-gallon plastic bucket will suffice for most chick waterers. Into this 5-gallon bucket of water, an amount of 2 1/2 cups of liquid household bleach is added. After removing the waterers from this solution, do not rinse or dry. Place them in an upright position on absorbent rags or towels. This will collect the drippings from the containers bottom that might be transferred and absorbed by the chicks' litter when replaced, causing damp litter near the waterers. Now simply refill with fresh water and "serve."

The small amount of chlorine left on the surface of the waterers will not hurt the chicks, but provides a prolonged disinfecting action on the waterers and in the drinking water itself.

A plastic bucket should be used so there is no problem with it rusting. The solution can be reused every day without changing for at least a week at a time. By sniffing the solution, you can tell if the chlorine has lost it's strength.

Keeping the solution covered in a cool, dry place will preserve it's disinfectant qualities. An occasional full-scale scrubbing will be needed for waterers, feeders, and equipment used between different broods of chicks or that have become excessively dirty. For this, use 1 cup of liquid chlorine bleach and 2 1/2 gallons of water mixed with a compatible cleaning agent that will not interfere with the action of the disinfectant. Cleaners containing sodium carbonate are inexpensive, readily available, and will not interfere with the disinfecting action of the bleach. Most laundry soaps contain this compatible ingredient and can be used with the chlorine for disinfecting while cleaning.

Remember that disinfecting is for killing germs and scrubbing is mainly for removal of germ holding-materials. Disinfect regularly. Scrub when needed.

IMPORTANCE OF CULLING

Chick culling usually means the disposing of bad chicks within a brood. I've often wondered why the subject of destroying animals is rarely mentioned. It is a rather awkward topic to write about. The fact may be the disapproval one might expect his readers to have. Instead of meeting with the topic face to face, the issue may be entirely avoided. This can prevent the needed culling of chicks by handlers who feel squeamish, "criminal," or unprepared to do such a deed.

Some parents move to the country so they and their children can experience the beginning of life among farm animals. It's easy to forget that with life there is also eventual death. Death occurs on a farm or ranch through natural and caused means. This too is a learning experience. The mode and attitude in which death is taught can be most important in teaching children to be humane and honest about dealing with death.

It's not very economical to keep chicks that are developing poorly. It's also not fair to healthy chicks to keep any that exhibit abnormalities or disease.

Unlike pets where economics is not usually involved, we do not keep chicks around with the idea they might feather out later, have more vitality later, catch up with the others in weight gain, or might become as good a specimen as the other chicks in the brood.

Systematic culling should be practiced by all handlers beginning with day-old chicks, and on through the entire growing period and equally through the laying life of hens. We must not be sympathetic with our chicks yet we must proceed to be humane at the same time when culling also means destroying.

One bloodless way to dispose of bad chicks is to drown them in a bucket of water. It will take about 30 seconds for day-olds to cease body functions. The older the chick the longer the process of drowning will take. If you feel squeamish about holding a chick under water until the bird's body stretches out, tremors, and relaxes, in that order, the body can be weighted down.

After disposing of hundreds of chicks, I still feel most comfortable with the drowning method for small chicks. Older and larger chicks will have their heads whacked off as if they are simply being butchered for the freezer.

Along with destroying an animal, the proper disposal of the remains is just as important to prevent infectious diseases from spreading or presenting a health hazard to wild or domestic animals. Proper disposal clearly means to guard against contamination of the soil, air, and water.

Unlike most large livestock, chicks can be burned quickly and efficiently in a "burn barrel" or incinerator. By making sure the fire continues long enough to completely destroy *all* remains and providing a heavy iron grate on top of the barrel, this will assure that wild animals and pets will not dig out remains and scatter them.

Burying a carcass always invites the danger of animals digging it up. Plus there is the danger of disease being spread through ground water and soil.

Starting with the day-olds, dispose of any chicks that have a deformity such as a crossed beak, one eye missing, unhealed navels, or broken or lame legs. Occasionally such chicks will pass through the hatchery without being detected. Also dispose of chicks severely weakened by stress or that appear dumpy, huddled, and chirp a lot.

At about five days of age, remove, and dispose of any chicks that have very dried and shriveled legs and are very light in weight. This indicates the chick is not drinking well and is dehydrating. The cause can be anything from a stressed chick that was unnoticed during the original culling, to a deaf or blind chick, to a lack of waterers.

Beginning at two weeks of age, it's wise to remove or wing band (Fig. 2-37) chicks that have not attained much wing feather growth. Because the wing feathers grow in before other feathers, it's an indication as to how fast the rest of the bird's body will feather out. Very slow feathering is hereditary and it is not a good quality. Poor feathering can result in pin feathers at butchering

time. Figure 2-38 shows how to band wings.

From two weeks on, most culling will consist of removing chicks that appear "dumpy." Dumpy chicks are usually runts. They sit around huddled a lot. They are not perky and are very quiet or chirp constantly. They appear with their heads tucked in toward their body or drooping down. They can be carriers of disease.

Others culled throughout the growing period will be the noticeable runts, chicks that appear sickly, or "barebacks."

If a handler finds many chicks at one time that should rightfully be culled, then overall management methods should usually be scrutinized more than the quality of the chicks at hand. The quality of the growing chicks should not be blamed if attention was given to the quality when purchased.

Under normal management, birds that are culled will represent approximately 6 to 12 chicks out of 100, up to the age of 20 weeks when pullet laying will commence.

Further culling can include the separation of cockerels from pullets and a variance in breed characteristics. For example, if the breed of chicks demands a single comb, any with a rose comb can be weeded out if your aim is to keep the flock breed pure. The same goes for a variance in skin or feather color. These off breeds or mixtures occasionally found in a brood of chicks sometimes will not be noticed until later in the brooding or growing period. They do not necessarily have to

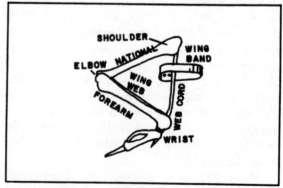

Fig. 2-37. Proper position to place wing band on a chick's wing (courtesy of National Band & Tag Co.).

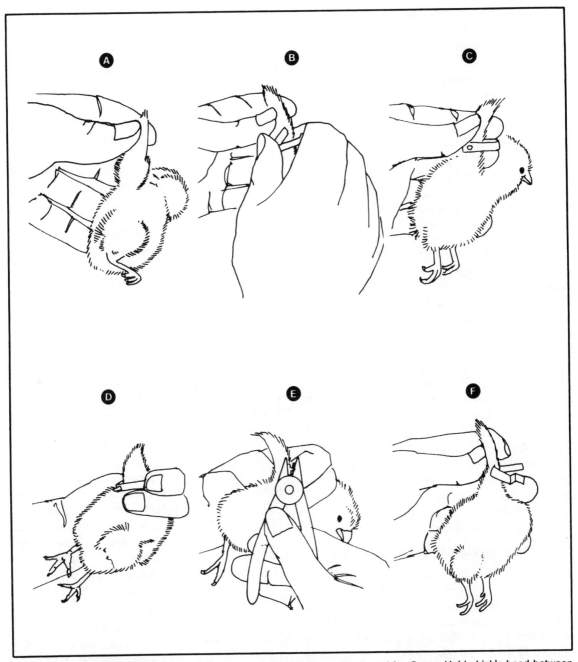

Fig. 2-38. (A) Hold chick in left hand with tip of right wing between thumb and forefinger. Hold chick's head between second and third finger. (B) With band between thumb and forefinger of right hand, push band through web of wing directly at the elbow joint. Be careful not to puncture the flesh or tear the tendon at the leading edge of the wing. (C) Band as applied before clinching. (D) With thumb and forefinger of the left hand, close the band until the rivet is inserted into the hole of the band. (E) While holding band closed, clinch the rivet with band pliers. (F) Turn band with rivet under wing. This will not allow the band to turn over end of wing. This will not allow the band to turn over end of wing. The chick is now permanently banded for life. (Photographs simulated with permission of Hy-Line International).

be destroyed—nothing is physically wrong with them—but rather they can be butchered with the extra cockerels or sold. Finding a couple of these nonconforming types in a brood by no way means the entire brood is not pure or that these oddballs are not good producers.

Because broiler crosses are butchered not long after the discontinuation of brooding, the only culling will be when they are day-olds and later if very bad runts or diseased chicks are found.

One other reason to cull is when cannibalism is first spotted in the flock. Begin by first discreetly watching which chicks are pecking at the already injured and pecked at chicks. Mark those spotted pecking.

Naturally, the longer chicks are kept the more culling and mortality there will be. Culling and mortality go hand in hand. If chicks are culled on a regular basis, there will be less mortality the handler will be confronted with. If there is substantial mortality, then more culling is in order.

The aim of culling layers is to provide high-quality pullets where few will need to be culled and removed from the laying house later after much expensive feed and manpower have gone into their upkeep.

A handler can have his own method of destroying bad chicks. The main concern is that the chicks are destroyed as necessary. Don't keep them longer than necessary or let them end up in another handler's flock of chicks through unscrupulous selling methods. Word gets around quickly among the poultry public of unfavorable sales by dealers.

PROTECTION AGAINST PREDATORS

Chicken handlers in various parts of the country will be bothered with the annoyance and the economic loss of their chicks caused by predators. Unless a handler is familiar with the obvious signs of the type of predator being dealt with, a great many chick losses can occur by the time the predator is identified.

Chicks that are allowed to range outdoors without supervision or chicks housed in buildings that have any unscreened opening of any size are the best quarry for a predator. A handler has only

himself to blame when chicks are lost to predators under these conditions.

Proper housing and fencing will keep chick losses to predators at a minimum. Here is a safe building checklist:

☐ Any opening, no matter how small, should be boarded up or as in the case of eaves vents, screened.

☐ A concrete wall foundation is a very good investment to keep rats and other burrowing animals from entering.

☐ Opaque or curtained windows will prevent other animals from seeing the chicks inside the building. Some animals, such as owls, will break through a glass window to get at chicks.

☐ Provide strong doors and hinges that can be closed tightly and securely latched and bolted. Small doors provided strictly for growing chicks to enter and exit should be constructed and be able to be closed with the same amount of care and consideration given to the building's larger entry doors.

☐ Keep all equipment, including large feeders and waterers, up off the floor to prevent hiding places for predators and to allow cats to hunt uninhibited.

☐ Feed that is stored should be in heavy metal containers with tight-fitting lids.

☐ Buildings constructed with wooden floors should be raised at least 1 foot off the ground and include thick sheet metal covering the underside of the floor. Rats can chew through thin sheets of metal and even concrete blocks. Raising the building allows air circulation under the floor and allows cats to hunt underneath. It does not prevent rodents from entering through the floor.

Fencing should be purchased and erected with the idea of protecting the chicks from predators. The fence quality and it's spacings should be considered. A fence with poor quality will rust quickly, causing the fence to acquire weak spots which any large animal can tear through. A large spade fence will allow small animals to enter pens. Here is a safe fencing checklist:

☐ Outdoor fencing should be checked for strength in the spring and fall by pulling on various areas of the constructed fence. Loose fence post should be held stationary in the ground.

☐ A wire fence should cover the entire top of outdoor pens to keep predators from flying or climbing into pens.

☐ Do not construct outdoor roosts in pens as this can encourage chickens to roost outdoors during the night.

☐ Construct well-made, sturdy gates that can be closed tightly.

☐ Construct an underground barrier to prevent burrowing animals from digging. Do this by either (A) Pouring a footing 2 feet deep around perimeter of pen, (B) digging a trench and filling with large rocks, blocks, or bricks, (C) sinking iron rods vertically 1 inch apart or, (D) extending fencing at least 2 feet over ground around perimeter of pen.

☐ Be sure all indoor pens have small access holes for your cats to enter. Rodents quickly learn if the pens are safe from cats and will visit pens even while the frustrated cats sit on the outside of the pens watching.

☐ Even small bantam pens should have a small access hole for the cats to enter and leave. Bantams won't usually go through these openings. They're pretty much content to stay where they belong.

A good cat will repay a handler by the amount of feed and chicks saved from rats. Rats love poultry houses. Begin by teaching a few kittens to respect and tolerate your chicks by housing them in the same building.

Watch the kittens closely at first for signs of playfulness. You do not want the kittens to play with the chicks because this playfulness can lead to hurting the chicks. It is normally wiser, when starting new kittens and chicks, to acquire kittens that are smaller than the chicks or wait until the chicks grow some.

The kittens must understand this building is their new home. They must be fed in the same building and have a place provided for just them. They must not be fed near your home or they will not stay in the building where they're needed most. Their area can be an isle, a loft, or a fenced-off corner where the chicks cannot go to devour the cat food.

You might even see the kittens occasionally sleeping under the brooder hover with the chicks. This is fine. The mingling together is good for everyone.

The chicks will soon tower over the kittens, but the kittens can take care of themselves. When housed together like this, the chicks will get accustomed to having the cats around. This is especially important for pullets being kept for laying because a strange cat walking in the coops will startle the chickens. In turn, cats not housed with the chickens might be very cautious of the chickens and shy away from mouse and rat infested corners of the building where the chickens congregate during the day. They might not even enter the building unless you go in too.

During cold winter months the warmth in the building from the grown chickens will keep the cats comfortable. It's a good feeling to walk into the poultry house and find your "rat exterminators" at work stalking, waiting, or sitting patiently in a nest, under a shelf, on a bale of straw, a rafter, or in a dark corner in quiet pursuit of vermin.

When kittens are raised with chicks in this manner, they will not bother chicks raised when they are grown cats.

Kittens sometimes fall prey to predators such as the great horned owl, dogs, tomcats, foxes, raccoons. Therefore, the kittens should not be allowed out of the building until they are almost fully grown. Provide a small ladder leading to an opening high up, such as under open eaves, so the cats can enter and exit the building on their own. In this way they can hunt around the outside of the building, too.

Some cats will not catch rats or small weasels. If you've raised a few kittens from the beginning, you can keep only those that prove to be good ratters. A cat that is only a good mouser will not be any help in protecting your chicks from attacks by rats or the small weasels.

I do not believe rodent baits are safe around

Purchase Date	Poultry, Feed,	Purchase Price	Source	Comments
4-01-85	6-1 qrt. wat.	$ 3.12	B.H.Store	plastic-tips easy
4-01-85	3-36 "feeders	12.48	B.H.Store	galvanized-reel
4-01-85	50# ch. st.	14.56	L. Co-op	20 1/2% protein mash.
4-03-85	102 N.H. chks.	45.00	H&H Hatch.	S-R, C.O.D.
4-15-85	50# ch. st.	15.08	N.B. Co-op	20 1/2% protein-med.
4-22-85	brooder bulb	4.16	B.H.Store	infra-red
4-22-85	400# ch. st.	116.48	L. Co-op	20 1/2 protein mash.
5-04-85	2-gal. fount	8.75	B.H.Store	double-wall, galv.

Table 2-2. Purchase Record Sample.

poultry houses. There are usually too many young children or pets around to consider baiting to be safe no matter where it's placed. Also, rodents eaten by the chickens or cats might contain some of the poisons. I haven't seen a good rodent bait yet that can outdo a good cat's work.

Trapping is another method. If spring traps are used for larger predators, be sure all pets, including the cats, are locked up while these are set. Live traps are good, but even these are inconvenient if pets keep ending up in them.

RECORD KEEPING

Without record keeping, a handler cannot possibly become proficient in raising chicks. There must be written records to look back on to review previous failures and successes. A handler must know, without guessing, which methods should be continued, done away with, or revised with future broods of chicks.

Table 2-2 will help a handler see more clearly how often certain equipment was purchased. If some items are purchased too often, could it be because of poor quality? Did the breed of chicks fit your need? How did other breeds compare in mortality rate, resistance to disease, speed of growth, ease of raising and price. A separate management record should be kept (Table 2-3).

Compare purchase prices yearly. Equipment and chick prices can cost you 10 percent more each year. This means a handler will have to cut cost elsewhere or sell his products at a higher price to

Table 2-3. Management Record Sample.

Date	Pullets	Cockerels	Losses	Cause	Med.	Vac.
4-03-85		S-R (100)	2	stress	-	-
4-11-85		S-R (100)	-	-	-	ND-IB,eye
4-30-85		S-R (98)	2	cannib.	-	-
5-14-85	55	43	-	-	-	LT,eye
5-28-85	53	43	2	coccid.	vineg	-
7-02-85	53	43	-	-	-	ND-IB,eye

keep up with inflation.

Were you satisfied with the hatchery you previously dealt with? How did the quality of chicks purchased compare to chicks purchased elsewhere? Did the total amount of pullets and cockerels raised meet your specific requirements? If not, adjust future chick orders accordingly.

Could feed cost be cut without shorting the chickens on nutrient needs? Would it have been worthwhile to purchase in half ton lots? Was the more expensive medicated feed necessary?

Always record the cause of a dead chicken. Good management is the number one factor for raising healthy chicks, a recorded number of deaths can give a clue to practices that must be changed. For instance, when a number of three-day-old chicks die and seem to have been dehydrated, it would indicate more or proper placement of waterers. If they were stressed or chilled during shipment, might the losses have been prevented by placing waterers under the heat the first few days? Chilling, confined overheating, and shipping stress causes most losses in the early part of brooding.

After three weeks of age, coccidiosis can be looked on as a major cause of mortality. Do the symptoms relate to coccidiosis? Could management practices be improved by providing more sanitary conditions? Were watchers disinfected regularly? Were the droppings watched for signs of diarrhea or blood? Was fresh litter material routinely placed over the brooding area?

If a large number of chicks turn out to be runts, was it from parasites, overheating, the wrong type of feed, or not enough good feeders and waterers?

All sorts of questions can be answered for raising the next brood of chicks when accurate records are kept. This can definitely save a handler money.

Chapter 3

Chick Feeding

Feeding chicks can be complicated or simple. This chapter will help you simplify feed requirements. If handlers can better understand the chick's feed requirements and the composition of those requirements, more economically prepared and nutritious feeds can be obtained.

Many handlers purchase commercially prepared chick feeds without ever knowing the feed's content. They rely solely on the feed manufacturer and the feed dealer. This is fine if the dealer knows his products. Ironically, I've seen and heard about many dealers who sell the wrong types of feeds to unknowing customers and, furthermore, make outrageous claims about what should be fed to the poultry.

If handlers do not acquaint themselves with their chicks' nutrient requirements and the composition of feed, they have only themselves to blame. If you are knowledgeable about feed and know what your birds need, you will not be intimidated when the dealer tells you to use turkey starter when you know you want a 23-percent broiler ration for your cornish crosses. You will not

be talked into using a medicated feed if you do not want to. You will not, under the implication that your chicks will die otherwise, succumb to unnecessary medications in your chicks' water if your aim is to stay away from medicated water additives.

The results of modern research on feeding chickens is available to everyone. Commercial broiler firms contract growers to raise the birds you see in the supermarkets. These companies provide the feed and medication growers give to the chicks. They also provide chicks that are hatched and vaccinated in their own hatcheries. See Fig. 3-1.

Because the company actually owns the chicks, which are delivered to the growers in huge vans, they take full responsibility as to what type feed is fed to the chicks. Their concern is proper nutrition combined with economy, which should concern every handler.

Computerized feed mills, in broiler firms do not buy prepared feeds. They know there is economy in producing their feed. The small raiser cannot purchase a feed mill and grain store to produce feed

Fig. 3-1. A hatch of 30,000 day-old-broiler chicks are headed to a grower farm from McCarty-State Pride hatchery (USDA photo by George A. Robinson).

more economically. Neither can he have small amounts of his own grains ground by a local feed mill to save money on feed. Feed dealers know this. As a result, the small-scale raiser might feel that he is at the mercy of these dealers.

What is left for the small-scale raiser to do in order to take the bite out of feeding his chicks?

☐ Get to know your feed. Study the following chapters on the composition and sources for the compositions.

☐ Know exactly what type of feed is needed for the type chicks being raised. Don't overfeed or underfeed with expensive protein.

☐ By comparing grinding rates at the mill and amount of feed purchased yearly, it might pay to purchase a small grinder or hammermill. Most such grinders use a tractor for power. The belt-driven ones having a higher rpm than one that runs off the power take-off (PTO) of a tractor.

☐ If local farm grains are available, compare ready-prepared feeds at the mill with grains bought, mixed with the proper concentrate, vitamins and minerals. Then find out the grinding rate to grind and mix these.

☐ You can usually purchase unmedicated feeds prepared by the local mill. If no then request it. Because if the medication is left out, these will be less expensive.

☐ By having 1/2 to 1 ton of feed ground at a time, a raiser usually will save money. Some nutrients are lost during storage even if antitoxicants, included in most concentrates, are used to preserve quality. If you find you can use 1/2 ton per month on your chicks, it should be a savings to purchase in half-ton lots.

Sometimes the same feed can be used by two broods of chicks at the same time even though they are different ages and different breeds. This can be done only if you know the nutrient requirements of both. For instance, by studying Tables 3-4 and 3-5, it will become obvious that a 0-to-6-week-old egg breed chick requires almost exactly the same nutrients as the 6-to-8 week-old broiler. By timing chick purchases or hatches so both egg breeds and broiler breeds are started the same time or two weeks apart, money can be saved by purchasing larger amounts and feeding them the same type feed.

"Free choice" feeding is the method most used for chicks. Feeders are kept filled constantly so the chicks eat when they feel a need to eat.

FEED COMPOSITION

Each nutrient in a balanced ration is used by the chick's body in a precise and sometimes peculiar way. Many nutrients are required because they cause other essential nutrients made useful and thus absorbed by the body. The importance of a balanced ration cannot be overemphasized. For example: vitamin D_3 must be available for calcium to be absorbed from feed. If vitamin D_3 is deficient, a calcium deficiency also occurs. A balanced ration can only be had by mixing various feed ingredients together to complement each other.

The bulk of poultry rations consists mainly of grains. Grains contain plant proteins. Protein contains amino acids that are necessary for protein to be absorbed within the birds' systems. Because these plant proteins are usually deficient in the amount of amino acids needed by chickens for protein absorption, animal protein must be added to rations for a substantially higher amino acid content.

A balanced formula for chick feed will contain both plant and animal products. When chicks are allowed to range, they will find worms, bugs, weed seeds, and leafy plants on their own.

GROWTH RATE

Hereditary factors will cause various breeds of chickens to grow slower or faster. Scientific research has brought about the tremendously fast rate of growth in today's broiler breeds. Many claim our limit has been reached in the creation of these fast growers.

There are also various degrees of differences between strains within a breed and between the sexes. Male chickens always grow faster than the females of the same strain and breed, although feed conversion is usually not as good. In egg breeds, the males' weight will not be as pronounced as in the general-purpose breed or the broiler breed, but it will be more so in the same age breed and strain.

For the normal growth rate of any particular breed, the right amount of protein must be contained in the chicks' ration. Protein stimulates growth.

It is the bird's growth rate—which is related to genetic makeup—that determines the need for various nutrients, including protein. It is not the nutrients that are solely responsible for growth rate. If the bird's body does not have the correct metabolism caused by genetics, no amount of excess protein will make a "super chicken" out of him.

The chicks' environment is a factor in their growth rate. More feed is eaten in cooler temperatures and less feed is eaten in warm temperatures. This is one important reason chicks should not be overheated. Consuming less feed because of overheating will also mean fewer nutrients are taken into the chicks' bodies. The result is stunted growth. The correct temperature means chicks will consume the proper amount of feed and protein (if the feed is balanced).

Chicks will eat only in the presence of light. Handlers must provide light during the fastest part of their growth period: the brooding period.

The average growth rate for chicks is shown in Tables 3-1, 3-2, and 3-3.

NUTRITION REQUIREMENTS

The nutritional feeding of chicks is not a new concept. Even 50 years ago the basic requirements were known and applied. Various nutrient deficiencies were also recognized. The nutrient requirements for the egg-laying chicks is much different than that of broiler chicks. See Table 3-4.

The broiler that reaches butchering size at 8 weeks needs quite a bit more nutrients in it's feed than the slower-growing layer type even though broilers eat more. Table 3-5 shows the nutrient requirements of a 6-to-8-week-old broiler to be almost the same as the requirements for day-old egg breeds up to 6 weeks old.

Considering that broilers eat more and that they eat the higher-nutrient ration, broilers are actually taking in an overwhelming amount of nutrients compared to egg breeds of the same age. Nutrients cost money. A handler will pay more to feed these broiler chicks up to 8 weeks of age than the egg breeds up to the same age, but he also will be done raising them at this age. While these broilers are taking up room in your freezer, the egg breed will still need feed to produce your eggs.

Tables 3-1, 3-2, and 3-3 will enable a handler to figure amounts of feed needed to grow egg breeds, broilers, and general-purpose breeds. The per-chick requirements need only be multiplied by the total amount of chicks grown to find the total amount of feed needed to raise them to butchering size for broilers or production size for egg breeds and general purpose. It takes about the same quantity of feed to raise a broiler chick to 8 weeks as it does to raise an egg breed chick to the

Table 3-1. Body Weights and Feed Requirements of Egg Breed Pullets.

Age (weeks)	Body Weight	Weekly Feed Consumption
0	.08 lbs. (35 g)	.10 lbs. (45 g)
2	.30 lbs. (135 g)	.20 lbs. (90 g)
4	.60 lbs. (270 g)	.40 lbs. (180 g)
6	.99 lbs. (450 g)	.57 lbs. (260 g)
8	1.37 lbs. (620 g)	.72 lbs. (325 g)
10	1.74 lbs. (790 g)	.85 lbs. (385 g)
12	2.09 lbs. (950 g)	.95 lbs. (430 g)
14	2.34 lbs. (1,060 g)	1.01 lbs. (460 g)
16	2.56 lbs. (1,160 g)	1.01 lbs. (460 g)
18	2.78 lbs. (1,260 g)	1.01 lbs. (460 g)

Adapted from *Nutrient Requirements of Poultry, 8th revised edition*, copyright 1984, National Academy of Sciences.

Table 3-2. Body Weights and Feed Requirements of Broilers.

Age (weeks)	Body Weights Males	Body Weights Females	Weekly Feed Consumption Males	Weekly Feed Consumption Females
1	.29 lbs. (130 g)	.26 lbs. (120 g)	.26 lbs. (120 g)	.24 lbs. (110 g)
2	.71 lbs. (320 g)	.66 lbs. (300 g)	.57 lbs. (260 g)	.53 lbs. (240 g)
3	1.23 lbs. (560 g)	1.14 lbs. (515 g)	.86 lbs. (390 g)	.78 lbs. (355 g)
4	1.90 lbs. (860 g)	1.74 lbs. (790 g)	1.18 lbs. (535 g)	1.10 lbs. (500 g)
5	2.76 lbs. (1.250 g)	2.45 lbs. (1,110 g)	1.63 lbs. (740 g)	1.42 lbs. (645 g)
6	3.73 lbs. (1,690 g)	3.15 lbs. (1,430 g)	2.17 lbs. (980 g)	1.76 lbs. (800 g)
7	4.63 lbs. (2,100 g)	3.85 lbs. (1,745 g)	2.41 lbs. (1,095 g)	2.01 lbs. (910 g)
8	5.56 lbs. (2,520 g)	4.54 lbs. (2,060 g)	2.67 lbs. (1,210 g)	2.14 lbs. (970 g)
9	6.45 lbs. (2,925 g)	5.18 lbs. (2,350 g)	2.91 lbs. (1,320 g)	2.23 lbs. (1,010 g)

*Adapted from *Nutrient Requirements of Poultry, 8th revised edition*, copyright 1984, National Academy of Sciences.

production age of 20 weeks.

Conversion of feed to meat is better for female broiler chicks than the males. It takes approximately 2 pounds of feed to make 1 pound of meat on the female. On the male, about 3 pounds must be eaten for each pound of meat they produce.

The average live broiler weight has almost doubled since 1935, when broilers weighed 2.86 pounds at 16 weeks of age. The conversion of feed to pounds of meat was just a little over what it is now for our broiler males. It took twice as long to get the birds to a decent butchering size (half the size today's birds). In other words, the birds ate as much feed as our broilers today but over an extended period of time. To grow those birds out to the current butchering size would have taken many more months and labor.

There are six requirements for nutrition of poultry:

☐ Protein
☐ Amino acids
☐ Fats
☐ Minerals
☐ Vitamins
☐ Water

Table 3-3. Body Weights and Feed Requirements of General Purpose Breeds.

Age (weeks)	Body Weights Males	Body Weights Females	Weekly Feed Consumption Males	Weekly Feed Consumption Females
0	.09 lbs. (40 g)	.09 lbs. (40 g)	.22 lbs. (100 g)	.17 lbs. (75 g)
2	.55 lbs. (25 g)	.50 lbs. (225 g)	.55 lbs. (250 g)	.50 lbs. (225 g)
4	1.20 lbs. (545 g)	1.00 lbs. (455 g)	.81 lbs. (368 g)	.71 lbs. (322 g)
6	1.75 lbs. (795 g)	1.46 lbs. (660 g)	.90 lbs. (406 g)	.75 lbs. (340 g)
8	2.25 lbs. (1,020 g)	1.85 lbs. (840 g)	.97 lbs. (440 g)	.83 lbs. (375 g)
10	2.76 lbs. (1,250 g)	2.20 lbs. (1,000 g)	1.13 lbs. (513 g)	.91 lbs. (415 g)
12	3.26 lbs. (1,480 g)	2.60 lbs. (1,180 g)	1.29 lbs. (582 g)	1.00 lbs. (452 g)
14	3.75 lbs. (1,700 g)	3.00 lbs. (1,360 g)	1.41 lbs. (637 g)	1.11 lbs. (505 g)
16	4.26 lbs. (1,930 g)	3.42 lbs. (1,550 g)	1.53 lbs. (695 g)	1.20 lbs. (547 g)
18	4.75 lbs. (2,150 g)	3.81 lbs. (1,730 g)	1.65 lbs. (745 g)	1.32 lbs. (597 g)

*Adapted from *Nutrient Requirements of Poultry, 8th revised edition*, copyright 1984, National Academy of Sciences.

Table 3-4. Nutrient Requirements of Egg Breed Pullets.

Calories	Energy Base kcal ME/kg Diet (per 2.2 lbs. feed) = 2,900 or, 1,318 Calories (per 1.1 lbs. feed)*				

			0-6 Weeks	6-14 Weeks	14-20 Weeks
	Protein	%	18 (Starter)	15 (Grower)	12 (Grower)
Amino Acids	Arginine	%	1.00	0.83	0.67
	Glycine and Serine	%	0.70	0.58	0.47
	Histidine	%	0.26	0.22	0.17
	Isoleucine	%	0.60	0.50	0.40
	Leucine	%	1.00	0.83	0.67
	Lysine	%	0.85	0.60	0.45
	Methionine + cystine	%	0.60	0.50	0.40
	Methionine	%	0.30	0.25	0.20
	Phenylalanine + tyrosine	%	1.00	0.83	0.67
	Phenylalanine	%	0.54	0.45	0.36
	Threonine	%	0.68	0.57	0.37
	Tryptophan	%	0.17	0.14	0.11
	Valine	%	0.62	0.52	0.41
	Linoleic acid	%	1.00	1.00	1.00
Minerals	Calcium	%	0.80	0.70	0.60
	Chlorine	%	0.15	0.12	0.12
	Copper	mg	8	6	6
	Iodine	mg	0.35	0.35	0.35
	Iron	mg	80	60	60
	Magnesium	mg	600	500	400
	Manganese	mg	60	30	30
	Phosphorous, available	%	0.40	0.35	0.30
	Potassium	%	0.40	0.30	0.25
	Selenium	mg	0.15	0.10	0.10
	Sodium	%	0.15	0.15	0.15
	Zinc	mg	40	35	35
Vitamins	Biotin	mg	0.15	0.10	0.10
	Choline	mg	1,300	900	500
	Folacin	mg	0.55	0.25	0.25
	Niacin	mg	27.00	11.00	11.00
	Pantothenic acid	mg	10.00	10.00	10.00
	Pyridoxine	mg	3.0	3.0	3.0
	Riboflavin	mg	3.60	1.80	1.80
	Thiamin	mg	1.80	1.30	1.30
	Vitamin A	IU	1,500	1,500	1,500
	Vitamin B_{12}	mg	0.009	0.003	0.003
	Vitamin D	ICU	200	200	200
	Vitamin E	IU	10	5	5
	Vitamin K	mg	0.50	0.50	0.50

Adapted from *Nutrient Requirements of Poultry, 8th revised edition,* copyright 1984, National Academy of Sciences.
*These can be considered the same as the Calories commonly used to denote human food, but by scientific measurements, kilocalorie (kcal) is the precise term of measurement.

Table 3-5. Nutrient Requirements of Broilers.

Calories	Energy Base: kcal ME/kg Diet (per 2.2 lbs. feed) = 3,200 or, 1,455 Calories (per 1.1 lbs. feed)*			
			0-2 Weeks	**3-6 Weeks**	**6-8 Weeks**

			0-2 Weeks	3-6 Weeks	6-8 Weeks
	Protein	%	23.00	20.00	18.00
Amino Acids	Arginine	%	1.44	1.20	1.00
	Glycine + Serine	%	1.50	1.00	0.70
	Histidine	%	0.35	0.30	0.26
	Isoleucine	%	0.80	0.70	0.60
	Leucine	%	1.35	1.18	1.00
	Lysine	%	1.20	1.00	0.85
	Methionine + Cystine	%	0.93	0.72	0.60
	Methionine	%	0.50	0.38	0.32
	Phenylalanine + Tyrosine	%	1.34	1.17	1.00
	Phenylalanine	%	0.72	0.63	0.54
	Threonine	%	0.80	0.74	0.68
	Tryptophan	%	0.23	0.18	0.17
	Valine	%	0.82	0.72	0.62
	Linoleic acid	%	1.00	1.00	1.00
Minerals	Calcium	%	1.00	0.90	0.80
	Chlorine	%	0.15	0.15	0.15
	Copper	mg	8.0	8.0	8.0
	Iodine	mg	0.35	0.35	0.35
	Iron	mg	80.0	80.0	80.0
	Magnesium	mg	600	600	600
	Manganese	mg	60.0	60.0	60.0
	Phosphorous, available	%	0.45	0.40	0.35
	Potassium	%	0.40	0.35	0.30
	Selenium	mg	0.15	0.15	0.15
	Sodium	%	0.15	0.15	0.15
	Zinc	mg	40.0	40.0	40.0
Vitamins	Biotin	mg	0.15	0.15	0.10
	Choline	mg	1,300	850	500
	Folacin	mg	0.55	0.55	0.25
	Niacin	mg	27.0	27.0	11.0
	Pantothenic acid	mg	10.0	10.0	10.0
	Pyridoxine	mg	3.0	3.0	2.5
	Riboflavin	mg	3.60	3.60	3.60
	Thiamin	mg	1.80	1.80	1.80
	Vitamin A	IU	1,500	1,500	1,500
	Vitamin B_{12}	mg	0.009	0.009	0.003
	Vitamin D	ICU	200	200	200
	Vitamin E	IU	10	10	10
	Vitamin K	mg	0.50	0.50	0.50

Adapted from *Nutrient Requirements of Poultry, 8th revised edition,* copyright 1984, National Academy of Sciences.
*These can be considered the same as the Calories commonly used to denote human food, but by scientific measurements, kilocalorie (kcal) is the precise term of measurement.

These are discussed individually in the following chapters. Water is listed because it is a necessary part of any feeding program.

The feed industry still keeps handlers in the dark when trying to chose nutrition for birds. Although most feed tags placed on prepared bags of feed show guaranteed amounts of crude protein, fat, and fiber. There are no amounts stated for the other listed ingredients.

Listing complete amounts of ingredients would be giving away trade formulas. The amounts listed pertain to the amount of energy the bag of feed contains. Animal protein can denote anything from processed baby chicks, feathers, poultry heads and feet, to unmentionables that end up also in most commercial soaps. This is truly recycling. If you've ever been in a rendering plant, you'll know what I mean.

Chick feeds are usually purchased under the names of a starter and a grower and sometimes the feed is called a starter-grower. The general rule of thumb is to feed starter to bantams, egg breeds, and general-purpose breeds for two months. Then use grower for the next two months. After that, the chickens will be ready to begin eating a layer feed in preparation for laying .

This is only a general rule to help you remember. The actual nutrient requirements should be followed as listed in Tables 3-4 and 3-5.

Protein and Amino Acids

Protein is the most expensive ingredient in any poultry ration but is required to stimulate growth. Chicks will only use so much of a given amount of protein. Any amount in excess of that required will be passed in their droppings.

Besides stimulating growth, protein repairs worn tissues and promotes fleshing and feathering. Protein makes productive use of consumed energy-producing feed ingredients. Chicks grow at a faster rate than adult birds so they require more protein. Broiler breeds grow at a faster rate than egg breeds, so their protein requirements are more.

It is really the amino acids contained in protein that are required by the birds. Amino acids allow the protein to be absorbed in the bird's system. See Table 3-6.

Deficiencies or excesses of certain essential amino acids cause feed intake to decline by influencing the areas of the brain controlling feed intake.*

Vitamins and Sources

Vitamins are added to commercially prepared feeds by using prepackaged supplemental vitamins in order to produce a balanced ration. Most everyone knows vitamins are good, but a handler should become familiar with the reasons individual vitamins are needed so deficiencies can be spotted and avoided.

The main, and probably the only, vitamin deficient in commercially packaged feeds is Vitamin D_3. A handler should provide this vitamin for any fast growers such as Cornish Rock Cross broilers. The best method is to administer cod liver oil in the broilers' drinking water. Packaged vitamins can be obtained, but the cod liver oil is more readily available in a more pure form.

The 13 essential vitamins, their functions, sources, and deficiency symptoms and treatments are listed in Table 3-7.

Mineral Needs

There are 12 minerals that should be included in chick feeds. See Tables 3-4 and 3-5. The functions, sources, deficiency symptoms, and treatment are shown in Table 3-8.

Although many feeds provide minerals in varying amounts, trace minerals may also be added in the form of a packaged mix added to prepared feeds. Some common mineral supplements are shown in Table 3-9.

GRIT . . . THEIR TEETH

Grit feeding is very important to confinement-reared birds who have no access to outdoor ground or soil that contains stones and gravel.

Grit looks like aquarium gravel. It comes in

Nutrient Requirements of Poultry, 8th revised edition, copyright 1984, National Academy of Sciences.

Table 3-6. Amino Acid Composition of Some Feeds Commonly Used for Poultry.

Entry Number	Feed Name Description	International Feed Number[a]	Dry Matter (%)	Protein (%)	Arginine (%)	Glycine (%)	Serine (%)	Histidine (%)	Isoleucine (%)	Leucine (%)	Lysine (%)	Methionine (%)	Cystine (%)	Phenylalanine (%)	Tyrosine (%)	Threonine (%)	Tryptophan (%)	Valine (%)
	ALFALFA *Medicago sativa*																	
01	meal dehydrated, 17% protein	1-00-023	92	17.5	0.80	0.90	0.77	0.32	0.84	1.26	0.73	0.23	0.20	0.79	0.56	0.70	0.28	0.84
02	meal dehydrated, 20% protein	1-00-024	92	20.0	0.92	0.97	0.89	0.34	0.88	1.30	0.87	0.31	0.25	0.85	0.59	0.76	0.33	0.97
03	**BAKERY** waste, dehydrated (dried bakery product)	4-00-466	92	9.8	0.47	0.82	0.65	0.13	0.45	0.73	0.31	0.17	0.17	0.40	0.41	0.49	0.10	0.42
	BARLEY *Hordeum vulgare*																	
04	grain, pacific coast	4-00-549	89	11.6	0.59	0.40	0.42	0.29	0.49	0.80	0.40	0.17	0.19	0.64	0.33	0.42	0.14	0.62
05	grain, pacific coast	4-07-939	89	9.0	0.48	0.36	0.32	0.21	0.40	0.60	0.29	0.13	0.18	0.48	0.31	0.30	0.12	0.46
06	**BROADBEAN** *Vicia faba* seeds	5-09-262	87	23.6	1.05	0.55	0.04	0.28	0.51	0.94	0.78	0.01	—	0.03	0.03	0.49	0.23	0.58
	BLOOD																	
07	meal, vat dried	5-00-380	94	81.1	3.63	4.59	3.14	3.52	0.95	10.53	7.05	0.55	0.52	5.66	2.07	3.15	1.29	7.28
08	meal, spray or ring dried	5-00-381	93	88.9	3.81	4.00	3.86	5.26	0.88	11.82	8.85	0.75	0.86	6.55	2.49	3.94	1.34	8.60
09	**BREWERS GRAINS** dehydrated	5-02-141	92	25.3	1.28	1.09	0.80	0.57	1.44	2.48	0.90	0.57	0.39	1.45	1.19	0.98	0.34	1.66
10	**BUCKWHEAT, COMMON** *Fagopyrum sagittatum* grain	4-00-994	88	10.8	1.02	0.71	0.41	0.26	0.37	0.56	0.61	0.20	0.20	0.44	0.21	0.46	0.19	0.54
11	**CANOLA** *Brassica napus-Brassica campestris* seeds, meal prepressed solvent extracted, low erucic acid, low glucosinolates	5-06-145	93	38.0	2.32	1.88	1.67	1.07	1.51	2.65	2.45	0.68	0.47	1.52	0.93	1.71	0.44	1.94
	CASEIN																	
12	dehydrated	5-01-162	93	87.2	3.61	1.79	5.81	2.78	4.82	9.00	7.99	2.65	0.21	4.96	5.37	4.29	1.05	6.46
13	precipitated dehydrated	5-20-837	92	85.0	3.42	1.81	5.52	2.52	4.77	8.62	7.31	2.80	0.15	4.81	5.17	4.00	0.98	5.82
	CORN, DENT YELLOW *Zea mays indentata*																	
14	distillers grains, dehydrated	5-28-235	94	27.9	0.97	0.49	0.70	0.62	0.99	3.01	0.78	0.40	0.24	0.94	0.84	0.49	0.20	1.18
15	distillers grains with solubles, dehydrated	5-28-236	93	27.2	0.98	0.57	1.61	0.66	1.00	2.20	0.75	0.60	0.40	1.20	0.74	0.92	0.19	1.30
16	distillers solubles, dehydrated	5-28-237	92	28.5	1.05	1.10	1.30	0.70	1.25	2.11	0.90	0.50	0.40	1.30	0.95	1.00	0.30	1.39
17	gluten, meal, 60% protein	5-28-242	90	62.0	1.93	1.64	3.07	1.22	2.29	10.11	1.00	1.91	1.11	3.77	2.94	1.97	0.25	2.74
18	gluten with bran (corn gluten feed)	5-28-243	90	22.0	1.01	0.99	0.80	0.71	0.65	1.89	0.63	0.45	0.51	0.77	0.58	0.89	0.10	0.05
19	grain	4-02-935	89	8.8	0.50	0.37	0.40	0.20	0.37	1.10	0.24	0.20	0.15	0.47	0.45	0.39	0.09	0.52
20	grits by-product (Hominy feed)	4-03-011	90	10.0	0.47	0.40	0.50	0.20	0.40	0.84	0.40	0.13	0.13	0.35	0.49	0.40	0.10	0.49

No.	Feed	Ref. No.	%															
21	COTTON *Gossypium* spp seeds, meal mechanically extracted, 41% protein (expeller)	5-01-617	93	40.9	4.26	2.28	1.70	1.08	1.57	2.47	1.51	0.55	0.59	2.17	0.69	1.38	0.55	1.97
22	seeds, meal prepressed solvent extracted, 41% protein	5-07-872	90	41.4	4.59	1.70	1.80	1.10	1.33	2.41	1.71	0.52	0.64	2.22	1.02	1.32	0.47	1.89
23	seeds, meal prepressed solvent extracted, 44% protein	5-07-873	91	44.7	4.77	1.80	2.17	1.48	1.36	2.44	1.73	0.61	1.12	1.55	1.45	1.49	0.55	1.91
24	FISH solubles, condensed	5-01-969	51	31.5	1.61	3.41	0.83	1.56	1.06	1.86	1.73	0.50	0.30	0.93	0.40	0.86	0.31	1.16
25	solubles, dehydrated	5-01-971	92	63.6	2.78	5.89	2.02	2.18	1.95	3.16	3.28	1.00	0.66	1.48	0.78	1.35	0.51	2.22
26	FISH, ANCHOVY *Engraulis ringen* meal mechanically extracted	5-01-985	92	64.2	3.66	3.59	2.32	1.53	3.01	4.83	4.90	1.93	0.59	2.70	2.18	2.68	0.74	3.38
27	FISH, HERRING *Clupea harengus* meal mechanically extracted	5-02-000	93	72.3	4.84	4.61	2.73	1.70	3.22	5.34	5.70	2.10	0.72	2.79	2.27	3.00	0.81	4.38
28	FISH, MENHADEN *Brevoortia tyrannus* meal mechanically extracted	5-02-009	92	60.5	3.79	4.19	2.25	1.46	2.85	4.50	4.83	1.78	0.56	2.48	1.98	2.50	0.68	3.23
29	FISH, WHITE *Gadidae* (family)-*Lophiidae* (family)-*Rajidae* (family) meal mechanically extracted	5-02-025	91	62.2	4.02	4.42	3.06	1.34	2.72	4.36	4.53	1.68	0.75	2.28	1.83	2.57	0.67	3.02
30	GELATIN process residue (gelatin by-products)	5-14-503	91	88.0	7.40	20.00	2.80	0.85	1.40	3.10	3.70	0.68	0.09	1.70	0.26	1.30	0.09	1.80
	HOMINY FEED—SEE CORN																	
31	LIVERS meal	5-00-389	92	65.6	4.14	5.57	2.49	1.47	3.09	5.28	4.80	1.22	0.89	2.89	1.69	2.48	0.59	4.13
32	MEAT meal rendered	5-00-385	92	54.4	3.73	6.30	1.60	1.30	1.60	3.32	3.00	0.75	0.66	1.70	0.84	1.74	0.36	2.30
33	with bone, meal rendered	5-00-388	93	50.4	3.62	6.79	1.85	0.90	1.40	2.80	2.60	0.65	0.25	1.50	0.76	1.50	0.28	2.00
34	MILLET, PEARL *Pennisetum glaucum* grain	4-03-118	90	15.7	0.74	0.47	0.74	0.31	0.37	1.14	0.45	0.25	0.24	0.56	0.35	0.48	0.08	0.49
35	MILLET, PROSO *Panicum miliaceum* grain	4-03-120	90	11.6	0.36	—	—	0.21	0.45	1.15	0.26	0.29	—	0.57	—	0.40	0.17	0.58
36	OATS *Avena sativa* grain	4-03-309	89	11.4	0.79	0.50	0.40	0.24	0.52	0.89	0.50	0.18	0.22	0.59	0.53	0.43	0.16	0.68
37	grain, pacific coast	4-07-999	91	9.0	0.60	0.40	0.30	0.10	0.40	0.30	0.40	0.13	0.17	0.44	0.20	0.20	0.12	0.51
38	hulls	1-03-281	92	4.6	0.14	0.14	0.14	0.07	0.14	0.25	0.14	0.07	0.06	0.13	0.14	0.13	0.07	0.20
39	PEA *Pisum* spp seeds	5-03-600	90	23.8	1.40	1.10	—	0.72	1.10	1.80	1.60	0.31	0.17	1.30	—	0.94	0.24	1.30
40	PEANUT *Arachis hypogaea* kernels, meal mechanically extracted (peanut meal) (expeller)	5-03-649	90	39.8	5.40	2.20	1.30	1.10	1.80	3.40	1.60	0.45	0.70	2.60	1.61	1.40	0.50	2.40
41	kernels, meal solvent extracted (peanut meal)	5-03-650	93	50.7	5.50	2.70	2.22	1.19	2.10	2.99	1.76	0.44	0.76	2.75	2.00	1.45	0.65	1.82

Table 3-6. Continued from page 83.

Entry Number	Feed Name Description	International Feed Number[a]	Dry Matter (%)	Protein (%)	Arginine (%)	Glycine (%)	Serine (%)	Histidine (%)	Isoleucine (%)	Leucine (%)	Lysine (%)	Methionine (%)	Cystine (%)	Phenylalanine (%)	Tyrosine (%)	Threonine (%)	Tryptophan (%)	Valine (%)
	POULTRY																	
42	by-product, meal rendered (Viscera with feet and heads)	5-03-798	93	58.0	4.00	5.90	3.68	1.50	2.00	3.70	2.70	1.00	0.69	2.10	0.54	2.00	0.53	2.60
43	feathers, meal hydrolyzed	5-03-795	93	86.4	5.42	6.31	9.26	0.34	3.26	6.72	1.67	0.42	4.00	3.26	6.31	3.43	0.50	5.57
	RICE *Oryza sativa*																	
44	bran with germ (Rice bran)	4-03-928	91	12.9	0.89	0.80	0.32	0.33	0.52	0.90	0.59	0.20	0.10	0.58	0.68	0.48	0.15	0.75
45	grain, polished and broken (Brewers rice)	4-03-932	89	8.7	0.62	0.63	1.36	0.17	0.35	0.52	0.24	0.15	0.08	0.36	0.41	0.29	0.13	0.50
46	polishings	4-03-943	90	12.2	0.78	0.71	1.36	0.24	0.41	0.80	0.57	0.22	0.10	0.46	0.63	0.40	0.13	0.76
	RYE *Secale cereale*																	
47	grain	4-04-047	88	12.1	0.53	0.49	0.52	0.26	0.47	0.70	0.42	0.17	0.19	0.56	0.26	0.36	0.11	0.56
	SAFFLOWER *Carthamus tinctorius*																	
48	seeds, meal solvent extracted	5-04-110	92	23.4	1.95	1.13	—	—	0.28	—	0.72	0.34	0.36	—	—	0.51	0.27	—
49	seeds without hulls, meal solvent extracted	5-07-959	92	43.0	3.65	2.32	—	1.07	1.56	2.46	1.27	0.68	0.70	1.75	1.07	1.30	0.59	2.33
	SESAME *Sesamum indicum*																	
50	seeds, meal mechanically extracted	5-04-220	93	43.8	4.93	4.22	2.96	1.09	2.12	3.33	1.30	1.20	0.59	2.22	2.00	1.65	0.80	2.41
	SORGHUM *Sorghum bicolor*																	
51	grain, 8-10% protein	4-20-893	87	8.8	0.34	0.35	0.39	0.19	0.42	1.18	0.21	0.16	0.16	0.42	0.38	0.29	0.10	0.53
52	grain, more than 10% protein	4-20-894	88	11.0	0.35	0.32	0.45	0.23	0.43	1.37	0.22	0.15	0.11	0.52	0.17	0.33	0.09	0.54
	SOYBEAN *Glycine max*																	
53	flour by-product (Soybean mill feed)	4-04-594	89	13.3	0.94	0.40	—	0.18	0.40	0.57	0.48	0.10	0.21	0.37	0.23	0.30	0.10	0.37
54	protein concentrate, more than 70% protein	5-08-038	93	84.1	6.70	3.30	5.30	2.10	4.60	6.60	5.50	0.81	0.49	4.30	3.10	3.30	0.81	4.40

#	Feed	IFN																
55	seeds, heat processed	5-04-597	90	37.0	2.80	2.00	2.17	0.89	2.00	2.80	2.40	0.51	0.64	1.80	1.20	1.50	0.55	1.80
56	seeds, meal solvent extracted	5-04-604	89	44.0	3.28	2.29	2.45	1.15	2.39	3.52	2.93	0.65	0.69	2.27	1.28	1.81	0.62	2.34
57	seeds without hulls, meal solvent extracted	5-04-612	90	48.5	3.68	2.29	2.89	1.32	2.57	3.82	3.18	0.72	0.73	2.11	2.01	1.91	0.67	2.72
	SUNFLOWER, COMMON *Helianthus annuus*																	
58	seeds, meal solvent extracted	5-09-340	90	23.3	2.30	—	1.00	0.55	1.00	1.60	1.00	0.50	0.50	1.15	—	1.05	0.45	1.60
59	seeds without hulls, meal solvent extracted	5-04-739	93	45.4	3.50	2.69	1.75	1.39	2.78	3.88	1.70	0.72	0.71	2.93	1.19	2.13	0.71	3.24
	TRITICALE *Triticale hexaploide*																	
60	grain	4-20-362	90	15.8	0.86	0.70	0.76	0.40	0.61	1.18	0.52	0.21	0.29	0.80	0.51	0.57	0.18	0.84
	WHEAT *Triticum aestivum*																	
61	bran	4-05-190	90	15.7	0.98	0.90	0.90	0.34	0.59	0.91	0.59	0.17	0.25	0.49	0.40	0.42	0.30	0.73
62	flour by-product, less than 4% fiber (wheat red dog)	4-05-203	88	15.3	0.96	0.74	0.75	0.41	0.55	1.06	0.59	0.23	0.37	0.66	0.46	0.50	0.19	0.72
63	flour by-product, less than 9.5% fiber (wheat middlings)	4-05-205	88	16.0	1.15	0.63	0.75	0.37	0.58	1.07	0.69	0.21	0.32	0.64	0.45	0.49	0.20	0.71
64	flour by-product, less than 7% fiber (wheat shorts)	4-05-201	88	16.5	1.18	0.96	0.77	0.45	0.58	1.09	0.79	0.27	0.36	0.67	0.47	0.60	0.21	0.83
65	grain, hard red winter	4-05-268	87	14.1	0.58	0.72	0.63	0.22	0.58	0.94	0.40	0.19	0.26	0.71	0.43	0.37	0.18	0.63
66	grain, soft white winter	4-05-337	89	10.2	0.40	0.49	0.55	0.20	0.42	0.59	0.31	0.15	0.22	0.45	0.39	0.32	0.12	0.44
	WHEY *Bos taurus*																	
67	dehydrated	4-01-182	93	12.0	0.34	0.30	0.32	0.18	0.82	1.19	0.97	0.19	0.30	0.33	0.25	0.89	0.19	0.68
68	low lactose, dehydrated (dried whey product)	4-01-186	91	15.5	0.67	1.04	0.76	0.10	0.90	1.15	1.47	0.57	0.57	0.50	0.20	0.50	0.18	0.30
	YEAST, BREWERS *Saccharomyces cerevisiae*																	
69	dehydrated	7-05-527	93	44.4	2.19	2.09	—	1.07	2.14	3.19	3.23	0.70	0.50	1.81	1.49	2.06	0.49	2.32
	YEAST, TORULA *Torulopsis utilis*																	
70	dehydrated	7-05-534	93	47.2	2.60	2.60	2.76	1.40	2.90	3.50	3.80	0.80	0.60	3.00	2.10	2.60	0.50	2.90

[a]First digit is class of feed: 1, dry forages and roughages; 2, pasture, range plants, and forages fed green; 3, silages; 4, energy feeds; 5, protein supplements; 6, minerals; 7, vitamins; 8, additives; the other five digits are the International Feed Number.

Nutrient Requirements of Poultry, 8th revised edition, copyright 1984, National Academy of Sciences.

Table 3-7. Vitamin Functions and Their Deficiency Symptoms.

Vitamin	Functions	Deficiency Symptoms	Treatments
Biotin	Promotes growth, prevents perosis.	Dermatitis on bottom of feet, lesions around mouth, swollen sticky eyelids, reduced hatchability. May lead to fatty liver and kidney syndrome.	Reversible. Check for randcidity of feed fat and mold. Strict diets of wheat or barley can cause.
Choline	Prevents perosis, provides good hatchability.	Suppressed growth, perosis induced.	Irreversible in mature cases. Adult birds have ability to synthesize.
Folacin (Folic Acid)	Strengthens blood.	Slow growth, poor feathering, loss of feather pigment, anemia, reduced egg production and hatchability.	Reversible. Administer in drinking water. New processing methods of feed may destroy if fish meal or soybean meal used . . . supplement.
Niacin (Nicotinic Acid)	Assists in the release of energy from nutrients.	Inflamed tongue and mouth cavity at 2 weeks of age called Black Tongue. Growth retarded, off feed, poor feather development, scaly dermatitis on feet and head. Sometimes hock disorder (swollen hocks, bowed legs).	Irreversible. Provide ample niacin in diet. Birds synthesize it from tryptophan, but slowly.
Pantothenic Acid (Calcium Pantothenate)	Participates in the metabolism of fat, synthesis of hormones, making of hemoglobin.	Retarded growth, ragged feathers, 12-14 days later-granulated eyelids stuck together, crusty scabs corner of mouth, dermatitis over toes, liver damage. Reduced hatchability. After 4-5 months-feather loss from head and neck.	Reversible. Try both calcium pantothenate and riboflavin in drinking water for scaliness.
Pyridoxine (B6)	Active in fat and protein metabolism.	Decline in body weight of adult birds reduced egg production and hatchability. Chicks abnormally excitable, slow growth, convulsions.	None specific. Rare in adult birds fed balanced diets.
Riboflavin (B2)	Promotes growth, hatchability, metabolism of energy nutrients.	Diarrhea, retarded growth, curled-toe paralysis(Chicks walk on hocks), high mortality beginning in 8 days.	Curable in early stages, otherwise irreversible. Addition of riboflavin if toe curling is not caused by infrared brooding.
Thiamin (B1)	Maintains appetite, obtains energy from carbohydrates and protein	Rare. Off feed, excitable, flighty (polyneuritis-lethargy, head tremors, head over back, emaciation, weakness, chemicals may interfere with action.	Nonreversible on lameness if caused from Amprol overuse. Add Thiamin to water and feed.
Vitamin A	To grow and maintain glands and cavity mucous membranes.	(Nutritional Roup) poor growth, stunting, droopy, ruffled feathers. Later, eyes swell with discharge from eyes and nostrils. Post mortem will show urate deposits in kidneys, ureters, cloaca, eye lesions, sticky eyelids and nervousness. Toxic.	Reversible. Vitamin A in water for one week.
Vitamin B$_{12}$	Promotes growth, hatchability. Small requirement.	Fatty heart, liver and kidneys. Poor feathering, anemia, gizzard erosion and perosis.	Reversible. Bacterial synthesis in intestine supplemented with B$_{12}$. Since droppings contain B$_{12}$, rare in floor raised chickens.
Vitamin D$_3$	Needed for calcium absorption.	Rickets, detectable in long leg bones-soft and springy. Birds become paralyzed. Growth and feathering affected. Rickets noticeable 4 wks. of age. Thin-shelled eggs. Toxic at over 100 times the requirement.	Irreversible once lameness sets in. Administer Vitamin D$_3$ source. Best to prevent than treat.
Vitamin E	Anti-sterility vitamin. Good fertility, good hatchability.	Encephalomalcia (Crazy Chick Disease) -staggering, stumbling, paralysis, incoordination. Post mortem lesions over brain. Damages nerves. Fluid swelling usually under skin on breast (exudative diathesis). Muscular dystrophy (lack of Vitamin E and selenium). Permanent sterility. Poor hatching.	Irreversible, but Vitamin E will prevent new cases. Prevent loss of Vitamin E in feed with antioxidants.
Vitamin K	Prevents excessive bleeding, shortens clotting time.	Chicks may bleed to death from minor injury. Accumulations of blood under skin.	Chicks generally recover on their own. Since Vit. K is synthesized by bacteria in intestine, sulfa drugs interfere with bacterial action, so supplement must be given then.

86

Table 3-8. Mineral Functions and Their Deficiency Symptoms.

Mineral	Functions	Deficiency Symptoms	Treatments
Calcium	Bone and shell formation, quality. Normal blood clotting, feed utilization, egg production.	Lack of either calcium, phosphorus and, or, Vitamin D will create rickets. Vitamin D_3 and, or calcium deficiency bones soft and springy, birds become paralyzed-begins 4 weeks of age. Poor growth. Older birds-cage layer fatigue (Osteomalacia). Bones easily broken, deformed sternum, and rib bones. Ruffled feathers, lame, stiff legged walk. Too much calcium-bad shells, nephrosis, visceral gout, deposits in kidney ducts found, high mortality. Calcium deficiency-poor shell quality.	Reversible if done immediately after paralysis-orally 1 gr calcium carbonate gelatin capsule daily 2 or 3 days. If bad shells, offer loose oyster shells and reduce limestone in feed. Check for molds and toxins in feed. Check level of calcium in starter feeds-sometimes lowered to 1/4 the need if tetracycline added. Also, excess of 2 to 1 ratio of calcium and phosphorous in diet.
Chlorine & Sodium (Salt)	Used with other minerals to develop bones and maintain good shells. For adequate water intake.	Decreased egg production, poor growth, cannibalism, reduced hatchability. Excess-loose and watery droppings, retarded-more than 2 % in water-toxic.	Adjust—decrease usually.
Copper	Elastin formation to prevent disecting aneurysms of the aorta. Builds blood cells.	Rare. Anemia, depigmentation of red feathers, bone deformities.	Supplement with copper.
Iodine	Synthesis of thyroid hormones.	Goiter, enlarged thryroid glands-results in poor growth, egg production and size.	Supplement.
Iron	Builds blood cells	Rare. Anemia, depigmentation of red feathers.	Supplement.
Magnesium	Used to maintain bones.	Rare. Poor feathering, grow slow-then stop growing, lethargic, irritable when disturbed, brief convulsions, sometimes death. Incoordination, ataxia, reduced hatchability.	Supplement with magnesium, feed balanced ration.
Manganese	In combination with calcium and Phosphorous-prevents perosis.	Decline in egg production, reduced hatchability, perosis (slipped tendon), thin-shelled eggs-break easy, shortened thick legs.	Irreversible if deformities occur. Aggravated by too much calcium or phosphorous. Poor egg shells-limit free choice calcium. Excessive phosphorous when meat, bone scrap soul protein.
Phosphorous	Works with calcium-bone and shell formation.	Lack of either calcium, phosphorous and, or, Vitamin D will create rickets If phosphorous-leg bones become soft and rubbery, joints enlarged, but bird does not become paralyzed.	Check phosphorous level in feed-an excess of calcium or phosphorous will cause rickets. Ratio should be 2 parts calcium to 1 part phosphorous for metabolism.
Potassium	Good egg shells.	Rare-feeds contain much more than poultry need. A deficiency will result in high mortality, retarded growth, decline in egg production, reduced egg shell thickness.	
Selenium	Works with Vitamin E for good muscle fibers	(Exudative Diathesis)-unthriftiness, ruffled feathers between 5-ll weeks. Poor growth, chick mortality, birds bruise easily-bruises may form scabs. Egg production affected.	Added to feed in form of sodium selenate, sodium selenite. Good sources also include dried brewer's yeast and fish meal. Toxic at 8-10 mg/kg in feed.
Zinc	Helps promote egg production, works with other minerals	Retarded growth, frayed feathers, legs and wings shorter and thicker, hock joints enlarged, lower egg production and hatchability. Skeleton abnormalities in chicks.	Supplement.

Table 3-9. Some Common Mineral Supplements.

	Calcium %	Phosphorous %	Potassium %	Magnesium %	Sulfur %	Sodium %	Crude Protein Equiv. %	Ash %	Bulk (Loose) Density lb/Cu. Ft.
Monocalcium-Dicalcium Phosphate	16.00	21.0	0.08	0.65	1.20	0.06	-	79.9	57.0
Dicalcium-Monocalcium Phosphate	22.00	18.5	0.07	0.60	1.10	0.08	-	85.6	58.0
Tricalcium Phosphate	32.00	18.0	0.08	0.42	-	4.90	-	99.9	81.0
Monoammonium Phosphate	0.27	24.0	-	0.45	1.42	0.06	68.75	45.0	57.0
Feed Grade Phosphoric Acid	0.06	-	18.00	11.0	22.00	0.76	-	94.7	90.0
Feed Grade Double Sulfate of Magnesium and Potassium	0.05	-	50.00	0.34	0.45	1.00	-	99.1	67.0
Feed Grade Potassium Chloride	0.06	-	18.00	11.0	22.00	0.76	-	94.7	90.0
Feed Grade Potassium Sulfate	0.15	-	41.00	0.60	17.0	0.09	-	98.8	90.0

(Courtesy of International Minerals & Chemical Corporation (IMC).)

small, medium and coarse (starter, grower, and layer) designations. It's found in most feed stores. Usually it's sold in 50-pound bags and runs about $3 per bag.

The grit is consumed by the chickens and goes to their gizzard, where the food is crushed before moving to the pancreas and small intestine for digestion. Grit is just as important for chicks as it is for adult birds.

A starter grit should be used for small chicks for the first two weeks. Then feed a grower grit for the next four weeks. Layer grit can be started anytime after the age of seven weeks.

Baby chicks not yet used to grit can mistake grit for feed and eat too much, causing digestive difficulties from lack of feed ingestion. The usual method is to feed small chicks grit by sprinkling fine grit over their feed the first few days. Later the grit can be fed in separate feeders. Chickens usually only eat the amount of grit that they need.

If the small, starter-size grit is unavailable locally, coarse, clean sand can be used in place of commercially prepared and packaged grit.

DRINKING WATER REQUIREMENTS

Water provides some trace minerals, but it's main purpose is to help maintain the normal body temperature and to prevent dehydration of the bird's tissues. Water further acts as a softening agent of food, a tool to help digest food and as an aid in the assimilation of nutrients eaten.

Normally, chicks consume about two times more water than the feed they will eat. Broiler chicks will drink one-half to two-thirds times more water than egg breeds. General-purpose birds will consume an amount between what broiler and egg breeds will consume. It's easy to figure waterer needs. See Table 3-10. Uncontrolled, excessive heat and humidity will cause chicks to drink more than usual. Some rations can cause more thirst among chicks.

Very young chicks should never be given ice-cold water or cold tap water. Warm the water to room temperature. Outdoors, fill 5-gallon buckets and warm the water in the sun. Ice-cold water can cause chicks to become chilled inside, and it can upset their digestive tract.

Table 3-10. Daily Water Consumption of Chickens.

Age (weeks)	200 Straight-Run Broilers		200 Egg-Breed Pullets	
	Gallons (U.S.)	Liters	Gallons (U.S.)	Liters
1	1.0	4.0	1.0	3.8
2	2.6	10.0	2.0	7.6
3	4.8	18.0	2.4	9.0
4	7.4	28.0	3.4	12.8
5	10.6	40.0	4.4	16.6
6	13.8	52.0	5.0	19.0
7	17.0	64.0	5.6	21.2
8	20.0	76.0	6.0	22.8
9			7.0	26.4
10			7.6	28.8
12			8.0	30.2
15			8.4	31.6
20			9.0	34.0

35 weeks . . . . Laying or Breeding 10.0   37.8

Consumption will vary considerably depending on temperature and diet composition.

*Adapted from *Nutrient Requirements of Poultry, 8th revised edition*, copyright 1984, National Academy of Sciences.

Soft water should not be given because of the salt content from mechanical water softeners. The salt can be toxic to chicks if given in large amounts. Water should always be fresh and pure. Change the water if it becomes fouled by feed, droppings, or litter.

WATER ADDITIVES

Some handlers feel the chicks' drinking water is not complete without some type of medication placed in it. I've seen many problems arise from handlers medicating drinking water. I advise no additives if a balanced ration is being fed and clean management is practiced because there is no medication that can take the place of these. I've seen many handlers lose chicks from medicating water needlessly.

If the ration is lacking essential vitamins, do not add vitamins to the water. Switch to another ration to correct the deficiency. Excessive use of some vitamins can be toxic, but a handler has no way of knowing how much is too much.

Some medications inhibit vitamins from doing their job. The only additives I rely on are cod liver oil and vinegar. When cod liver oil is administered to broilers and tall-legged breeds such as Langshans and Modern Games, it will prevent the very common crippling of these birds associated with rickets. The vinegar is used to clear up coccidial infections.

Perhaps you have an additive you rely on heavily and feel you must use. Fellow handlers and salesman are good at instilling this need in unexperienced handlers. If it works good for you in combination with your management and type feed used, fine, but don't be afraid to try serving the water without it. You might find it's only fear that causes you to use it. It might be healthier for both you and your birds to try omitting the additive.

Chapter 4

Chick Problems

Most problems with chicks can be corrected easily and inexpensively without great losses. Management is the main concern in keeping chicks healthy. Always be on guard for signs of disease and problems. Probably 90 percent of the chicks lost yearly could have been avoided with a combination of observation and a quick response by handlers.

If handlers become familiar with symptoms of trouble and appropriate remedies are applied, chick losses can be kept very low. Many handlers mistakenly believe a certain percentage, as many as one-half, of the chicks raised will automatically die. Years ago losses were greater. Today's chicks have much more vitality and stamina bred into them. Combined with modern vaccinations, medicine and improved management practices, today's chicks are easier to raise and there is less mortality.

Beyond this, small-scale handlers must never forget that new is not always better. Sometimes there are tradeoffs. One example is when commercial feed processors lower the calcium level in an important feed, such as starter feed for chicks, just so it does not interfere with absorption of a medication such as tetracycline. The overuse of the coccidiostat Amprol can interfere with the actions of Vitamin B_1 and can cause deficiency symptoms. Because flies can be a problem in commercial laying houses, a chemical larvicide was introduced into the layers feed so the poultrys' droppings would work to kill fly larva in dropping pits. The Environmental Protection Agency wanted further testing done, and it was ordered off the market.

Knowledge from both the old and the new can sometimes be combined with a compatible medium resulting, but we must never overdo that which has not been proven from long-standing use.

Always remember to carefully follow medication directions and precautions. Wash your hands after handling any medication or vaccination solutions, and keep such materials out of reach of children—even in outbuildings.

Observe withdrawal times. This is the time that elapses between the last dose and the time the birds are butchered or their eggs were gathered. This will help prevent residues of the medication from appearing in your meat and eggs.

BEAK TRIMMING

The following is reprinted with the permission of Lyon Electric Company, Inc.

Beak trimming, as the words imply, is the removal of a portion of birds beak(s) by trimming and cauterization or by searing the upper beak only. The major advantages of beak trimming is to curb fighting and cannibalism. Birds with trimmed beaks tend to be quieter because a major reason for fear of other birds has been eliminated. Other advantages of beak trimming are reduced feed wastage, the elimination of toe and feather picking, reduced egg loss, and reduced spreading of disease.

The method and age to beak trim will depend on the use of the bird, broiler, layer, etc., and the convenience and desire of the grower. Broiler beaks are generally trimmed at day-old or at an early age by either the hatchery or producer. The most popular method of beak trimming layers is the precision 6- to 10-day-old method. Some egg producers, however, prefer to beak trim at an early age and again before the birds are placed into production. Because so many methods are used, the producer or grower must, in the final analysis, select the method most suitable to him.

Do's and Don'ts of Beak Trimming

1. Don't beak trim when birds are under stress.

2. Don't rush the beak trimming. See that operators are trained first. Speed will follow.

3. Do keep plenty of feed available after beak trimming.

4. Do keep water available, deep enough so the bird can drink easily.

5. Do keep cauterizing blade clean and in good condition.

If beak trimming is important enough for you to include it in your operation, it is important enough to be done right. Failure to beak trim properly can damage bird livability and uniformity. It can cause starve outs, feed wastage, and even cannibalism. This adds up to lost profits. A good beak trimming program can save you money. Management evaluation should be used for beak trimming as for any other operations you perform. Make it a regular practice to see that quality is maintained and new operators are properly trained. Beak trimming is not the most enjoyable job so don't overlook the operators work area. It should be arranged for maximum efficiency yet comfortable to assure minimum operator fatigue. The human factor alone can cause poor beak trimming quality.

Observe safety precautions. A beak trimmer is used to cut or sear and cauterize. It is an electrical device and should be treated accordingly. Replace worn or frayed cords, and clean the important front-end area daily to ensure good electrical contact. Be certain the blade is cleaned and in good condition at all times.

Day-Old Beak Trimming of Broiler Chicks

Beak trimming of broilers at one day old is the most widely used method of broiler producers. While some producers actually cut off a portion of the upper beak with a cauterizing blade (Fig. 4-1), the most popular method is to trim by beak heat treating or searing (Figs. 4-2 and 4-3).

Upper Beak Trimming

In this method a small portion of the upper beak is cut off and cauterized as shown in Fig. 4-1. To do this the Super Debeaker is fitted with the IR Upper Beak Removal Attachment, Catalog No. 940-14 Water Cooled or 940-15 Waterless. The upper hole in the attachment gauge allows only a small amount of the beak to be removed, but enough to last until market time. Setup and operation instructions are included in the accessory package.

Beak Trimming by Searing Methods

Two types of upper beak heat treating are in use.

Fig. 4-1. Line indicates the portion of the upper beak to cut off when using a cauterizing blade (courtesy of Lyon Electric Company, Inc.).

Both methods may be done on the Super Debeaker, using the BHT attachment, Catalog No. 940-06 or by using the Beak-Heat-Treator Debeaker, which was designed specifically for upper beak heat treating by searing.

Beak Trimming by Angle Searing

This method is accomplished using a cauterizing blade with a 45-degree angle bend in it. The top curved surface of the beak is touched to the hot cauterizing blade (as shown in Fig. 4-2). Notice that the tip of the beak is *not* seared. When using this method, care must be taken so that the seared portion is a dimes-to-nickel width (.045 to 1075) *in front of the nostrils*. Proper setting of the blade and attachment will prevent this from happening. When properly done, the tip will drop off in 8 to 12 days, during which time the bird has learned to eat and drink properly, and is off to a good start. Blades used for this type of beak trimming are the BT,

IRXN, IRXW, LD and MN2. For Super Debeaker, there is a special MN attachment, Catalog No. 940-08, for use with the MN blade. No attachment is needed for use on the Beak-Heat-Treator Debeaker.

Beak Trimming by Notch Searing

Notch beak trimming shown in Fig. 4-3 is done by using a cauterizing blade with a curved lip along the entire bottom edge. The machine is adjusted so that when the upper beak is touched to the blade it is trimmed a dimes to nickels width (.045 to 1075) in front of the nostrils, by searing a notch in it. This method leaves a thin part of the beak at the front but the tip is eliminated. The bird retains full use of it's beak however while learning to eat and drink before the remaining seared part drops off. As with the angle sear, care should be exercised to keep the notched area forward of the nostrils. The blades used on this method are the DL, DLX, DL2, and MN2. The wide lip area of the DL2 and MN2 makes it easy to beak trim two birds at once. This method can be used with BHT attachment No. 940-06 on the Super Debeaker, but works best on the Beak-Heat-Treator Debeaker.

Precision 6 to 10-Day-Old Beak Trimming of Layer Chicks

This method of beak trimming layer chicks is widely used. Properly done it is one of the most accurate methods of beak trimming available. The Super V Precision Debeaker or the Dual Debeaker

Fig. 4-2. Day-old broiler angle sear trim (courtesy of Lyon Electric Company, Inc.).

Fig. 4-3.Day-old broiler notch searing (courtesy of Lyon Electric Company, Inc.).

Fig. 4-4. Line indicates where part of beak is removed on a 6-to-10-day-old chick (courtesy of Lyon Electric Company, Inc.).

are designed for this method of beak trimming. To use this method with a Super Debeaker, a power unit is required. The timed 2+ seconds of cauterization provided by these units is necessary to inhibit the growth of beak roots. Figure 4-4 shows how the bird will look after trimming. Notice that the lower beak is slightly longer than the upper beak. This is accomplished by applying a slight choking action to the birds throat during the trimming operation to withdraw the tongue and lower beak. Figure 4-5 shows how the beak will look when the bird reaches maturity. Complete instructions covering this method are supplied and should be carefully adhered to. Properly done this method of beak trimming will suffice for the productive life of the bird. The Super V Precision Debeaker and the Dual Precision Debeaker are available in water cooled and waterless models. Three types of attachments for this method are available for Super Debeaker, the B Attachment, Water Cooled No. 940-11, the BP Attachment, Waterless No. 940-12 and No. 8BC Water Cooled Attachment No. 940-10.

3 to 6 Week Beak Trimming

The TT method of beak trimming was designed primarily for beak trimming birds from 3 to 6 weeks of age. It has been used to trim beaks of birds up to 12 weeks of age, but proportionally less beak is removed at this age. It is NOT recommended for beak trimming birds less than three weeks old. With the TT method, the bird is held sideways at a 90-degree angle to the blade. Both beaks are trimmed and cauterized simultaneously with an inward slant, as shown in Fig. 4-6. Using this method the birds beaks are trimmed permanently. The special beak guide and blade used in the TT method greatly reduces the variations in beak trimming caused by too little or too much in other methods. Because this method of beak trimming is different, careful operator training is required.

Fig. 4-5. This is how the bird will look at maturity (courtesy of Lyon Electric Company, Inc.).

Fig. 4-6. Line indicates where trimming and cauterizing are simultaneously accomplished on a 3-to-6-week-old bird (courtesy of Lyon Electric Company, Inc.).

BREAST BLISTERS

Breast blisters can occur as early as 6 weeks of age in any breed of chick but it seems to occur more in heavy chicks. It appears as a soft swelling anywhere on the breast or where the neck meets the body. Depending upon how long the chick has had it, the swelling will contain a clear or blood-tinged fluid or a thick pus.

Blisters appears mainly on chicks raised in battery brooders. The problem is caused from a constant irritation from sharp edges on the feeders or waterers. Sharp edges should be located in brooders and bent smoothly back in shape. Feeders and waterers set on litter should be checked for sharp edges if floor raised chicks get blisters.

If the blisters have not turned to a thick pus, they can be drained using a sterilized syringe and needle. After completely draining, rinse with a diluted solution of potassium permanganate, flushing and syringing. Potassium permanganate is purchased at drugstores in small tablet form. A 300 mg. (5 gr.) tablet should be diluted with 1 quart of boiled water to make a main stock solution. One-half cup of this solution is then mixed with about 1 cup of clear boiled water and cooled.

If a blister has turned to pus, or if blister continues to fill with fluid, a small incision can be made with a sterilized razor blade and then flushed. It's a good idea to spray the top of a wound with a methyl violet or gentian violet antiseptic to kill bacteria and to show which bird was operated on later.

BROODER PNEUMONIA (ASPERGILLOSIS)

Caused by fungus contained in moldy feed or litter, this respiratory disease is not highly contagious. Check for mold and compare symptoms. Symptoms include labored breathing, gasping, increased thirst, sleepiness, loss of appetite, emaciation, cyanosis (dark bluish coloring of skin), and nervous disorders such as a twisted neck. Young birds are more susceptible.

Treatment consists of removing moldy litter or feed and cleaning. Raise the humidity of the house, and then medicate with a fungistat such as gentian

violet, mycostatin, sodium or calcium propionate, mold curb, Rocon, nystatin, amphotericin B, brilliant green or copper sulfate (1:2000 solution). The litter should be sprayed lightly with a 1 percent copper sulfate or an oil-base germicide to control dust that might contain fungus spores. Copper sulfate corrodes metal so plastic or glass containers should be used. Severely affected chicks will usually die. Mortality can run from 5 percent to as high as 50 percent, depending how long the birds have been in contact with a certain amount of the fungus.

CANNIBALISM

Cannibalism must be stopped as soon as chicks are seen pecking on one another. Causes can include the use of bright brooding lights, a large ray of sunlight coming into an enclosed brooding area, a change of environment, overcrowding, high temperatures, insufficient feeders and, or waterers, unbalanced ration (see sodium deficiency in Table 3-8), injuries, lack of variety in feed consistency, and lack of entertainment.

Immediately remove injured or dead chicks. Spray injuries with an antiseptic wound dressing that contains methyl violet or gentian violet. Keep injured chicks brooded separately from rest of brood. Examine causes and remedy. The ideal time to remedy the situation is when pecking of the vent, toes, wings, tails, nose, and backs is first spotted. If just one or two chicks seem to be doing the pecking, clip their beaks. This usually puts an end to the beginning of cannibalism caused by just a few chicks.

If chicks are being brooded under bright lights and pecking is spotted, look to see if some chicks are pecking at feed clinging to other chicks. This is usually the case. Dim lights will have to replace the brooder lights being used. This can be done easily with red brooder bulbs.

After injured chicks are completely healed, in about five to seven days, and the cause has been remedied, they can be safely put back in with the rest of the brood. Always keep an eye on any brood of chicks that have been moved to different brooding quarters. The frightening experience can stimulate them to begin pecking. Keep the area dimly lit at first and make sure feeders and waterers are where all chicks can easily find them.

Injured chicks can be placed in a small box with a small lamp hung over them which contains a colored bulb. Be sure to check for correct brooder temperature for them.

COCCIDIOSIS

If the chicks' droppings have been faithfully watched, a severe case of coccidial infection should not occur. Coccidiosis usually appears in chicks. Adult chickens eventually build up an immunity to the organisms. Chicks brooded on litter will build up an immunity quicker than battery-brooded chicks.

If the ceca is cut open, it's lining would be bloody from the irritation caused by the protozoan organisms. (See Fig. 4-7.) A coccidiostat such as Amprol will bring on an attack of coccidiosis at around four weeks of age. This medication gives the disease to the chicks so an immunity can be built up within the chicks' bodies. A handler is suppose to ride this infection out unless the chicks are really uncomfortable. Then a sulfa drug should be given.

Because Amprol is actually a Vitamin B_1 antagonist, that is, it interferes with the function

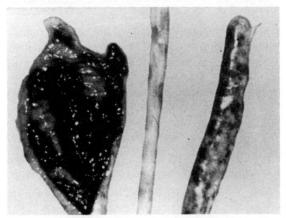

Fig. 4-7. Ceca cut open exposing bloody lining from a severe coccidial infection (courtesy of L. Dwight Schwartz, D.V.M., Senior Pathologist, Michigan State University).

of Vitamin B_1 (Thiamin), the mild case of enteritis it will bring on will cause growth depression, lack of appetite, and possibly even blood in the droppings.

Usually only one-half the legal allowable dose is added to chick starters, but it's enough to interfere with the function of the Vitamin B_1. If symptoms are noticed, especially when you are not feeding a medicated feed, sulfadimethoxine or sulfaquinoxaline can be used. Liquid Amprol can be used according to label directions also.

Plain vinegar can also be used by adding about a quarter cup to each gallon of the chicks' drinking water for about three days until the chicks' droppings no longer look watery or contain blood. Remember that too much cod-liver oil also will cause loose droppings. Blood in droppings is caused by something irritating the lining of the digestive tract. Do not give cod-liver oil when feeding the vinegar.

Begin watching for signs in the droppings as early as two weeks of age. If the droppings are watched, the vinegar can be given before chicks are lost.

Cornish Rock broilers do not need to build up an immunity to coccidiosis. Medications are definitely not needed for them.

FEATHER PULLING

Chicks sometimes grab feathers and pull them out of the skin of other chicks. Feather pulling can be distinguished from poor feathering "barebacks" by the little holes left in the skin where the feathers have been removed. In dark feathered chicks, there will be a small quantity of dark pigment in each hole. Feather pulling can lead to cannibalism if not kept in check.

If only a few chicks seem to be pulling feathers, trim their beaks. This can be done easily with a pair of nail clippers. Grasp the chick's beak with the thumb and index finger of one hand, and with the other, clip about one-sixteenth of an inch of the top beak off on small chicks. Larger chicks can have a bit more clipped off. Just make sure you do not cut past the lighter white spot of the mandible. If bleeding does occur, quickly dip the chick's beak into some fine feed mash until the blood clots.

The beak trimming will allow the feathers to slip out from the chick's beak as it is grasped.

INFECTIOUS BRONCHITIS

An acute and highly contagious viral respiratory infection that shows mainly gasping, coughing and sneezing. Infectious bronchitis begins suddenly and is rapidly spread. There will be fluffed out feathers, because chicks feel cold, a lot of chirping, coughing, labored breathing, and gasping in young chicks. Feed and water intake declines and there will be wet-looking eyes and a slight nasal discharge. Usually all of your chicks will get the disease. Young chicks have the highest mortality; it might reach as high as 60 percent. Adult layers will drop egg production severely even months after they recover. The disease causes a loss of mucin cells in the magnum of the reproductive tract of the hens and other uterine cells. The result will be many egg-laying problems in the bird's reproductive system and bad quality eggs with thin whites and bad and thin shells. The egg quality is frequently a permanent problem so hens should be butchered.

There is no medication to hasten the course of the disease. It must run it's course naturally. The disease is spread through the air, infected equipment, crates, feed bags, human clothing and boots, infected dead birds, and rodents. So far the disease is limited to chickens.

Chicks should be made as comfortable as possible by raising the brooding temperature 5 to 10 degrees. Every effort should be made to get the chicks to eat and drink. The virus is destroyed by heat, disinfectants, and sunlight that is not filtered through windows.

Most states allow immunization with a live-virus vaccine. The vaccine is usually given in the drinking water. Extreme care should be used when using and administering any vaccine—especially a live one.

INFECTIOUS SYNOOVITIS (MYCOPLASMA SYNOVIAE-MS)

An infectious joint and respiratory disease, synovi-

tis most often occurs in chicks 4 to 12 weeks of age. Because it is egg transmissible, many hatcheries and breeder farms do blood tests for breeding stock. Flocks formerly infected should not be used to obtain hatching eggs.

Symptoms include lameness with swollen joints, loss of weight, green droppings, breast blisters, inactivity, and limping. In the respiratory form, the chicks will show respiratory distress. A yellow exudate is found in the joints, mainly the keel, hocks, wings, bursa, and feet. Internally there is an enlarged liver and spleen, with a stringy type of exudate around the heart. In the respiratory form, the air sacs will be filled with cheesy looking exudates.

There is nothing to be gained in treating broilers that will soon be butchered. Layer chicks can be treated with spectinomycin, chlortetracycline, erthromycin, tylosin, lincomycin, or any tetracycline antibiotics administered in the feed. Labels should contain the correct dosage.

The disease is spread by direct contact with infected birds, through the air, and on equipment and people.

LICE

There are no sucking lice that infest domestic chickens, but there are at least seven species of biting-chewing lice that might give you trouble. The four most common are *shaft lice* that concentrate on the feather shafts, *head lice* that are found mainly about the head and neck, *wing lice* found about the wing feathers, and *body lice* on the skin (Fig. 4-8). The three less commonly found species are *fluff lice* found in the fluff, *large chicken louse*, which is very large and distinctively marked a blue-gray, and the *brown chicken louse* found on the feathers in southern areas.

Lice live, feed, and breed—spending their entire life cycle—on the chickens. The adult lice have flat bodies, six legs, and a rounded broad head. Their mouth contains serrated teeth on the underside of the head. All contain two claws at the bottom segment of each leg.

There is irritation to the chicken as the lice crawl over the body feeding on feathers, dry skin

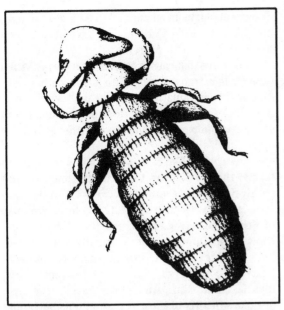

Fig. 4-8. An enlarged view of a chicken body louse, showing two small claws at the bottom segment of each leg (courtesy of L. Dwight Schwartz, D.V.M., Senior Pathologist, Michigan State University).

scales, blood particles and scabs on the skin. This constant irritation will cause chickens to have a lack of appetite, diarrhea, sleeplessness and a 10 to 20 percent drop in egg production. Because of the stress, the chickens are weakened and are more susceptible to disease. It is important to keep the pests from the chickens.

Lice multiply more in the warm months but they also bother the chickens in cold months.

By parting a chicken's feathers, a handler can usually find the lice or the egg masses adhered to the feathers near the skin (Fig. 4-9). Around the vent and under the wings are a good place to look. All chickens get lice to one degree or another, so periodic dusting is in order. A dusting box can be made to handle infestations between this periodic dusting. Even young chicks enjoy dusting.

Once chicks are out in buildings on litter, they are then prey to lice. Because roosters usually don't take dust baths, it's important to individually dust them with the lice powder. Lice love young skin and tender feathers. Large amounts of lice will quickly kill young chickens and small chicks.

Treatment consists in thorough cleaning of the house between broods. After a building is cleaned and empty of birds, an insecticide should be sprayed. Pay particular attention to cracks, crevices, corners and rough wood areas. Keep feed (even if in bags) and water and feeders out of the building while spraying. Sprays can be made with 4 percent malathion or 0.5 percent coumaphos, and applied with a hand sprayer.

Dusting the chickens and litter can be accomplished with sodium fluoride. It can be shaken right from the can. Be sure to part the feathers and powder right down to the skin of each bird. For laying hens be sure to powder inside of nests, too.

Roosts should also be "painted" by mixing insecticides with diesel oil, kerosene, or water. Use about 1 ounce for every 15 feet of roosts. This can be applied with a brush or a small oil can. Nicotine sulfate in a 40 percent strength can be applied full

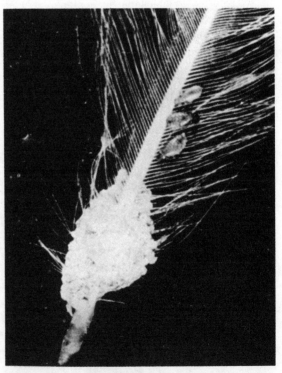

Fig. 4-9. Chicken feather lice with their egg mass near bottom of feather (courtesy of L. Dwight Schwartz, D.V.M., Senior Pathologist, Michigan State University).

strength with the brush or diluted with the same quantity of water for use with the oil can.

Painting the roosts kills the lice as the chickens are roosting because fumes are created from the chicken's body heat when it comes in contact with the insecticide.

Some of the new sonic devices work great in keeping lice and other pests off chickens. The quality and effectiveness varies with different brands. Ask that a trial period or guarantee be given as to its effectiveness in your poultry house before you fully commit yourself to its purchase. Most must be positioned just right in the building for the sonic waves to disperse evenly. Have the salesman set it up for you. Results should be noticed in just a few days if the device is doing its job. You might even find dead rats laying about the building floor, or bugs coming out from the cracks and crevices in the walls.

Chicken lice do not live on humans but they can be transported to chickens by humans. Besides making chickens uncomfortable and lowering egg production, the lice cause the feathers to become dull and ragged looking.

MAREK'S DISEASE

Marek's Disease is usually a highly contagious disease in chicks from about 3 to 20 weeks of age, but chickens as old as 18 months have been known to come down with Marek's.

The virus that causes Marek's is a herpes virus, type B. It is transmitted by air from feather dander, as the virus matures, to it's infectious form in the follicles of the feathers. Most dust, manure, and saliva contain particles that are a further source for spreading.

The cancer like disease can show up in three forms: the nerve form that causes lameness and paralysis from nerve tumors (Fig. 4-10); the skin form is seen with enlarged feather follicles because of skin tumors (Fig. 4-11); and the viscera forms show up as tumors most commonly found in the liver, kidney, heart, lungs, spleen, gonads, pancreas, bursa of Fabricius, proventriculus, muscles and skin. An ocular form, gray eye, discolors the iris of the eye gray; pupils becoming irregularly shaped and blindness follows.

There presently is no cure, although there is a vaccine available that must be given at one day of age for positive effectiveness. If delayed, chicks can be exposed to the dangerous virus. Vaccinated birds can become infected but they will not develop tumors. The vaccine used is a live turkey herpes virus. It is available only in 1000-dose bottles for about $12. Unused contents should be disposed of

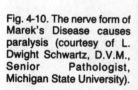

Fig. 4-10. The nerve form of Marek's Disease causes paralysis (courtesy of L. Dwight Schwartz, D.V.M., Senior Pathologist, Michigan State University).

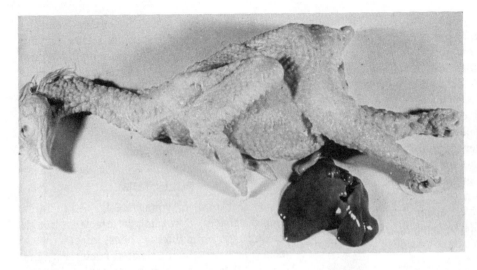

Fig. 4-11. Note enlarged feather follicles in skin form of Marek's (courtesy of L. Dwight Schwartz, D. V. M., Senior Pathologist, Michigan State University).

safely. If chicks are ordered from a hatchery, ask if they perform the vaccination. Some don't.

OMPHALITIS (MUSHY CHICK DISEASE)

This is an inflammation of the navel in baby chicks caused by bacteria entering an improperly closed navel. The cause is usually from unsanitary conditions within an incubator. Dirty and exploder eggs, poor quality shells, and thin and cracked shells allow bacteria to enter eggs and thus infect the chicks. The infection does not spread from chick to chick but is only an occurrence in chicks with the unhealed navels.

Chicks will appear weak and unthrifty. The abdomen will be enlarged and puffy (mushy) feeling. The navel will be moist and inflamed (Fig. 4-12). Most infected chicks die within a week. Outward signs are chicks huddling (usually with drooping heads) to try to keep warm near the heat source.

An antiseptic can be placed over the navel, but the affected chicks should be disposed of because they usually turn out to be poor-quality runts.

Incubators should be fumigated with 40 percent formaldehyde. About 30 ml of the formalin and 15 gr of potassium permanganate are used per 20 cubic

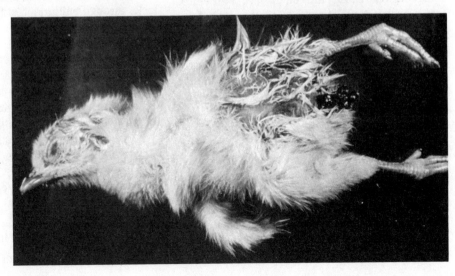

Fig. 4-12. Mushy Chick Disease shows a puffy abdomen and inflamed navel on this dead chick (courtesy of L. Dwight Schwartz, D.V.M., Senior Pathologist, Michigan State University).

99

feet of inside capacity of incubator. (Or 1 teaspoon of formalin to 1/2 teaspoon of postassium permanganate.)When the chemicals come in contact, they form a gas that is the fumigant. The required amount of potassium permanganate is placed in a glass bowl in a (90 to 100 degree Fahrenheit dry bulb reading and a wet bulb reading of 90 degrees Fahrenheit) incubator. The formalin is quickly poured over the potassium permanganate and the door and vents are quickly shut. The fumes will burn your mucous membranes. Eyes should keep protected from the fumes. The incubator should be kept shut for about three hours. Then neutralize the solution by pouring ammonia water over it—keeping your face and eyes covered.

POISONING

Signs of toxic poisoning vary but include uneasiness, wing paralysis, vomiting, nervous symptoms, circling, loss of weight, leg deformities, soft-shelled eggs and malformed eggs, tremors, convulsions, prostration, internal bleeding, dilated pupils, retarded growth, fluid in the abdominal cavity, depression, watery droppings, listlessness, and thirst.

When any unusual symptoms occur in a flock, think back to any methods of cleaning, disinfecting, or parasite control that was recently done. Some compounds can cause burns on the face, wattles and feet. Check if medications or wormers could have been overdosed. Are there fly or insect baits where chickens can get to them? Are rodent poisons out of reach? Overuse of some chemicals, either organic or inorganic, can be toxic. Were chickens ranging near where crops or orchards were recently sprayed?

The feed can be questioned if other sources can be ruled out. Cottonseed meal, for example, contains gossypol that will cause a swelling around the heart, labored breathing, weakness, and lack of appetite.

Soybeans contain compounds that are toxic unless heat-treated. Rapeseed meals contain compounds that can depress growth rate and egg production.

Treatment for most poisonings requires removing the offending substance after playing detective to the cause. Some poisoning does not produce highly visual symptoms, such as PCB (polychlorinated biphenyl). PCB's have been found in some poultry meat and egg products in excess of permitted levels. Some of the chemicals were traced to plastic bags used on bakery products that were ground into poultry feeds.

PULLORUM

This is a disease of young chicks. Adult birds become carriers. Spreading is attained through hatching eggs from infected hens, infected chick boxes, incubators, contaminated equipment, and houses and feeds containing infected poultry by-products.

If pullorum is egg-transmitted, mortality begins the first few days of life and peaks at two to three weeks of age. Symptoms include huddling near heat, no appetite, depression, sleepiness, droopiness, diarrhea, white pasting around vent (sometimes containing green bile material), gasping and weak knees. Commonly found lesions include spotted decay of the internal organs of chicks (Fig. 4-13). Survivors should not be used to produce hatching eggs. Infected chicks infect others through the droppings. This disease was once very common but has now been eliminated from commercial flocks through pullorum testing and by destroying infected birds.

Pullorum testing can be done at home by purchasing the pullorum stained antigen and bleeder loop. The bleeder loop draws the right amount of blood from the vein, under the wing, at the same time it pierces the skin. The blood is then mixed with a drop of the antigen on a glass plate and compared with photos (supplied with purchase) after two minutes of drying.

The antigen can only be purchased in 1000-dose bottles for under $30 but it can be re-capped with the dropper cap and refrigerated.

RICKETS

This is a nutritional disorder of young chickens

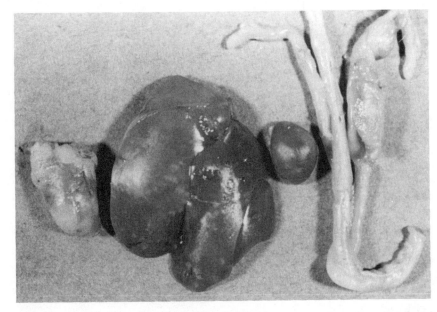

Fig. 4-13. A spotty liver and other internal organs of a 3-week-old chick that contacted pullorum disease (courtesy of L. Dwight Schwartz, D.V.M., Senior Pathologist, Michigan State University).

caused by a deficiency of Vitamin D_3 and calcium, or an imbalance of calcium and phosphorus. If calcium is lacking, it is simply unavailable for the body's use. If Vitamin D_3 is lacking, the available calcium cannot be absorbed and used by the body. Vitamin D_3 is needed for calcium to be utilized. If Vitamin D_3 or both calcium and Vitamin D_3 are deficient, the young growing bones of chicks will become soft and springy with eventual crippling (Fig. 4-14).

For proper metabolism, a ratio of 2:1 should be present for calcium and phosphorus in the feed. An excess of either will cause rickets, with bones becoming soft and rubbery.

Rickets will begin to be noticed as the chick starts to put on a bit of weight at about four weeks of age. Fast growers such as Cornish Rock Cross broilers are more prone because of the extra weight their legs must carry. Tall-legged breeds, such as Langshans, are prone to rickets also because they seem to be top heavy. Any chick whose diet is deficient or imbalanced can get rickets: it's just not as readily apparent as in the larger type broilers.

Rickets cannot be cured once the crippling has begun (the first sign). Birds with rickets cannot get around properly to feed and their growth is severely stunted. It's usually more economical to dispose of such birds rather than to try and grow them out.

Fig. 4-14. This 5-week-old broiler with rickets, caused from a lack of Vitamin D_3 should be disposed of because she will not make economical growth.

Most rickets with broilers (or other chicks for that matter) are caused from a deficiency of Vitamin D_3 in commercially prepared chick starters. Because there is no way of knowing just how much of the vitamin is in the starter feed, it's better to administer the vitamin on your own (with cod-liver oil) beginning at five days of age. Giving the oil sooner can produce loose droppings. Watch the condition of the droppings so you can tell if the right amount is being given. Four ounces of a good, fresh poultry cod-liver oil should be enough for 25 chicks until four weeks of age, when they have access to sunlight.

Ironically, commercial starter feeds that should contain a good amount of calcium for baby chicks is sometimes lower in it's calcium level to intensify the action of antibiotics such a tetracycline. The calcium content may be lowered to as much as one-fourth the amount chicks need.

Sailors long ago knew the values of cod-liver oil in preventing rickets. During their long journeys on galley ships where the sun was not seen for days, but fish was plentiful, men were seldom troubled with rickets.

Chicks should not be troubled now with such an old nutritional disease, but many are. There are handlers who matter of factly assume broilers cripple and that nothing need be done.

SPRADDLE LEGS

Spraddle legs is caused when chicks are allowed to walk over slippery surfaces before their young bones have hardened enough to support their weight. Tall-legged breeds are most prone. The legs begin to flex sideways, eventually becoming fixed turning straight out from each side of the body. Once this happens nothing can be done.

New chicks should always be placed on top of bunched up rags or towels until they gain footing. This usually takes about three days.

Folded newspapers and some types of straw can be slippery enough to cause spraddle legs. Wait until chicks are about a week old before placing them directly on straw or sprinkle gravel or dirt over the top.

TOE CLIPPING

The following is reprinted with the permission of Lyon Electric Company, Inc.:

Toe clipping utilizing a cauterizing blade offers many advantages including some not possible with mechanical cold clipping. It retards bleeding. Back Ripping is eliminated. Birds tend to be quieter. It can be used as a marking method to identify strains.

Many broiler producers have found that cutting the middle toe of each foot solves the ripped back problem. Some owners make it a regular practice of removing cackeral nails to protect the hen.

Crossed-lot birds are sometimes nervous and will pile up at the slightest provication. When this occurs they claw each other severely on the back, resulting in an unsightly carcass at market time. Toe clipping tends to eliminate this problem.

Manual Toe Clipping

Manual toe slipping using a Super Debeaker is accomplished using a flat beak support (Cat. No. 120-01) and a K Blade (Cat. No. 930-11) or IR Blade (Cat. No. 930-08). This type of toe clipping is almost always done using a foot pedal to operate the Debeaker. It can be done using a Pow-R-Pak Power Unit, but careful adjustment of the stroke must be made to cut fully through the toe without forcing the blade down on the beak support too hard, which will materially shorten blade life. A B11T Attachment cuts toes and wing tips with a shearing/cauterizing action.

To clip any of the forward toes, hold the bird with its back to the operator. A scratch mark on the flat anvil will aid in positioning the toes. Toes not to be cut are curled under the anvil (Fig. 4-15).

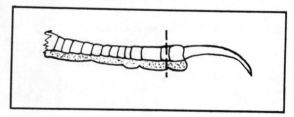

Fig. 4-15. Toe clipping is done through the middle of the second scale from the end of the toe (courtesy of Lyon Electric Company, Inc.).

Table 4-1. Toe Clipping-Marking Combinations.

L = Left Foot R = Right Foot				Total Marks
L1 L2 L3	L1-2 L1-3 L2-3	R1 R2 R3	R1-2 R1-3 R2-3	12
L1-R1 L1-R2 L1-R3	L2-R1 L2-R2 L2-R3	L3-R1 L3-R2 L3-R3		9
L1-2-R1 L1-2-R2 L1-2-R3	L1-3-R1 L1-3-R2 L1-3-R3	L2-3-R1 L2-3-R2 L2-3-R3		9
L1-R1-2 L1-R1-3 L1-R2-3	L2-R1-2 L2-R1-3 L2-R2-3	L3-R1-2 L3-R1-3 L3-R2-3		9
L1-2-R1-2 L1-2-R1-3 L1-2-R2-3	L1-2-R1-2 L1-3-R1-3 L1-3-R2-3	L2-3-R1-2 L2-3-R1-3 L2-3-R2-3		9 — Total = 48
*Courtesy of Lyon Electric Company, Inc.				

The toe is clipped through the second scale from the end of the toe.

Toe Clipping as a Marking System

Based on an article by George D. Quigley, University of Maryland for use by the Lyon Electric Company, Inc.):

Toe clipping can be used to advantage to identify strains, age in replacement programs, etc. Use a definite system, thinking in terms of the left and right foot. Marking two toes per foot gives 48 combinations (Table 4-1). Additional combinations are possible using the rear toe (Fig. 4-16).

VACCINATING

The choice to vaccinate is entirely up to the

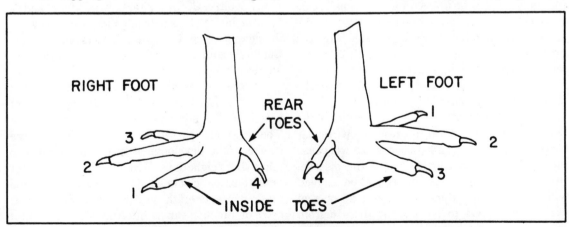

Fig. 4-16. Additional combinations of toe clipping as a marking system can be made by utilizing the rear toes.

handler. The amount of vaccinating because of the various types is also up to the handler. This section is only to be used as a guide to determine if vaccinating should be done, what vaccines are available, the procedures, and the cautions in handling.

There are other factors besides the chickens' health that should be considered. Some people are sensitive to poultry and even canine vaccines. A handler can be affected by handling the live vaccine or by eating vaccinated chickens. Symptoms will vary and the cause is sometimes undetected. There are sometimes pains felt in the joints. If this is the case, the only way a handler can be sure is to stop eating the vaccinated chickens and to stay away from the vaccines. If the pains stop and only occur again when the vaccinated chickens are eaten or vaccinated, then you are probably sensitive to the vaccines. It may be hard to differentiate as to which vaccine is the problem if more than one has been used.

This is not meant to scare a handler from needed vaccinating, but only to warn of possible consequences. If a certain disease has been known to be prevalent in your area, you would be wise to vaccinate for the particular disease. The more money invested into a flock, the more a handler might be inclined to protect them through vaccination.

Most vaccines are fairly inexpensive, although they are only available in 500-dose and 1000-dose containers. It can be a waste for most small-scale to invest in as the unused contents must be destroyed after mixing. Perhaps one day the pharmaceutical companies will think of the small-scale raisers and make small does vials available for them. This would also help many 4-H clubs who must vaccinate smaller lots of birds.

Vaccines are made from large quantities of the organism or virus known to cause the particular disease. Most are live virus vaccines that will cause the chickens to get a mild case of the disease. Because they are live, vaccines should be handled with extreme care. Burn or disinfect all opened vaccine containers to prevent the disease from spreading accidentally to other birds or poultry. Do not open containers until ready to use.

Always make sure instructions are included with the vaccine. Follow the directions to the maximum. Vaccines are usually stored under the refrigeration and must be warmed to room temperature if given as an injection.

There are various methods employed in administering the vaccines. Some are injected subcutaneously (under the skin), some can be sprayed, or mixed into the drinking water, dropped into the eye or nasal passage or applied using the wing-web stab method.

The drinking water method is for mass innoculation and is not as reliable as most other methods. Some vaccines, such as Erysipelas, Fowl Cholera and a Coccidiosis Vaccine, are available only commercially.

A suggested schedule for vaccination is shown in Table 4-2. There are many good books and pamphlets available that will explain vaccination procedures. Specific questions can be answered by local agricultural extension offices.

WORMS

There are four main species of worms that affect domestic chickens: thread, cecal, round and tape.

Thread (Capillaria) Worms

These worms are long and very thin and thread like (Fig. 4-17). Six species of this particular worm infect poultry. C. obsignata, C. caudinflata, and C. bursata infect the small intestine, especially the duodenum. The C. retusa infects the cecum. Capillaria annulata and C. contorta infect the crop and esophagus.

These worms are tough to eliminate. Their control consists mainly of good management practices. The adult worm lays eggs in the bird. The eggs are passed in the droppings of the chicken. The development of the worm embryo takes six to eight days. When most infective after embryonation, chickens pick up these eggs in the infected litter or off the ground and eat them. If this cycle of infection can be interrupted, their control will be much better. This calls for cleaning up,

Table 4-2. Vaccination Schedule.

Age	Disease	Agent	Procedure	Repeat
1-day	Marek's Disease	Turkey herpes-virus, live	Injection under skin on back of neck.	
10-days	Newcastle-Bronchitis Combination	Chick embryos, live virus	Optional-drinking water, eye drop, nasal or spray If spray method, must be originally done when chicks.	8 wks 14-wks 26-wks every 3 months
6-wks or older	Laryngo-tracheitis	Chick embryo or chicken tissue culture origin	Eye drop or vent.	
8-20 weeks	Avian Encephalomy-elitis	Chick embryo (Picornavirus), live	Drinking water. Primarily for breeder flocks.	
8-wks	Coryza	Strains of Haemophilus gallinarum, inactivated	Injection under skin on back of neck.	12-wks
10-wks	Fowl Pox	Chick embryo, live	Wing-web method. (or in feather follicle)	
12-wks	Fowl Cholera	Bacterial, usually live	Wing-web method or beneath the skin.	

disinfecting, fumigating, and using plenty of clean litter to cover and top dress old litter between cleanups. When the house is empty, steaming the floor with 140 degree Fahrenheit steam will kill remaining worm eggs. Threadworms cause poor growth, poor egg production, poor fertility.

Gentian violet prevents embryonation of the capillaria eggs. Meldane-2 (coumaphos) is the most

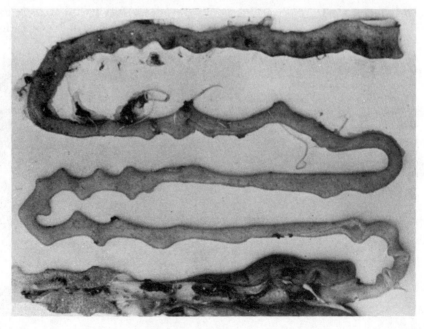

Fig. 4-17. A heavy infestation of Thread worms like this calls for strict management practices (courtesy of L. Dwight Schwartz, D.V.M., Senior Pathologist, Michigan State University).

effective treatment approved for use. It requires three-quarters of a pound to be mixed with 500 pounds of feed and fed for 14 days. It is effective against thread, cecal, and roundworms. Hygromix (hygromycin b) will control populations of thread, cecal, and roundworms when mixed at the rate of 3 gr. per 500 pounds.

Always follow directions for use and withdrawal times for any wormer.

Cecal Worms (Heterakis Gallinae)

These worms are found in the cecum (blind pouch) of the chickens. The adult worms are from three-eighths to one-half inches long. They do little damage but they are the cause of the spread of blackhead that will most seriously affect and kill turkeys and peafowl. Chickens contact blackhead also, but are not as seriously affected.

The protozoan parasite responsible for blackhead is carried in the cecal worm egg, and this is how it is transmitted. Birds swallow the infected worm eggs. Earthworms also carry the blackhead protozoan and birds that eat the earthworms then become infected.

Blackhead can be seen as yellow circles on the liver, with slightly depressed centers in infected birds.

Birds usually show no outward signs; they just

unexpectedly drop over and die. This death will usually occur around 16 weeks of age in turkeys. Because the cecal worm eggs will remain infective in soil for many months, it's advised that turkeys and peafowl be kept off ground where chickens have been for at least 18 months.

To eliminate cecal worms, medicate with phenothiazine, hygromycin B or Meldane-2. Follow manufacturer's directions.

Roundworms (Ascardia Galli)

This is the most common of worms found in chickens. They damage the lining of the intestine so badly that bleeding (enteritis) can occur. The chickens are unable to properly digest and assimilate food so the growth is retarded. This is especially true in young, growing chicks.

Roundworms have occasionally been found inside chicken eggs, where the worm has gone up the cloaca and was trapped in the forming egg. Although gross in all respects, it apparently does no harm to humans who eat these chicken eggs.

Older chickens develop a resistance to roundworms. Young chickens are most susceptible to them. A few worms in each hen are not seriously harmful, but as many as 75 or more are a problem. Heavily infested birds will show droopiness, diarrhea and emacittion. Death occurs in very

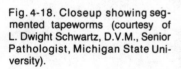

Fig. 4-18. Closeup showing segmented tapeworms (courtesy of L. Dwight Schwartz, D.V.M., Senior Pathologist, Michigan State University).

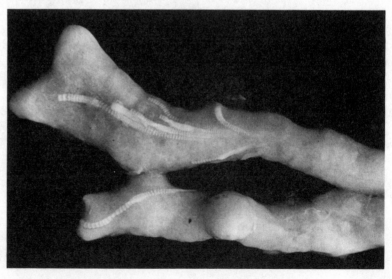

heavy infections. Mainly there is reduced efficiency in the birds. Birds become infected upon eating the worm eggs during their infective stage.

Clean range aids in their control. Piperazine is the most common wormer used for these worms. Other treatments are hygromycin B, Meldane-2 and Wormal. Fortify feed with Vitamin A for about one week after worming to help weakened birds recover.

Tapeworms

These are flat, segmented ribbon like worms (Fig. 4-18). They vary from only one-sixteenth of an inch long to several inches in length. In young birds heavy infestations will cause slow growth.

Tapeworms spend part of their life in intermediate hosts. These includes slugs, beetles, ants, snails, earthworms, flies, grasshoppers, etc. These intermediate hosts become infected when tapeworm eggs are eaten. Chickens become infected when these intermediate hosts are eaten, naturally, chickens that have access to range will become more readily infected than confined birds.

Control means controlling the intermediate hosts. Flock medication to eliminate tapeworms can be accomplished with a butynorate compound, but unless the whole head (scolex) of the worm is removed and chickens are kept from the intermediate hosts, new infestations will prove to be as bad as before.

Chapter 5

Pullets and Hens

Although the management of adult chickens is definitely not as complex as managing chicks, it is also not the time for a handler to sit down on the job. There are still important details to bring the chickens into full production. You cannot just sit back and wait to see what happens.

Many species of animals will not perform well in an improper environment. Chickens are more sensitive to their environment than other livestock. Chickens must be scrutinized, manipulated, deceived, and prodded into efficient production. Not that the hen cannot lay eggs on her own, but pullets and hens must be made to pay for their upkeep. They must be under a handler's control at all times.

Chickens must be discouraged from laying eggs on the floor. Chickens who eat eggs must be stopped. Those who do not want to lay eggs must be culled from the flock early. Broody hens must be forced to lay eggs.

All these problems and more will keep handlers on their toes. For efficiency with your chickens, trouble must be dealt with because lost eggs and lost chickens are lost dollars.

If you are not conscientious about management practices with your chickens, at least be conscientious about accurate record keeping. Many handlers would be surprised as to how much money is lost yearly because of poor management. The recorded facts might cause you to either quit while you're ahead or proceed with more gumption.

The following topics consist mainly of information on female chickens 20 weeks of age and older. This is when egg production begins and is maintained.

PURCHASING WISELY

There are also plenty of people offering chickens for sale who know too little about the chickens they have. Check classified advertised prices for chickens in your area.

Usually live chicken prices are highest when market egg prices are the highest. Because of supply and demand this can vary. For most areas, prices will be highest in the fall. Many handlers will dispose of their 18-month-olds at this time and replace with ready-to-lay pullets they started in the spring. It may be tough to find layers in the spring because most handlers keep their birds while egg production is at its peak. Most simply will not part with their chickens until the birds molt at the end of summer.

Many handlers do not want to bother with chicks. They prefer to obtain started pullets, ready-to-lay pullets, or producing hens. Started pullets, six to eight weeks of age, sometimes can be obtained. Their cost will naturally be higher than day-old chicks because they are female. The extra money covers feed and brooding, and perhaps initial chick cost the seller-raiser has incurred. There will be a wait of approximately four months after purchase before the birds will begin to lay eggs the first time. Their availability is usually late spring through late summer.

When purchasing these started pullets, first check for growth size. A 6-week-old pullet's body should look 6 inches long and an 8-week old pullet should be 8 inches long. This is important because many nutrient deficiencies, parasites, and diseases will stunt the growth of chicks.

Ready-to-lay pullets should look like adults when sold at 16 to 20 weeks of age. The cost is relatively high for chickens that have been raised carefully, culled, vaccinated, and will lay eggs shortly within a month. Their availability is usually late summer through fall.

If a seller does not know which of his chickens is laying brown eggs or white eggs, you can use this fairly accurate rule if the chicken has white ear lobes, it usually lays white eggs. Colored ear lobes (anything other than white) mean you can assume the chicken lays brown eggs.

Hens are female chickens about 1 1/2 years old, usually going through their first molt and beginning their second year of laying. They become mostly available late summer to fall.

It's usually uneconomical to purchase older hens because egg production begins to decline sharply after second year of laying. Hens are less expensive because of this fact. If hens are obtained for nothing, then it might pay (slightly) to keep them for eggs through their third productive laying period.

If the owner of the chickens is a reliable source, have him tell you how many eggs are being laid by the hens in question. A little arithmetic will tell whether the hens will pay for their feed through the eggs you'll receive. Use Tables 6-1 and 6-2 to figure the amount of feed the hens will eat during the time you care for them, and multiply by the cost of the feed. Take the egg amount expected and multiply by market cost of similar eggs.

Look at the condition of the feathers. Ruffled feathers, with the chicken pulling its head in toward its body ragged feathers will indicate disease or parasites. Determine if dull or ragged feathers, along with loss of feathers, is due only to a molt. A molt should occur at the end of summer or fall and the bird should not have its head pulled in toward its body as if it were cold. If birds are sick, they will not appear lively. They will sit around with their heads drawn in towards their bodies with their feathers fluffed (ruffled) out. A bald spot on very top of head, or a larger bald spot on back, is the result of housing roosters with hens.

If all seems good so far, continue by randomly checking the eyes and nostrils of a few birds. You must hold the bird out in front of you. Check for small bubbles in the eyes or crust formations that indicate respiratory disease. The nostrils should be clean and dry, with no watery substance, crusts or dirt coming out of or adhering to nostril openings. If you see problems, forget about these chickens.

Stay clear of the entire brood of chickens if any show watery fecal material smeared over the hind end. Further, watch that chicks walk normal and are not pecked on. A long standing habit of cannibalism is hard to break.

With ready-to-lay pullets, check legs for good color and smoothness of the scales. Young legs will be smooth and thin looking. Hens legs will be lighter in color, thicker and not quite as smooth looking (Fig. 5-1). The older the bird the older the legs will look. Severely thickened legs with raised scales, white dust, scabs, and crust indicates scaly leg, mite infestation. Although treatment is quite successful, if birds have not become lame, mites are time consuming to treat.

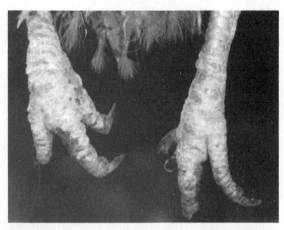
Fig. 5-1. Hens at three years old or more will have legs and feet that look old. A slight raising of the scales here could indicate the beginning of scaly leg mite infestation.

Keep new birds penned and from any other poultry you have for no less than two weeks. Many diseases will show more advanced symptoms within this period of time. During this "lock up" period be especially careful of transporting disease. Keep feeders, waterers, and other equipment confined to the same birds during this time.

When tending the chickens, take care of the home flock before tending to the needs of the new birds. This helps to prevent spreading disease from the new birds to the home flock. Change boots on entering and leaving the building in which new chickens are housed as another precautionary measure. In other words, proceed and think as though the new birds *are* diseased.

These safety measures will pay you many times over should the new birds come down with something. It will also serve to prove your case if the new birds are indeed sick and your other chickens aren't.

Know the name and address of the source for your chickens. At flea markets and livestock actions, a buyer might forget to get this pertinent information.

Persistent egg eaters are tough to distinguish when first purchased. It's a bit sneaky, but you might want to bring an egg along with you when the birds are inspected. Tell the owner you've been troubled with egg eaters and ask if you can place the egg in the middle of the pen. Either the owner's reaction or the birds' should tell you what you want to know.

Always wear different clothing and shoes when visiting other places that raise any type of poultry.

TRANSPORTATION

When transporting chickens in any moving vehicle, the birds will get bounced around some and be knocked over from being unbalanced while trying to stand. During this process, wings can be scraped, legs sprained, and feathers broken. Bleeding can cause the chickens to peck at such injuries while traveling.

To avoid such mishaps, chickens should be transported in a container that will not allow the birds to stand up. Chicken crates (Fig. 5-2) are ideal for grown birds. They can be stacked without much worry of shutting off air to the birds because they have ridges that prevent the crates from being moved together tightly.

Boxes and cages short enough to restrict a full standing position can also be used. If they are too tall, place enough straw in bottom to make the height shorter. Place enough chickens in each container so the birds are sitting side by side. Too much space will allow the chickens to be bounced to and fro.

Proper ventilation is very important to successful transporting of chickens. Too little ventilation and birds will become overheated and suffocate. Too much air and the birds will get chilled and contract a respiratory infection. No matter what type of container is used, openings must be available for air to enter and escape.

In boxes, cut enough openings so that when chickens are placed inside and the top is closed, they will remain comfortable. Check their comfort by allowing body heat to accumulate a few minutes after the top is closed. Then slide your hand down into the closed box top and feel the air around the chickens. It should not feel overly hot. If it is too hot, usually dampness can also be felt from the birds' trapped respiration.

A thermometer can be used to measure comfort. Place the thermometer in the closed box of chickens for two minutes, remove, and read. Grown birds will be comfortable at about 65 degrees fahrenheit (18.33 degrees C.) but during hot weather it will be tough keeping it at this temperature. if it is very hot outdoors, more vent holes will have to be cut and fewer chickens should be transported in each box. At no time should the temperature ever go above 80 degrees.

Because chickens do not have sweat glands, excess heat is diffused mainly through the respiratory system. This causes them to pant when overheated. If chickens are panting, cut more vent holes and remove chickens until they are no longer panting and are comfortable. Holes cut should be as large as a chicken's head (about 2 inches round). This will allow enough air to pass through but prevent chickens from escaping.

Load containers of chickens into the vehicle while making sure the sides of boxes do not touch and thereby restrict ventilation. If necessary, place spacers (bricks, rocks, wood) between boxes to keep them apart while the vehicle is moving.

Open crates and cages in an open pickup truck

should be covered lightly with a tarp or drop cloth to shield birds from sun and wind. Plastic tarps should not be used because body heat and carbon monoxide will build up quickly under plastic. The covering used should be a porous type that breaths.

With an enclosed vehicle, such as a van, all that might be needed is the opening of some windows if you notice that the chickens are panting while you are traveling. Enclosed toppers on the back of pickup beds should have windows cracked for ventilation.

An old-time favorite of many handlers is the gunny sack-feed bag method of transporting chickens. I do not recommend transporting chickens in this fashion because they can suffocate and be hurt in the process.

Tying a chicken's legs together and placing the chicken gently on a bed of straw on the floor of an enclosed vehicle is much better in a pinch. Occasionally, chickens are unexpectedly obtained without chicken crates, boxes, or cages on hand. Straw or rags will help prevent the chickens from rolling around and bruising themselves.

For some reason, there are people who believe

Fig. 5-2. These commercial, ready-to-lay pullets have been stacked and trucked safely to their destination with only a curtain drawn over the sides of the truck to keep out drafts while traveling.

Fig. 5-3. A convenient way for a handler to grab and hold a chicken is by grasping the top of the wing firmly near the body with one hand while simultaneously using the thumb to balance the bird.

they can transport chickens in a closed trunk of a car, in 80 degree Fahrenheit (26.66 degree C.) weather for 20 miles. They seem quite surprised when they open the trunk and find chickens sprawled out, barely moving, or barely breathing—with some already dead.

If chickens are transported comfortably, they can safely travel for many hours without feed and water. Handling the chickens should be done in a way to avoid excessive wing flapping. The bird is more calm and is easier to hold and catch when only one wing is grabbed (Fig. 5-3). Do this by grabbing the top of the wing firmly near the body; use your thumb to balance the bird. Grabbing a bird by it's legs (Fig. 5-4) is much more difficult, and the bird frantically flaps it's wings—because it's scared.

SPACE REQUIREMENTS

If chickens have access to pens outdoors, somewhat less housing space is required than for confined chickens. If partial confinement is used, have quarters large enough to meet cold-weather needs. Very cold climates call for more confinement. Very warm climates will allow chickens to be outdoors much of the time. Buildings will be used mainly for sleeping and eating purposes.

The following overall figures can be used to estimate space for confined adult chickens raised on the floor. For lightweight egg breeds, such as Leghorns, 2 square feet per bird is needed. General-purpose breeds, such as New Hampshire Reds or White Plymouth Rocks, should have 3 square feet per bird.

If your flock consists of very large Cochin or Jersey Giant breeds, you will need about 4 square feet for each bird. Bantams, either floor or cage raised, need about one-half to three-quarters square feet (depending upon how much space feeders and waterers take up in a cage or if nests are used on the cage floor).

With proper ventilation and insulation, these figures should provide comfortable quarters in cold weather without further crowding. Always keep any unused feeders, waterers, and other equipment off the floor space. Just a couple pieces of unused equipment laying underfoot in the pens can take up space needed for a half dozen chickens.

SHELTER REQUIREMENTS

Seven main requirements for housing adult chickens are:

☐ Allowing the proper living space.
☐ Supplying ventilation.
☐ Providing a draft-free environment.
☐ Protecting against predators.
☐ Building on high ground.
☐ Providing easy access to buildings by vehicles.

Fig. 5-4. Grabbing a chicken by its legs will cause excessive wing flapping.

□ Being within comfortable walking and watching distance from the handler's home.

Floor Space. Space can also include headroom space with the inside height being just tall enough to allow the handler to stand on top of 2 feet of litter. A ceiling height any taller will not contain the chicken's body heat in cold seasons. The right amount of chickens in a building, with a low ceiling, will keep the chickens' drinking water from freezing in cold winter months. A comfortable environment with continued access to drinking water will induce better egg production.

Large, open barns and sheds do not allow heat to accumulate for use by the chickens in cold weather. If the chickens are cold and the water constantly freezes, there is definitely too much open space being allowed for the chickens.

Some handlers use plastic stapled in place to close off and bring down ceiling height in high-ceiling buildings. There is more of a need for ventilation in rooms that have the cubic footage reduced in this way.

Dryness. Dryness, a by-product of proper ventilation, is a requirement for healthy chickens. Insulation will help in keeping buildings dry and temperatures more stable, but it is only through ventilation that the ideal environment will be maintained.

Drafts. Providing a draft-free environment adds to the comfort of the birds and is a guard against respiratory infections.

Chickens do not catch "colds" but they are susceptible to stress that can induce respiratory infections. Chickens are stressed if they must roost nightly with constant cold air being blown on them. When chilled they become stressed. When stressed, their resistance to infections is lowered. Hence, if there is disease, their body will not fight it off full force. Sick hens do not lay; they take money from a handler's pocket.

Drafts can be checked by first closing down ventilators, doors, windows or vent boards in the building. Next, by simply holding a 1-foot piece of thread by one end and slowly moving it over the area where the chickens roost, a handler can detect the worst draft areas. By moving the string slowly toward the incoming draft, a handler can tell which opening should be closed.

When ventilators, vent boards, and windows are open, there should be an exchange of outside air with inside air. Drafts must not be created over the roosting area. Windows should be installed so that the tops open inward.

Predators. All poultry buildings should be built to keep out predators. Prevention is the key, do not wait until the problem is encountered. A handler can lose all his chickens in one night.

Location. Constructing buildings on high ground will help keep the area around the building dryer and aids in air circulation for ventilating. Low grounds and high water tables keep areas damp. Damp grounds promote diseases and deteriorates wood and metal buildings.

If low ground must be used, the addition of gravel sloped away from the building and gutters to drain rain water from the roof of the building will usually suffice.

Access. Easy access means no mud to get stuck in and no squeezing between buildings or other obstacles. For convenience, feed should be stored right where it will be used—near the chickens. Providing a good drive will eliminate problems getting feed and straw to the building. It will also make the job of loading and unloading birds much more pleasant.

Hauling manure away from the building will be much easier, too. Plus, a drive of this sort, when blanketed with snow, can be shoveled with a snowplow. Bringing feed, water, and visiting the building to collect eggs will be much easier.

Convenience. A short walking distance from your home to the chickens' building will prove to be convenient when eggs are gathered. As many as four trips a day will be needed whether the weather is hot or cold. Just having a building 50 feet closer to your home could save you almost 7 miles in one year if eggs are collected only once a day!

Only after learning the shelter requirements for chickens can a handler decide on the type of building to construct or remodel. Then he can

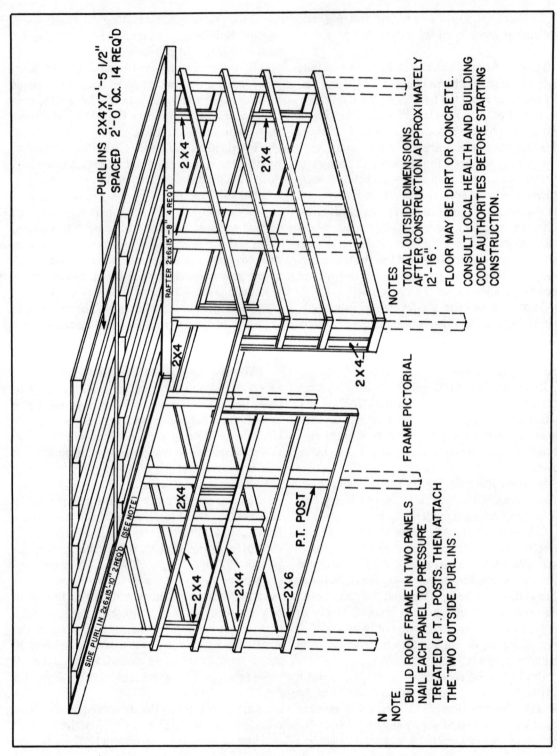

PURLINS 2X4 X 7'-5 1/2"
SPACED 2'-0" O.C. 14 REQ'D

RAFTER 2x6x15'-8" 4 REQ'D

2 X 4

2 X 4

2 X 4

2 X 4-

2 X 4

2 X 4

2 X 4

2 X 6

P.T. POST

SIDE PURLIN 2x6x15'-10" 2 REQ'D (SEE NOTE)

FRAME PICTORIAL

NOTES

TOTAL OUTSIDE DIMENSIONS AFTER CONSTRUCTION APPROXIMATELY 12'-16".

FLOOR MAY BE DIRT OR CONCRETE.

CONSULT LOCAL HEALTH AND BUILDING CODE AUTHORITIES BEFORE STARTING CONSTRUCTION.

NOTE

BUILD ROOF FRAME IN TWO PANELS NAIL EACH PANEL TO PRESSURE TREATED (P.T.) POSTS. THEN ATTACH THE TWO OUTSIDE PURLINS.

Fig. 5-5. A 157" × 16'2" poultry house for 80 birds. Sunken pole construction is used (USDA, Cooperative Farm Building Plan Exchange).

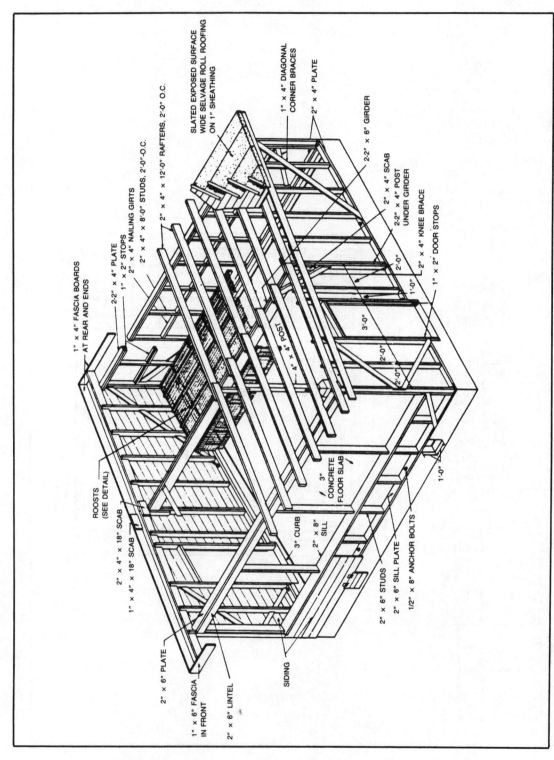

1" x 4" FASCIA BOARDS
AT REAR AND ENDS

SLATED EXPOSED SURFACE
WIDE SELVAGE ROLL ROOFING
ON 1" SHEATHING

1" x 4" DIAGONAL
CORNER BRACES

2" x 4" PLATE

2-2" x 6" GIRDER

2" x 4" SCAB

2" x 4" POST
UNDER GIRDER

2-2" x 4" KNEE BRACE

1" x 2" DOOR STOPS

2'-0"

2'-0"

3'-0"

1'-0"

2'-0"

2'-0"

2'-0"

4" x 4" POST

2-2" x 4" PLATE
1" x 2" STOPS
2" x 4" NAILING GIRTS
2" x 4" x 8'-0" STUDS, 2'-0"-O.C.
2" x 4" x 12'-0" RAFTERS, 2'-0" O.C.

ROOSTS
(SEE DETAIL)

2" x 4" x 18" SCAB
1" x 4" x 18" SCAB

2" x 6" PLATE

3" CURB

3"
CONCRETE
FLOOR SLAB

2" x 8"
SILL

SIDING

2" x 6" STUDS

2" x 6" SILL PLATE

1/2" x 8" ANCHOR BOLTS

1'-0"

1" x 6" FASCIA
IN FRONT

2" x 6" LINTEL

Fig. 5-6. A poured concrete floor and foundation are the base for this 20-x-20-foot house for 100 hens (USDA, Cooperative Farm Building Plan Exchange).

115

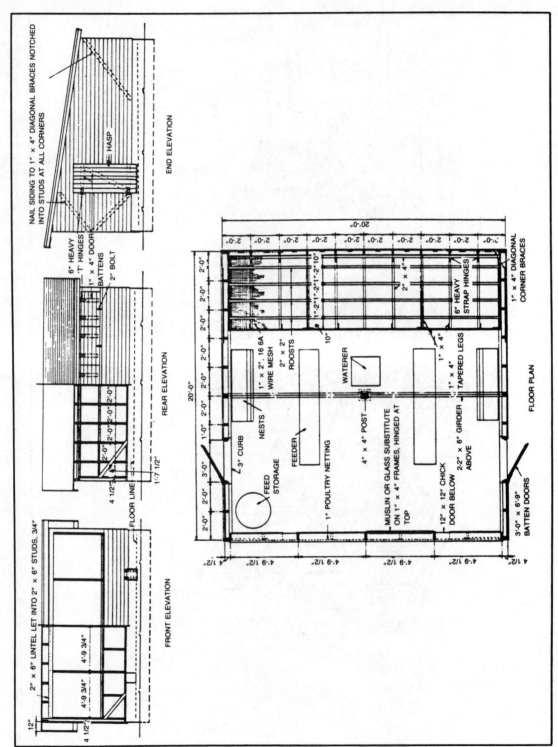

NAIL SIDING TO 1" x 4" DIAGONAL BRACES NOTCHED INTO STUDS AT ALL CORNERS

HASP

END ELEVATION

6" HEAVY 'T' HINGES
1" x 4" DOOR
BATTENS
2" BOLT

REAR ELEVATION

FLOOR LINE
1'-7 1/2"
4 1/2"
2'-0" 2'-0" 2'-0"
2'-0"

2" x 6" LINTEL LET INTO 2" x 6" STUDS, 3/4"

4'-9 3/4"
4'-9 3/4"
12"
4 1/2"

FRONT ELEVATION

20'-0"
2'-0" 2'-0" 2'-0" 2'-0" 2'-0" 2'-0" 2'-0" 2'-0" 2'-0" 2'-0"

1" x 4" DIAGONAL CORNER BRACES
6" HEAVY STRAP HINGES
2" x 4"
1"-2"-1"-2"-10"

1" x 2", 16 6A WIRE MESH
2" x 2" ROOSTS
10"
WATERER
1" x 4"
TAPERED LEGS

NESTS
FEEDER
4" x 4" POST
2-2" x 6" GIRDER ABOVE

3" CURB
1" POULTRY NETTING
MUSLIN OR GLASS SUBSTITUTE ON 1" x 4" FRAMES, HINGED AT TOP
12" x 12" CHICK DOOR BELOW

FEED STORAGE

3'-0" x 6'-9" BATTEN DOORS

FLOOR PLAN

20'-0"
2'-0" 1'-0" 2'-0" 2'-0" 2'-0" 2'-0" 2'-0" 2'-0"
3'-0" 2'-0" 2'-0"

4 1/2" 4'-9 1/2" 4'-9 1/2" 4'-9 1/2" 4'-9 1/2" 4 1/2"

Fig. 5-6. Continued.

116

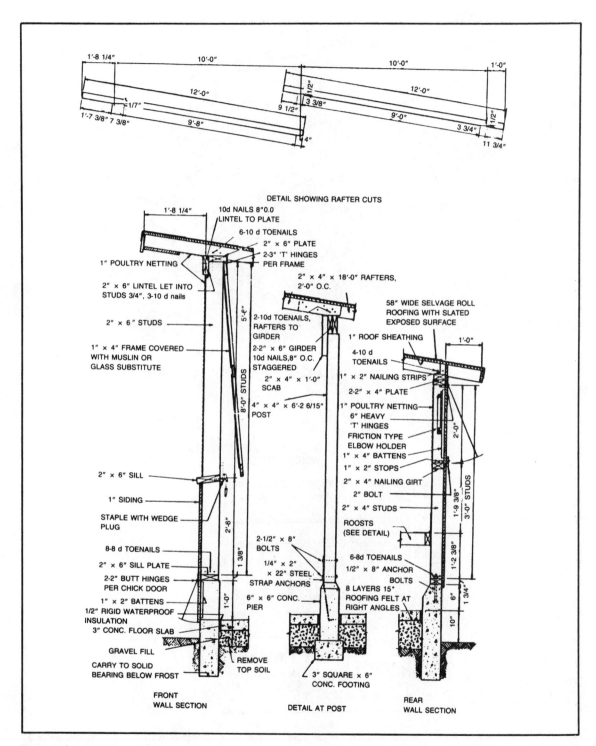

DETAIL SHOWING RAFTER CUTS

FRONT
WALL SECTION

DETAIL AT POST

REAR
WALL SECTION

Fig. 5-6. Continued.

117

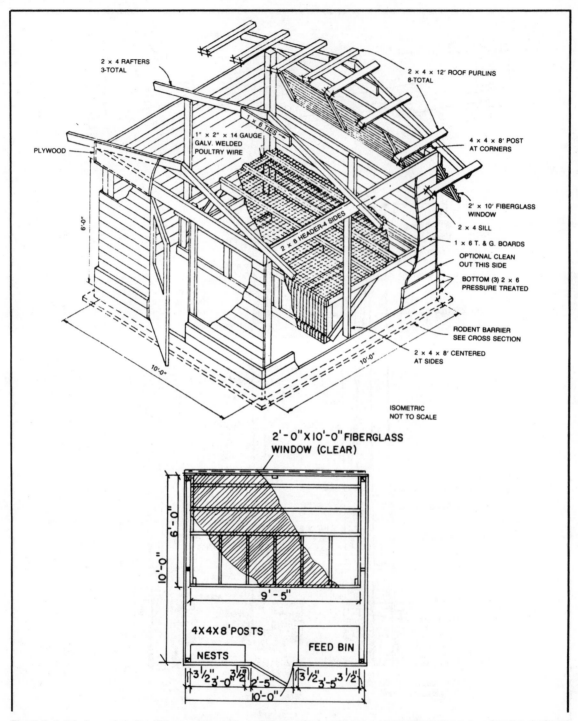

Fig. 5-7. A 9-hole nest and a 400-pound feed bin can be built into this 10-×-10-foot New Jersey poultry house for 30 birds (USDA, Cooperative Farm Building Plan Exchange).

118

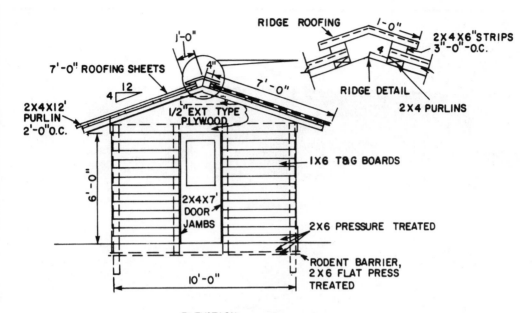

RIDGE ROOFING

1'-0"

2X4X6"STRIPS
3"-0"-O.C.

RIDGE DETAIL

2X4 PURLINS

7'-0" ROOFING SHEETS

1'-0"

4"

7'-0"

2X4X12'
PURLIN
2'-0"O.C.

4 12

1/2"EXT TYPE
PLYWOOD

1X6 T&G BOARDS

2X4X7'
DOOR
JAMBS

6'-0"

2X6 PRESSURE TREATED

RODENT BARRIER,
2X6 FLAT PRESS
TREATED

10'-0"

ELEVATION

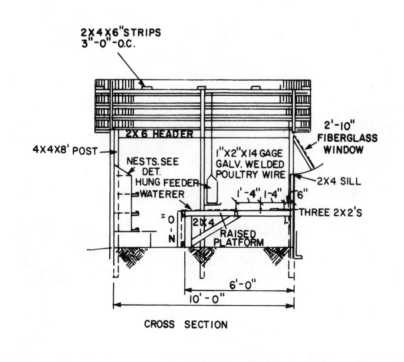

2X4X6"STRIPS
3"-0"-O.C.

2X6 HEADER

4X4X8' POST

NESTS.SEE
DET.
HUNG FEEDER
WATERER

1"X2"X14 GAGE
GALV. WELDED
POULTRY WIRE

2'-10"
FIBERGLASS
WINDOW

2X4 SILL

1'-4" 1-4" 6"

THREE 2X2'S

2X4

RAISED
PLATFORM

6'-0"

10'-0"

CROSS SECTION

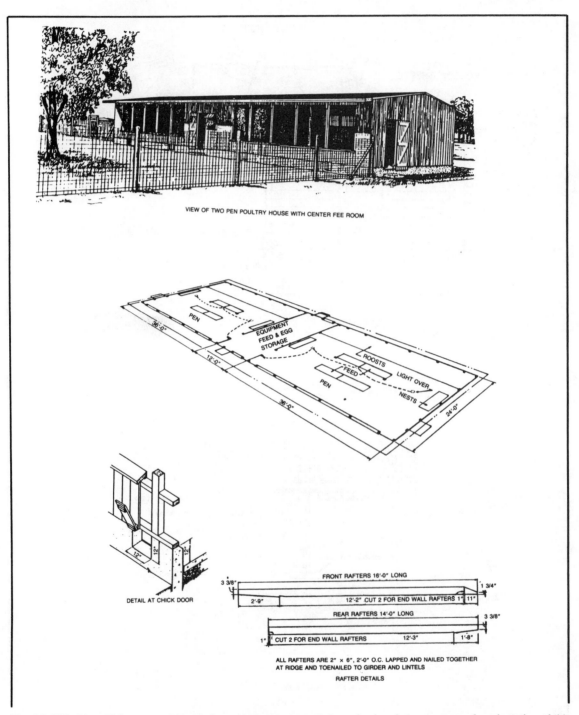

VIEW OF TWO PEN POULTRY HOUSE WITH CENTER FEE ROOM

DETAIL AT CHICK DOOR

FRONT RAFTERS 16'-0" LONG

REAR RAFTERS 14'-0" LONG

ALL RAFTERS ARE 2" × 6", 2'-0" O.C. LAPPED AND NAILED TOGETHER
AT RIDGE AND TOENAILED TO GIRDER AND LINTELS

RAFTER DETAILS

Fig. 5-8. This 24- × -72-foot poured foundation and pier house contains a feed and storage room. An adaptation of this 500-bird house can be made for 250 birds by building only one-half of the unit (USDA, Cooperative Farm Building Plan Exchange).

120

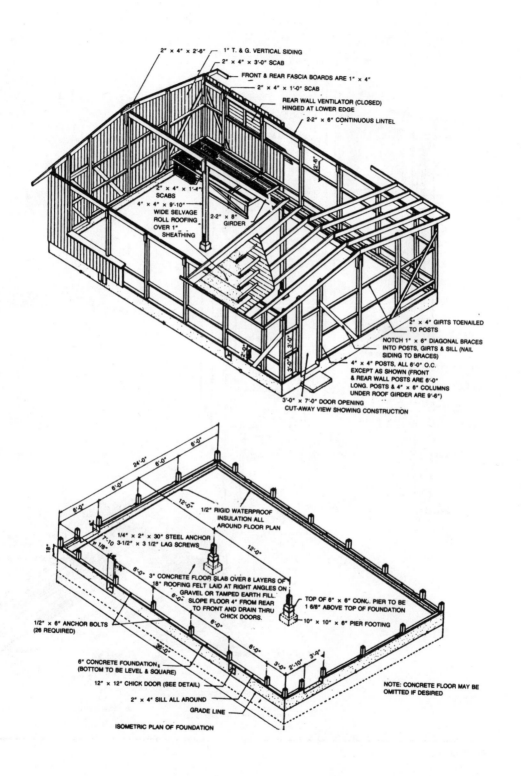

2" × 4" × 2'-6"
1" T. & G. VERTICAL SIDING
2" × 4" × 3'-0" SCAB
FRONT & REAR FASCIA BOARDS ARE 1" × 4"
2" × 4" × 1'-0" SCAB
REAR WALL VENTILATOR (CLOSED) HINGED AT LOWER EDGE
2-2" × 6" CONTINUOUS LINTEL
2'-8"
2" × 4" × 1'-4" SCABS
4" × 4" × 9'-10"
WIDE SELVAGE ROLL ROOFING OVER 1" SHEATHING
2-2" × 8" GIRDER
2" × 4" GIRTS TOENAILED TO POSTS
NOTCH 1" × 6" DIAGONAL BRACES INTO POSTS, GIRTS & SILL (NAIL SIDING TO BRACES)
4" × 4" POSTS, ALL 6'-0" O.C. EXCEPT AS SHOWN (FRONT & REAR WALL POSTS ARE 6'-0" LONG. POSTS & 4" × 6" COLUMNS UNDER ROOF GIRDER ARE 9'-6")
3'-0" × 7'-0" DOOR OPENING
CUT-AWAY VIEW SHOWING CONSTRUCTION

24'-0"
6'-0"
6'-0"
6'-0"
6'-0"
12'-0"
1/2" RIGID WATERPROOF INSULATION ALL AROUND FLOOR PLAN
1/4" × 2" × 30" STEEL ANCHOR
7'-10"
3-1/2" × 3 1/2" LAG SCREWS
18"
12'-0"
6'-0"
3" CONCRETE FLOOR SLAB OVER 3 LAYERS OF 18" ROOFING FELT LAID AT RIGHT ANGLES ON GRAVEL OR TAMPED EARTH FILL. SLOPE FLOOR 4" FROM REAR TO FRONT AND DRAIN THRU CHICK DOORS.
6'-0"
TOP OF 6" × 6" CONC. PIER TO BE 1 6/8" ABOVE TOP OF FOUNDATION
10" × 10" × 6" PIER FOOTING
1/2" × 6" ANCHOR BOLTS (26 REQUIRED)
38'-0"
6'-0"
3'-0" 2'-10" 3'-0"
6" CONCRETE FOUNDATION (BOTTOM TO BE LEVEL & SQUARE)
12" × 12" CHICK DOOR (SEE DETAIL)
2" × 4" SILL ALL AROUND
GRADE LINE
NOTE: CONCRETE FLOOR MAY BE OMITTED IF DESIRED
ISOMETRIC PLAN OF FOUNDATION

121

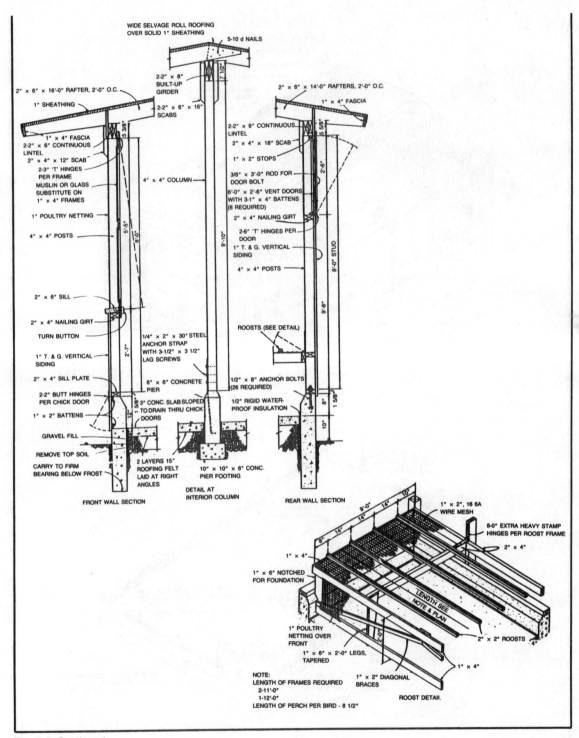

WIDE SELVAGE ROLL ROOFING
OVER SOLID 1" SHEATHING

5-10 d NAILS

2" × 6" × 16'-0" RAFTER, 2'-0" O.C.

1" SHEATHING

2-2" × 8" BUILT-UP GIRDER

2-2" × 6" × 16" SCABS

1" × 4" FASCIA
2-2" × 6" CONTINUOUS LINTEL
2" × 4" × 12" SCAB
2-3" 'T' HINGES PER FRAME
MUSLIN OR GLASS SUBSTITUTE ON 1" × 4" FRAMES

4" × 4" COLUMN

1" POULTRY NETTING

4" × 4" POSTS

2" × 6" SILL

2" × 4" NAILING GIRT

TURN BUTTON

1/4" × 2" × 30" STEEL ANCHOR STRAP WITH 3-1/2" × 3 1/2" LAG SCREWS

1" T. & G. VERTICAL SIDING

2" × 4" SILL PLATE

2-2" BUTT HINGES PER CHICK DOOR

6" × 6" CONCRETE PIER

3" CONC. SLAB SLOPED TO DRAIN THRU CHICK DOORS

1" × 2" BATTENS

GRAVEL FILL

REMOVE TOP SOIL
CARRY TO FIRM BEARING BELOW FROST

2 LAYERS 15" ROOFING FELT LAID AT RIGHT ANGLES

10" × 10" × 6" CONC. PIER FOOTING

FRONT WALL SECTION

DETAIL AT INTERIOR COLUMN

2" × 6" × 14'-0" RAFTERS, 2'-0" O.C.

1" × 4" FASCIA

2-2" × 6" CONTINUOUS LINTEL

2" × 4" × 18" SCAB

1" × 2" STOPS

3/8" × 3'-0" ROD FOR DOOR BOLT

6'-0" × 2'-6" VENT DOORS WITH 3-1" × 4" BATTENS (8 REQUIRED)

2" × 4" NAILING GIRT

2-6" 'T' HINGES PER DOOR

1" T. & G. VERTICAL SIDING

4" × 4" POSTS

ROOSTS (SEE DETAIL)

1/2" × 8" ANCHOR BOLTS (26 REQUIRED)

1/2" RIGID WATER-PROOF INSULATION

REAR WALL SECTION

1" × 2", 16 6A WIRE MESH

8-0" EXTRA HEAVY STAMP HINGES PER ROOST FRAME

2" × 4"

1" × 4"

1" × 6" NOTCHED FOR FOUNDATION

LENGTH SEE NOTE & PLAN

2" × 2" ROOSTS

1" POULTRY NETTING OVER FRONT

1" × 6" × 2'-0" LEGS, TAPERED

1" × 2" DIAGONAL BRACES

1" × 4"

NOTE:
LENGTH OF FRAMES REQUIRED
2-11'-0"
1-12'-0"
LENGTH OF PERCH PER BIRD - 8 1/2"

ROOST DETAIL.

Fig. 5-8. Continued.

decide on the type of construction: sunken poles (Fig. 5-5), piers, regular foundation (Figs. 5-6 and 5-7), a combination of foundation and piers (Fig. 5-8), block walls and foundation, or no foundation for a summer range shelter.

If the span is not too great, trusses can be built from 2 x 4's without many braces using plywood plates glued and nailed in place. This allows for storage space through the trusses (Fig. 5-9).

Trusses can be set on top of pole framed walls or conventional walls and foundation that are sheathed overall. Finishing touches can be put on later (Fig. 5-10).

If possible, construct a feed storage room within the building (Fig. 5-8). If not feed bins can be built in (Fig. 5-7).

The environment requirements for chickens can be integrated into existing buildings, but many handlers still insist on throwing their chickens into any building on the property with only the addition of straw, nests, and feeders. They later wonder why their chickens aren't producing eggs well. Usually the breed of chickens is blamed. Sometimes the feed is scrutinized. Very rarely is the housing blamed.

Even if only a doghouse is provided for a couple chickens, the shelter requirements should be adhered to as much as possible. Years ago, I found myself looking for emergency shelter to winter some extra flock breeds. Winter had already arrived and my plans for construction of a new building consisted of not more than preparatory ground breaking. I knew the chickens could not go all winter crowded in the old buildings. Besides, I had to separate breeds for hatching eggs in late winter.

I put together a very primitive looking "hut," trying to keep the shelter requirements in mind. Looking for elevated ground, I found the perfect spot in among our flourishing pines. The pines afforded protection from high winds and blowing snow (and hid the eyesore too!). The hut was quickly erected by putting together four large sections of an extra chain link fence from a dog kennel, complete with hinged door.

I used 2-×-10-inch planks, covered with tar pa-

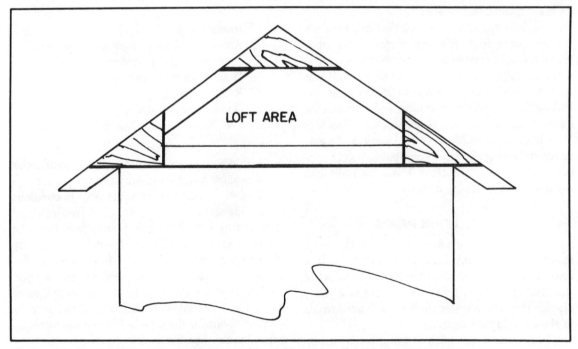

Fig. 5-9. An open truss can allow storage space through the trusses if the span is not too great.

Fig. 5-10. Finishing touches on a poultry building can be useful. A Mail Pouch thermometer, aluminum-roofed cupola, galvanized ridge covers, crossbuck door and wooden furring strip details over the outer walls of this building.

per, for the roof. Bales of straw were stacked around the sides, brick fashion, to insulate the enclosure. Plastic feed bags were stretched across the door . . . Voila! One of the most perfect make-do chicken houses I've seen.

The straw insulated so well that drinking water was kept from freezing most of the time. Enough cracks existed in the structure to ventilate without drafts, thus keeping litter dry, too. It was so cozy walking into this hut to collect eggs and finding the chickens so comfortable looking in the midst of the blizzards that prevailed outdoors.

I did have a problem with oppossums digging under and killing a few chickens, but stringent trapping took care of the problem. The straw walls later became good mulching material for the garden.

VENTILATION NEEDS

The ventilation of chicken houses is the most misunderstood of any shelter requirements. It is also the most important factor for the comfort of the chickens and in prevention of disease. Only disease-free, comfortable chickens will perform up to their productive capacity.

Ventilation is intended to bring fresh air and oxygen into the building while driving foul air,

gases, carbon dioxide, and excess vapor out. For a dry atmosphere at a comfortable temperature, the whole system depends on a combination of various factors:

☐ Insulation provided.
☐ Amount and rate of air being moved.
☐ Amount of birds housed.
☐ Desired temperature.
☐ Relative humidity.
☐ Outside temperature.
☐ See Table 5-1 and Fig. 5-11.

Inside house temperatures will be much easier to maintain at a stable temperature when buildings are insulated. Insulation prevents large fluctuations in temperatures and prevents maintained temperature loss. The builtup body heat from the chickens in winter will not dissipate too quickly through the walls and ceilings. In summer, cooler air brought into the building will be held longer.

The R-value rating is labeled on packages of insulation. Most salesmen will be glad to figure insulation needs for the type building constructed in your climate. See Table 5-2.

Proper ceiling insulation values can be quite

Table 5-1. Current Recommended Practices for Laying Houses.

Poultry laying houses have two systems of management, one with the birds on builtup litter or slatted floors and the other with the birds held in cages (from one or two birds per cage up to 25 or 30 birds in wire floor colony pens). Current recommended practices for laying houses with birds on litter and slatted floors are given below.
Temperature: 44°F. (7°C.) minimum 86°F. (30°C.) maximum.
Relative humidity: 50 to 80%.
Ventilation rate: 0.5 to 1 λ/s (liters per second) per bird in winter and 2 to 3 λ/s per bird in summer. The cubic feet per minute conversion would be: 1.06 to 2.12 cfm per bird in winter and 4.24 to 6.36 cfm per bird in summer.
Space: On litter, 0.28 to 0.37 m² (about 3-4 square feet) per hen (may be reduced for small breeds). On litter with utility pit, 0.09 to 0.23 m² (about 1-2 1/2 square feet) per hen. On slats, 0.09 to 0.18 m² (about 1-2 square feet) per hen. Current recommended practices for laying houses with birds in cages are:
Temperature: 44°F. (7°C.) minimum to 86°F. (30°C.) maximum.
Relative humidity: 50 to 80%.
Ventilation rate: 2.5 to 3 λ/s per hen with provisions for opening windows or side walls in summer. The cubic feet per minute conversion would be: 5.3 to 6.36 cfm per hen.
Space: 0.09 to 0.18 m² (about 1-2 square feet) per hen.
Reprinted with permission of the American Society of Heating, Refrigerating and Air-Conditioning Engineers (ASHRAE), Inc., Atlanta, GA

easily attained with fill insulation materials. Another method for insulating ceilings in an outbuilding is called the "straw loft," where either baled straw or loose straw is piled over the top of the ceiling. This method works extremely well in buildings where such space is used for storing straw.

Of the total amount of heat produced by chickens, mainly through their respiratory system, only part is available to heat the air. This part is called the *sensible heat* or the *usuable heat*. The rest is contained in the water vapor and is called *latent heat* or *unusable heat* (Fig. 5-12). Latent heat cannot warm the air so it can be removed along with

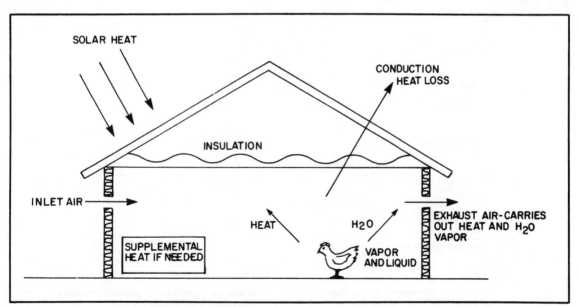

Fig. 5-11. Heat and moisture is produced and lost from a poultry house (courtesy of the Cooperative Extension Service of Michigan State University, North Central Regional Bulletin #183).

Table 5-2. Insulation Values of Materials.

Material	Thickness	R (resistance) values per inch thick I/k	thickness listed I/C
Building Materials			
Building board-			
Asbestos-cement board		0.25	
Asbestos-cement board	1/4 in.		0.06
Gypsum or plaster board	1/2 in.		0.45
Plywood (Douglas Fir)		1.25	
Plywood (Douglas Fir)	1/4 in.		0.31
Plywood (Douglas Fir)	3/8 in.		0.47
Plywood (Douglas Fir)	1/2 in.		0.62
Plywood or wood panels	3/4 in.		0.93
Fiber board sheathing	1/2 in.		1.32
Fiber board sheathing	25/32 in.		2.06
Hardboard-medium density		1.37	
Particleboard-medium density		1.06	
Wood subfloor	3/4 in.		0.94
Insulation			
Blanket or batt-			
Glass wool, mineral wool or			
fiber glass, *approximate	3-3 1/2 in.		11
	5 1/2-6 1/2 in.		19
	6-7 in.		22
	8 1/2-9 in.		30
	12 in.		38
Rigid-			
Glass fiber		4.00	
Expanded perlite		2.78	
Expanded rubber		4.55	
Expanded polystyrene extruded		4-5.00	
Cellular polyurethane			
(R-11 exp.,unfaced)		6.25	
Loose fill-			
Milled paper or wood pulp		3.13-3.70	
Sawdust or shavings		2.22	
Perlite, expanded		2.70	
Glass or mineral wool	3 3/4-5 in.		11
(*approximate)	6 1/2-8 3/4 in.		19
	7 1/2-10 in.		22
	10 1/4-13 3/4 in.		30
Vermiculite		2.13-2.27	
Masonry			
Concrete, solid		0.08	
Brick, common		0.20	
Brick, face		0.11	
Concrete blocks-			
Sand and gravel, 8" 12"			1.11
			1.28
Cinder, 8" 12"			1.72
			1.89
Lightweight, 8 12"			2.00
			2.27
with vermiculite, perlite			
or mineral filled cores, 8" 12			5.03
			5.82
Roofing			
Asphalt roll roofing			0.15
Asphalt shingles			0.44
Wood shingles			0.94
Siding			
Wood shingles, 16", 7 1/2" exp.			0.87
Wood, 8" drop	1 in.		0.79
Wood, 8" beveled	1/2 in.		0.81
Wood, 10" beveled	3/4 in.		1.05
Alum. or steel (residential)			
hollow backed			0.61
insulation backed			1.82
Alum. or steel			
(farm buildings) unbacked			0.00
Woods			
Hardwoods: maple, oak, etc.		0.91	
Softwoods: fir, pine, etc.		1.25	

*Insulation is produced by different densities; therefore, there is a wide variation in thickness for the same R-value among manufacturers. No effort should be made to relate any specific R-value to any specific thickness. See individual manufacturer's label.
Adapted and reprinted with permission of the American Society of Heating, Refrigerating and Air-Conditioning Engineers (ASHRAE), Inc., Atlanta, Ga.

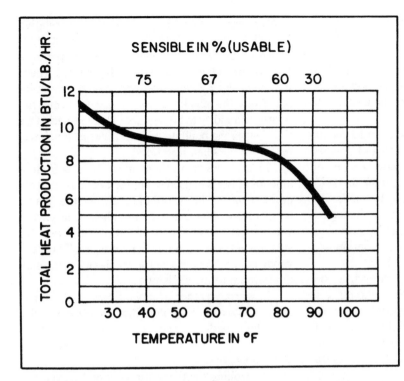

Fig. 5-12. Hourly sensible and latent heat production for laying hens: (1)Find house temperature on bottom. (2)Move vertically to curve. (3)Then move horizontally to left to get the Btu of total body heat produced per hour per pound of body weight. (4)Multiply the body weight by the Btu amount to get the total heat production per bird per hour. (5)Find the sensible percent on the top scale and subtract from 100 percent. The answer is the percentage of No. 4 answer that is latent (unusable) heat tied up in water vapor. (Graph courtesy of the Cooperative Extension Service of Michigan State University, North Regional Bulletin #183).

the water vapor to keep the building drier.

Air has a moisture-holding capacity. The warmer the air the more moisture it will hold. See Fig. 5-13.

The more chickens housed the warmer the air. The warmer the air the more moisture that is trapped and contained in the latent (unusable) portion of the air. Thus, more inside air can be exchanged with fresh air to remove most of the moisture. If the fresh air coming in is cooler, it will naturally contain less moisture than the warmer air going out.

Accordingly, if the indoor temperature is lower when fewer chickens are housed, there will be less moisture contained in the cooler air. Because the cooler air will not hold much moisture, it must go somewhere. It collects as condensation on walls and ceilings, causing damp conditions. If an exchange of inside and outside air (ventilation) is attempted, the building's air will become even more cold. If air is not exchanged, the litter and interior of the building will become damp.

Research has shown that for every drop of al-most 2 degrees Fahrenheit, between 75 degrees and 45 degrees, there is an increase in feed consumption by about 1 1/2 percent. Because egg production does not vary much between these temperatures, it proves to be less economical to

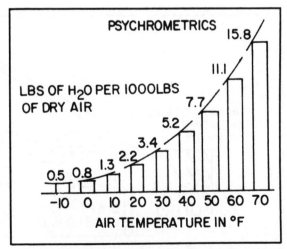

Fig. 5-13. The moisture-holding capacity of air (courtesy of the Cooperative Extension Service of Michigan State University, North Regional Bulletin #183.

keep chickens any cooler than this.

This could mean saving approximately 2 1/2 pounds more feed weekly for 100 ready-to-lay egg breed pullets housed at 73 degrees Fahrenheit to as much as 35 1/2 pounds more feed weekly for 100 7 1/2-month-old, egg-breed hens housed at 45 degrees Fahrenheit.

For a month, the figures range from 10 pounds of unnecessary feed consumption to 143 pounds! At 21 degrees Fahrenheit, the extra feed eaten monthly would be a whopping 265 pounds. With heavy breeds it would stagger to 374 pounds. Imagine all the labor and money that can be saved, while still reaching production, just by providing the correct temperature through ventilation and body heat.

During very cold weather conditions, as the cooler outside air is drawn into the building, it is warmed and therefore will pick up and hold moisture. Although the outdoor air might be cooler, it could have a completely saturated relative humidity of 100 percent because it can hold only so much water vapor at a given temperature.

Relative humidity is the ratio produced when water vapor in the air is compared with the amount of water vapor the air can hold at a given temperature.

Figure 5-14 shows how 1 pound of 20 degree

Fahrenheit outside air at 100 percent relative humidity enters the building through a vent. This air is then heated to the inside building temperature of 60 degrees Fahrenheit (15.55 degrees C.) where it expands by 2.3 cubic feet and absorbs water vapor from the chickens and house to bring the relative humidity to 80 percent. The ventilation air thus leaves the building with 28 times as much water vapor as when it entered.

In cold weather, there must be a sufficient amount of birds housed or supplemental heat in order to warm the ventilation air to the inside temperature of 60 degrees Fahrenheit while excess water vapor is being carried out of the house. Insulation helps maintain the temperature. Thus, the vapor-holding capacity of the air should determine a minimum of air exchange.

In warm weather, if moisture-saturated air is brought into a building more than 10 degrees cooler than the outside air, the excess moisture will deposit itself on walls, ceilings, and litter in the form of condensation.

Controlling ventilation in cold or hot weather can be done best with a thermostat that controls a fan. These fans are simply set to the desired temperature, between 45 and 86 degrees Fahrenheit (7.22 and 30 degrees C.), in relation to the temperature that will keep the relative humidity

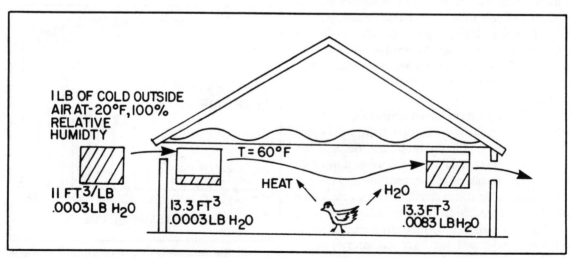

Fig. 5-14. Ventilation air exchange through a poultry house (courtesy of the Cooperative Extension Service of Michigan State University, North Regional Bulletin #183).

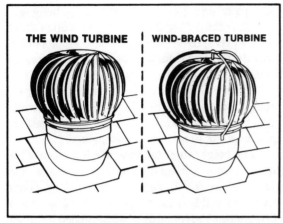

Fig. 5-15. High-wind areas should use a braced turbine like the one on the right (courtesy of Leslie-Lock, Atlanta, GA).

from 50 to 80 percent. The use of a hygrometer, the same used in incubators, can be of help in determining the humidity.

Vent boards, cupolas (Fig. 5-10) or manually operated fans are more difficult to control because they must be readjusted constantly as the outdoor weather conditions change. Turbine fans are dependent upon outside wind for drawing air from buildings. Installed on the roof, they can be made semi-adjustable by installing a sliding panel directly underneath them to restrict air leaving the building. High-wind areas should use a wind-braced turbine (Fig. 5-15).

LIGHTING

When chickens have a continual 14 to 15 hours of light per day, their systems will be stimulated to continue producing eggs. The months of peak production is when the hen is stimulated to produce eggs by naturally long hours of daylight. As winter approaches, the natural daylight decreases and so does egg production, unless supplemental light is provided in the building. The light's intensity should be only enough so that hens can walk around and see their feed, water, and nests.

If there are problems with hens eating eggs, do not have bright lights shining directly on any area where eggs are laid. Curtains can keep the interiors of nests dark for this purpose. Floor-laid eggs will

not be protected unless lights do not shine in these corners.

The extra lighting should be controlled by a timer to turn lights on and off as set. Drastic fluctuations in lighting the birds can cause premature molt, and egg production will be upset. The timers cost no more to operate than their initial expense.

Timers can be used in various ways. First, a brighter light can be set to come on as natural daylight disappears during the evening. Then, just before all lights will automatically turn off, a very dim light—representing dusk approaching to the chickens—can be set to come on for a few minutes. The chickens, believing nightfall is coming, go to their roosts for the night.

If the bright lights were just abruptly turned off at night, there would be quite a commotion inside the dark building as chickens wandered around, bumping into feeders, flying up and missing roosts completely, and crying. Chickens can get hurt during such activity. Of course, this won't bother caged layers. Imitating dusk for them would be more of a kind gesture to make them comfortable with their surroundings.

Having the lights come on at night means chickens will sleep until later hours in the morning, and begin laying eggs later in the morning.

Another timer method is to have only the brighter light come on a few hours before daybreak. A dimmer light is not needed because birds will not be going to roost. They will stay awake until the natural dusk occurs toward evening. Because the chickens are awake sooner, they will thereby begin laying eggs sooner in the morning, and therefore should be collected sooner.

If a handler knows he'll be gone all morning, the lights can be set to turn on a couple hours later than usual to delay laying that morning. If the handler will be gone all afternoon, the timer can be set to turn lights on a few hours earlier so the majority of eggs, which are laid in the afternoon, will be laid late morning for collection before the handler leaves.

Fooling the chickens in this way should only be done occasionally, but it is necessary if floor-raised birds are eating egg frequently and you are trying to correct the bad habit.

To figure the length of time to supply artificial light, subtract the natural daylight hours from the needed 14 to 15 hours. In winter, longer hours of artificial lighting will be needed because of naturally shorter winter daylight hours. In the spring, when natural daylight is close to 14 hours long, the artificial lights can be discontinued gradually.

Periodically check the timer clock for unnoticed power interruptions and proper working condition.

Fluorescent tubes can be purchased in daylight-cool blue or warm-red colors. If you use fluorescent lighting, be sure that the tubes are the warm red hue type because chickens cannot see well in the cooler blue, violet, or green wavelengths.

Both incandescent (ordinary lamp bulbs) and natural sunlight emit rays in the red range that stimulates production and helps chickens to see better. Accordingly, feed consumption will be increased, not solely because of the lights, but because of the extra energy that will be used to produce more eggs as the birds are stimulated.

PURPOSE OF ROOSTS

Roosts are used by chickens mainly in an effort to air-condition their bodies against heat and cold. Comfortable, rested chickens will perform better throughout the day.

As a chicken roosts, its body covers its feet, keeping feet and legs warm. Feathers are fluffed while roosting so that body heat can circle the entire body is not obstructed.

Roosts keep chickens from constant contact with cool, damp floors. Enough roosting space must be made available for the amount of chickens housed or they will roost on other available objects. By measuring the length of roosting lumber, allow 7 inches in length for each egg breed type chicken and about 10 inches for heavier general-purpose breeds.

The roosting material should not be too wide or too narrow because the chickens' toes must curve in a natural position around the roosts for balance. A 1 1/2-inch wood pole or a 2 x 4 turned with the narrow edge up would be ideal. Old wooden ladders make very good roosts, and can be hung with wire from the ceiling. Make sure roosts don't swing and that they are secure and stable. Wood ladders provide the right amount of space between the rungs so the birds aren't crowded.

When making a series of roosts extending out from the wall, allow from 12 to 15 inches between each roost. Roosts can be placed side by side or graduated as in a stair-step fashion.

The height to install roosts is important. Too low and litter will build up to the roosts in a short time. Chickens with cannibalistic tendencies and predators will be able to reach roosting chickens. Too high and heavy birds or wing-clipped birds will have a difficult time reaching roosts. High roosts also can cause bumblefoot because the chickens have to jump down, bringing all their weight in fuller force down onto their feet.

Roosts should be no taller than 2 feet unless you use the stair-step pattern where back roosts are naturally higher. If you use dropping boards or pits under roosts, take this 2 feet into consideration when installing roosts 6 to 8 inches above the pit or board.

INDOOR-OUTDOOR PENS AND FENCING

Indoor pens can be made to section off the inside of a building in order to separate breeds, sexes, or chickens from feed storage areas or to provide a work area for the handler to vaccinate and wing clip birds. If the building is large enough, pens can serve to confine birds in a smaller area during the cold months in order to conserve heat. This can be done with a wall of plastic covering a wire partition. In warm months, the plastic wall can be taken down to aid in ventilation and to give the birds more room.

Indoor pens can be sectioned off with chicken wire or welded wire. Make sure the bottom 2 feet of wall is rot-proof material because having the wire extend down to the floor level will quickly deteriorate wire as it comes in contact with corrosive manure and damp litter. When this happens, the chickens will be squeezing through the holes in the wire where rusting has taken place and they will gain access to other pens and stored feed.

Although welded wire does not hold up outdoors, it does last longer indoors and can be more economical to use. Indoor pens can be arranged so there is an isle or separate feed storage area. This requires doors on each pen for access to the birds and in tending to their needs.

Interior doors of this type can be made with 1-x-3 inch frames made stationary where they join with L brackets and are covered with welded wire stapled or tacked into place. Install the finished door with hinges.

Having the door open out toward the aisle seems more troublesome when bringing feed and water into a pen. When other factors are taken into consideration, a door opening out will be convenient. It can serve as an isle blockade to corral chickens back into pens. Chickens will not be able to escape as easily when the door is opened by the handler (with his arms full of feed). Usually a door opening out will provide a somewhat large entrance when opened. Locks or wood stops can be installed and closed easier. Space is not unused on the floor area where ordinarily an inside door would open over. A waterer, grit pan, or nest box can be used in the unobstructed area.

Long metal springs, the kind used extensively years ago for keeping screen doors shut, should be installed so pen doors will close on their own as you enter or leave a pen. They must be long enough to allow door to open fully. They can be installed on hooks so they can be detached if desired.

Elastic ropes, similar to those used in body building equipment, can also be used to close doors automatically.

On dirt floors, heavy railroad ties can be used to section off buildings. They are heavy enough to stay put, other lumber can be nailed to them, poles will not have to be sunk in the ground to provide nailing members, and the ties are already preserved to prevent rotting and will serve to protect walls placed on top of them. I believe their cost will not outweigh the cost of replacing other materials that will not last as long near the damp litter.

Outdoor pens should be constructed with the heaviest chicken wire available. Thin-gauge chicken wire will only last a few years. The thicker gauge should last three times as long.

Most woven wire has spacings (openings) that are large enough to admit predators. They last long

Fig. 5-16. These chickens are fully protected from digging crawling, and flying predators.

outdoors, but the large openings should be avoided.

Chickens are less likely to fly over the tops of pens if given a large pen area. The larger the pen the shorter you can make the sides of pens. A wire netting should be stretched across the top to keep predators out. Chicken wire works fine for this (Fig. 5-16).

If you are not in the habit of closing up the chickens entry nightly, predators will effortlessly go into an open pen and use the chickens' entrance to enter the building. Do not provide outdoor roosts in outdoor pens or chickens may want to roost there at night, becoming good game for predators and a good target for inclement weather.

Outdoor pens are unnecessary for total confinement, but many handlers consider it cruel to not let chickens outdoors to eat bugs, smell the breeze, and bath in the sun's rays.

FEEDERS

Four main types of chicken feeders used by small-scale raisers are: the hanging tube, hoppers, trough feed pans, and ordinary feed pans.

A feeder should provide at least one day's amount of feed for the number of chickens it will serve. It should prevent feed wastage by chickens who scratch feed out or dig and push feed out with their beaks. The feeder should be one where droppings are not accessible to the feed. It should be non-corrosive if it is to be placed on top of litter. A feeder should be easy to fill, clean, and maintain.

A hanging tube type feeder (Figs. 5-17 and 5-18) fits these requirements best. Because of the heavy weight of feed, hanging feeders usually hold 25 to 40 pounds of feed. If a handler wants more feed available to the chickens, extra hanging feeders must be used.

The hanging tube of these feeders can be purchased separately from their bottom pans at some poultry supply houses. This allows a handler to purchase only 2-inch-deep pans with large capacity tubes for use with chicks or bantams, too. The 4-inch-deep pans are used for large, adult chickens.

Tube feeders have adjustable bottoms or grills to restrict the amount of feed flowing down into pan

in order to prevent feed wastage (Fig. 5-19). This can only be done with gravity-type feeders. Occasionally fine mash will get caught up in the tube and must be shaken down manually by rocking the tube back and forth.

Because tube feeders are hung from the ceiling, they are not in direct contact with corrosive manure and damp litter. Therefore, they last longer than most feeders.

Covers should be purchased or made for tube

Fig. 5-17. A version of a tube feeder uses chains for balance (courtesy of Shenandoah Manufacturing Company, Inc.).

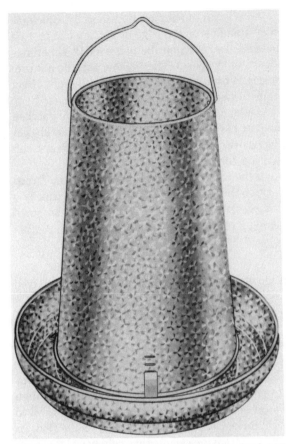

Fig. 5-18. Galvinized 40-pound feeder with feed pan designed to keep birds from billing out feed (courtesy of The Warner Corporation).

feeders. Some chickens enjoy roosting on the top edge and they will foul the feed inside with their droppings. Also, it seems to be a most inviting dark tunnel for some hens to lay eggs in.

The only thing I find wrong with tube feeders is the top width of the tube. It seems the tops could be somewhat wider without interfering with the feed flow. This would make filling them much more easier. It's tough trying to steady the swinging feeder as feed is being dumped into it. If a handler isn't careful, he's liable to spill more feed on the floor than the feeders are preventing the chickens from wasting.

Hoppers are another type of feeder. Large floor-mounted hoppers hold as much as 150 pounds. They are made to be placed on bricks to prevent

the bottom from rusting out or they can be purchased with adjustable legs.

It's a good idea to keep hopper feeders far enough above the litter so that barn cats can get to mice and rats that love to visit underneath and eat spilled feed. Nevertheless, you must keep the feeder low enough for the chickens. Tops should also be provided to keep chickens and droppings off the feed.

Hopper feeders are easy to fill because of the extra-wide tops. These feeders can serve as extra feed storage while in use too.

Hopper feeders are also called range feeders. For this purpose, rain shields are needed to protect the feed. See Fig. 5-20.

There are some wall-mounted hopper feeders such as those used for rabbits. Most have a small capacity but they can be used to supply grit and oyster shells. Wooden feed and storage hoppers can be made fairly easy and at low costs.

Fig. 5-19. A cutaway view of one type of adjustable bottom (courtesy of Brower Manufacturing Company, Inc.).

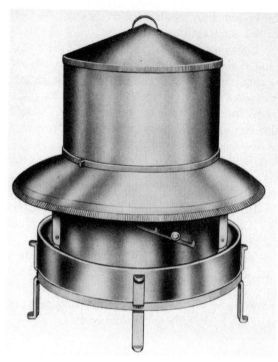

Fig. 5-20. A 150-pound hopper with a rain shield for outdoor use (courtesy of Brower Manufacturing Company, Inc.)

Trough feeders can be made of wood or metal. Manufactured feed troughs can be purchased that will hold as much as 80 or 130 pounds of feed. Most trough feeders made for adult chickens contain hinged vertical wire spacers that cover feed to prevent feed wastage and roosting. Most have legs and some have perches (Fig. 5-21).

Trough feeders can work out well if a handler doesn't object to periodically lifting the feeders off the floor when adding new litter material.

Pan feeders are the old standby with most small-scale raisers because they are usually less expensive and easier to obtain than the others. Pan feeding will do for a couple chickens, but for flocks larger than 12 they can be more of a nuisance for feeding purposes.

Metal pans, even if galvanized, rust through quickly because they are difficult to keep off damp litter. Rubber pans are better but cost more. The black rubber pans do allow ice clumps to be knocked out easily without fear of damaging the container.

Both types of pans are tipped easily. Chickens enjoy standing on the edge or placing one foot on the edge and flipping the pan over (I sometimes believe on purpose). The shallow pans do not prevent feed from being scratched and thereby flung to all corners of the pen.

Taller pans prevent feed from being scratched out, but they have been known to completely get flipped over, trapping chickens underneath and suffocating them.

If the pan is too tall, the chickens will be forced to get in the pan to eat. It's better to use pans only if necessary or for grit, oyster shells, or small amounts of warm-wet mash treats.

WATERERS

A good waterer can be cleaned and disinfected easily, will prevent the fouling of drinking water from droppings and litter materials, will provide ample freshwater for the amount of chickens it will serve, and can be made to keep water from freezing.

Larger flocks, where indoor temperatures always remain above freezing, can use trough waters (Fig. 5-22). Because they are only 1 1/2 to 3 1/2 inches wide and either stand on the floor or are hung from the ceiling, they help keep litter from

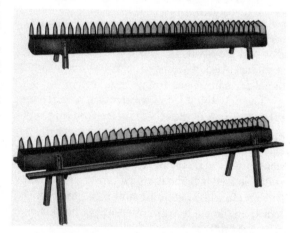

Fig. 5-21. An 80-pound capacity, short-leg feeder and a 130-pound-capacity galvanized trough feeder with perch 16 inches above the floor (courtesy of Brower Manufacturing Company, Inc.).

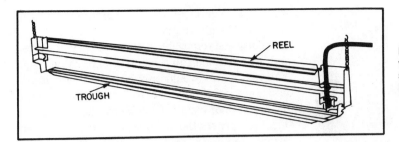

Fig. 5-22. This 8-foot-long galvanized, hanging-trough waterer will serve 200 birds (courtesy of Brower Manufacturing Company, Inc.).

being scratched into the drinking water. As the birds drink, a water valve will automatically admit more water into the trough. Some of these are designed so tipping does not occur as readily. All have reels to keep birds from roosting and all can be used for chicks by adjusting a chain or stand.

Waterers can be hooked up to a pressure supply, a gravity tank, or a drum of water. Most are stainless steel and some containing porcelain coatings. They will last a long time because harsh water and medicines will not corrode them.

Although such waterers are very convenient for watering large flocks of chickens, they will not work properly if allowed to freeze. There is a special heater designed just for trough waterers. One wider trough comes equipped with a float valve and hose ready to screw on to an existing water hose. The trough can be set up on blocks or hung. Although there is a revolving reel on its top, birds still manage to roost on it and foul the water.

There are poultry shockers made to keep chickens from roosting over waterers (or anything else you want them off of). They are of low voltage and will not harm the chickens.

Bowl fountains are usually made of plastic. Water is delivered automatically (the same as troughs) but some are for low-pressure water systems only. These are fairly easy to maintain and clean, but, again, they must be kept from freezing to work.

Double-wall fountains (Fig. 5-23) hold 2, 3, 5, or 8 gallons of water—according to size purchased. The bottom is filled with water and then the top is placed down over forming a "double wall." The vacuum created inside controls the water level in the attached pan.

The larger fountains of this type must be filled where they are placed. They are too heavy to carry

once filled. This requires carting buckets of water to the waterer or the use of a hose.

Algae accumulates easily inside waterers and this necessitates disinfecting the interior occasionally.

Electric base heaters can be purchased to fit under the base of double-wall fountains to keep water from freezing (Fig. 5-24). Both should be kept off damp litter.

When metal pans are purchased with the addition of a roost guard and float, the ordinary water

Fig. 5-23. Cutaway view exposing the inner wall and handle of a double-wall fountain (courtesy of the Brower Manufacturing Company, Inc.).

135

Fig. 5-24. Electric base heaters operate only when temperature goes below 50 degrees Fahrenheit, keeping drinking water between 50 and 55 degrees Fahrenheit (courtesy of the Brower Manufacturing Company, Inc.)

pan then becomes an automatic modern type of watering system (Fig. 5-25). As with others, keep metal from damp litter if you do not want to replace pans every few years.

Water warmers can be used with pan waterers if they can be secured in the pan. Otherwise, chickens will trip over the cord and pull the waterers completely out of the drinking water. Electric heating bases are less troublesome.

Use Table 3-10 to figure water consumption and provide waterers that will contain the right capacity per day. Over half of each egg is composed of water. The same is true of the body of a hen. This is why a chicken can go longer without feed then without drinking water.

Chickens will drop in egg production if water is made unavailable to them for one day. Most will hold up laying until the needed water is given. Chickens also will not drink as much water if the water is dirty and smells foul from litter and droppings. This also, will cause a drop in production.

NESTS

The type of nests used and how they are used can greatly influence the overall quantity of eggs collected by the handler. Nests are usually metal or wood construction (Fig. 5-26).

Manufacturers claim metal nests provide more ventilation only because of the vent holes they have in the sides and the mesh removable bottoms, but wood nests can have holes drilled into their sides and bottoms for ventilation, too.

The mesh removable bottoms are plastic coated and are intended to prevent rust marks on eggs. The rust marks would only be on the eggs in the first place if the eggs were to come in contact with the metal floor installed just below the mesh rack. This only proves the metal nests do rust when corrosive droppings come in contact with the metal floors.

Metal cannot "breath" as wood can because of the lack of natural pores. Ventilation holes are needed to help dry the metal nests.

Wood nests have been unduly charged with harboring parasites. Even metal nests, if not cleaned regularly or dusted, can lead to parasite infestation.

With 12- x -12-inch nests, there should be one separate compartment provided for every 5 hens. Metal nests are usually made to accommodate 50 or more hens as they contain 10, 14, and 16 compartment holes. A new four-hole metal nest is on the market. Designed especially for trap-nesting in small pedigree breeder pens, the nest is ideal for raisers with only 20 hens.

Metal nests come with folding perches attached

Fig. 5-25. Three-gallon galvanized water pans should be purchased with a wire guard to keep chickens from walking in pan. The float will transform the pan into an automatically filled waterer (courtesy of the Brower Manufacturing Company, Inc.).

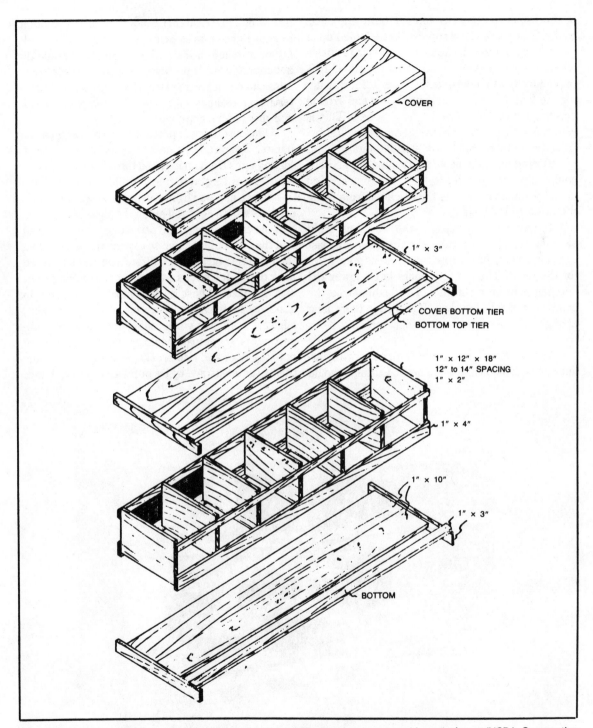

COVER

1" × 3"

COVER BOTTOM TIER
BOTTOM TOP TIER

1" × 12" × 18"
12" to 14" SPACING
1" × 2"

1" × 4"

1" × 10"

1" × 3"

BOTTOM

Fig. 5-26. A simple, 1933-circa, 12-hole nest plan for 60 hens that can be constructed for today's use (USDA, Cooperative Farm Building Plan Exchange).

to the fronts so chickens can get up to the nests easily. The perches are suppose to be folded up at night to discourage chickens from sleeping in nests where droppings will soil the nests interiors. This procedure would have excellent merit if it was not for the fact that most chickens are up and around before their handlers are in the morning. This is especially true with the use of supplemental artificial lights for production stimulation.

Closing off their nests by raising the perches could cause early risers to lay "floor eggs." You do not want to discourage the chickens from using the nests to lay eggs.

To partially discourage the chickens from sleeping in nests, first raise the perches at the last egg collection or just before the chickens go to roost for the night. Then, a few hours later, lower the perches with only the use of a flashlight so the chickens are not disturbed. If you're in there long enough, the hens just might hop into the nests before you leave.

Another method is to supply all nests with curtains on both metal and wood nests. Curtains should be of thick material that is not transparent enough to emit light into the nests. It should be nonraveling or stitched on raw edges so loose threads do not entangle the hens' legs. On wood nests the curtains can be tacked in place. Duct tape will hold material on metal nests if the metal is completely clean and dry before applying.

The curtains will prevent or correct egg-eating habits. Rear roll-out nests are available for collecting eggs from an isle, and these also help to prevent egg eating, too. See Fig. 5-27.

There are also front roll-out nests that provide sections where eggs roll out of the sight of the hens. To collect these eggs, the perch must first be raised and the flap pulled down to expose the eggs. Then the flap must be put back up and the perch lowered back down. It's not as convenient as reaching right into the nests. These devices must also be kept in good repair because, if the metal flaps are bent, eggs are restricted when rolling down into the compartments. If compartments are bent, eggs can roll onto the floor and risk breakage. It's good to know this if the nests are to be purchased secondhand.

Fig. 5-27. Rear roll-out nests are used when isle collection is desired (courtesy of Shenandoah Manufacturing Company, Inc.).

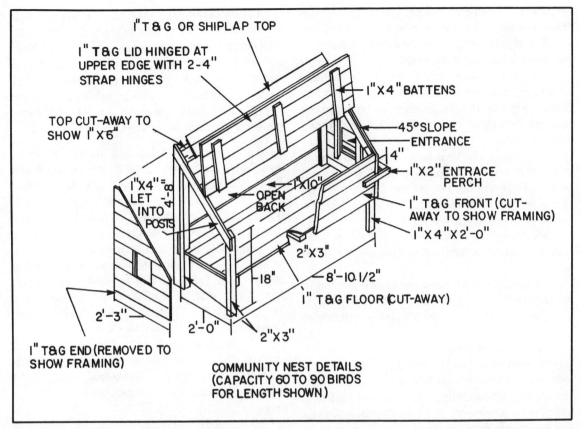

1"T & G OR SHIPLAP TOP

1" T&G LID HINGED AT UPPER EDGE WITH 2-4" STRAP HINGES

1"X 4" BATTENS

TOP CUT-AWAY TO SHOW 1"X 6"

45° SLOPE ENTRANCE

4"

1"X 2" ENTRACE PERCH

1"X4" LET INTO POSTS

1"X10"

OPEN BACK

1" T&G FRONT (CUT-AWAY TO SHOW FRAMING)

1"X 4"X 2'-0"

2"X3"

18"

8'-10.1/2"

1" T&G FLOOR (CUT-AWAY)

2'-3"

2'-0"

2"X3"

1" T&G END (REMOVED TO SHOW FRAMING)

COMMUNITY NEST DETAILS (CAPACITY 60 TO 90 BIRDS FOR LENGTH SHOWN)

Fig. 5-28. Plan for a colony nest, also called a community nest, for 60 to 90 birds (USDA, Cooperative Farm Building Plan Exchange).

Trap nest fronts can be made or purchased to fit all compartment type nests. Trap nest fronts allow the chicken to enter the nests but prevents her from leaving. In this way, eggs from individual chickens can be collected for pedigree hatching or for sorting out "undesirables" in the culling process.

I prefer colony nests over all others for floor-reared chickens. These consists of a large box hung on the wall or standing on legs with a hinged, slant-top roof to collect eggs when raised and prevent roosting when closed. There is only one access hole for all chickens to enter and leave. The hole should not have bright lights or sunlight shining into it. The interior stays dark. The completely darkened interior really helps to keep egg-eating hens from readily finding the eggs. Chickens prefer very dark

nesting quarters and a colony nests fits the purpose best. Eggs would be collected just as often as any other nest setup.

I know of no company today that manufactures this type of nest, but it can be built quite easily from wood (Fig. 5-28). A nest must provide protection for the eggs and be a convenience to the handler who collects the eggs.

LAYER CAGES

A small system of cage laying can be incorporated for use by small-scale raisers. The main advantages of the layer cage system is fewer broken, eaten, and dirty eggs. Hens cannot promote bad habits among the entire flock (such as feather pulling and egg eating). Hens are never walking on damp litter, droppings or in feeders and waterers. A handler can tell which hen is doing her job and when because the eggs roll out front over wire trays before her.

The disadvantages are the extra time and labor required in filling the smaller feed and water troughs. Nevertheless, most small-scale handlers would find it uneconomical to install an automatic feeder. Also, the droppings must not be left to collect underneath or they will attract flys during warm months.

Floor-raised chickens help manure and litter to dry as they scratch around in it. Cage birds cannot do this. Hens will become fat and lazy if a low-fat diet is not fed. Floor-raised birds burn up these extra calories as they move about.

Smaller egg breeds fit better into the cages, and dust created from their flying about is cut down some.

It's possible to purchase one or two sections of secondhand layer cages. Sometimes egg factories will know where some are available. Otherwise check classified ads.

Each section usually contains 12 compartments. Sections can be cut with wire cutters to provide smaller sections for use in small buildings. Remember, when cutting, that you will be losing a couple compartments in the process because you will be cutting through these.

Cages can be hung singly in rows against the wall, doubled and hung back to back in the middle of the pen, or arranged stair-step style.

Freezing water in the small troughs will become a problem unless a lot of birds are caged in a small, but ventilated room or regular trough heaters are installed.

Colored plastic or wooden clip style clothespins can be attached above cages in order to show who's laying and how many eggs per week. Marks placed on wooden clothespins or the use of colors representing numbers can be used to count eggs.

Layer cages can also be used in culling floor-reared chickens in order to find who might not be laying at all.

One pair of bantams can comfortably fit into each compartment without discouraging breeding. The feeders and waterers will need to be adjusted in order for the bantams to comfortably reach them.

Colony cages can also be used for layers. These consist 3- x -4-foot cages placed off the floor. Usually about four layers are in each cage. They are better than single layer cage compartments because the chickens get more exercise as they compete for the feed. This can help to prevent the caged-layer fatigue syndrome. Figure 5-29 shows plans for a colony layer cage.

☐ Construct a frame as shown by using 2-by-4-inch lumber and slope floor supports A and B to allow eggs to "roll away" after being laid.

☐ Use a piece of 1- x -2-inch welded wire 4 x 6 feet long and cut as shown on dotted lines. Fold wire upward at 90-degree angles, lengthwise, along the line of the inner cuts as indicated.

☐ Slide wire into position on A and B leaving an overlap of about 1 foot on each end. Stretch tightly with claw of hammer or garden rake, and fasten into place with staples over each wire strand. Shape egg collection tray as shown.

☐ Use 2- x -4-inch welded wire for top and sides. Cut and staple into place leaving a 2 1/2-inch opening between the floor and bottom edge of front wire so eggs will freely move out into collection tray.

☐ Cut a 10- x -12-inch opening (preferably in front or top) and use the cutout for a door using wire for hinge and hook.

☐ Waterers and feeders are made from rain guttering cut the length of cage. Cut slots 3 inches high and 6 to 8 inches long in wire above feeders and waterers for access holes, turning sharp wires away from hole so chickens don't get cut.

TYPES OF LITTER

The best litter material is one that does not pack down, absorbs moisture quickly, has no signs of mold, and is economical and readily available in the area where you live. Crushed corn cobs are used extensively on broiler farms because it is available, its small form suits chicks well, and it is used until the chicks (Fig. 5-30) are fully grown eight weeks later.

The constant removal of litter between commercial broiler broods every 4 to 8 weeks demands

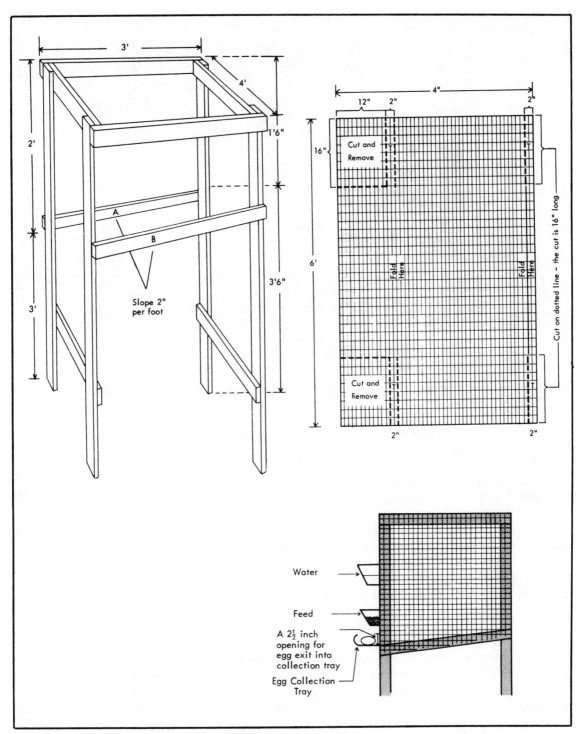

Fig. 5-29. Plans for 2 colony cage showing framing, wire floor, waterer, feeder and egg collection tray (USDA).

141

Fig. 5-30. These broiler chicks will be raised until market age, using crushed corn cob litter extensively (courtesy National Archives).

a litter that can be quickly picked up, easily carted away, and composted or spread over soil to be worked in immediately.

Most cage egg factories require little or no litter because manure is contained and scraped automatically from pits below the birds. There are still some egg factories where heavier type New Hampshires are floor raised. There is the extra cost for litter purchase, but if there is a local market for brown eggs they usually will command a higher price than white eggs which should offset litter costs.

The main concern of any handler obtaining litter for his hens should be to make sure litter to be used is not musty or moldy. By sniffing the litter before purchasing or using it, a handler with a good nose can smell musty, moldy odors. Moldy litter usually appears gray or black.

Moldy litter contains toxins that have been found to cause various respiratory and organ-related diseases. Besides being a health hazard to the chickens, the mold contains specific antigens that can cause a handler to contact Farmers' Lung Disease.

Hay should never be used for bedding because it's green nature causes it to quickly decompose and heat up when added to poultry manure. It has poor absorbing qualities, anyhow, and money is only wasted using it.

Straw is usually available at a reasonable cost in most areas. It should be bright golden, clean, and fresh smelling. Straw can be used to insulate open lofts in cold weather. When warm weather comes, the same straw can then be used as litter material if it's been kept dry.

Many by-products of farm crops are used for litter in many areas. "Sweetening litter" to help keep down ammonia fumes can be accomplished by occasionally sprinkling powdered agricultural lime over litter to neutralize it.

142

Proper ventilation will aid in keeping litter dry. In turn, this keeps litter costs down substantially.

When trying to overcome floor laying habits, the litter can be omitted for a while in order to discourage nesting on floors until the hens are using the nests provided.

DUST BATHS

Dirt floors should have a layer, preferably 1 foot deep, of absorbent sand spread over soil. If the floor is clay, 2 feet or more is recommended. Sand will dry faster than heavy soils and will be a more sanitary medium on which to place litter. Chickens will enjoy digging holes in the sand to satisfy scratching instincts.

They'll further enjoy laying in sand gullies they've created. With one leg stretched straight out, and feathers fluffed on end, they'll flap their wings vigorously to throw the sand over their bodies. As the sand and dust filters down through the feathers and settles on the skin, lice can be smothered by the dust and shaken loose.

Even chicks only a few weeks old can be found trying to take a dust bath in their feed, although this does not mean they have lice. The vigorous dusting also proves to be soothing as the sand gently scratches over the skin. Dust bathing should not be relied on to completely eliminate lice on chickens.

When a dirt floor is unavailable in the chicken house, a dusting box can be added. Place loose sand, at least 6 inches deep, in a 2-foot tall wood box measuring at least 2 feet square. Occasionally sprinkle wood ashes or lice powder over the sand and mix thoroughly. Be sure to place the box out from under the roosting areas to keep sand free of manure. If placed in an open area of the pen in direct sunlight, the chickens will enjoy the box even more and will not be as tempted to use it for nesting.

EGG PRODUCTION

Beginning when pullets are 20 weeks old, all extra roosters should be culled from the flock. One good rooster for every 15 pullets is plenty if breeding is desired. Too many roosters "bothering" young pullets will keep pullets hiding and worried when they should be seriously thinking about the egg-laying process.

Start the pullets off by feeding a layer ration and a grain-oyster shell mixture in separate feeders so they can eat all they want. Both layer ration and grain mixture together should equal 14 1/2 percent protein.

Use artificial lights in combination with natural daylight to bring the total lighting period up to 14 hours to stimulate egg production.

Tuck clean bright bunches of straw into nests and keep curtains on nests pinned up so pullets can see the straw. The curtains are used to discourage egg eating. The curtains can safely be raised until laying commences and most pullets have caught on to their purpose.

Don't be too eager. It will take a few weeks for young pullets to even begin checking the nests. Soon they will follow each other's maneuvers and begin wondering what other pullets find so inviting in the nests.

When you first come across pullets sitting in nests, do not disturb them because they will only be frightened and run from the nests immediately. Handlers must be patient with their pullets during what can be a most confusing period as the reproduction process takes over.

Pullets further along in the process will abruptly "squat" to the ground as a rooster (or her handler) approaches. Just reach down and pet her and tell her to get on with it!

Don't worry about first eggs that are sometimes "dropped" almost indiscriminately anywhere on the floor. The time to worry about floor eggs is when chickens are seen constantly nesting in floor corners.

If young pullets, or older hens for that matter, seem to refuse to use nests provided or definitely are not interested in even checking the nests by 24 weeks of age for egg breeds or 28 weeks for general-purpose heavy breeds, remove all litter material from the floor. Or just stop adding new litter. Make sure the chickens can see the straw sticking out of nests.

Because chickens like to feel comfortable they will begin to inspect the nests containing straw. This usually occurs within a few days. A few egg-shaped rocks or fake eggs can be placed in a few nests. This usually sparks the idea.

In the beginning, as stubborn nest seekers are seen in the nests, they may be found using them for sleeping purposes during the night. I wouldn't worry much about this problem until all pullets are visiting the nests frequently. You want the pullets to become accustomed to the nests. Many young pullets seem to have a fear of nest holes while others act as though they were raised in them.

When the egg-laying process begins and chickens no longer prefer the floor over the nests, replace litter on the floor (lightly at first because you don't want the floor to be more tempting then the nests). Watch the chickens and gradually increase litter material.

Turn the nest curtains down, sit back, and relax awhile. Then begin collecting eggs daily.

Some 80 percent production can be expected with egg breeds while general-purpose breeds should work up to about 70 percent production. The daily rate of production is figured by dividing the amount of chickens into the total amount of eggs, after multiplying the number of eggs collected by 100%. Example: 48 eggs collected × 100% = 4800 ÷ 80 hens = 60% production for the day.

Weekly percentages can be arrived by adding percentages for seven days and dividing by 7, or by adding all eggs gathered for one week and figuring as above, and then dividing by 7.

After beginning to lay, chickens should double their production of eggs in about one month's time.

A sample of an actual egg laying schedule of performance for 100 heavy breed pullets for their beginning month of laying is shown in Table 5-3.

Table 5-3. Beginning Laying Month Sample for 100 General Purpose Breeders.

SUNDAY	MONDAY	TUESDAY	WEDNESDAY	THURSDAY	FRIDAY	SATURDAY
FEBRUARY						
19 12-eggs (gave wet mash)	20 11-eggs (3 eggs eaten)	21 19-eggs (clipped beaks)	22 25-eggs	23 31-eggs (warm- 60°)	24 42-eggs	25 42-eggs
26 37-eggs	27 49-eggs (cold)	28 43-eggs (cold- 28°)	29 33-eggs (very cold-22°)			
MARCH						
				1 46-eggs (25°)	2 51-eggs	3 45-eggs
4 47-eggs	5 43-eggs	6 45-eggs	7 44-eggs	8 43-eggs (cold)	9 52-eggs (cold)	10 42-eggs (cold)
11 46-eggs (cold)	12 46-eggs (cold)	13 47-eggs	14 44-eggs	15 48-eggs	16 44-eggs	17 47-eggs
18 50-eggs	19 48-eggs	20 60-eggs	21 41-eggs	22 55-eggs	23 44-eggs (warm)	24 58-eggs (warm)

It should be noted that these are pullets used for breeding where egg laying is not forced until late winter. Results for fall laying pullets would be similar. Notice how egg production almost spontaneously goes up and down in sequence daily. Also note that 60 percent production was only reached on time during the four week period.

If chickens of the same age are receiving 14 hours of light, plus the correct rations, and they still are not producing up to the 70 or 80 percent rate, then culling is needed. When poor layers or nonlayers are removed from the flock, the rate of production increases because of the decrease in birds.

The expensive "formulas" on the market—to promote quicker starts in laying or for use when chickens might be stressed as when cold temperatures suddenly prevail—work fairly well but will be costly if you have a large flock. Similar results are obtained by using a broad-spectrum antibiotic such as oxytetracycline hydrochloride that is purchased in powdered form and mixed with powdered, packaged vitamins and water. The mixture is then administered and mixed with the chickens' drinking water daily until egg production reaches a peak after about one week.

Usually about 5 teaspoons (1000 mg) are all that's needed of the O.H. daily for 100 chickens. Mix this with about 3 teaspoons of packaged multivitamins made especially for poultry. Then add to 1 quart of water and shake vigorously to mix. Then add to the drinking water.

Because mixed solutions are unstable, mix only as needed and used. Carefully observe all label directions and precautions.

Be especially careful in observing withdrawal times which should be included on bags of O.H. but isn't always. A withdrawal time is the period during treatment and after the last dose is given in which the eggs or meat will be safe to eat (meaning residues do not remain). A handler will be safer by extending the withdrawal period on his own. The O.H. is also administered to chickens as an aid in controlling infectious synovitis and chronic respiratory disease (CRD).

Another "booster" is to feed small amounts of moistened mash to birds daily only to get them started. If continued too long, the chickens will pester you daily for this treat until their dying days. If given at a certain time each day, the chickens even quickly learn at what time they should pester you for the treat! Just one or two scoops, moistened with diluted powdered milk or water, is plenty for 100 chickens per day. It can be fun watching the chickens fight for each morsel of this "treat."

Warm, cooked cull potatoes are also a good booster. These should be given toward evening so birds can roost full of this warm food and wake early with energy to produce.

A chart should always be kept as to the amount of eggs collected per pen or building. A drop in production will be noticed quickly. A drop in the average amount of eggs can mean sickness or drastic temperature changes but most likely it can mean eggs are being eaten. Egg eating is more detectable and curable when several pens house the flock because the problem can be pinpointed to one pen of chickens instead of the whole flock.

At 20 weeks of age layers that are to become caged layers should be placed in their cages with the required layer ration. Because only one feed tray is hung on layer cages, an occasional sprinkling of scratch grains over the top of the layer ration mash is appreciated by the hens. If pellet feeding, the grains can be mixed with the pellets, making sure both add up to the right amount of protein when mixed. Top-dress with oyster shells and grit.

Give cage layers 14 hours of lighting and be sure there is always a constant supply of drinking water. Keep distractions and loud noises away from the building when chickens are expected to begin a new season of laying, and make sure other livestock or pets do not frighten them.

EGG QUALITY

The quality of an egg depends on four parts of the egg: the shell, air cell, yolk and the white. See Table 5-4.

The exterior factors involve the shape, soundness, and cleanliness of the shell. All but soundness quality can be determined by casually glancing at

Table 5-4. Summary of U.S. Standards for Quality of Individual Shell Eggs.

	Specifications for each quality factor		
Quality Factor	**AA Quality**	**A Quality**	**B Quality**
Shell	Clean. Unbroken. Practically normal.	Clean. Unbroken. Practically normal.	Clean to slightly stained.* Unbroken. Abnormal.
Air Cell	1/8 inch or less in depth. Unlimited movement and free or bubbly.	3/16 inch or less in depth. Unlimited movement and free or bubbly.	Over 3/16 inch in depth. Unlimited movement and free or bubbly.
White	Clear. Firm.	Clear. Reasonably firm.	Weak and watery. Small blood and meat spots present.**
Yolk	Outline——slightly defined. Practically free from defects.	Outline——fairly well defined. Practically free from defects.	Outline——plainly visible. Enlarged and flattened. Clearly visible germ development but no blood. Other serious defects.

*Moderately stained areas permitted (1/32 of surface if localized, or 1/16 if scattered).
**If they are small (aggregating not more than 1/8 inch in diameter).

For eggs with dirty or broken shells, the standards of quality provide two additional qualities. These are:

Dirty	**Check**
Unbroken. Adhering dirt or foreign material, prominent stains, moderate stained areas in excess of B quality.	Broken or cracked shell but membranes intact, not leaking.***

*** Leaker has broken or cracked shell and membranes, and contents leaking or free to leak.

an egg. Soundness should be examined by candling the egg for positive verification quality.

The interior factors involve the size of the air cell, the distinctness of shadow, the size and shape of the yolk, condition of germ, and the viscosity and clarity of the white

Shell Shape. The ideal egg shape is shown in Fig. 5-31. Abnormal shells have ridges, rough areas, or thin spots.

Soundness. Shells may be either sound, checked, or cracked or leaking.

Abnormal shells may result from improper nutrition, disease, or the physical condition of the hen. A crack in a shell can occur while still in the hen's body. An additional deposit of shell forms over these "body checks" to repair the crack, leaving a slight ridged area that usually then affects the shell's shape, too.

Other checks in an egg occur where there is a broken or cracked shell but the shell membranes remain intact so egg does not leak. The checks might be plainly visible or fine and hairlike, termed

Fig. 5-31. An ideal egg shape (courtesy of the Brower Manufacturing Company, Inc.).

blind checks, that can go unnoticed if not candled slowly. These blind checks usually become visible after much cooling and contraction takes place, causing the crack to separate.

Gently tapping two eggs together will assist in detecting blind checks at home. This procedure is call *belling.* A duller sound will be heard if an egg contains a blind check. Take two eggs and gently tap both large end together. If the sides are tapped together, a blind check will not be detected on the opposite side unless the egg is rotated Therefore, the large ends are tapped. By practicing with both checked and sound-shelled eggs, a handler will notice the difference in sound immediately.

Leaking eggs should be removed from nonleakers or the good eggs will be damaged by sticking to each other. Bits of the shells will be pulled off when you attempt to separate them.

Clean, fresh leakers can be used for cooking but they should be used immediately. Leakers with dirty shells contain a higher amount of bacteria and should be disposed of.

Cleanliness. Clean egg shells are classified as shells free from visible foreign material, stains, or discolorations. An egg is considered clean if it has only very small specks, stains, or marks, and if the amount does not detract from the generally clean appearance of the egg.

Dirty shell eggs do not include broken shells as these should be disposed of. Dirty shell eggs that are still of eating quality are those with less than one-thirty-second of the shell surface covered with dirt, foreign material and stains in one area or one-sixteenth of the surface if scattered (Fig. 5-32).

Air Cells. The depth of the air cell determines the quality in grading. Because of evaporation of moisture from the egg in the presence of air, older eggs always have a larger air cell. A very old egg will have an air cell so large it will cause the egg to float if placed in a bowl of water.

The air cell gauge can be used to determine the depth and quality of an egg's air cell (Fig. 5-33). The egg must first be candled to locate the bottom of the air cell. Use a pencil to mark this point. Then the gauge is placed over the top of the air cell for measurement.

A ruptured air cell will cause one or more separate air bubbles to float beneath the main air cell. These are caused by rough handling, cracked, or frozen eggs.

Yolk Shadow. This determines the thickness of the white, the condition of the yolk, and it's color.

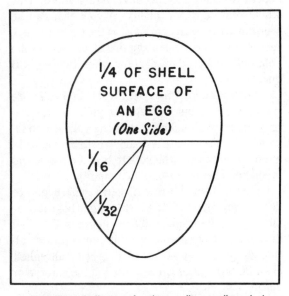

Fig. 5-32. Dirty shell eggs of eating quality are allowed when less than one-thirty-second of the shell surface is dirty or one-sixteenth if scattered.

147

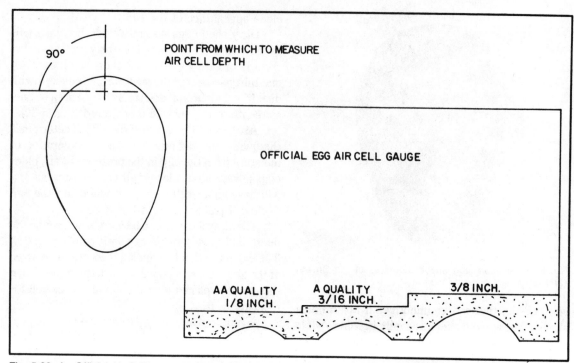

Fig. 5-33. An Official Air Cell gauge used to measure the depth of an egg's air cell to determine freshness.

When candled, if the egg is twirled, the yolk should appear to blend into the surrounding white. This would represent AA quality. A yolk that can be seen but is not clearly outlined, as the egg is twirled, represents A quality. An egg that clearly shows the yolk outline as a dark shadow when twirled is B quality.

Yolk Size and Shape. Freshly laid yolks are round and firm, but with age the yolk absorbs water from the white. This causes the yolk size to increase. It also stretches and weakens the yolk membrane, causing the yolk to become more oval in shape. This represents a B quality.

Germ Condition. A germ will begin to develop rapidly anytime a fertile egg is held at over 80 degrees Fahrenheit (26.66 degrees C.). Cell development ceases below this temperature, although cooling at 40 to 80 degrees Fahrenheit (4.44-26.66 degrees C.) does not kill the embryo or germ.

If germ development is present, it will be visible, upon candling, as a circular dark area or spot near the center of the yolk shadow. Either germ development or yolks that show up as olive yolks or other defects are B quality. If blood is visible as definite lines or as a blood ring, incubation has advanced. Such eggs are classified as inedible. Yolks showing no germ development at all but that show only slight surface defects are AA and A quality.

Condition of White. On candling, two conditions are looked for in the white: viscosity and clarity. Viscosity pertains to the thickness of the white. If the egg is twirled near the candling light, the amount of freedom of movement of the yolk can be seen. Thick whites permit only limited movement of the yolk with an indistinct shadow. Thin whites permit free movement of the yolk with a distinct shadow resulting.

Weak and watery whites permit the yolk to come near the shell closely, causing the yolk shadow to appear plainly and dark when the egg is twirled while candling. These are B quality.

A fairly firm white of A quality will permit the yolk to come a bit close to the shell but they do not

148

appear dark, only well defined. Firm whites, when twirled, prevent the yolk outline from being seen clearly.

Inedible eggs by U.S. standards include mixed rots, sour eggs, green whites, white rots, musty eggs, moldy eggs, black rots, cooked eggs, blood rings, chick embryos, bloody whites, large blood spots, meat spots, and severe shell damage.

Mixed Rots. This occurs when the vitelline membrane of the yolk breaks and the yolk mixes with the white. It shows up as a murkiness throughout the interior when candled.

Sour Eggs. These are hard to detect when candling but usually show up in weak whites with a murky shadow around an off-centered, swollen yolk. The organisms responsible for sour eggs produce material that shows up as a green sheen under ultraviolet (black lights) lights. These always have a sour odor.

Green Whites. The same bacteria, pseudomonas, that cause sour eggs, cause green whites. These whites are seen as a definite green color when using the standard candling light. These sometimes smell sour.

White Rots. Upon candling, these appear as threadlike shadows in the thin white, later appearing as a severely blemished yolk. When broken open, it shows a crusted appearance. Frequently there is a fruity odor that classifies this type egg as a mixed rot.

Musty Eggs. These are detected by the smell that comes from the unbroken egg. Musty eggs are caused by musty odors absorbed from egg cartons, nesting material, or storage containers.

Moldy Eggs. These might or might not show mold spots on the shell. Mold growths inside the shell can be seen by candling. A smell might or might not be present. The causes are the use of dirty water for washing eggs or storage in areas of high humidity.

Black Rots. Any rot in advanced stage will cause egg contents to appear black when candled. When broken, the contents are a muddy brown color and give off a repulsive, putrid odor.

Cooked Eggs. These eggs have been subjected to heat for a long enough period of time to cause the contents to congeal and show up as threadlike shadows in the white or a dark opaque appearance.

Blood Rings. These are caused when fertile eggs are held above 80 degrees Fahrenheit (26.66 degrees C.) for up to 24 hours and then the egg is cooled down below 40 Fahrenheit (4.44 degrees C.) The embryo, which began to develop a circulatory system, dies at this temperature. The blood that began to circulate in the system drains to the outer edge of the germ disc and causes the blood ring shown as a brilliant red circle one-eighth to three-eighths of an inch wide.

Chick Embryos. If incubation temperatures are maintained for days, an embryo will begin to form and a dark spot will be seen about the third day with a white-shelled egg or at about the fifth day for a brown-shelled egg. The spot in a green- or blue-shelled egg of an Aracauna breed chicken might take seven days to notice this spot. After the fourth or fifth day, blood vessels will be seen spreading out along the inside of the shell when candled.

Bloody Whites. These are eggs that have blood mixed in with all the white. Such a condition can be present in eggs just laid.

Blood Spots. These are clots of red blood larger than one-eighth of an inch wide caused by germ development or blood from the oviduct.

Meat Spots. These might be blood spots that have lost their red color, turning brown, or bits of tissue picked up from the oviduct. These eggs are considered inedible if the spot is larger than one-eighth of an inch wide.

Shell Damage. Any shell that has the membrane broken and allows the egg to leak it's contents. Broken or cracked shells with membranes intact are classed only as checked eggs.

The final U.S. grading is based on the percentage of standard qualities given to each lot of eggs. A lot consists of one or more cases of eggs. Cases contain 30 dozen eggs. Ultimately, some B-standard eggs can end up as A or AA quality (Tables 5-5 and 5-6).

Weight classes further are given to eggs for a size classification (Table 5-7).

U.S. consumer grade (origin)	Quality required[1]	Tolerance permitted[2] Percent Quality
Grade AA	87 percent AA	Up to 13 .... A or B[5]
		Not over 5 .... Checks[6]
Grade A	87 percent A or better	Up to 13 .... B[5]
		Not over 5 .... Checks[6]
Grade B	90 percent B or better	Not over 10 ...... Checks

U.S. consumer grade (destination)	Quality required[1]	Tolerance permitted[3] Percent Quality
Grade AA	72 percent AA	Up to 28[4] .... A or B[5]
		Not over 7 .... Checks[6]
Grade A	82 percent A or better	Up to 18 .... B[5]
		Not over 7 .... Checks[6]
Grade B	90 percent B or better	Not over 10 ...... Checks

[1] In lots of two or more cases, see table 4 of this section for tolerances for an individual case within a lot.

[2] For the U.S. Consumer grades (at origin), a tolerance of 0.50 percent leakers, dirties, or loss (due to meat or blood spots) in any combination is permitted, except that such loss may not exceed 0.30 percent. Other types of loss are not permitted.

[3] For the U.S. Consumer grades (destination), a tolerance of 1 percent leakers, dirties, or loss (due to meat or blood spots) in any combination is permitted, except that such loss may not exceed 0.30 percent. Other types of loss are not permitted.

[4] For U.S. Grade AA at destination, at least 10 percent must be A quality or better.

[5] For U.S. Grade AA and A at origin and destination within the tolerances permitted for B quality, not more than 1 percent may be B quality due to air cells over 3/8 inch, blood spots (aggregating not more than 1/8 inch in diameter), or serious yolk defects.

[6] For U.S. Grades AA and A Jumbo size eggs, the tolerance for checks at origin and destination is 7 percent and 9 percent, respectively.

Table 5-5. Summary of U.S. Consumer Grades for Shell Eggs.

EGG COLLECTING

Because too many handlers take egg laying and collecting for granted, countless numbers of eggs never show up in some handler's egg baskets owing to nonproduced eggs, broken, or eaten eggs. Eggs that should never appear in the handler's basket include soiled, overheated, frozen, incubated and unsightly shell informations.

Many handlers find egg collecting a pleasurable deviation from other chores. In the beginning, you might enjoy it so much that eggs are collected often and thoroughly. That is the way it should be done. Family members might even argue over who has the right to perform this pleasurable task.

Soon, the "fun" might wear off—there's quiet over the homestead and in the chicken coop. Family members no longer argue over their privilege to collect eggs, but rather over the other members' reluc-

Table 5-6. Tolerance for Individual Case Within a Lot.

U.S. consumer grade	Case quality	Origin	Destination
		Percent	
Grade AA	AA (min)	77	62
	A or B	13	28
	Check (max)	10	10
Grade A	A (min)	77	72
	B	13	18
	Check (max)	10	10
Grade B	B (min)	80	80
	Check (max)	20	20

Size or weight class	Minimum net weight per dozen	Minimum net weight per 30 dozen	Minimum weight for individual eggs at rate per dozen
	Ounces	Pounds	Ounces
Jumbo	30	56	29
Extra large........	27	50-1/2	26
Large	24	45	23
Medium	21	39-1/2	20
Small.............	18	34	17
Peewee	15	28	—

Table 5-7. Weight Classes of U.S. Consumer Grades for Shell Eggs.

tance to perform the chore. Eggs are then collected only once daily, resulting in a drop in production, broken, cracked, unedible, overheated, frozen, or partially incubated eggs. This is mismanagement or no management at all.

Quality eggs can be produced by small-scale raisers through good feed, housing, and care. But to preserve this quality, certain measures must be taken from the time the egg is laid until it arrives in the kitchen for cleaning and storing.

First, to prevent egg breakage, the nests bottoms must be made soft and bouncy. This entails the use of litter material to line the nests bottoms. Chickens do not lay eggs while sitting. As the egg moves down the egg tract and enters the cloaca, the hen feels the pressure of the egg near the vent. She stands, squats just a little, then pushes the egg with surrounding muscles. The egg, covered with a protective cuticle material, is still set as it drops from the vent.

Within a minute the cuticle substance drys, further sealing the shell's pores, and the egg shell's finish takes on a sheen as though polished. This dryed cuticle material helps to keep the egg's interior from becoming contaminated by germs that would otherwise enter through the pores. Some people call the substance *bloom.*

Handlers should take advantage of this protective covering by making sure eggs do not come in contact with damp litter, manure, or broken eggs that can cause the cuticle to be removed and thereby admit germs. When eggs are carried in open baskets from the building to the handler's home, eggs should be shielded from rain or snow.

By providing clean nest material you can help prevent broken eggs and also preserve the cuticle

layer over the shells. For clean eggs, enough nests, one to every five hens, should be provided to prevent chickens from fighting over nest space and causing broken eggs. In rainy or snowy weather, outdoor pens become muddy, and it's best to confine the chickens to their house continuously. Muddy feet will make nest material and eggs dirty and wet.

If there are problems with hens who want to lay eggs outdoors, confine the flock until about 2 P.M. when the majority of the eggs are already laid.

Inexperienced handlers are frequently intimidated by snapping, biting hens as they reach under them to retrieve eggs. This cannot be completely avoided. Young pullets are the ones most likely to act in this manner because they are scared and they also don't know who's the boss yet. They soon realize you have full rights to the eggs and they then learn to act civil.

Most hens will sit in a compartment type nest with their backside toward the entrance. Not many pullets peck at your hand in this position. A handler should then reach under, gently pushing the hen upward, and feel around in a circle below her for any available eggs. The gentle push upwards will teach young pullets to later raise themselves up from the nest as your hand goes under them, making the collecting easier for all concerned.

There might be young pullets, broody hens, or just plain nasty ones who will continue to snap at your hand. A handler can wear a long thick glove on one hand to block her snapping attempts while reaching under her with the other hand feeling for eggs. Usually most chickens quit snapping when they learn you won't give up.

Sometimes, if a handler is skillful, he can grab

the neck of a snapping hen, reach under and quickly retrieve the eggs. If he's not careful, the hen will be impulsively raise upwards, kicking her feet and breaking eggs.

Some flighty breeds constantly startle their handlers as they run screaming out of their nest throughout the laying season. Then there are some seemingly docile hens who will snap at a stranger's hand reaching under them.

An egg's quality is maintained best at temperatures between 45 and 55 degrees Fahrenheit (7.22 and 12.77 degrees C.). At 68 degrees Fahrenheit (20 degrees C.) a fertile egg will begin to incubate. It will actually begin the process of forming an embryo. Although a constant 68 degrees Fahrenheit will not hatch a chick after 3 weeks, the changes that take place within a 68-degree-Fahrenheit egg after a few hours is enough to begin deterioration of the egg's quality. Because the embryo growth is not rapid enough at 68 degrees Fahrenheit, after a few days the embryo would die and you would have a rotten egg.

Between 32 and 45 degrees Fahrenheit (0-7.2 degrees C.) condensation occurs on eggs and they will "sweat." This sweating removes the protective cuticle. At 32 degrees Fahrenheit and below, the egg's shell will crack as the contents expand from the cold. Sometimes just the shell only cracks. If contents ooze from the crack when slightly warmed, the membrane has also cracked.

A hen's body temperature is about 106.5 degrees Fahrenheit (41.38 degrees C.). From this temperature, a freshly laid egg must rapidly be cooled to 60 degrees Fahrenheit (15.55 degrees C.) or less to stay fresh. The rate at which freshly laid eggs cool will depend first on the temperature of the interior of the chickens building. Next, the cooling rate is reliant upon how soon the eggs are collected after being laid. The container into which the eggs are placed upon gathering is another point to keep in mind.

Always use a container that "breaths." Wire baskets are best and will immediately begin to cool eggs by ventilation. Some straw stuck to eggs will fall through. Most wire baskets (Fig. 5-34) made especially for egg collecting have a raised center in the bottom to prevent the eggs from rolling from side to side and breaking. Most are also plastic coated to help prevent rusting that might mar eggs. My old trusty and semirusty baskets have never

Fig. 5-34. Left-rear: a plastic-coated egg basket that holds 180 eggs is usually too large for most small-scale handlers. Right-rear: this small woven basket will not ventilate as well as the wire baskets. Left-front, plastic pails do not "breath" and should not be used for egg collection. Right-front: small wire baskets suit small-scale handlers beautifully but are hard to find. Front: a Jiffy-Way egg scale.

spotted eggs, even while dipping in sanitizers. They can be painted using two good coats of an oil-base paint made especially for metal surfaces.

Today's new type of wire egg baskets are too large for small-scale egg collecting. The extra space will allow the few eggs collected to roll around the bottom edge in a circle and break. The new baskets hold up to 180 eggs. A bunched-up towel can be placed in the bottom of these to prevent eggs from rolling, but this will defeat the purpose of these baskets in restricting the ventilation. They do come in handy for gathering vegetables from the garden and in scalding poultry during butchering.

The old type wire baskets can occasionally be found second hand. They were designed for small-scale producers; two small sizes were made. The smaller one was made to hold about 30 eggs and the larger one about 60 eggs.

Wire baskets can be custom made by a local welding shop. Be sure to have the basket's bottom center arched to prevent egg rolling. Have the spacing of wires designed so the smallest eggs you'll be collecting will not fall through all the way to the top edge.

If you will be using a small automatic egg washer, purchase the 120-egg basket that goes with the washer. The eggs can be collected all day and left in the basket until they are washed at the end of the day.

Loosely woven wood baskets ventilate but not as well as the open-wire type. Plastic and galvanized pails cannot ventilate and should not be used. A handler might believe there is no harm in placing eggs in a pail if they will be washed and refrigerated as soon as brought into the kitchen. Nevertheless, it takes some time to gather the eggs, and 10 minutes or more of cooling time is already lost. If you take time to pet the family dog, look for the first red tomato, in the garden or uses the same egg collecting period to feed and water the chickens, a pile of warm eggs in a pail will most likely be the same temperature an hour later as when collected.

If the eggs were already cool when collected and kept in a cool room for an hour, this would not pose a problem because it's the heat we are to worry about. A single freshly laid egg will take over one hour to cool to below 60 degrees Fahrenheit (15.55 degrees C.) in a 50 degree Fahrenheit (10 degree C.) room. Imagine how long a dozen or more would take to cool if piled atop one another. The eggs act as their own insulation.

Styrofoam is an excellent insulator, and cardboard insulates, too, so never place warm eggs into egg carons. Let the eggs cool to 45 degrees Fahrenheit (7.22 degrees C.) first.

Collecting eggs often and in the right containers will maintain quality at it's peak. Collecting often will cut down on the amount of eggs available to tempt potential egg eaters and further will allow the handler to catch them in the act.

On the other hand, collecting too often, such as hourly, will bother nesting hens and frighten young pullets enough to put off laying until you're not around.

Usually a schedule of 10 A.M., 1 P.M., and 5 P.M. will do for flocks of about 50 chickens. A larger flock might need collecting at 10 A.M., 12 P.M., 2 P.M.., and 5 P.M.. Cage layers do not need collecting as often as floor-raised chickens. The amount of collecting will depend on the amount of caged layers.

STORING EGGS

It's best to store eating eggs at temperatures between 45 and 55 degrees Fahrenheit (7.2 and 12.77 degrees C.). High humidity is also needed in order to prevent eggs from losing their moisture. Egg quality is maintained at relative humidity levels (between 75 and 85 percent). Humidity levels above 85 percent cause molds to grow within the egg, especially if the storage area is not ventilated.

Most refrigerators do not contain a humidity this high or temperatures above 45 degrees Fahrenheit. An "egg room" is recommended. You can check for the correct temperature with a meat thermometer. They can also be used for testing smoked and cooked meat temperatures, incubator temperatures, and air temperatures. They are made to give an instant reading because there is no waiting for mercury to rise up the tube.

An ordinary incubator hygrometer will give humidity readings within a refrigerator or egg room and can be further used to give humidity readings within the chicken house for ventilation purposes.

Many basements are ideal areas for eating-egg storage because most will stay cool and damp without much fluctuations in temperature or humidity. Check temperature and humidity there during very warm and humid weather conditions. Try not to wash eggs and store in egg cartons with the large end up. Root cellers are another option for egg-storage. Again, check temperature and humidity for various seasonal changes.

A small egg-storage room, providing proper temperature and humidity, can be built into the corner of a basement. Store eggs off the floor and away from walls in case of flooding or damp surfaces.

After eggs are gathered and brought in for storage, they should be washed only if dirty. Washing destroys the protective cuticle covering and leaves the shell's pores open to bacteria and odors. Properly sorted unwashed eggs will keep their quality better and longer. Unwashed clean eggs can be washed just before using if you feel the need to wash them.

Even though a handler practices good management through careful handling of eggs, there will be a small percentage of dirty eggs collected.

Dirty eggs are covered with bacteria that will cause spoilage or food poisoning if the bacteria enters the egg. More damage can be done if dirty eggs are washed carelessly than if the dirt is left on the shell. Providing moisture to the dirt causes bacteria to breed, grow, and penetrate the shell.

To minimize chances of bacteria or odors penetrating the shell, use a mild detergent or sanitizer with water at least 20 degrees warmer than the eggs and at a minimum of 90 degrees Fahrenheit (32.22 degrees C.) and a maximum of 120 degrees Fahrenheit (48.88 degrees C.).

Washing in cool water will help bacteria to be "sucked" into the egg as the egg contents contract with the shell while being cooled. Warming the egg expands the contents and thereby hinders the introduction of bacteria. Bacteria cannot be removed once it enters the egg. Immerse in water no longer than three minutes for hand washing.

To make your own sanitizer, mix about 2 tablespoons of detergent with 4 tablespoons of chlorine bleach to 1 gallon of water. Use a very soft brush or terry cloth to remove dirt. Hardened accumulations can be scraped off with the side of a butter knife blade.

Rinse thoroughly with clear water at the same temperature or slightly warmer than the wash water. Special sanitizers for washing eggs can be purchased at poultry supply houses.

Do not place wet eggs in an egg carton. Let eggs dry thoroughly on a towel or in a rack and then place them in egg cartons, with large end of the egg facing up, and refrigerate. Bowls or baskets can be used to store small amounts of eggs in the refrigerator. Self-defrosting refrigerators pull moisture from food and will begin to dry fresh eggs (and thereby lower the quality).

Most small automatic egg washers are built to hold 120 eggs and are too large for most small-scale raisers. If you wash only dirty eggs such washers are not needed. For raisers of 250 to 400 layers, who want to wash all eggs, these small automatic washers will save an enormous amount of work. Eggs can be collected in baskets purchased with the washers and the filled baskets are just placed down inside of the washer with a sanitizing detergent. In three to eight minutes, the eggs are washed. If a separate heating element is also purchased, the right washing temperature can then be maintained throughout the wash cycle.

Cracked eggs can be used if the contents are not oozing from crack. Cook cracked eggs, where membranes are still intact, thoroughly or use in baked goods, casseroles or other food products that will be thoroughly cooked.

Eggs will pick up odors from other foods, chemicals, petroleum products, paints, etc. Make sure your eggs are not stored near any strong odors, especially if eggs have been washed.

Cover leftover egg yolks with a small amount of water and store in refrigerator in a tightly closed container for later use. Egg whites should also be stored in a tightly closed container but need no water over them.

During the high production period in the summer, there might come a time when extra eggs are a problem. Instead of storing these unsafely for long periods, they can be frozen or water glassed to be used later when production is down because of the molting period or changeovers between young and old flocks.

Frozen whites do not whip well after being thawed. The usual procedure is to thoroughly mix both yolks and whites together. A blender mixes the two very well. This mixture can then be placed in plastic freezer containers or pint or quart plastic freezer bags. The yolk and white will separate while freezing takes place, but upon thawing and cooking they are mixed again. Frozen eggs can be used for any cooking purpose except for beating into a stiff mixture.

A quart freezer bag will hold about 20 broken out eggs.

If the heavy duty zipper locking freezer bags are used, a low-fat omelette can be made right in the bag in a microwave.

Although microwave manufacturers suggest not cooking eggs in the appliances because the eggs might explode, the frozen plastic bags of egg mixture can be cooked in a microwave on medium heat at 10 minutes for a quart bag. When pressure builds up within the closed bag of eggs while microwaving, open the door and turn the bag occasionally—while mixing egg mixture with your fingers through the bag. When the mixture begins to puff and solidify, open one small corner of the bag to let steam escape. Continue cooking and occasionally mixing for the remainder of time.

When done, open the bag completely and slide the contents onto plate. You'll get a very fresh tasting, light and firm type of scrambled egg. And, because no fat is used for cooking, the only fat will be what the egg contains (about 10.5 percent per egg).

Additional ingredients such as mushrooms, onions, pepper, and cheese can be added. Just be sure the bag is resealed, with the extra air squeezed out, before beginning to cook and allow built-up pressure to escape as the bag puffs.

An old-time method of preserving eggs on the farm is with the a sodium silicate solution. This egg preserver is also called *water glass.* Most country drug stores carry quart and pint bottles of this thick, clear liquid. The solution is mixed with boiled and cooled water in a crock or stone jar, and the clean, fresh eggs are placed into this mixture that seals the pores of the egg and thus preserves them.

I understand the sodium silicate is also purchased for the use of sealing car and truck radiators and waterproofing boots. I have not tried this myself.

Do not let the versatility of this product scare you from using it for preserving your overabundance of eggs. If done correctly, you can easily eat last June's eggs at Christmas and swear they were just laid. One quart of water glass will do about 12 dozen eggs in a 4- or 5-gallon crock, at a cost of around $3.

Because unfertile eggs keep longer, these are recommended for storage, but I've always used my breeder eggs for storage which are definitely fertile and found them to store very well. The eggs should be strictly fresh. Make sure no cracked or dirty eggs are used.

Mix 1 quart of the liquid sodium silicate with 12 times the amount of water. Water must first be boiled and allowed to cool before mixing. Manufacturer's directions say to pack eggs in the crock with the small end down. This is impossible to do as eggs constantly roll around. I simply place the daily excess of eggs in the crock in any direction. The solution is a bit slippery. Care must be taken to gently lay eggs in one by one with a good hold on each egg.

As eggs take up space in the crock, the mixture solution naturally rises. Accordingly, as eggs are taken from the crock the solution height is lowered. Keep a few inches of solution over all eggs to allow for some evaporation that might occur.

Directions also state to cover eggs with a glass plate to hold the eggs under the solution. Fresh eggs do not float and there should be no need for any type of covering other than a clean towel over the top to keep out dust and rodents.

After a few weeks, do not be alarmed when you find the top of solution has turned from a very cloudy liquid to a thick white mixture that clings to your hands and the eggs like thick pudding. This is normal and helps the preserving (Fig. 5-35).

Keep the container of eggs covered lightly in a cool place. Unheated basements or cool storage rooms are good. As the eggs are needed, take a bowl with you, reach into the crock, and take out the desired number of eggs. Make sure the eggs left in the crock are covered with the solution before you leave. Rinse the eggs with clear water before cooking.

Eggs preserved in this way will keep for many months and can be used any way fresh eggs are used. The whites will even beat up into a beautiful meringue for holiday pies. It's hard to distinguish these eggs from fresh. I've found the yolks tend to break easier if you're not careful when laying them into a pan for frying. The whites are also thinner.

Another way to use up extra eggs is to cook up some large pans of eggnog for the holidays (if it will last that long). Freeze eggnog in plastic milk jugs; allow space at the top for expansion. Thoroughly defrost until no ice chunks remain, shake, and pour.

For variety, pickled eggs can be made. A dozen eggs will surprisingly fit into a 1-quart jar. Use the following recipe or obtain one from a canning books.

Pickled Eggs

- [ ] 1 dozen boiled and peeled eggs, cooled (do not overcook).
- [ ] 3 cups white vinegar.
- [ ] 1 teaspoon peppercorns.
- [ ] 1 dryed and crushed red hot pepper.
- [ ] 2 tablespoons sugar.
- [ ] 1/4 teaspoon dill seed or small sprig of dill.
- [ ] 1 clove of garlic, chopped.

Pack peeled eggs into a sterilized quart jar. Combine vinegar, spices, and sugar in an enamel pan. Bring to boil, reduce heat, and simmer for 5 minutes. Pour hot liquid over the hard-cooked peeled eggs in jar to within 1/2 inch of the top jar edge. Seal. Process in boiling water bath for 20 minutes.

Tumeric or food coloring can be used when canning for coloring the bottled eggs or beet juice can be added a few days before serving.

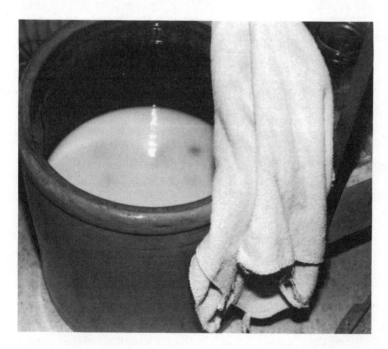

Fig. 5-35. A crock of water glassed eggs will normally turn cloudy after a few weeks.

Many farm wives know the difficulty in removing shells from fresh eggs. To peel eggs easily, take them out from the refrigerator 24 hours before cooking.

Eggs held in water glass solution can be taken right from crock, rinsed, and hardboiled in the shell and easily peeled because they are already "aged." Do not overcook eggs or cook eggs at high temperatures because the eggs will toughen. Use low to moderate temperatures and gently boil for hard-cooked eggs.

Being able to store your bounty of food grown yourself is one of the great features of growing your own.

CULLING

To prevent spending unnecessary amounts of money on feed a handler must perform strict culling among his flock beginning at 20 weeks of age and throughout the entire laying period. Culling results in cutting down on pullet and hen mortality because the poor-quality birds are weeded out before mortality occurs.

Stringent culling also raises the percentage of egg production because the rate for figuring is based only on good-quality birds and not a combination of both poor and good.

At 20 weeks of age, all unnecessary roosters must be taken out of the flock because having too many upsets young pullets. Roosters will also delay pullets from beginning to lay. They will keep pullets hiding and worried by constant mating attempts. Pullets can be so worried that they might be found hiding under nests or afraid to come out and eat.

One rooster for every 15 hens is plenty even for breeding purposes. Roosters are not required for chickens to lay eggs and are totally unnecessary unless fertile eggs are desired.

Next take out unlikely layer prospects. These are mainly runts among the same age birds who have not attained proper growth. No sick, weak, or lame birds should be kept. Most culling will be done with general-purpose heavy breeds because bred-to-lay chickens normally lay well unless stunted, sick, or stressed. As laying progresses and

production seems to stay at about 50 percent for a few days at a time nonproducers can be culled from the flock.

There are a number of ways to cull these birds if they are floor raised. One is to mark each bird as seen in the nests for three days or one week. Three days of constant marking will show the best layers and nonlayers but not the poorest layers. Seven days will show all chickens who are laying and the nonlayers. This is done upon frequent egg-collection visits to the building.

Begin when the first day's egg is to be laid. While looking for eggs, spray the back of each bird found in the nests with an indelible type marker. One such spray is an antiseptic purple colored wound dressing that contains methyl-violet. It stains the backs of all but black feather very well and stays put for a good six weeks.

An anti-infection medicine called gentian violet can also be used because it stains purple and does not rub off. It is available at most drug stores in small bottles in liquid form and is usually provided with a dabber for application.

Both products can also be used for open wounds the birds encounter. The dabber is a bit messy. The spray is quicker and less messy. Just be sure the nozzle is pointed in the proper direction when spraying or you'll have purple marks on you, too.

During the first few days also notice, but do not mark, birds that seem to be laying eggs on the floor. Toward the end of the period, if eggs have been found on the floor in these same spots, then proceed to mark the backs of these floor layers, too.

At the end of three days, only the best layers will be marked if eggs are collected three or four times daily. At the end of 1 week, if a handler collects eggs five times a day, all producers will be marked.

If unmarked birds are checked, they will be found to have pubic bones that are very close together when measured with the finger. The hind end will look narrow instead of rounded and full. The vent opening will be small and dry instead of wide and moist. The yellow pigment from the beaks, shanks, vent, and skin surrounding the eyes in yellow skin breeds will be a much brighter yellow in a nonproducer.

Because nonproducers and poor producers are not messed up from the marking, they can ultimately be sold if desired without their appearance being affected. Although mark culling seems to take longer, it is sometimes more convenient than individually handling each chicken for regular culling. Regular culling for nonlayers and poor layers consists of first caging all hens and pullets, then picking up each one individually and looking at the following:

Vent. The vent of a layer will appear large, oval, and moist. A nonlayer has a vent which is small, round-looking, and dry.

Pubic Bones. These are the two sharp bones that protrude on each side of the vent. By holding the bird against you with one hand, take the fingers of your other hand and place them down between the two bones. The two bones are spread far apart in a layer. Two or three fingers should fit between the two bones. If only one finger will fit between the two bones, this indicates a nonlayer.

Note: This type of quick check can be made indiscreetly when purchasing pullets or grown hens from a seller. All you need to do is ask to handle a couple of the birds you're interested in buying.

Keel Bone. The keel bone (sternum) is centered directly below the two pubic bones. Place your hand horizontal to the rear of the chicken. A wide spread, usually three or four fingers placed between the pubic bones and this keel bone—plus soft, puffy and doughy feeling skin there—will indicate laying condition. If the pubic bones and keel are together, such as only one or two fingers—and skin there is tight and tough feeling—this is a nonlayer.

Comb and Wattles. A layer will have a large, warm, shiny-looking comb and wattles. The nonlayer will possess a small shriveled-looking, cold, faded comb that sometimes has white flakes of scruff resembling dandruff powdered over the surface.

Broody hens do not lay eggs. Either break up their broodiness, use them for hatching, or sell them as brood hens.

Poor layers should be culled from the flock if feed expenses seem high. Poor layers can be found be examining the following areas.

Skin. The bright yellow skin and fat of yellow skin breeds get coloring from the xanthophyll pigments contained in the chickens' diet. Corn and alfalfa meal are the main sources of coloration. When chickens are laying, this yellow coloring in the beak, skin around the eyes, the vent, the shanks, feet, toes, and nails gradually fades and becomes paler as the yellow pigment from the feed goes instead to the egg yolks the hens produce.

It's easy to tell at a glance which chickens have laid the longest because they will have the largest majority of pale body parts. These parts will naturally fade in a orderly progression I call VELBS.

V—is for the vent.

E—is around the eye.

L—is for the ear lobes.

B—is the beak.

S—the shanks.

A pullet whose yellow coloring is only faded around the vent, eye, and lobe has only been laying a few weeks. The addition of a faded beak means the hen has been in production a couple months. The shanks, feet, toes, and nails fad last and occurs at about six months of production.

Parasite infestation can also cause the fading. Be sure the chickens do not have worms. This is done by periodic worming with a suitable vermifuge. Lice are prevented by powdering with lice powder.

When hens quit laying, the yellow coloring will come back to these parts of the body (usually in the progression in which the coloring left). Do not color cull during a regular molt.

By also examining a hen's head, you can further distinguish productivity. The head of a good producer will show a well proportioned beak and head with a full-looking face. A poor producer will exhibit a long, narrow-looking beak and head with a small sunken looking face and eyes.

Because a chicken's bad disposition can be indictive to a poor layer, be suspicious of any who are especially flighty, squawky, or difficult to handle and catch. The good producers are always more friendly, energetic, easier to handle, and are off the roosts more than a poor producer.

Hens that molt early are out of production longer than normal and should also be culled from the flock. Culling should be practiced even during a second laying season if hens are held over. If a handler becomes familiar with signs of laying and nonlaying, he'll be able to almost cull on site.

MOLTING

Many inexperienced handlers believe that if a pullet or hen has feathers missing from the top of her head and back she is molting. They ridiculously refuse to purchase excellent hens in this condition. Such handlers probably have heard about molting but have no idea what is actually is or how a molting chicken looks.

Feathers missing from the top of a chicken's head making her appear bald and a bare back just shows the results of aggressive mating attempts by roosters. As the rooster grabs the top of her head with his beak to steady and balance himself, he also places his feet upon her back to further hold her down. A few weeks of this type of treatment will ruffle and remove any hen's feathers! Roosters have their own favorite hens and a handler can tell by looking just which ones they are.

A molt (also spelled moult) is used by hens to recondition their protective covering of feathers for a new season. The length and time of molt will depend on the breed strain and individual hens. Hens that are very good producers will molt late and fast. This will begin anywhere between September and October and will last from two to three months. Early molters are usually not good producers. They will begin a molt as early as July and stay in molt for about five months.

Because poor-producing early molters can begin production the same month as the good-producing late molters, it's wise to cull these early molters when they are seen in the earlier months.

The first complete annual molt begins after the first full season of laying. This is approximately after 12 months of laying for April-hatched chicks. A second year of laying will provide about nine or ten months of additional egg production.

Molting involves the "shedding" of feathers from a chicken. Chickens molt from the head on down through the the body in the following order:

- ☐ Head
- ☐ Neck
- ☐ Breast
- ☐ Body (abdomen and back)
- ☐ Tail
- ☐ Secondary feathers
- ☐ Primary flight feathers.

A molting chicken will appear more ragged than bald, as if the feathers were thinned out. Feathers will lack lustre with the color appearing spotty. A molt is not considered complete unless the body and wing feathers are shed.

The molting of the wings is the most important part of the molt in determining a good producer. When spreading the wing of a hen and studying the basic parts, you will find two sections contain the longest feathers of the entire wing. These two sections are called the primary flight feathers and the secondary feathers. Many handlers refer to both sections as flight feathers, although this is incorrect. Between the two sections of feathers is a short small feather in the wing joint called the axial feather.

The 10 primary flight feathers are shed before secondary feathers. Primaries are shed in a consistent and regular pattern, secondary feathers are not. It is the shedding of the primary flight feathers that will tell a handler how long a hen has been molting in order to determine her productivity.

The very first primary feather to be shed is the one next to the axial feather. Then the rest of the primaries are shed as they grow in the row. Good producers, being fast molters, will shed several of these primaries at one time until the last one in the tip of the wing is shed. A poor producer that molts slowly will shed one primary every two weeks. With 10 primary feathers, this will take 20 weeks! For a good producer that molts fast, the time will only be about half that.

By checking which chickens have primaries missing in late fall or early winter, you can find the good producers. Those with all primaries intact have most likely molted early, having already grown the new feathers back.

As each primary is shed, a new one will begin to grow (taking over 6 weeks in doing so). The secondaries are shed last with the small axial feather.

Many good producing chickens, especially egg breeds, will lay during the entire molting period if proper rations are continued.

FORCED MOLTING

Force molting is not a new procedure. As early as 1900, chickens were induced into molting by stressing them in order for them to produce larger eggs with a better quality of shell and a longer production period for hens.

It wasn't practiced commercially on a very large scale until egg and poultry meat prices were down during the 1960s. Today it is practiced quite freely. California still leads the way as more than 90 percent of it's poultry farms participate.

Force molting can be done any time of the year, and this enables handlers to have the highest production in the life span of the flock at a period when poultry and egg prices are higher. Good production can be had for up to three years of age by force molting.

Because it will cost about $250 to purchase and raise 100 lightbreed pullets until they're into production, it can pay to keep 18-month-olds through another period of laying. One-hundred egg breed hens will cost about $520 to keep during the same amount of time it takes to raise 100 chicks until laying. At 50 percent production for this amount of time, the hens will produce about $600 worth of eggs. Therefore, a handler is ahead of his costs. But if the costs of raising 100 chicks is also added, the costs will be about $770. He is then unprofitably

in the red by $170 (not counting the labor involved in raising any of them)!

Hens that have never molted naturally are easier to molt than hens that have molted. Most pullets will have to be molted before the age of 17 to 18 months when a first natural molt usually occurs. Older hens that have naturally molted before will need more stressful conditions during a force-molt program.

The very early practice of force molting resembled the natural molting. Today's methods are much more stressful. Of the following four types of force molting, there are also three methods: Rapid molt, normal molt, and slow molt. The slower the molt, because of the increased rest the birds obtain, the better and longer the resulting production.

A rapid molt returns the hens to 50 percent production in less than six weeks. A normal molt returns them to 50 percent production in 6-8 weeks. A slow molt takes nine or more weeks to return to 50 percent production.

The three main types of force molting employed in the industry are: the low-nutrient molt, the feed-additive molt, and the restricted or no-feed or no-water molt.

The low-nutrient molt is not used much. It consists of feeding a ration low in protein or calcium during the "rest" period of the molt.

The feed-additive molt uses antiovulatory drugs. It is a method not used commercially but mainly in laboratory experiments.

The restricted or no-feed or no-water molt is considered by most researchers to produce the best results. Basically the method is carried out in the following way.

☐ Culling should first be done. Eliminate any birds that are poor or ones you haven't got around to pulling from the flock. Birds molted together should be of same age. This is also the time to perform worming, touch-up debeaking or revaccination (if you were planning to do these tasks). Weigh a few birds so you will know how much weight will be lost from the stressing which will take place. This is not as important for very heavy hens. Extra calcium can be fed two days before feed will be removed from top-dressing over clean litter at the rate of 5 pounds per 100 hens. This improves the shell quality of the last eggs to be laid during the molt and provides an extra margin of safety when nutrients are taken away.

☐ Take all feed from the chickens but leave clean drinking water available to them. The fasting will continue for 10 days.

☐ At the same time feed is removed, make sure birds only receive eight hours of total light (this includes natural daylight).

☐ If a rapid molt is desired, provide free choice oyster shell feed for all 10 days, along with the water. If a normal molt is desired, the oyster shell feeding is optional or can be given in small quantities. The slow molt requires no feeding of oyster shell at all—just water.

☐ During the fifth day of no feed, birds can be weighed again. Body weight should not go below the recommended body weight for a 20-week-old pullet of the same breed and strain you're molting.

☐ On the eleventh day of no feed, for a rapid molt, feed the usual layer mash but restrict the amount to 12 to 14 pounds per 100 hens for the first two days to avoid overeating and crop compaction. For a normal molt, feed a high-fiber mash, also called a molting mash, consisting of cracked grains for two to three weeks before feeding the regular layer ration. Supplement with vitamins and minerals in the water. Restrict this feed also for the first two days and then feed free choice. For a slow molt, feed cracked or whole grains consisting of corn, oats, barley, and milo for best results. Do this for four or more weeks before feeding a layer ration. Restrict these also for first two days and then feed free choice.

☐ The lighting is gradually increased a few hours each day. Rapid molting requires lights be increased starting the eleventh day. Normal molting begins adding lighting at about the twenty-eighth day. Slow molting should have lighting increased beginning about the forty-second day.

Force molting must be used properly, and hens should be in good condition in the beginning because the procedure stresses the birds enough so a few will most likely be lost to stress. This is normal.

Force molting will not make a poor flock good. It's purpose is to make good flocks even better for a longer period of time. This can save much money in replacement-pullet costs by extending the hen's reproductive life.

Although hens will lay for seven to 10 years, you must consider investments to increase the dollar return per each dollar invested in your birds. This calls for production and egg quality. Anything less can be considered an expensive hobby.

HOW TO HANDLE BROODY HENS

Broody hens want to hatch eggs and become mothers. In a production flock, there is no time or space for "broodies." A broody must either be broke, used to hatch eggs, or culled from the flock and sold to someone who wants a broody hen.

One day, as you are collecting eggs, you may reach toward a hen who immediately raises her feathers on end and loudly err-a-w-ks at you in a forbidding tone.

If you don't do something with her, you might find others wanting to become mothers, too: it seems to be a "catching" idea. This can be bad because brooding hens do not lay eggs. They simply brood over the thought of possible motherhood.

Further, a broody will constantly steal eggs she spots near her nesting area. By using her beak, she rolls and shoves all the eggs she can underneath herself. If she spots a clutch of eggs she thinks is too much trouble to move to her nest, she might just go to the clutch of eggs and continue sitting instead. All this fuss can create broken and dangerously heated eating eggs.

Most egg-breed chickens will not get broody. They have no desire to sit because most of the instinct to want to sit has been genetically bred out of these breeds in order to keep egg production going. It's mainly the hybrid chicks that will not sit. Many old-time standard breeds of heavies, lights, and bantams will sit if the opportunity—such as other broodies, a pile of uncollected eggs, a nice dark secluded corner, or a demanding and aggressive rooster—is there.

Most broodies can be broke fairly easy. Remove her from the pen and place her in a completely wire cage with no access to straw or litter of any kind. Do not place the cage directly on the litter of the building floor because she will pull the litter through and make a nest. Place the cage on blocks so that droppings fall through bottom of cage. Keep her out of dark corners by making sure the cage is in light as much as possible.

Keep clean water and the layer ration available to her at all times so she will stay in good condition for laying. Feed should be placed in a small, narrow trough. If placed in a pan large enough for her to fit into, she may make it into a nest, with the feed being used as nesting material.

Sometimes even bringing a quiet family dog around the caged hen will "upset" her out of her broodiness. Do not bring a barking dog into the coop because it could upset the other layers.

Usually two to three days is all that's needed to break her. If she acts normal again—no fluffing out feathers, squawking or biting—she is broke. This does not mean she will not go broody again. You might place her back in with the rest of the flock today and find her broody again tomorrow or next month.

It's a good idea to mark broody hens with a staining material or place a band on her leg. A thick string can also be used for identification purposes by loosely tying the string around the joint that attaches the wing to the body.

There are some hens who never completely break or who break but continue a series of broodiness. Although worthless for egg production, broody hens are usually sold at a higher price than ready-to-lay pullets to someone who wants to hatch chicks.

Insistent broodies will sit anywhere and on anything (Fig. 5-36) even if given a new home. That's all she needs is a clutch of good fertile eggs to occupy her in a dark secluded area away from pets, predators, other poultry, and disturbances.

A dozen eggs is plenty for a heavy general-purpose hen to hatch. The new nest and the mother should be lightly sprinkled with lice powder as large amounts of lice will kill baby chicks. The hen will occasionally eat and drink while she's in her sitting "trance" so make food and water available near her.

After the eighteenth day of sitting, the eggs should begin to hatch and will continue to hatch for a few more days. The mother will usually keep the chicks under her for a day or two before bringing them to food and water.

Fig. 5-36. This insistent broody Barred Plymouth Rock hen hatched and raised the five Mammouth White Pekin ducks shown with her.

162

There occasionally is a fickle hen who decides at the last minute she doesn't enjoy the idea of motherhood anymore. She might leave the nest before the eggs are hatched or wretchedly kill the chicks as they hatch. This is uncommon.

The chicks will go where they shouldn't so you must think ahead to protect them. Be sure there are no open dishes of water they will fall into. The bottoms of nearby fencing should be screened if other chickens, livestock, or pets are in the nearby fenced area. The chicks will walk through the fencing and meet their doom for sure.

Mother hens usually raise their babies until about six to eight weeks of age. Friends of mine had a mother hen who raised her chicks to production size! It was a late-season hatch, and I think the hen believed the chicks needed extra care during the colder weather.

GROOMING FOR SHOW

Many 4-H children must spruce up their chickens for fair time in order to place the final touch upon tender loving and knowledgeable care given to their birds over the summer. These children know nothing can top good feed and management to produce winners.

The shape, conformation, and vitality of a chicken is given more consideration at a show pen than any other factor. Therefore, it's wise to choose the ideal body first and put the crowning glory on feathers and skin later.

Early maturing roosters who bother hens or fight should be kept separate from the hens in order to keep feather quality looking good. To brighten plumage and provide that little extra weight that makes most show birds look so great, a milk-and-fish-oil mash can be fed as an extra treat about six weeks before the birds are to be shown. Mix grower crumbles or mash with warmed, powdered milk and about 1/2 teaspoon of fresh cod liver oil. Remove any leftover mash not eaten in a few hours to avoid spoilage.

Feed this mixture once a day for two weeks. Do not feed this cod liver oil mixture to meat birds within 3 weeks of showing or the meat might taste fishy and white feathers might take on a yellow cast.

There's no doubt that free ranging over lush greens and access to insects will produce healthier looking birds. Be sure your prize specimens are under constant watch and locked tightly at night. I've seen too many prospects destroyed by predators just before show time.

During this time, pluck the occasional black feather from a white chicken. Allow all white-feathered chickens, whether meat breed, general-purpose heavy or fancy, in sunlight as often as possible the last month of conditioning to bleach normal yellowing of white feathers. Do not overexpose to weather as the white feathers can become brassy. Brassiness that shows up over the hackle and back feathers of males is genetic and cannot be removed. A snow-white chicken with gleaming red wattles and comb is a very striking specimen.

Because you do not want your colored-feathered chickens to lose their rich color tones, they must be kept out of direct sunlight. Even black feathers will bleach sometimes, giving a molted effect.

The feeding of an iron supplement will enrich breeds whose feathers contain red pigments. Most colors except white contain red pigments.

Practice the correct method of removing and placing chickens through cage entrance doors. For practice sessions, use a chicken who will not be shown in case feathers are broken during practice. Most anyone can do this, but the practice is meant to improve the tenseness of the handler when the actual procedure is demonstrated in front of the judge. I remember one tearful little girl who, in spite of constant practice, got so flustered when she had to do this in front of the judge, she placed her bird through the opening completely tail first and lost First Prize because of it.

Never keep show chickens in a small cage because cages can take their toll on feather quality and beauty. Begin actual grooming one week before show time by completely separating the specimens to be shown from other chickens. Place these specimens in a separate pen containing lots of clean, soft deep litter. Litter can serve as a grooming aid by it's gentle abrasive action against the skin and feathers.

I do not suggest water bathing chickens as some handlers will do. Oils in the feathers, that cause them to shine, will be lost from the use of any soap. There's always a chance of ruining feathers when wetting. The use of dyes and bleaches is strictly forbidden. The chilling effect of bathing can cause birds to get sick.

An extremely dirty area on feathers can be spot shampooed. Gently rub shampoo in the direction of the feather grain so feathers do not break. Rinse thoroughly, partially blow dry, and then air dry.

The use of plain cornstarch will clean up white birds. Powder the cornstarch down through the feathers. The bird will work the cornstarch out of the feathers by shaking them. Some raisers completely submerse and wash chickens with mild soap, rinsing with diluted laundry bluing to whiten and remove yellowing.

The day before the show use a soft nail brush and plain water to gently clean around the beak, face, eyes, comb, and wattles.

To clean shanks, feet, toes, and nails, mix a small amount of liquid dishwashing detergent to make suds along with a cap full of peroxide to about four cups of warm water. Use a soft nail brush to gently scrub dirt from the top of the shanks down over the top of the feet, around toenails, the bottom of feet, and the underside of toenails. Scrub in the direction scales grow down over hanks. Rinse thoroughly with clear water. The peroxide is not used as a bleaching agent but only as an aid to remove and soften dirt and dead skin as in manicuring.

The final step is the grooming is oiling the comb, wattles, and ear lobes so they take on a gleaming, rich red appearance. Even white ear lobes will look better. After the bird is completely dry, rub a small amount of mineral oil, cod-liver oil or vegetable oil into the comb, wattles, and ear lobes. A final buffing of the beak and toenails with a nail buffer can add to the appearance.

When transporting, use a shallow box in which the bird cannot stand in.

BUTCHERING STEPS

It is not economical to overfeed meat birds. An eight-week-old cornish rock broiler cross should be more than ready (although not particularly willing) to be butchered.

If extra fat is desired on the carcass, these crosses can be fed out another two weeks. Cornish rock cross broilers have excellent flavor at four weeks of age and up if good rations have been provided.

I have tasted very unpleasant bad spots in fresh pork because of feed additives. Therefore, I do not recommend feeding broilers anything containing chemicals or medications. Fast growers do not need these additives as these birds are not around long enough to require strong medications that will leave residues in the meat.

In fact, the feeding of a coccidiostat in the starter feed can bring on an infection at four weeks of age as the medication works to afford immunity within the birds to fight later infections. This can place stress on your fast growers and somewhat retard growth.

Use only organic additives, such as vinegar, for coccidiosis and cod-liver oil to prevent the crippling rickets these birds can get. Discontinue cod-liver oil when birds are receiving full sunshine. Make sure the oil is discontinued two weeks before butchering to prevent a fishy taste in meat.

Cornish rock broilers that are to be butchered at only four weeks of age for cornish game hens will not need the oil.

Occasionally small processors are available for dressing and killing birds. These processors cater to the small-scale raiser and are very convenient for handlers who cannot find the time or the inclination to butcher at home. The steps these processors use would be similar to those used at home. Exceptions are that equipment might be a bit larger and feathers are not usually hand picked. See Figs. 5-37 through 5-50.

If possible, plan outdoor home butchering for cooler weather. Because most hatcheries stop selling chicks in June, it's better in some areas to pur-

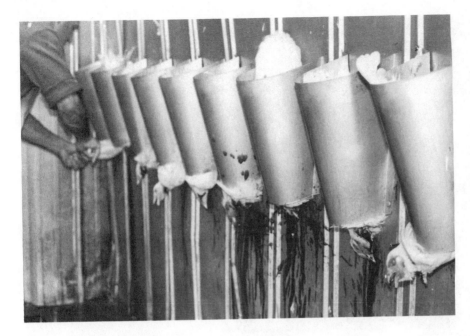

Fig. 5-37. Broilers are placed into killing cones. The jugular veins in the top of throat are cut for a thorough bleeding.

chase February-hatched broiler chicks for April butchering. Cooler weather helps prevent the butchered carcasses from staying warm. If summer butchering is planned, arrange the time before the heavy fly season comes.

An alternative for home butchering is to kill, scald and pick the feathers outdoors, placing birds with feet cut off into chilled ice coolers of cold water. Then drain the birds and finish the dressing procedure indoors where cooler, cleaner (free of

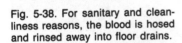

Fig. 5-38. For sanitary and cleanliness reasons, the blood is hosed and rinsed away into floor drains.

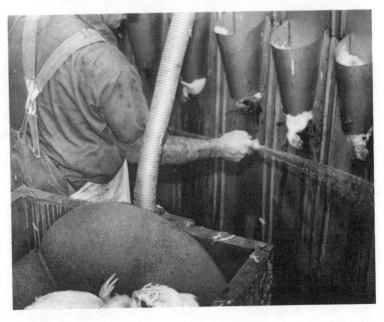

Fig. 5-39. The interior of this scalding tank revolves so all parts of the feathers are thoroughly saturated and scalded.

flys) conditions usually prevail. Whatever building, room, or area is used should be reasonably clean for the actual killing and scalding, but extremely clean and sanitary for the eviscerating process when body cavities are cleaned of their contents.

Have the birds, a 55-gallon drum, and a scalding pot ready (Fig. 5-51). The procedure for butchering your own birds begins with the scalding pot. The pot should be large enough in order to submerse the birds in the contained hot water, and

Fig. 5-40. The scalded birds are placed into this stainless steel revolving picker that can defeather from 500 to 200 broilers per hour, depending on the model used.

Fig. 5-41. When the picker's time cycle is over, the door will automatically unlock and open, throwing the birds out onto the bird catch table.

at the same time avoiding a flow of water over the sides of the pan. A large canning kettle will do. A 16- or 22-quart pressure canner pot is even better and heavier.

A small fiberglass chicken scalder is on the market for small-scale raisers at about $100. The scalder contains a heating element that automatically keeps water at the proper scalding temperature.

For just three or four birds, the water can be

Fig. 5-42. This tool was specially made for use with a hammer for fast head removal.

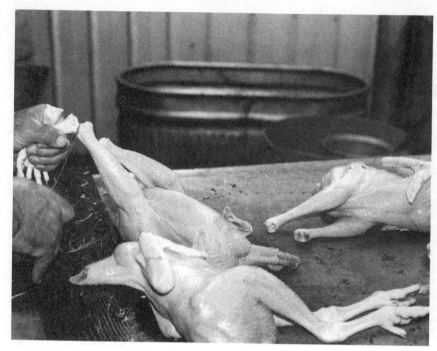

Fig. 5-43. The feet and shanks are removed in one operation by cutting through hock joints.

heated to almost boiling in the kitchen over the range. For a larger number of birds, a constant supply of heat should be provided to maintain the water temperature. This can be done directly over an open fire outdoors by using a 5-gallon metal bucket with air vents pierced toward the bottom. Fill the bucket one-third full with charcoal, light it, and be sure bucket is held stationary by placing large blocks around it. When the coals are red, place the scalding pot on top of the bucket and fill

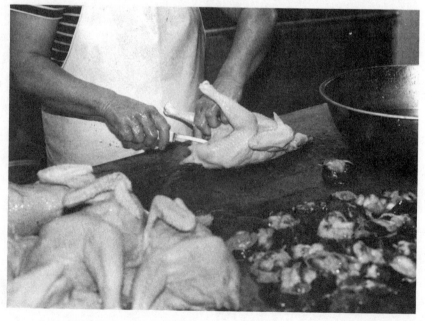

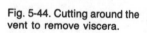

Fig. 5-44. Cutting around the vent to remove viscera.

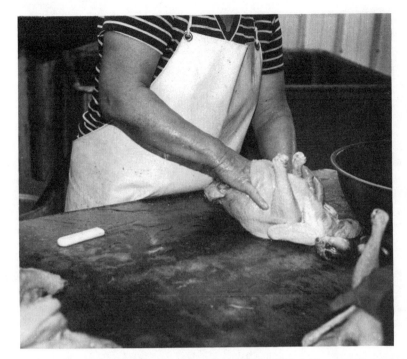

Fig. 5-45. Reaching into the cut opening to remove viscera.

with 125 to 130 degree Fahrenheit (51.66-54.44 degree C.) heated water.

A more expensive way to supply heat is by placing a roll of toilet tissue in a 26- or 32-ounce coffee can and pouring about 1 quart of denatured alcohol over the top of the rolled paper. After about one to two hours when the roll of tissue has swelled and absorbed all the alcohol, place the entire can, including the roll of paper, into the bottom of a metal 5-gallon can. Puncture air vent holes around the

Fig. 5-46. The giblets are separated from the viscera by cutting the gizzard loose.

169

Fig. 5-47. The green bile sac is pinched loose near it's bottom, where it's attached to the liver.

bottom of the 5-gallon can. Then carefully light the roll of alcohol and place the scalding pot filled with water over the top of the 5-gallon can.

This amount of alcohol with one roll of paper will provide heat long enough to do about 15 chickens. If only a few chickens will be done, the coffee can can be smothered to put out the flame. When cool, cover the can with the plastic lid (usually provided) to prevent the remaining alcohol from evaporating so it can be used later.

Fig. 5-48. One method of removing the gizzard contents is to simply slice it open. The lining will then need to be removed in a separate procedure.

170

Fig. 5-49. Removal of the gizzard lining is easily accomplished with this machine.

Caution should be exercised when using the flammable substances such as the denatured alcohol. It's a good idea to become familiar with it's capabilities before using it full-scale. A camp stove can be used to heat smaller pots of water in which to add to the larger scalding pot as it's water cools down. The incinerator shown in Fig. 5-52 can also be used to keep water in scalding pots hot enough for dipping.

Beginners should check the water temperature

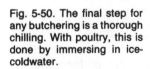
Fig. 5-50. The final step for any butchering is a thorough chilling. With poultry, this is done by immersing in ice-coldwater.

Fig. 5-51. A 55-gallon drum to be used for feather and viscera collection, with the scalding pot in foreground heating over a fire.

with a small commercial dial meat thermometer available at restaurant supply wholesale stores. The cost is about $15. These are used commercially to test internal heat of smoked meats and can be used at home, too. A candy thermometer can also be used, but you will not get an instant reading because with these you must wait for the mercury to rise.

Scalding the birds with hot water softens and relaxes the muscles that hold the feathers, making feather removal easier. The addition of a small amount of detergent to the scald water allow the water to penetrate the oil of the feathers better in order to thoroughly wet them. Wet feathers allow picking machines and hands to more readily grasp and pull feathers loose.

At scalding temperatures above 130 degrees Fahrenheit (54.44 degrees C.), the very thin yellow outer covering of the skin will come off. This will happen more quickly on young birds. A "semi-, soft-, or slack-scald" should be used for young birds. This consists of a temperature of about 128 degrees Fahrenheit (53.33 degrees C.) into which the bird is immersed and swished around for about one minute.

In this "semi-scald," soft water will loosen feathers much better than hard water. To soften hard water, place a couple of teaspoons of baking soda into the scald water.

A "sub-scald" can be used on older hens and cock birds by immersing them in 138 to 140 degree Fahrenheit (58.88-60 degree C.) water for about one minute. This hotter water will loosen more stubborn feathers of older birds, but there will be a tacky feeling to the dried skin because the outer covering has been removed causing moisture loss.

When water has almost reached the correct temperature, prepare the birds for killing. It is easier and more sanitary to dress chickens that do not have a full crop of grain. Plan to remove their feed and keep them off litter a half day before butchering. If allowed to remain on litter, the litter will be found in the crop.

Use wire cages raised off the ground (Fig. 5-53). Electric stunning knives are much too expensive for most small-scale raisers. The purpose of the commercial electrical stunning is to prevent bruises and broken wings on commercially dressed birds and to provide a quicker and more thorough bleeding out. When birds are stunned, they become

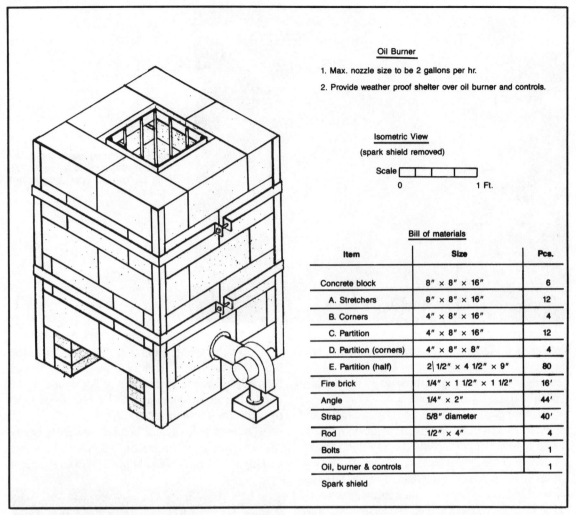

Oil Burner

1. Max. nozzle size to be 2 gallons per hr.

2. Provide weather proof shelter over oil burner and controls.

Isometric View
(spark shield removed)

Scale ☐☐☐☐☐
0   1 Ft.

Bill of materials

Item	Size	Pcs.
Concrete block	8″ × 8″ × 16″	6
A. Stretchers	8″ × 8″ × 16″	12
B. Corners	4″ × 8″ × 16″	4
C. Partition	4″ × 8″ × 16″	12
D. Partition (corners)	4″ × 8″ × 8″	4
E. Partition (half)	2 1/2″ × 4 1/2″ × 9″	80
Fire brick	1/4″ × 1 1/2″ × 1 1/2″	16′
Angle	1/4″ × 2″	44′
Strap	5/8″ diameter	40′
Rod	1/2″ × 4″	4
Bolts		1
Oil, burner & controls		1
Spark shield		

Fig. 5-52. An outdoor incinerator.

rigid and the inevitable flopping around is avoided.

Sticking is a bit tricky and bleeding is not as good. Sticking involves the insertion of a knife into the mouth of the bird and, with a quick twist of the hand, severing the jugular veins near the groove in the back roof of the mouth. Stunning or sticking is unnecessary for home butchering.

To kill and bleed out, the jugular veins in the top of the throat should be severed. The use of a meat cleaver and chopping block is somewhat dangerous unless the chicken is kept from flopping around. Beginners can tie a thin rope or twine around the feet and the top of the neck. With

someone on each side pulling down and out on the ropes, the chicken can be made to lie still.

With practice, the chicken can be laid across the chopping block with the neck stretched out against it's surface. Most chickens will quietly assume this position long enough for the cleaver to come down over the top of the neck. Never hold the neck while chopping. It's both stupid and dangerous and there's no need.

If the neck is not severed exactly right, don't worry. You should end up with a fairly nice carcass even if not perfect.

Immediately upon severing the neck, allow the

Fig. 5-53. Holding cages should be raised from ground to prevent birds from picking up litter, grass, and stones.

chicken to hang upside down in a barrel to drain the blood from the body's veins. The barrel will prevent blood from being splattered on you as the bird will flap around around quite a bit.

A killing cone can be bought or made and mounted on a tree, a building, or an upright board. It will hold a chicken upside down while you use a knife to cut through the jugular veins. Gravity assists in quickly draining blood. The cut does not need to be deep. Try to avoid complete severing of the windpipe and neck. This procedure will cause the least amount of splattering and flopping around.

When killing chickens, you must be concerned about satisfactory bleeding. Otherwise the skin will turn red, appearing frostbitten. The nice yellow-looking skin of a nice plump broiler will not look tempting if not bled thoroughly. Let bleeding continue for 60 to 90 seconds before being scalded.

After bleeding, take the bird by both legs and lower it in to the hot scald pot (Fig. 5-54). Slowly twist the bird in a circular motion, back and forth, to help water penetrate feathers. Be sure all feathers on legs past the hock joints are covered with water or there will be small feathers left on the bottom of the resulting drumsticks.

After the proper timing has elapsed, raise the bird from the water, slightly drain (Fig. 5-55), and then either hang it by the feet or lay it on a board over a barrel for picking. The barrel can be used to catch the feathers taken off.

To hang the carcass, bend a loop from heavy wire to construct a convenient shackle to hold feet quickly in place for suspending at shoulder height

Fig. 5-54.Grabbing both feet, the fully bled bird is lowered into the scalding water to release feathers from the follicles.

Fig. 5-55. After timing, raise the bird and slightly drain excess water.

grabbed, pulled, and rubbed almost simultaneously. With an automatic picker, the bird is held near rubber "fingers" that rotate and "grab" feathers off the carcass. For a small automatic picker to be an economically sound investment for small-scale raisers, 450 chickens will have to be processed in order for the picker to pay for itself.

I find the automatically heated small scalding tank to be more of a convenience to have because heating kettles and pans of water can be a chore. Really, scalding the birds at the correct temperature is far more important and harder to accomplish than rubbing feathers off the chicken. Feather removal will be tougher if the scalding is not done correctly at the right temperature.

After feather removal, cut shanks and feet off in one operation by cutting through hock joints. The sooner dirty shanks and feet are removed, the less chance of contaminating the carcass with bacteria.

Cooling the carcass by immersing in cold water before eviscerating (gutting) helps clean the carcass and makes the job easier.

Plastic cutting boards, like some used commercially, can be purchased at a butcher supply for about $15 to $20 for a 2- × -3-foot size. Used for the final dressing process, the boards are claimed to be more sanitary than the wood cutting boards. Nevertheless, they will need to be scrubbed with a stiff brush to remove accumulations left in between cutting marks that appear after use.

Begin by cutting a small V where the tail bone meets the body on the back side. This is where the

from a tree branch, beam, ceiling hook, or similar sturdy tie-off. A hanger can also be used (Fig. 5-56).

Large feathers such as tail and wings should be removed first because they are somewhat tougher to remove later and they get in the way of picking the rest of the carcass. Even if an automatic picker is used, the large, annoying feathers should be removed first by hand.

Large feathers must be removed almost singly in a yanking motion. Body and leg feathers are

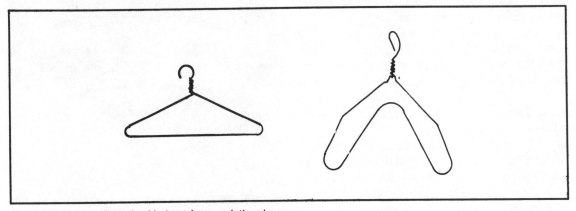

Fig. 5-56. A convenient shackle bent from a clothes hanger.

175

oilgland, called the uropygium gland, is located. Chickens are frequently seen using their beaks to expel the oil from the sac to groom their feathers. The oil sac removal will prevent an odd flavor from developing in the meat.

Next, slit the skin a couple inches near where neck meets the body by the breast to remove crop and windpipe (the hollow looking tube). Carefully grab the bag type sac (the crop). If the chicken was fasted long prior to butchering, the crop will be harder to find—looking only like a thick fold of skin. A crop full of grain is easier to find but if broken, as they tear easily, it can contaminate meat and be messy besides.

Gently pull the crop out through the slit skin and cut it loose close to the body. Pull the windpipe loose if possible. It usually will break and the remainder is then removed from the inside cavity. Cut off the neck if desired as close to body as possible.

Now, make a shallow slit just below the pointed rear of the breastbone (also called keel-bone or sternum). Widen the slit carefully by not cutting too deep as the intestines are right there. Puncturing the intestines accidentally will allow the foul fecal contents to leak into the cavity and contaminate the meat.

If the opening is still not wide enough to admit your hand, a vertical slit can be made from the center of the first horizontal cut to form a T. As soon as the horizontal slit is wide enough, reach in above the viscera (all the internal organs) and move your fingers back behind the mass. Gently pull back toward the opening to work the mass out.

After the mass of viscera is pulled from the cavity, you will notice it is still attached at the vent. Push the viscera to one side of the vent while cutting along one side and the bottom edge of vent. Repeat on the other side of vent. Make certain the knife does not puncture any part of the attached intestine.

The lungs still remain in the cavity, sometimes along with the heart and part of the windpipe, and they must be removed. The lungs lie far up into the cavity along each side of the backbone. The pink-and-spongy-looking lungs are scraped loose from the backbone crevices with the finger or by using a handy gadget called a lung remover. This gadget looks like a screwdriver with a rounded series of teeth on it's end. It saves a lot of broken fingernails!

With young birds, the kidneys and sex organs can remain attached to the backbone. In older birds, they should be removed at the same time as the lungs.

The giblets are separated from the viscera by cutting the gizzard loose, then with index finger and thumb, pinch the greenbile sac (gall bladder) near it's bottom where it's attached to the liver, and pull off. If not pinched near the bottom tightly, the sac will break and contaminate the meat with it's contents. The heart will either be attached to the viscera or still be way up inside the body cavity.

The gizzard is cleaned by removing the interior sac. First begin a cut on one side (placing your thumb over the hole Fig. 5-57). Next, cut down slowly and carefully until the white colored lining is noticed (Fig. 5-58). By cutting about one-sixteenth of an inch more, the sac will be seen (Fig. 5-59). Pull apart to remove the sac (Fig. 5-60). This sac is usually filled with grit, stones, and grain (Fig. 5-61).

Dressed carcasses are chilled to extract all body heat and to prevent bacterial growth. The chilling procedure helps birds to stay moist as they are kept immersed in cold, icy water until thoroughly chilled throughout the meat before storage. It can take a few hours to bring carcass temperatures to below

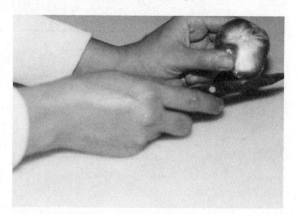

Fig. 5-57. To clean a gizzard, begin by cutting on one side, placing your thumb over hole.

176

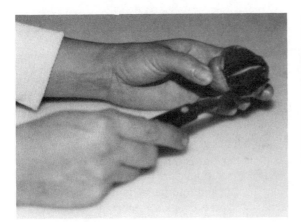

Fig. 5-58. Cut down carefully until a white-colored lining is noticeable.

40 degrees Fahrenheit (4.44 degrees C.), but it definitely should take no longer than four hours for 4-pound birds and not longer than eight hours for 8-pound birds.

A clean and sanitized utility sink, bathtub, or stock tank can serve as a chilling vat for a few dozen birds.

CUTTING AND STORING PROCEDURES

After the carcass is butchered, dressed, and cooled, what you'll have is a ready-to-cook (RTC) chicken that can be frozen whole, cut into halves for broiling, quartered, or cut into parts for frying.

Cutting up the carcass completely and storing

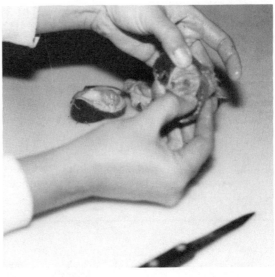

Fig. 5-60. Carefully pull the sides apart to remove the sac.

parts in the freezer will take up less space than freezing whole chickens. The choice is yours. Whole chickens can quickly and easily be thawed faster than a frozen lump of parts placed in a pan of water. When thawed, whole chickens can then be cut into parts.

Whole chickens should be drained in a sink, a large colander, or a rack after butchering and com-

Fig. 5-59. Cutting about one-sixteenth of an inch more will reveal the sac, usually filled with grit, stones and grain.

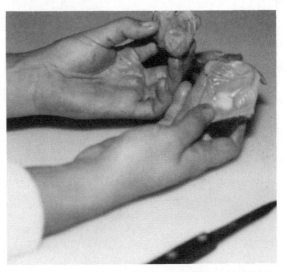

Fig. 5-61. The enclosed sac is removed in one neat wad.

ing out of the chilling water. This prevents leaking in the freezer and ice from forming in freezer storage bags.

Whole eight-week-broiler crosses fit neatly into 1-gallon "heavy duty" freezer bags. The zipper-type bags can have the excess air squeezed out for more protection, and they do not rip easily and leak blood all over before the birds have had a change to freeze.

Large and much older chickens will present a problem in bagging them because the larger bags are often harder to find locally. Freezer paper does not keep quality long and it tears easily. (Pressure canning tenderizes older birds beautifully.) Foil is expensive to use, gets brittle after long freezer exposure, and it tears, also.

For whole bird freezing, hold a freezer bag with one hand. With the other hand, grab one leg while shoving the neck end into the bag corner first and then pushing on the leg to neatly bring this end of carcass down into the bag.

Squeeze out air with your hands or use a straw to suck excess air out. Seal and freeze.

The most important thing to remember, in cutting the chicken into parts, is to cut between the joints or where bones are more or less naturally

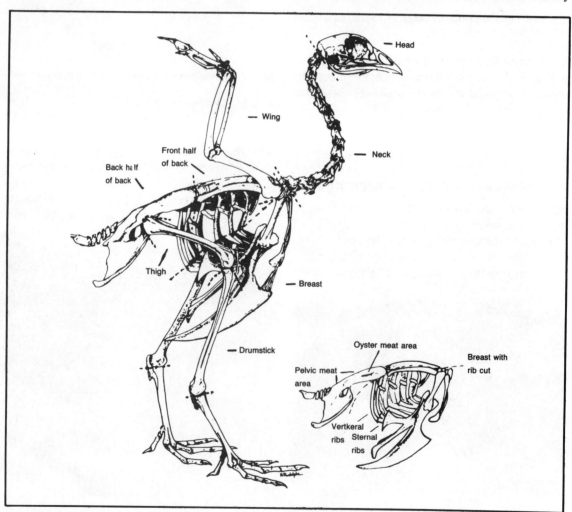

Fig. 5-62. Skeleton of chicken indicating points to sever parts.

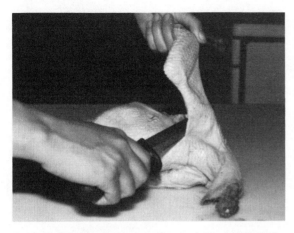

Fig. 5-63. Remove wings where they are jointed to the body.

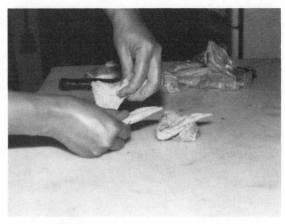

Fig. 5-65. Fold wing tip back behind joint for a more compact and attractive piece of meat.

separated. Otherwise disjoining the parts will be hard to do. Figure 5-62 shows where the various joints and separations are made. The following steps can be used for cutting into parts:

☐ Remove wings where they are jointed to body (Fig. 5-63). Bend wing back and cut between the joint (Fig. 5-64). The wing part can be made to look more compact and tempting by folding the tip back behind the joint (Fig. 5-65).

☐ Cut through joint between upper thigh and body to remove drumstick and thigh (Figs. 5-66 and 5-67). Technically, a drumstick is the lower thigh, with "drumstick" being a sort of slang word for this part. The legs are actually discarded at butchering

time and are properly called the shanks.

☐ Separate thigh from drumstick. The correct place to cut is across the visible line of fat which can be used as a guide (Figs. 5-68 and 5-69).

☐ Separate breast from back by running knife down across the top of backbones (Fig. 5-70). Standing the carcass on end will help to finish the cut (Fig. 5-71). When the knife reaches the bottom near the neck, the parts are separated by pulling down and apart (Figs. 5-72 and 5-73).

☐ The neck is removed by cutting as close to

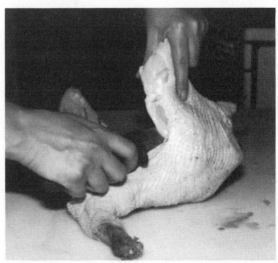

Fig. 5-66. To remove thigh and drumstick, begin to cut between upper thigh and body.

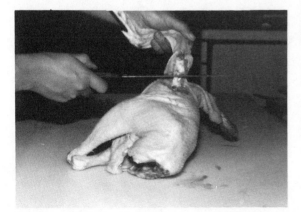

Fig. 5-64. Bend the wing back and cut between the exposed joint.

179

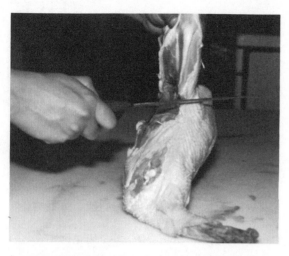

Fig. 5-67. Folding back will help expose the joint between the thigh and body.

Fig. 5-69. A perfect cut made through joint of thigh and drumstick.

the back as possible (Fig. 5-74).

  □ The back can be further cut in half by following the last small cage bone down to the main backbone (Fig. 5-75). The back is then snapped in two pieces (Fig. 5-76).

  □ To split breast, press down firmly in center of breastbone to crack bone (Fig. 5-77). Beginning at widest end of breast, slide knife down into center of V (Fig. 5-78). Proceed to finish cut toward other end to separate (Fig. 5-79).

  Each chicken can actually be cut into 11 pieces (Fig. 5-80). I regularly will thaw two broilers weighing 3 to 4 pounds each by placing them in a sink of hot tap water. In one hour, the birds are thawed. In another 10 minutes, the birds are completely cut and separated into 4 wings, 4 drumsticks, 4 thighs, and 24 white meat chunks cut from strips of the breast (Fig. 5-81).

  Breast fillets are removed by cutting along both sides of the breastbone. Remove skin first. By pulling the meat away from the breastbone along one of the cuts, two distinct strips of meat will be seen—a wide strip and a narrow one. The narrow strip will need to be loosened somewhat to free it from the bone. Do the same on the other side of the breastbone.

  These breast strips can then be cut into about 1-inch pieces. Each broiler breast will provide about 12 chunks to fry into chickenettes (with the follow-

Fig. 5-68. To separate thigh from drumstick, begin to cut over the visible line of fat for a perfect cut every time.

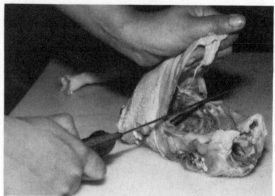

Fig. 5-70. Separate the breast from back by running a knife down across the top of backbones as shown.

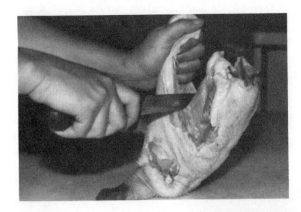

Fig. 5-71. Stand carcass on end to help finish removal of breast from back.

Fig. 5-72. Pull down and then apart. See Fig. 5-73.

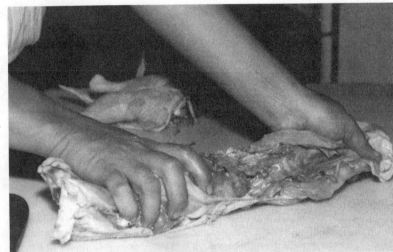

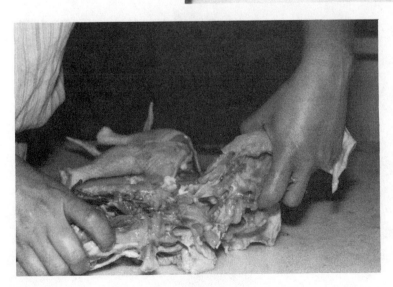

Fig. 5-73. Pulling apart will completely separate the breast from the back.

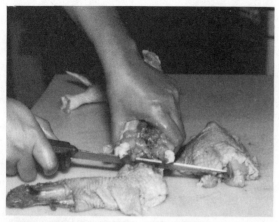

Fig. 5-74. Remove the neck by sliding a knife down toward body as close as possible.

Fig. 5-77. To split a breast, press down firmly over center bone to crack.

Fig. 5-75. The back can be cut in half by following the last small cage bone down to the main backbone with the knife.

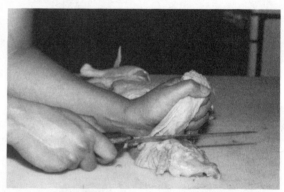

Fig. 5-78. At the widest end of the breast, slide the knife down into center of the V.

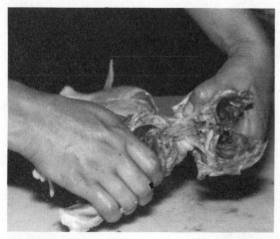

Fig. 5-76. Finish separating the back into two pieces by snapping apart.

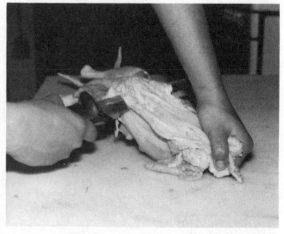

Fig. 5-79. Finish splitting the breast by cutting back toward the end.

182

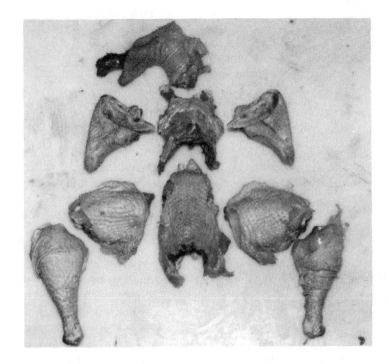

Fig. 5-80. All finished cuts but the two split breast pieces arranged in the position removed from the whole bird. The breast would lie under the two middle back pieces.

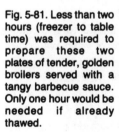

Fig. 5-81. Less than two hours (freezer to table time) was required to prepare these two plates of tender, golden broilers served with a tangy barbecue sauce. Only one hour would be needed if already thawed.

ing recipe) and then dipped into sauces contained in the other recipes. The backbones, necks, and bare breastbones are put back into one of the reusable freezer bags and refrozen to be used for soup later.

Chickenettes and Fried Chicken

4 cups dry pancake mix.
1 small pkg. dry Italian seasoned salad dressing mix.
1 egg.
2 cups water.

Beat egg, water, and 1/2 the salad dressing mix together in a bowl.

Mix the dry pancake mix with the other half of the dry salad dressing mix in the plastic freezer bag used previously to store one of the chickens. Make sure the bag is completely dry before placing these two dry ingredients inside.

Dip all chickens parts and breast chunks in the seasoned egg and water mixture first. Then place a few pieces at a time into the seasoned pancake mix in the bag. Shake to coat. Set on wax paper or flattened brown paper bags for about 10 minutes so the coating has time to set up.

Heat the cooking oil until small bubbles appear and place chickenettes into oil, a few at a time, and cook until light, done and golden brown. Drain on paper toweling.

Repeat the procedure with chicken parts. Fry eight to ten minutes until golden brown. Then place on towel lined platter and microwave on high for 15 minutes or place on baking sheets and oven fry remaining time for 30 minutes at 350 degrees Fahrenheit.

Tangy Barbecue Sauce

Mix:
1 cup prepared ketchup.
1/4 cup brown sugar.
1/4 teaspoon garlic powder.
1/4 teaspoon onion powder.

Sweet-"N"-Sour Plum Sauce

Mix:

1/2 cup heated, melted plum or apricot jelly.
1 tablespoon vinegar.
1/2 teaspoon grated green pepper.
1/4 teaspoon grated red pepper.

SANITATION GUIDELINES

Older chickens, although more resistant to germs than chicks, must drink clean water from clean containers. Chickens will barely drink fouled water. They will be found to peck at it quickly, shaking their heads because of the bad taste.

A hen's body and her egg contains about 65 percent water. The main source is drinking water. If the right ingredients, including water, are not made available to the hen, eggs cannot and will not be found in the hen, and therefore not laid.

A hen will "hold up" laying until drinkable water is available. Drinkable water is devoid of feed, manure, and litter that causes water to quickly sour, ferment, and foam. In warm temperatures, water is also needed for the chickens body to get rid of excess heat.

Warm drinking water in the sun will provide conditions for algae growth that will eventually turn water green. In unsanitary, germ-laden waterers, these conditions appear more quickly.

If roost-free waterers are situated above litter material, as on a stand, most fouling of water will be prevented. An occasional scrubbing with a stiff brush and disinfecting will be all that's needed.

Disinfecting equipment, feeders, and waterers can be done by using old fashion pine oil available at drug stores. For general disinfecting, cleaning and odor removal, pour 1 gallon of warm water over 4 tablespoons of pine oil in a bucket. Rinse equipment well after washing with the mixture.

Household chlorine bleach can be used on waterers and feeders, if done outdoors, away from the chickens and manure. Bleach on manure will cause fumes. The feeders and waterers should first be scrubbed, rinsed, then washed with diluted bleach and rinsed lightly to leave a small amount on surface to mix with the drinking water when filled for continued germ killing.

To further disinfect water and prevent algae

build up, potassium permanganate can be used in the drinking water. The tiny purple 300 mg. tablets can be obtained at the drug store. Make a stock solution by mixing 1 tablet into 1 quart of hot water. It takes a long time to dissolve so mix a day ahead. Use 1 tablespoon to 2 gallons of water. For disinfecting equipment, use 1 tablespoon to 1 gallon of water. Do not store stock solution for long periods as the solution loses it's disinfecting properties.

Before new flocks are placed in an empty building the interior should be cleaned. To keep dormant or active disease from infecting flocks between different broods using the same building, all old litter should first be removed down to bare earth or wood floors.

Cobwebs and dust are unsightly and are known to carry disease. These should be removed as carefully as possible to avoid inhalation of the dust. The use of a good respirator and a very long handled broom or mop will help. If conditions get very dusty, leave the building for awhile until the dust settles. Do not worry about every little speck as a disinfectant can be sprayed. Just get the large accumulations out of the way.

It use to be common practice years ago for every dedicated poultry raiser to scrub all bare walls and floors with boiling hot lye water. The use of modern vaccines and medicines has caused many small-scale raisers to relinquish dreaded fears of many diseases so such drastic measures of disinfecting the poultry house have pretty well ceased for small raisers. Commercial raisers cannot afford to relax disinfecting efforts but modern equipment helps speed today's disinfecting a bit more.

Many smaller raisers can get by with an ordinary spraying or whitewashing between flocks housed. An old disinfectant called cresol can be purchased at the drug store. Mixed according to label directions or at the rate of 1 pint bottle to 2 gallons of water, the mixture is sprayed over the interior walls and ceilings of the vacant building. Allow the building to air dry completely for a few days before placing birds inside.

Whitewashing, a common management practice for disinfecting poultry houses years ago, is still used today. A whitewashing mixture for disinfecting (when disease has been a problem) can be made by using lye (sodium hydroxide). Certain precautions must be taken in mixing and handling any lye preparation. Observe all label warnings to avoid being burned. Lye should always be added (slowly) to the surface of water. Lye becomes a boiling hot, spattering mixture when added to water. Wear goggles or a face shield and keep off skin, eyes, mucous membranes and clothing.

Whitewash Formula No. 1

4 gallons cold water.
1 to 13 ounce can of lye.
3 pounds of powdered agricultural lime.

Mix lime with water in a 5-gallon or larger nonaluminum container. Always add lye to the surface of water and do it slowly to avoid violent spattering as the cold water boils from the lye addition. The mixture is then painted on the vacant building walls when cool. Allow to dry before chickens are placed in building. The mixture will harm paint or varnish surfaces but does not affect metal and wood.

Another whitewash formula, which is not so dangerous to use, but does not kill disease germs as the lye formula does, can be sprayed or painted on to brighten the interior by mixing the following.

Whitewash Formula No. 2

4 gallons of water.
14-pound box of powdered milk.
50 pounds of agricultural lime.
Thin and strain for spraying.

SELLING TIPS

Many handlers give little or no thought to the possibility of culling, which may necessitate the disposal of part of his flock. When the decision is made, it might be at an inconvenient or unmarketable time of the year. If a handler is aware of some facts before selling is required, the procedure will become less of a problem or the need to sell can be avoided. Culling in order to reduce flock size is done for various reasons:

□ Feed and litter cost too high.
□ Chickens are not producing.
□ Chickens are producing too much.
□ Do not want to butcher.
□ Lack of food storage space.
□ Too many roosters.
□ Excess broody hatches.
□ Not enough shelter.
□ Too demanding.

Costs. Some inexperienced handlers do not realize that chickens are an investment. They are part of a handler's assets that require reinvesting to realize returns. Like the purchase of a house on time payments, their upkeep cost must also be figured into the budget so the capital does not become a loss.

If the chickens' upkeep costs are figured before the initial investment is made, their upkeep should not become a hardship for any handler, causing him to later cut down flock size.

Feed and litter are the prime concerns when figuring upkeep costs. By using Tables 3-1, 3-2, and 3-3, a handler can judge feed consumption per week, month, or year. Then by investigating area feed costs and availability, an approximate estimation can be made as to what actual feed costs will be (allowing 10 to 20 percent more for winter feed purchases).

Litter costs will vary because of individual housing circumstances that depend upon litter type used, climate, ventilation attained, amount of birds housed, whether floor or cage raised, if birds are ranged or allowed outdoors, and if provisions are made to prevent damp conditions around waterers.

An approximate average of $2 per week can be used to figure litter costs for 100 floor reared hens on straw in a fairly well insulated and ventilated building. This includes nest material used in 20 nests.

Low Production. When mature chickens are not producing, a handler quickly loses money. This calls for an overall review of management practices or a search for symptoms of disease. It is rare for laying age chickens to completely halt egg production unless under stress. Stress can result from molting, incorrect feed, parasites, disease, or uncomfortable environmental temperatures.

If you are to have a clear conscience, you cannot sell chickens under these conditions. First a handler should not burden other handlers with diseased or parasitic chickens. Second, if management is to blame, it should be corrected instead of allowing others to profit from your mistakes by purchasing good chickens that are only mismanaged.

When chickens are laying poorly under good management, then it is time to renew the flock or cull out poor or nonproducers. This can occur when chickens are going into their third season of laying or occasionally when fancy breeds have been chosen for production. Both can be a problem to sell.

Many inexperienced poultry buyers, because they are not familiar with breeds of chickens, consider the old-time general purpose breeds as being fancy. This is incorrect for most breeds, but you'll have a hard time trying to convince some of them that the breed is a good standard breed.

High Production. Occasionally, you find production so good that you cannot handle the excessive amount of eggs produced. If the excess of eggs daily is more than double the amount you normally use, then the flock is too large and should be reduced in size. Having an excess of only double enables the storage of such eggs for the use during period of time when production normally slacks. Storage of more than double the amount needed will bring an excess of storage eggs.

For example, if 50 egg breed hens are kept originally because 25 eggs daily are needed, during the high production period in the summer, almost 50 eggs can be produced almost daily for about 60 days total. The extra 25 eggs daily can be frozen or water glassed to be used during the molt period and colder weather, which may cause a slack in production totaling about 60 days.

If the correct amount of chickens have been purchased initially, there will not really be an overabundance of eggs that cannot be used through storage and daily use.

Butchering. A handler might not want to butcher extra chickens for various reasons. Some believe it's a waste to butcher good pullets or fancy breeds. Or maybe the handler cannot find the time to arrange for butchering and decides to sell instead. If a handler is beginning a new, young flock, he may prefer to sell the older hens rather than butcher for stewers. Stewers are the best type of chicken to use for pressure canning in jars. They have more flavor than others this way and they tenderize right in the jars when processed.

Storage. Lack of freezer space will cause some handlers to sell. Again, think of possible pressure canning poultry. There's no need to bone as the birds are canned with the bones and the meat comes off the bones easily for salads and sandwiches.

The decision to sell chickens should be made at a time when there is a market for them. Chickens do not sell well if the weather is cold. I suppose most people are put off by the idea of taking care of livestock in inclement weather. So plan to sell in good weather unless you have patience and time on your hands.

The best source of advertising is usually a local rural newspaper. Local farmers can tell you which newspaper is best. The latest edition of the *Ayer Directory of Publications* can be of some help in locating local rural newspapers, especially if you're new to the area. This directory can be found at most libraries.

If you're new to the area, you will still have to purchase some of the local newspapers to see which classify a larger amount of livestock. The best newspaper to advertise in is the one that reaches the most readers interested in chickens. The advertising rate is only secondary.

If you have a large number of chickens to sell, say 50 or more, it could pay to advertise in two papers if both seem good. Make it a habit to ask callers to identify the paper so next time you'll know which paper brings the most response.

When placing the ad, be as brief as possible. It's sometimes a good idea not to place the selling price in the ad. You might want to lower the asking price or make a deal with a potential buyer who might take all the chickens at a quantity price.

When placing an ad over the phone, have the person read it back to you slowly to avoid errors that could cause a delay in selling the chickens. For instance, the wrong phone number, price, or age of chickens placed in a weekly paper may delay sales. By then, the 25 chickens you want to sell will have eaten enough money in feed to pay for the ad. Errors can be costly even if the ad is run free another week as a courtesy gesture.

If you've done your homework and feel your chickens are worth what you're asking, do not be intimidated by callers who immediately ask you to lower your price. Take their phone number down and tell them you can call them in a couple of weeks if you decide to lower your asking price. Be polite. Tell them the ad has not been running long enough yet for you to realize the response you will get.

Do not fall for lines. Many people love to play with human nature. You may have callers exclaim, "I just called another ad, and they're selling their chickens at half the price you're asking!" If you know you're in the ballpark on your pricing, calmly and politely tell these callers, "Well, that sounds like a good deal. I would suggest you hurry over there and check it out." That will put most of those type of callers in their place. They will then either make up an excuse to come see your chickens or they were really not that interested, anyhow.

Another line from dealers is, "Well, I called earlier and someone there said the chickens were only $2 apiece." Don't get angry and tell him how wrong he is . . . he already knows. Politely tell him, "There must have been a misunderstanding earlier . . . The price of the chickens is $3 apiece."

A note of caution about potential buyers who come out to your place. Never, never let anyone—no matter how clean they appear—set one foot into your chicken coop, yard, pen, or building. This is one of the easiest ways for disease to enter your flock. Have the customer wait outdoors away from the chickens. Always try to have another member of your household assist you by watching the customers. Customers can inch their way into the building before you know it.

Chicken people are great, but they have this mysterious inner urge to want to see other handler's chickens and how they're "set up." Resist the urge to show off your flock. Bring out one of the available chickens for your customer to look at. Politely tell them you practice strict disease control by keeping strangers out of the coop.

An outdoor pen will help customers see the chickens. Do not let the visitors walk where your chickens walk. Do not allow them to come into the pen to help catch the chickens either. Catch them yourself or have a member of the household help and hand them out the door of the pen or building to the customer. You will later have a clear conscience and the rest of your flock may thank you for it.

PROTECTION AGAINST PREDATORS

Many people believe chickens should be allowed to range and scavenge for insects, seeds, and grass. They think it's cruel to keep chickens confined. It's not any crueler to confine them than it is to allow wild animals, pets, and livestock to maim, kill and devour. Cattle accidentally and purposely trample chickens and pigs eat live chickens quicker than you can say ah-oh—.The chickens do look good and healthy outdoors but they also look good to other animals.

Most predator losses can be avoided just by becoming aware of the problem and working to prevent predators from gaining access to your chickens. Chickens locked up tight are rarely bothered by predators. This should be a handler's first concern when predator proofing.

Weak and rusty stays and wires in fencing, broken windows, loose hinges and doors, faulty closures, and open top runs and pens should all flash warning lights to handlers because they don't always see these ways of entry before the predators do. A thorough inspection should be made by walking slowly over and around the entire building and any attached pens.

Weak sections of fencing should have square patches of fencing cut, placed over weak areas, and wired on in a weaving pattern with galvanized 17 gauge electric fence wire. If the fencing can be ripped when pulling it in two directions with your hands, the spot is weak. If numerous areas are weak, it's time to replace all the fencing involved.

Open top pens outdoors should be covered. Simply stretching lengths of chicken wire over the top will discourage many predators. Having a pen's top covered does not mean the small entry door to the building can be left open at night. This small door should still be closed up. If inconvenient to do so, perhaps because you must crouch down to enter a covered pen, a sturdy rope attached to the door and running through a couple of eyes (Fig. 5-82) can be used to close the door after the chickens are all in for the night.

Upon inspecting the buildings, pay particular attention to ground-level areas for possible predator entries. Even holes as small as 1 inch should be repaired because there are small predators and pests such as the least weasel that will go through.

On very old buildings, the entire bottom edge might be rotted. Do not let this keep you from performing the needed repair. By using utility-grade furring strips, boards, strong glue, caulking, and a few nails, the building can be made safe.

New buildings should have a concrete footing (rat wall) installed below ground level and under exterior walls. On existing buildings dig as close to the exterior wall as possible. If you do not want to invest much money in an older building, quite a bit of concrete costs can be saved by substituting some of the concrete mix with rocks, old metal fence posts, and iron stakes. First pour about 6 inches of mixed concrete into the trench. Then place the scrap iron and rocks over the concrete and tamp down well. Finish the fill with more concrete and pack down, sloping the top from a couple inches over the edge of the building and out so rain will be diverted away from building.

The trash fill will help cut costs and serve to discourage rats and other animals from digging under. Rats can chew through almost anything, including concrete, but the idea is to discourage their attempts and possibly keep them out long enough until the barn cat takes care of them.

Knowing the kind of predator that is preying on your chickens will help a handler know how to handle the situation and further take steps to end the problem. This calls for a bit of knowledge about

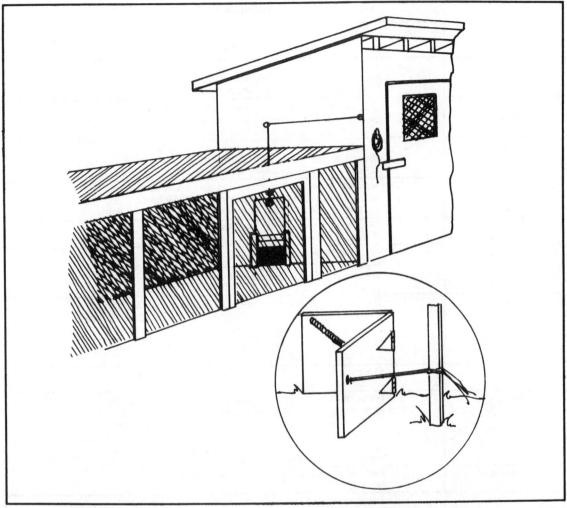

Fig. 5-82. Close the poultry house door for the night by using a thin rope run through eyes and attached to a loose sliding door (top) or use a spring between the door and entrance so the door will close when the attached rope is loosened (below).

signs left behind and the basic habits of predators. See Table 5-8.

Most states have many similar wild animals that will prey on domestic poultry. Some states have wild animals that frequent their area only. A few states have such an individual problem with some wild animals that federally funded organizations and programs are set up to research and control predatory animals. In California, for instance, coyotes are considered the main problem. Bobcats are a minor problem where turkeys are grown.

Studies were conducted on large chicken ranches where bobcats were monitored and radioed while locked in buildings with the chickens. The bobcats seemed to be less of a problem than thought when monitored in this way. The experiment included darkening the buildings to induce the cats' preying instincts. The cats remained up in the building's rafters and only harassed the chickens. None of the chickens were attacked and killed.

Table 5-8. Predator Indication Guide.

Predator	Signs
Bobcat	Said to be minor problem with chickens on the West Coast. Usually they attack ranged turkeys.
Cat (domestic)	Usually only 1 or 2 chicks devoured (on premises by tomcats) with evidence of wings and legs left only. Will kill nightly. Trap near entries.
Coyote	Usually seen by handlers as they are not very shrewd in their attempts to gain entry into the poultry house. Fairly easy trapping.
Dog	Maimed, missing birds, wires and doors torn down. Will kill and maim many or just one. Usually takes bird home but may hide and eat (usually) the whole bird.
Fisher	Said to be a problem on the East Coast only. Will store extra food, returning later to eat it.
Fox	Will remove whole birds, day and night, usually night. Chicken legs can be found at fox den entries. Will travel 1/2 mile or more with the kill. Tough to see and trap.
Hawk	Bothers ranged chickens. Hunts during the day. Swoops down and takes whole bird. Depending on how adept the hawk is, you might not hear chicken squawk when attacked.
Mink	Usually remove smaller chicks only. Discharges an acrid musk which can be smelled hours later.
Muskrat	Prefers pond foods, but will attack chickens, eating insides out, leaving rest of carcass.
Owl	Great Horned Owl mainly. Usually takes head off only on large chickens, small chicks taken whole, at night, but will hunt daylight, enter through 1 foot square openings in building. Will attempt flying through panes of glass upon spotting chickens. Will take roosting chickens from trees. Headless chicken carcasses found in area.
Opossum	Eats insides out on premises, likes eggs, picks away at bones.
Raccoon	Takes whole carcass, eats fresh kills, sometimes breast eaten only, hunts every other night. Bits of coarse fur may be attached to entry.
Rat	Contusions and bites on legs, chicks dragged into rat tunnels usually with part of body (such as head and neck) down in tunnel, eaten around bone. Look for tunnels going under building walls and rat droppings near feed pans. Will come out and eat right with chickens. Will travel from building to building. Pull and eat feathers for protein off roosting chickens.
Skunk	Eats insides out on premises, likes eggs. Will take a broody's eggs out from under her. Sometimes faint skunk odor noticed around building, but not usually.
Weasel	Bites on neck found, will attack only a few or a lot, bluish coloration of skin about head and under wings. Sometimes run in family packs. Occasionally a faint skunk odor may be evident. Least Weasel will enter 1 opening.
Wolf	Usually chickens are considered too small a game for them.

I wouldn't say this experiment proved bobcats do not attack chickens because I've trained some chicken-eating dogs this same way with good results. By beginning when the dog first goes after the chickens, even if the chickens are actually killed and eaten, I place the dog into the pen with the chickens and lock him in there for two to three days. Of course I watch him closely when first put in. Most dogs cower and look a bit embarrassed, but the chickens aren't killed. Some may romp around after the chickens at first, but they're immediately scolded when I hear the commotion. Always train a dog by having it near you and the chickens often. Of course, a real chicken killer won't be trained to leave the chickens alone when you're gone.

RECORD KEEPING

One of the most common mistakes handlers make is to not keep records of egg production, feed costs, litter costs, and equipment costs (Tables 5-9 and 5-10). Without a record of these figures and costs, a handler cannot possible know which way he is headed. If he's going in the hole, he should definitely be the first to know so amendments can be made. If he's doing great, he will not know for sure unless he can show it on paper.

Keeping a record of laying production, mortalities, and upkeep costs can help a handler to spot areas that should be improved. Different broods of chickens can also be compared so the handler can ascertain whether the breeds he has chosen are good for his circumstances.

Table 5-9. Purchase and Sales Record Sample.

	Month-Paid Out			Month-Received	
Date	April	Amount	Date	April	Amount
Ap-11	1,000# lay. mash L. Co-op	$103.00	Ap-1	5 doz. eggs	$4.50
Ap-20	6 pkgs. terra. H. Store	12.60	Ap-3	4 doz. eggs	3.00
			Ap-5	10 doz. eggs	9.00
Ap-23	500# cr. corn Mr. Jones	35.00	Ap-6	8 doz. eggs	7.20
			Ap-8	5 doz. eggs	4.50
Ap-23	500# wheat Farmer Brown	35.00	Ap-11	10 doz. eggs	9.00
Ap-23	100# oyster shell L. Co-op	7.00	Ap-18	10 doz. eggs	9.00
			Ap-24	5 roosters-W.R.	15.00
Ap-23	600# oats Kellerman	36.00	Ap-27	5 doz. eggs	4.50
	Subtotal	228.60	Ap-28	10 culled hens-W.R.	30.00
			Ap-29	10 doz. eggs	9.00
Date	May	Amount	Ap-29	5 roosters-R.I.	15.00
Ma-18	1,000# lay. mash L. Co-op	$103.00	Ap-29	5 doz. eggs	4.50
Ma-20	5-day classified	10.00		Subtotal	124.20
			Date	May	Amount
Ma-21	pkg. multi-vitamins @$4.95	4.95	Ma-1	8 doz. eggs	7.20
	4 hanging feeders H. Store	24.00			

Table 5-10. Production and Management Record Sample.

SUNDAY	MONDAY	TUESDAY	WEDNESDAY	THURSDAY	FRIDAY	SATURDAY
	1 BA- 47 WR-10 BM- 9 Tot.- 66	2 BA- 38 WR-12 BM-10 Tot.- 60	3 BA-48 WR- 9 BM- 9 Tot.- 66	4 BA- 40 WR-11 BM-10 Tot.-61	5 BA-50 WR- 9 BM- 8 Tot.-67	6 BA- 45 WR-12 BM- 9 Tot.-66
7 BA-47 WR- 8 BM- 9 Tot.-64	8 BA- 51 WR- 7 BM-10 Tot.-68	9 BA-47 WR- 6 BM- 9 Tot.-62	10 *clipped beaks BA- 45 WR- 9 BM-10 Tot.-64	11 BA- 55 WR-12 BM-12 Tot.-79	12 BA- 48 WR-10 BM- 9 Tot.-67	13 *1 WR broody BA- 52 WR-12 BM-12 Tot.-76
14 *Pen up broody BA- 49 WR-10 BM- 9 Tot.-68	15 *Sold 5 BA- 55 WR-12 BM- 10 Tot.-77	16 BA- 50 WR-10 BM- 15 Tot.-75	17 BA- 54 WR-13 BM-13 Tot.-80	18 *hen killed BA- 52 WR-14 BM- 14 Tot.-80	19 BA- 55 WR-13 BM- 12 Tot.-80	20 *hen killed BA- 50 WR-10 BM-11 Tot.-71

If their are many purchases for any one item of equipment, perhaps it is because the equipment is not of good quality and another brand should be tried. Did the total amount of pullets and cockerels raised meet your specific requirements? If not, you'll know exactly how many to purchase the following year if a record was kept of what was previously raised.

Recording the loss of any hens or roosters will help to later identify the cause, especially if quite a few are lost. Any symptoms they displayed should also be recorded.

By checking over records kept, you might find that egg production is better when certain procedures or feed practices are used, but you will not readily see this unless it's written down.

The main reason for keeping accurate records is to save money when an overall view is made of the records at the end of the season. The little time it actually takes to keep records is money well saved the next time around. Even if the extent of your record keeping consists only of jotting down figures over the days on a calendar, a handler will find the answers to many questions later when this is reviewed.

Table 5-10 is a sample record for a flock of 100 hens and 12 roosters, with the three breeds penned separately. Breed names can be easily abbreviated because of the variety of letters the various names begin with. Simply abbreviate the breed in the pen, the pen number or the building and write down how many eggs are collected daily from each group of chickens. Record keeping will be easier if a large flock is divided into smaller groups by penning. It will be tough to identify problems in a large floor-raised flock if this is not done.

In Table 5-10, there are 65 Black Australorp hens with three roosters in 3 pens. Another pen contains 15 White Rock hens with two roosters. A fifth pen contains 20 Black Minorca hens with seven roosters.

A handler should be able to spot four pertinent problems in this sample calendar record.

□ First, at this time of the year, a handler will expect to receive 70 to 80 percent production from his hens. In this flock, the 65 Black Australorps should be laying 45 to 52 eggs per day (70 percent × 65 = 45 and 80 percent × 65 = 52), the White Rocks 10 to 12 and the Black Minorcas 14 to 16. By glancing at the calendar's recordings, you can clearly see the WR's have not attained this goal by the 9th, so perhaps there are egg eaters here. The beaks are clipped on the 10th. A significant improvement in production begins on the 11th. The BM's pick up in the same time meaning there were a few egg eaters here, too.

☐ The calendar also tells you that the hen that went broody on the 13th, is still broody on the 19th after your attempt to break her on the 14th. Because she is good and broody, eggs can be set under her if desired.

☐ The handler further sees the BM's should be doing better. The five extra roosters (he first thought wouldn't matter) are removed and sold. The BM's production improves almost imme-diately–a sign the overabundance of roosters were affecting laying.

☐ The handler finds a hen killed on the 18th and 20th from the same pen. The insides have been eaten only. There is no place for a skunk or op-possum to enter, and this sign indicates no other predator. The handler assumes cannibalism is pres-ent in the flock. He watches more closely and finds one culprit, removes her, and that ends the deaths.

Chapter 6

Feeding Pullets and Hens

The correct feeding of adult chickens is just as important as it was when they were chicks. It takes certain vitamins, minerals, fats and water to make the incredible egg.

Chickens seem to know what they need in the way of nutrients. It's just an instinct nature has bestowed upon all animals. When domesticated animals must rely on man to provide the correct nutrients, they are under the handler's care not nature's care.

FEED CONSUMPTION

As with chicks, adult chickens do not eat in order to feel full. They eat mainly to acquire energy their brain tells their body it should have. This energy is converted from the fats available in the chickens' ration.

Pullets and hens need extra energy to lay eggs. Their bodies also need extra energy in colder temperatures in order to keep them warmer. This extra energy calls for extra fat consumption, not necessarily extra fat in the ration, because the chickens will eat the right amount of feed to acquire the right amount of fat to be turned into energy.

To prove this point, a very low fat diet was recorded as causing birds to eat as much as 30 percent more than similar birds fed a high energy-high fat ration.* A well-balanced 14.5 percent layer ration contains just the right amount of fat in relation to the quantity of feed the chickens are known to consume for their age. Because of these facts, certain amounts of proteins, vitamins, and minerals can be placed in the feed with the knowledge and assurance that the chickens will consume a certain percentage of nutrients because they will be eating a specific amount of feed. On the other extreme, a very high fat diet will cause birds to eat less but the nutrient requirements will not be met and neither will egg production.

The higher the temperature the less feed the

*Nutrient Requirements of Poultry, 8th revised edition, copyright 1984, National Academy of Sciences.

chickens consume. The lower the temperature the more feed consumed. Each temperature drop of almost 2 degrees in a building's interior will induce the chickens to eat 1 1/2 times more feed. Much money can be saved on feed costs by providing housing temperatures as close as possible to 75 degrees Fahrenheit (23.88 degrees C.) through the use of ventilation and body heat.

In very cold weather, allowing the chickens' house to stay at below-freezing temperatures can cause 100 heavy breed layers to consume an extra 374 pounds of feed a month. This would be around $50 worth of extra feed in most areas. This extra money would be better spent on proper ventilation and housing that would also bring a winter supply of eggs because of the heated environment.

It's no wonder chickens won't lay eggs in the winter when their handlers keep them at below 45 degrees Fahrenheit (7.22 degrees C.). The handler then thinks the chickens are eating too much (which they are) and he proceeds to give them a cheaper feed (which is normally higher in fat). He might even add extra protein and think this will do the trick. The chickens eat less of this feed because they acquire their energy needs quicker with this extra-fat diet. They are, however, receiving way fewer nutrients because of the decrease in feed consumption. The lack of nutrients causes the egg production to plummet to zero. Now the handler believes he has a very bad strain of chickens. This handler is actually working against himself.

Because the feed consumption of chickens will vary depending upon the available fat and calories in the ration, the weather, housing temperatures and the chickens' rate of production, Tables 6-1 and 6-2 can only be used as a basic guide.

NUTRITIONAL REQUIREMENTS

Pullet and hen feeding is entirely different from the feed used to start and grow chicks or, for that matter, most other types of poultry. This is because you are aiming for something other than growth, good feathering, and skeletal formation. You now want good egg production, and this calls for different quantities of protein, fats, minerals, and vitamins to enable the reproduction system to properly function.

Because protein is so highly regarded when growing chicks, many handlers make the false assumption that protein is what also causes hens to lay. They believe the more protein fed the more eggs produced. Chickens have a very limited capacity for the storage of protein in their bodies to use toward the production of eggs.

Egg production will increase some if more protein is fed, but not from an economical standpoint in comparison with the extra cost of a higher-protein feed. A balanced ration also takes into consideration the highest egg production to be received weighed against cost factors. The increased egg production from a costly higher protein feed just does not justify or outweigh it's use.

Table 6-1. Body Weights, Feed Requirements, and Production of Egg Breed Pullets.

Age (weeks)	Body Weight	Weekly Feed Consumption	Daily Egg Production
20	2.99 lbs. (1,360 g)	1.01 lbs. (460 g)	-
22	3.00 lbs. (1,425 g)	1.16 lbs. (525 g)	10%
24	3.31 lbs. (1,500 g)	1.31 lbs. (595 g)	38%
26	3.47 lbs. (1,575 g)	1.47 lbs. (665 g)	64%
30	3.80 lbs. (1,725 g)	1.70 lbs. (770 g)	88%
40	4.00 lbs. (1,815 g)	1.70 lbs. (770 g)	80%
50	4.12 lbs. (1,870 g)	1.69 lbs. (765 g)	74%
60	4.19 lbs. (1,900 g)	1.66 lbs. (755 g)	68%
70	4.19 lbs. (1,900 g)	1.63 lbs. (740 g)	62%

Adapted from *Nutrient Requirements of Poultry, 8th revised edition,* copyright 1984, National Academy of Sciences.

Table 6-2. Body Weights, Feed Requirements and Production of General Purpose Breeds.

Age (weeks)	Body Weights Males	Body Weights Females	Average Weekly Feed Consumption Each bird	Daily Egg Production
20	5.29 lbs. (2,400 g)	4.26 lbs. (1,930 g)	1.43 lbs. (650 g)	-
22	5.82 lbs. (2,640 g)	4.65 lbs. (2,110 g)	1.57 lbs. (715 g)	10%
24	7.06 lbs. (3,200 g)	5.40 lbs. (2,450 g)	1.90 lbs. (862 g)	15%
26	7.81 lbs. (3,540 g)	6.02 lbs. (2,730 g)	2.20 lbs. (1,000 g)	30%
28	8.27 lbs. (3,750 g)	6.35 lbs. (2,880 g)	2.45 lbs. (1,109 g)	56%
30	8.60 lbs. (3,900 g)	6.61 lbs. (3,000 g)	2.45 lbs (1,109 g)	75%
32	9.02 lbs. (4,090 g)	6.81 lbs. (3,090 g)	2.45 lbs. (1,109 g)	80%
34	9.31 lbs. (4,220 g)	6.90 lbs. (3,130 g)	2.45 lbs. (1,109 g)	78%
36	9.57 lbs. (4,340 g)	6.97 lbs. (3,160 g)	2.45 lbs. (1,109 g)	76%
38	9.81 lbs. (4,450 g)	7.01 lbs. (3,180 g)	2.43 lbs. (1,102 g)	73%
40	10.01 lbs. (4,540 g)	7.01 lbs. (3,180 g)	2.41 lbs. (1,095 g)	72%

*Adapted from *Nutrient Requirements of Poultry, 8th revised edition*, copyright 1984, National Academy of Sciences.

Most pullets are not yet fully grown when egg production begins. Extra protein can be used for their growth but there really is no need. They will attain the correct adult size slowly on their own with a balanced 14 1/2 percent layer ration. There is no need to grow them faster unless you plan to butcher them soon. In that case, there is no longer a need to speak of layers and their nutriment needs for egg production.

Over the years researchers have caused the basic nutrient requirements of chickens to teeter. Basically the principles of nutritionally feeding layers has been the same. Researchers have known the needs for the basic proteins, fats, minerals and vitamins. Today's requirements for layers is just more balanced. Next year's research will balance the requirements for rations even more, and so on. Because poultry producer's are commercialized now more than any other time in history, there is more research being done to help the industry.

There is no secrets about on the nutritional needs of poultry because there are too many commercial feed companies competing to sell good feed to consumers. Thank goodness for competition! If there were no competition between feed companies, the poultry industry might have owned all that knowledge, too.

Various poultry companies in the industry perform their own research on the nutritional requirements of broilers and layers. Feed companies also perform their own research in their own company laboratories. The U.S. Department of Agriculture, in a effort to help growers, conducts similar research activities. Then there's a multitude of universities researching poultry needs on top of all this other research, with the reports from the committees involved with the National Academy of Sciences (National Research Council) considered, by most, to rank highest. See Table 6-3.

SOURCES AND NEED FOR PROTEIN

Luckily the amount of protein needed for adult chickens is less than when they were chicks or there would be quite a monthly feed bill. Protein is the most expensive ingredient per pound, aside from all labor involved, in making up any ration.

If a high percentage of protein was required constantly for layers, store-bought eggs would reflect this price and it would still be an attainable ideal to raise our own chickens for eggs.

Because protein is no longer needed to stimulate growth in adult birds, the protein content of the ration is lowered. Chickens can only utilize a certain amount of protein. This amount is the recommended 14 1/2 percent for layers. Any ex-

Table 6-3. Nutrient Requirements of Egg Breed Layers and Breeder Pullets.

			Laying	Breeding
Calories	Energy Base kcal ME/kg Diet (per 2.2 lbs. feed) = 2,900 or, 1,318 Calories (per 1.1 lbs. feed)*			
	Protein	%	14.5	14.5
Amino Acids	Arginine	%	0.68	0.68
	Glycine and Serine	%	0.50	0.50
	Histidine	%	0.16	0.16
	Isoleucine	%	0.50	0.50
	Leucine	%	0.73	0.73
	Lysine	%	0.64	0.64
	Methionine + cystine	%	0.55	0.55
	Methionine	%	0.32	0.32
	Phenylalanine + tyrosine	%	0.80	0.80
	Phenylalanine	%	0.40	0.40
	Threonine	%	0.45	0.45
	Tryptophan	%	0.14	0.14
	Valine	%	0.55	0.55
	Linoleic acid	%	1.00	1.00
Minerals	Calcium	%	3.40	3.40
	Chlorine	%	0.15	0.15
	Copper	mg	6.00	8.00
	Iodine	mg	0.30	0.30
	Iron	mg	50.00	60.00
	Magnesium	mg	500.00	500.00
	Manganese	mg	30.00	60.00
	Phosphorous, available	%	0.32	0.32
	Potassium	%	0.15	0.15
	Selenium	mg	0.10	0.10
	Sodium	%	0.15	0.15
	Zinc	mg	50.00	65.00
Vitamins	Biotin	mg	0.10	0.15
	Choline	mg	?	?
	Folacin	mg	0.25	0.35
	Niacin	mg	10.00	10.00
	Pantothenic acid	mg	2.20	10.00
	Pyridoxine	mg	3.00	4.50
	Riboflavin	mg	2.20	3.80
	Thiamin	mg	0.80	0.80
	Vitamin A	IU	4,000.00	4,000.00
	Vitamin B_{12}	mg	0.004	0.004
	Vitamin D	ICU	500.00	500.00
	Vitamin E	IU	5.00	10.00
	Vitamin K	mg	0.50	0.50

Adapted from *Nutrient Requirements of Poultry, 8th revised edition,* copyright 1984, National Academy of Sciences.
*These can be considered the same as the Calories commonly used to denote human food, but by scientific measurements, kilocalorie (kcal) is the precise term of measurement.

cess is not stored in the body; it is passed in droppings.

The protein requirements for layers is actually a requirement for the amino acids the protein contains. Amino acids allow the protein to be absorbed in the chicken's body. Deficiencies or excesses of certain essential amino acids cause feed intake to decline by influencing the areas of the brain controlling feed intake.*

Roosters actually have less need for the amino acids than laying hens, but the layers have less of a need for amino acids than fast growing broilers. Protein makes productive use of consumed energy (fats). Not enough protein in the ration will cause fat deposits. Fat chickens do not lay eggs; they only lay around.

The highest quantity source of protein comes from animal by-products and soybean concentrates. Animal by-products includes fish scales, hides, blood, feathers, hair, bones, intestines (viscera), feet, legs, heads, chick culls (usually eggs breed cockerels), and other organic animal and fish matter from slaughter houses and rendering plants. These by-products have gone into animal and pet feeds for years. Commercial soap is also made from these and other recycled by-products. If you look closely at your favorite dry dog food, you may find some animal hairs mixed in.

Recycled by-products from animals are fed, rubbed on, worn, sprinkled, dusted, plowed in, poured, compressed, woven, bottled, chunked and pelleted daily. I'm sure nature intended these "leftovers" to be put to good use and not wasted.

Heat-treated soybeans, not those fresh from the field should be used for poultry feed. Whole fresh soybeans are toxic, along with a few other protein sources. Overheating will deteriorate the protein, but it must be heat-treated to dry and remedy the toxic substances. All soybean concentrates are heat-treated.

Protein concentrates are always used and mixed in conjunction with other products—mainly grains. They are not fed alone. All are ground together evenly to produce a mash or are molded and broken down to form pellets. The concentrates will not mix with whole or cracked grains because it will sift down between the grains and end up in the bottom of the feeder to be scratched out or undesirably eaten in its concentrated form.

Companies producing concentrates determine recommended formulas for their use in mixing various types of poultry feed. Feed dealers, co-ops, feed and grain stores and elevators have the formulas for mixing the concentrates into a starter, grower, broiler, or layer mash.

If you do your own butchering of beef, you can let the hens peck clean some of the excess bones. Make sure the bones are fresh and do not remain in the pen to decay before being fully eaten. This won't cause cannibalism. Chickens are meat eaters. Their nutrient requirements prove this. They would make very poor vegetarians.

The excess bones have bits of meat, fat, and muscle attached that the chickens will devour. Bits of scrap fat and meat can also be fed. Some can be frozen in large garbage bags and taken out daily to feed the chickens. There is no need to defrost. Young chickens sometimes turn their beak up to this treat at first until they get a taste. So be careful not to leave these uneaten scraps in the pen long enough for them to decay.

FATS AND ENERGY

Fats and carbohydrates are utilized by hens when being converted into energy. Adult chickens need more energy and thereby more of these ingredients in the diet as compared to young chicks. Adult males will need more to produce energy than hens because the larger the bird the more energy required to maintain the body.

This energy is measured in calories. A calorie is the amount of heat required to raise the temperature of 1 gram (28.35 ounces) of water from 16.5 degrees Celsius (329 degrees Fahrenheit) to 17.5 degrees Celsius (347 degrees Fahrenheit). A kilocalorie (Kcal) is 1,000 small calories or 1 large Calorie. This is the nutritional unit term used most often. Scientists can measure the energy that will

---

Nutrient Requirements of Poultry, 8th revised edition, copyright 1984, National Academy of Sciences.

be available to chickens from various feeds by burning the feeds and measuring the heat produced during the process.

Not all energy produced by feeds goes into maintaining the chickens' body or producing eggs. Some is lost through the droppings . It is the energy used for the body's maintenance in which you should be interested. This is called the *metabolizable energy* (ME) value of a feed. This is how the energy values in feed are measured.

If an excess of these calories is consumed, because other nutrients, such as protein, are lacking (causing birds to eat more in trying to obtain the needed nutrient) the calories are not utilized by the chickens, and they become fat deposits on the carcass of the bird. Fat birds do not breed or lay well. This is why commercial breeder hens are limited as to the amount of feed they consume. Limiting the calories alone would not keep the hens from gaining weight because chickens will eat until they obtain enough calories.

An overweight hen is caused mainly by the increased level of estrogen hormones and an overconsumption of total energy. When estrogen hormones are produced in a hen when reproduction begins, it causes fat to naturally deposit in areas of the body. This is why the estrogenic compound, diethyl-stillbestrol, was implanted in pellet form into the necks of chickens years ago to produce fat on broilers. This was much less expensive than overfeeding in order to produce the fat. It was banned from use in the 1950s when it was found the pellets did not completely dissolve and left residues of the hormone in the butchered carcass.

An overconsumption of total energy occurs when chickens are fed an imbalanced diet. They thereby eat to acquire a certain level of nutrients the imbalanced ration is deficient in, and they accordingly overeat the fat-producing ingredients they actually need.

Further, chickens fed low-energy diets of about 2,600 kcal/kg (or 1,182 calories per 1.1 lbs. feed) have been recorded as eating as much as 30 percent more than similar birds fed diets containing 3,200 kcal/kg (or 1,455 Calories per 1.1 lbs. feed). Thus, in comparison to high-energy diets, low to moderate energy levels allow birds to eat more and, therefore, to consume greater amounts of nutrients unless lesser concentration of nutrients are used.*

If the total ingredients in a ration are balanced to meet the hen's functioning needs, there will be no chance of her overeating and thereby consuming more calories than needed. The free choice method of feeding is used so the chickens can balance their needs.

Most energy producing fats and carbohydrates in poultry feeds come from animal and poultry by-products acquired from rendering plants, restaurant greases, and vegetable and plant oils.

VITAMINS

Vitamins not sufficiently found in feed ingredients are supplemented by adding prepackaged vitamin mixes to feed as it is ground. Handlers knowledgeable about vitamin needs for their hens can avoid deficiencies in rations. There are 13 main vitamins used poultry rations: Biotin, choline, folacin, niacin, pantothenic acid, pyridoxine, riboflavin, thiamin, and Vitamins A, B_{12}, D, E, and K.

☐ Biotin promotes growth and prevents perosis. A deficiency of biotin can cause fatty liver disease and kidney syndrome. Sources are dried brewer's yeast, liver, molasses, and green leafy plants.

☐ Choline also prevents perosis.

☐ Folacin (folic acid) prevents loss of egg production, anemia, loss of feather pigment and poor feathering. Sources are soybean meal, wheat bran and middlings, fish meal, liver meal, etc.

☐ Niacin. A niacin deficiency can cause hock disorders and poor feather qualities.

☐ Pantothenic acid. A severe deficiency causes loss of feathers from the head and necks, liver damage and reduced hatchability. The source for pantothenic acid is calcium pantothenate.

☐ Pyridoxine (B_6). Deficiencies are rare but if they occur in hens it will cause a lack of appetite,

---

Nutrient Requirements of Poultry, 8th revised edition, copyright 1984, National Academy of Sciences.

thereby reducing body weight, egg production, and hatchability.

☐ Riboflavin. Promotes growth and hatchability. There are few sources.

☐ Thiamin (B₁). Maintains the appetite and obtains energy from carbohydrates and protein. Sources include cereal grains and their by-products.

☐ Vitamin A. Used to grow and maintain glands and the mucous membranes in body cavities. Sources are yellow corn, legumes, grasses, fish oils, and supplements.

☐ Vitamin B_{12}. Promotes growth and hatchability. A deficiency causes perosis and a fatty heat, liver, kidneys. Sources are animal origin feeds and poultry droppings.

☐ Vitamin D_3. Is needed for calcium absorption to prevent rickets. A good source is cod-liver oil.

☐ Vitamin E. Is the antisterility vitamin for good fertility and hatchability. Alfalfa meal is rich in Vitamin E.

☐ Vitamin K. Prevents excessive bleeding and shortens the time for blood to clot. A deficiency can cause death from less of blood during a minor injury. This vitamin is synthesized by bacteria in the intestine.

Vitamin C is not needed in poultry rations as chickens are able to synthesize the vitamin on their own.

MINERAL NEEDS

Minerals are needed by hens to perform various functions within the body. They furnish no energy but they are essential for the utilization of energy and protein. The minerals known to be needed by chickens are calcium, chlorine, copper, iodine, iron, magnesium, manganese, phosphorus, potassium, selenium, sodium and zinc.

☐ Calcium is required for maintenance of the hen's bones. If a ration is deficient in calcium while a hen is laying, the available calcium will go to the shell of the egg (which is 95 percent calcium). This leaves little for bone maintenance. Too little or too much calcium in diet, and eggshells become thin.

It is also used for efficient feed utilization and blood clotting.

☐ Chlorine is used with other minerals to develop bones and to maintain good-quality shells.

☐ Copper prevents anemia in birds because it builds blood cells. It prevents depigmentation of red feathers.

☐ Iodine prevents poor growth and poor egg production. It is also used to produce thyroid hormones.

☐ Iron builds blood cells and prevents depigmentation of red feathers.

☐ Magnesium is used in the bones along with other minerals.

☐ Maganese is used in combination with calcium and phosphorus to prevent malformations of the bones and to prevent thin-shelled breakable eggs.

☐ Phosphorus provides good shell and bone formation. Lack of phosphorus can cause rickets.

☐ Potassium is needed in small quantities. A complete absence of potassium can cause poor egg production and thin shells.

☐ Selenium works with Vitamin E. Lack of selenium will produce poor growth and egg production, and birds that bruise easily.

☐ Sodium is needed for hens to consume adequate amounts of drinking water. Because an egg is over 65 percent water, the intake of water must be adequate.

☐ Zinc helps promote egg production. It works with other minerals.

The majority of minerals mixed into poultry feed are provided as supplements because grains do not provide mineral needs. Most calcium is furnished by the addition of bone meal, calcium carbonate, phosphates, limestone, calcite grit, and oyster shell.

Oyster shell is usually fed free choice by handlers to assure calcium needs are met. Too much calcium can actually cause bad shells and deposits in the kidney ducts. This is why the mineral in shell form should be fed free choice. Combining too much calcium in the mixed ration forces the chickens to consume too much calcium.

MASH VERSUS PELLET FEEDING

Because of the extra processing that must be done to pellet feeds, they are more expensive to purchase. Pelleting feeds involves keeping the ground-up feed at a higher than normal moisture level so it can be pressed through various die molds while being heat-treated. It's similar to the procedure used when potatoes are squeezed through a ricer utensil when cooking. The final product is then cooled and bagged. A smaller form called "crumbles" is processed mainly for chicks.

Pelleted feeds that get scratched out of feed pans by the chickens can be seen by them before it's lost forever in the litter. Mash that is scratched out of feed pans onto litter quickly sifts into the litter, and is therefore uneaten and wasted. Therefore, feed wastage is claimed to be less with pellets. Also, because pelleted feed takes longer to fully digest, it allows for better assimilation of the nutrients it contains.

Chickens can taste food. When the palatability of grains is similar to that of a mash, chickens will prefer the grains over the mash because of the larger form of the feed. The same is true of pellets. This is the same reason some people enjoy crispy pizza or crispy chicken.

When chickens eagerly eat a mash, they occasionally will seem to be choking because the crop is being impacted quicker with this fine feed. They do not enjoy eating this way. Chickens love to eat a moistened mash, and grains and pellets help chickens enjoy their feed.

Pelleted feeds can be mixed with the right amount of scratch grains for the balanced nutrients needed daily. The high cost of commercially prepared layer pellets usually deter handlers from using them.

SCRATCH GRAINS

Scratch grains are nothing more than different grains mixed together. Chickens love them as they add variety to their diet. Large grains should be cracked so they are more digestible, but it's all right to feed all whole grains.

It's better to mix your own grains than to purchase commercial scratch feeds because most packaged scratch mixtures contain about three-quarters corn and very little wheat and oats. The proportions should be listed on the label.

Begin by purchasing equal amounts of grains available in your area. Usually grains will be less expensive if it is purchased directly from the grower. You might even be able to buy grains that are already cracked or crimped.

The usual ingredients in a scratch mixture are cracked corn, whole oats, and whole wheat. Other nutritious grains such as millet, barley, buckwheat, rye and sunflower seeds can be used but are not as readily eaten. Sometimes leaving a different scratch before the chickens a few days will encourage them to try and eventually like the odd grains.

The protein content of equally mixed scratch grains can be figured by referring to Table 6-5. Then divide by the number of grains used to figure the protein content (if mixed unequal, the proportions are broken into parts and then figured). Example for equally mixed grains:

Corn at 8.8 percent protein + oats at 11.4 percent protein + wheat at 10.2 percent protein = 29.14 Then, the total 29.14 ÷ 3 grains = 9.71% total protein.

If 100 pounds of each grain is used, there would be 9.71 percent protein in the 300 pounds of grains.

When scratch grains are fed in combination with the layer mash or pellets, consideration should be given to the protein content of both the scratch mixture and the layer ration so chickens receive the correct amount of total protein.

The layer requirements for protein are 14 1/2 percent, but if a 9.71 percent scratch feed is fed along with this layer ration the amount of total protein is then reduced. Example: Scratch feed at 9.71 percent + layer mash at 14.50 percent = 24.21 percent. The total is 24.21 percent ÷ 2 feeds = 12.10 percent.

With a 9.71 percent scratch feed and a 14.5 percent layer mash, a handler is actually feeding only a 12.10 percent total ration because chickens will usually consume an average of one-half of each daily. This calls for an increase in the protein and other nutrients in the layer ration. This is especially apparent in cold weather when chickens might overeat grains only to acquire extra energy from fat in the grains in order to keep warm.

The percentage of the lacking protein must be doubled and added to the layer mash to make up for protein that cannot be added to the scratch grains. In warmer weather, when chickens are not consuming as much fat, the layer mash protein will not need quite as much protein added because the chickens will usually be eating a slight bit more mash than scratch.

An example of doubling the lacking protein would be: 14.50 percent protein needed (12.10 percent total protein of mash and scratch = 2.40 percent). Multiply this difference by 2: 2.40 percent x 2 = 4.80 difference. Then: Mash containing 14.50 percent protein + 4.80 percent difference = 19.30 percent protein of mash needed (to be fed with a 9.71 percent protein scratch feed).

Now the total ration provides the required 14.5 percent protein. Example: 9.71 percent protein scratch feed + 19.30 percent mash = 29.01 percent. The total is 29.01 percent of both (two feeds = 14.5 percent).

Although chickens will eat to acquire the nutrients they feel they need, they might enjoy eating the scratch grains more because of their texture, and then the nutrients in the lower nutrient mash are not consumed as needed. It does not usually work the other way around unless a pellet ration is provided.

The assorted grains can be easily mixed by hand or with a shovel in a 55-gallon drum by pouring in small amounts of each grain into the drum and mixing a little at a time.

Oyster shells can be mixed with the scratch feed. If the hen's calcium intake has been low or if grit is unavailable because of deficiencies in the layer ration, you might find them scratching the grains out of the pan to pick out the needed oyster shells.

GRIT

Grit is the name given to coarse minerals to aid birds in grinding food for digestion. Unlike mammals, poultry cannot chew food in their mouth because of the absence of teeth.

A chicken does have a tongue—shaped like a thin arrow or heart—that is used to swallow food. After leaving the mouth, the food must first go to a temporary storage area within the crop. From there the food passes to the gizzard, which is in reality a large muscle, situated about midway in the body. The gizzard crushes food into very small particles for further digestion in the pancreas and small intestine that lay directly behind it.

When grit is swallowed it, too, goes into the gizzard with the food. As the gizzard muscle contracts, the feed is crushed against the bits breaking it into more digestible size pieces. Whole and cracked grains need to be broken down more than a fine mash. The need for grit is greater with these feeds.

Most grit particles are indigestible and passed in the droppings after going through the digestive system.

It's more important for confined chickens to be given grit than chickens allowed outdoors to find their own small stones. Chickens raised on dirt floors will find a fair amount of grit but they must dig for it. This will cause the chickens to dig large, unsightly holes in the floor.

Each layer will consume as much as one-third of a pound of grit per month. That is about 33 pounds for a flock of 100 birds.

An occasional shovelful of coarse sand and gravel can be placed in the pens to provide grit needs. This will save an owner of 100 birds about $2 a month if grit is not purchased. Most feed stores sell grit in 50-pound bags. There are three sizes available for different size chickens: starter, for chicks, grower for larger chicks, and the layer size made especially for the adult birds. The right size is important so the grit does not go through the digestive system too quickly.

OYSTER SHELLS

Oyster shells are mainly for supplying chickens with free-choice additional calcium as oyster shells are high in calcium content. Oyster shells are partially crushed in the gizzard where they release

Table 6-4. Common Sources of Calcium and Phosphorus.

Source	Percentage of Element	
	Calcium	Phorphorous
Ammonium phosphates	-	20-24
Bone meal, steamed	23-36	8-18
Calcite grit	34	-
Deflourinated phosphates	30-36	14-18
Dicalcium-monocalcium phosphates	15-23	18.5-23
Dicalcium phosphate	24-26	18-22
Fish meals	2-14	2-7
Limestone	38	-
Meat and bone meals	4-14	2-7.5
Oyster shell	38	-
Phosphoric acid	-	23-24
Sodium phosphates	-	25-26

Courtesy of International Minerals and Chemical Corporation (IMC).

calcium to later be absorbed in the body's system. The shells are to be used as a supplement only and not as the sole source of calcium in a diet. The shells are fed free choice by the handler. Other forms of calcium are ground into the feed. See Table 6-4.

Many handlers believe the more calcium the better the egg shells will be. This is not true. Chickens can receive too much calcium. This is why excess calcium should not be ground into the feed.

Because chickens will consume the right amount of calcium if a supplement of shells is provided, there is no need to provide excess calcium in the mash. This can cause birds to overeat their calcium needs, and that can cause problems such as nephrosis, visceral gout, deposits in the kidney duct, and bad shells.

HOME-MIX RATIONS

Most handlers are interested in saving money on feed costs. This should not be done at the expense of nutrition because the chickens will suffer and so will you when you're not collecting eggs.

Nutritious feed formulas can be ground from your own grains or grains purchased. Also, the grains must be obtained at a very reasonable price to make the effort worthwhile. It will not pay unless a handler uses at least a half ton every four to six weeks because many nutrients are lost during prolonged storage even when antioxidation compounds are used. This means a flock of about 100 to 125 birds would be needed to consume this amount of feed.

If scratch feed is also fed, a mash will have to be stored even longer with this size flock. Be sure storage containers are air tight. Do not store mash in feed bags because both air and rodents will get at feed. Store in wood or metal bins or drums with tight fitting lids (Fig. 6-1). Be sure grains purchased have been thoroughly dried for storage and grinding or you'll end up with toxic molds in the damp feed and it will have to be destroyed.

Knowing the farmer you purchase the grains from should avoid some problems. Ask if the particular grain involved has been dried in a grain dryer. If not, and if you are not sure of the reputation of the farmer, it's usually better to purchase elsewhere. It's no fun dumping a half ton of feed into a compost pile where the chickens cannot touch it.

Feed mills wouldn't dare sell and grind undried feed. Table 6-6 shows weights per bushel for various grains depending upon maturity and dryness. Corn will constitute the major portion of the mash. The next largest portion is the protein concentrates.

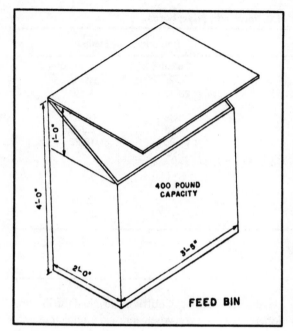

Fig. 6-1. Plan for a 400-pound capacity feed bin to store mash or grains (USDA, Cooperative Farm Building Plan Exchange).

The feed mill will have layer ration formulas for mixing the correct amount of grains with protein concentrates, salt, vitamin premixes, and minerals (including calcium). If you are unfamiliar with mixing feeds at the mill, just tell the sales clerk how much protein you want in the feed and what type of feed it will be for. In this case it is a layer mash. Then let him look up the formula and mix it for you.

It's a good idea to call ahead and get prices of grinding or purchasing grains and the hours the grain can be ground. Don't expect to go into the mill 5 minutes before closing to have a half ton ground and bagged.

You will have to bring or purchase your own bags to take the feed home. Always bring a few extra bags because not all bags are the same size. If you purchase the bags from the feed mill, make sure they are not paper bags that can't be reused. Some mills charge the same amount for these as they do the plastic or burlap. The plastic bags last longest.

The *Pearson's Square* can also be used to calculate how much protein supplement should be used to make a mixture or how much grain should be used. To calculate the amount of grains to use with a protein supplement to produce a desired protein content of a mash, the following steps would be involved in the use of the square method.

☐ Draw a square and put the desired percent of crude protein in the middle of the square (A of Fig. 6-2).

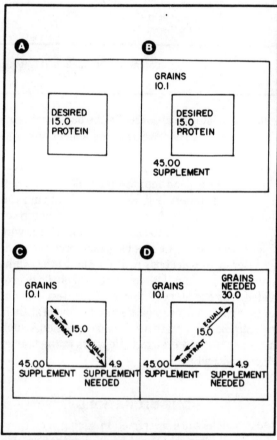

Fig. 6-2. After drawing a square (A) write in the desired percent of crude protein in the middle; (B) the averaged percentage of grain protein goes in the upper left-hand corner with the supplement protein percentage in the lower left hand corner; (C) subtract the grain percentage diagonally from the desired protein in the middle and place answer in the lower right-hand corner; (D) subtract the desired protein in the middle from the supplement in the lower left-hand corner and place answer in the upper right-hand corner, then finish beginning with the last step.

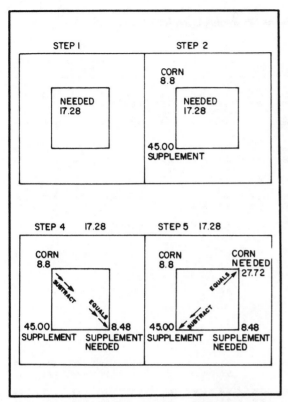

Fig. 6-3. An adaptation of the Pearson Square is used when a certain percentage of some nutrient is to be added to a fixed percentage of one or more ration ingredients.

□ Next, place all the feeds into a group, but specify the proportion of each feed in the group. Determine the average percentage of protein in the group by using the protein percentage given for various grains in Table 6-5. Our example would show:

Proportion of corn-5   at 8.8% protein
Proportion of oats-2   at 11.4% protein
Proportion of wheat-3   at 10.2% protein

8.8 + 11.4 = 10.2 = 30.4 ÷ 3 (feeds) = 10.1 average percent protein.

□ Place the averaged percentage of grain protein in the upper left-hand corner of the square and the protein percentage of the supplement in the lower left-hand corner. In this example we are using a 45 percent protein supplement (B of Fig. 6-2).

□ Now subtract the grain protein percentage diagonally in the upper left-hand corner from the desired protein in the middle and place answer in the bottom right-hand corner (C of Fig. 6-2). This amount is supplement.

□ Next, subtract the percent of crude protein desired in the middle from the percent of crude protein in the supplement and place the difference in in the upper right-hand corner (D of Fig. 6-2). This amount is the grain.

□ Add both the grain needed and supplement needed and convert into a per hundred weight (per cwt.) basis to find the percentage of each. Our example would be finished this way: 30.0 grain needed + 4.9 supplement needed = 34.9 total. To convert: 30.0 grain ÷ 34.9 (total = 0.8596 × 100 = 85.96 percent cwt. 4.9 supplement ÷ 34.9 (total) = 0.1404 × 100 = 14.04 percent cwt.

The parts of the various grains to be used as mentioned in the second step are now converted into percentages. In our example there was a total of 10 parts of grain. These parts are divided into the total percentage of grain needed: 85.96 percent grain needed ÷ 10 parts grain = 8.59 percent each part.

The 5 parts of corn would be: 5 x 8.59 percent = 42.95 percent corn (or 43 pounds of corn).

The 2 parts of oats would be: 2 × 8.59 percent = 17.18 percent oats (per 100 pounds of mix).

The 3 parts of wheat would be: 3 × 8.59 percent = 25.77 percent wheat.

On a 1-ton (2,000 pounds) basis, the total percentage figures would be further multiplied by 20 because the percentages are equal to the pounds needed for each 100 pounds of feed.

If a handler wants to find a certain percentage of some nutrient to add to a fixed percentage of one or more ration ingredients, an adaption of the Pearson Square is used. Let's say a handler definitely wants 20 percent wheat and 5 percent of a vitamin-trace mineral premix to be in the final ration. These two ingredients make up 25 percent of the ration (20.0 + 5.0 = 25.0). He will then need to know what combination of corn and soybean supplement

Table 6-5. Composition of Some Feeds Commonly Used for Poultry.

Entry Number	Feed Name Description	International Feed Number[a]	Dry Matter (%)	ME_n* (kcal/kg)		Protein (%)	Ether Extract (%)	Linoleic Acid (%)	Crude Fiber (%)	Calcium (%)	Total Phosphorus (%)	Non-phytate Phosphorus (%)	Potassium (%)	Chlorine (%)
	ALFALFA *Medicago sativa*													
01	meal dehydrated, 17% protein	1-00-023	92	1370	(623)	17.5	2.0	0.47	24.1	1.44	0.22	0.22	2.17	0.47
02	meal dehydrated, 20% protein	1-00-024	92	1630	(741)	20.0	3.6	0.58	20.2	1.67	0.28	—	2.21	0.47
	BAKERY													
03	waste, dehydrated (dried bakery product)	4-00-466	92	3862	(1755)	9.8	11.7	—	1.2	0.13	0.24	—	0.49	1.48
	BARLEY *Hordeum vulgare*													
04	grain	4-00-549	89	2640	(1200)	11.6	1.8	0.83	5.1	0.03	0.36	0.16	0.48	0.15
05	grain, pacific coast	4-07-939	89	2620	(1191)	9.0	2.0	0.85	6.4	0.05	0.32	—	0.53	0.15
	BROADBEAN *Vicia faba*													
06	seeds	5-09-262	87	2431	(1105)	23.6	1.4		6.7	0.11	—	—	—	—
	BLOOD													
07	meal, vat dried	5-00-380	94	2830	(1286)	81.1	1.6	...	0.5	0.55	0.42	—	0.09	0.27
08	meal, spray or ring dried	5-00-381	93	3420	(1555)	88.9	1.0	0.10	0.6	0.06	0.09	—	0.41	0.27
	BREWERS GRAINS													
09	dehydrated	5-02-141	92	2080	(945)	25.3	6.2	2.94	15.3	0.29	0.52	·—	0.09	0.12
	BUCKWHEAT, COMMON *Fagopyrum sagittatum*													
10	grain	4-00-994	88	2660	(1209)	10.8	2.5	...	10.5	0.09	0.32	0.12	0.40	0.04
	CANE MOLASSES—SEE MOLASSES													
	CANOLA *Brassica napus-Brassica campestris*													
11	seeds, meal prepressed solvent extracted, low erucic acid, low glucosinolates	5-06-145	93	2000	(909)	38.0	3.8	—	11.1	0.68	1.17	0.30	1.29	—
	CASEIN													
12	dehydrated	5-01-162	93	4130	(1877)	87.2	0.8	—	0.2	0.61	1.00	—	0.01	—
13	precipitated dehydrated	5-20-837	92	4118	(1872)	85.0	0.6	—	0.2	0.68	0.82	—	0.01	—
	CORN, DENT YELLOW *Zea mays indentata*													
14	distillers grains, dehydrated	5-28-235	94	1972	(896)	27.8	9.2	—	11.3	0.10	0.40	—	0.17	0.07
15	distillers grains with solubles, dehydrated	5-28-236	93	2480	(1127)	27.4	9.0	4.55	9.1	0.17	0.72	0.41	0.65	0.17
16	distillers solubles, dehydrated	5-28-237	92	2930	(1332)	28.5	9.0	4.55	4.0	0.35	1.33	1.24	1.75	0.26
17	gluten, meal, 60% protein	5-28-242	90	3720	(1691)	62.0	2.5	—	1.3	—	0.50	0.19	0.35	0.05
18	gluten with bran (corn gluten feed)	5-28-243	90	1750	(795)	22.0	2.5	—	8.0	0.40	0.80	—	0.57	0.22
19	grain	4-02-935	89	3350	(1523)	8.8	3.8	2.20	2.2	0.02	0.28	0.10	0.30	0.04
20	grits by-product (hominy feed)	4-03-011	90	2896	(1316)	10.4	6.9	3.28	6.0	0.05	0.52	—	0.59	0.05
	COTTON *Gossypium* spp													
21	seeds, meal mechanically extracted, 41% protein (expeller)	5-01-617	93	2320	(1055)	40.9	3.9	2.47	10.8	0.20	1.05	—	1.19	0.04
22	seeds, meal prepressed solvent extracted, 41% protein	5-07-872	90	2400	(1091)	41.4	0.5	—	13.6	0.15	0.97	0.29	1.22	0.03
23	seeds, meal prepressed solvent extracted, 44% protein	5-07-873	91	1857	(845)	44.7	1.6	—	11.1	0.15	0.91	—	—	—
	FEATHERS—SEE POULTRY													
	FISH													
24	solubles, condensed	5-01-969	51	1460	(664)	31.5	7.8	—	0.2	0.30	0.76	—	1.74	2.65
25	solubles, dehydrated	5-01-971	92	2830	(1286)	63.6	9.3	0.12	0.5	1.23	1.63	—	0.37	—
	FISH, ANCHOVY *Engraulis ringen*													
26	meal mechanically extracted	5-01-985	92	2580	(1173)	64.2	5.0	0.20	1.0	3.73	2.43	—	0.69	0.29
	FISH, HERRING *Clupea harengus*													
27	meal mechanically extracted	5-02-000	93	3190	(1450)	72.3	10.0	0.15	0.7	2.29	1.70	—	1.09	0.90
	FISH, MENHADEN *Brevoortia tyrannus*													
28	meal mechanically extracted	5-02-009	92	2820	(1282)	60.5	9.4	0.12	0.7	5.11	2.88	—	0.77	0.60
	FISH, WHITE Gadidae (family)· Lophiidae (family)-Rajidae (family)													
29	meal mechanically extracted	5-02-025	91	2593	(1179)	62.6	4.6	0.08	0.7	7.31	3.81	—	0.83	0.50
	GELATIN													
30	process residue (gelatin by-products)	5-14-503	91	2360	(1073)	88.0	0.0	—	—	0.50	Trace	—	—	—
	HOMINY FEED—SEE CORN													
	LIVERS													
31	meal	5-00-389	92	2860	(1300)	65.6	15.0	—	1.4	0.56	1.25	—	—	—
	MEAT													
32	meal rendered	5-00-385	92	2000	(909)	54.4	7.1	0.28	8.7	8.27	4.10	—	0.60	0.91
33	with bone, meal rendered	5-00-388	93	1960	(891)	50.4	8.6	0.36	2.8	10.30	5.10	—	1.02	0.74
	MILLET, PEARL *Pennisetum glaucum*													
34	grain	4-03-118	91	2554	(1161)	13.1	4.3	0.84	4.3	0.05	0.32	—	0.43	0.14
	MILLET, PROSO *Panicum miliaceum*													

Entry Number	Iron (mg/kg)	Magnesium (%)	Manganese (mg/kg)	Sodium (%)	Sulfur (%)	Copper (mg/kg)	Selenium (mg/kg)	Zinc (mg/kg)	Biotin (mg/kg)	Choline (mg/kg)	Folic Acid (Folacin) (mg/kg)	Niacin (mg/kg)	Pantothenic Acid (mg/kg)	Vitamin B6 (Pyridoxine) (mg/kg)	Riboflavin (mg/kg)	Thiamin (mg/kg)	Vitamin B12 (µg/kg)	Vitamin E (mg/kg)
01	480	0.36	30	0.12	0.17	10	0.34	24	0.30	1401	4.2	38	25.0	6.5	13.6	3.4	4	125
02	390	0.36	42	0.13	0.43	11	0.29	25	0.33	1419	3.3	40	34.0	8.0	15.2	5.8	4	144
03	28	0.24	65	1.14	0.02	5	—	15	0.07	923	0.2	26	8.3	4.3	1.4	2.9	—	41
04	50	0.14	16	0.04	0.15	10	0.10	17	0.15	980	0.7	55	8.0	3.0	1.8	1.9	—	20
05	110	0.12	16	0.02	0.15	8	0.10	15	0.15	1034	0.5	48	7.0	2.9	1.6	4.0	—	20
06	—			—				—							—			
07	2020	0.16	5	0.32	0.32	10	0.01	4	0.08	695	0.1	29	3.0	4.4	2.6	0.4	44	—
08	3000	0.40	6	0.33	0.32	8	—	306	0.20	280	0.4	13	5.0	4.4	1.3	0.5	44	—
09	250	0.16	38	0.15	0.31	21	0.70	98	0.96	1723	7.1	29	8.0	0.7	1.4	0.5	—	25
10	44	0.09	34	0.05	0.14	10	—	9	—	440	—	19	12.0	—	5.5	4.0	—	—
11	159	0.64	54	—	—	10	1.00	71	0.90	6700	2.3	160	9.5	—	3.7	5.2	—	—
12	18	0.01	4	0.01	—	4	—	33	0.05	205	0.5	1	3.0	0.4	1.5	0.5	—	—
13	17	0.01	4	0.01	—	4	—	32	0.04	206	0.5	1	2.7	0.4	1.5	0.4	—	—
14	209	0.07	22	0.09	0.43	45	0.45	33	0.49	1180	0.9	37	11.7	4.4	5.2	1.7	—	—
15	280	0.19	24	0.48	0.30	57	0.39	80	0.78	2637	0.9	71	11.0	2.2	8.6	2.9	—	40
16	560	0.64	74	0.26	0.37	83	0.33	85	1.10	4842	1.1	116	21.0	10.0	17.0	6.9	3	55
17	400	0.15	4	0.02	0.43	26	1.00	33	0.15	330	0.2	55	3.0	6.2	2.2	0.3	—	24
18	460	0.29	24	0.95	0.22	48	0.10	7	0.33	1518	0.3	66	17.0	15.0	2.4	2.0	—	15
19	350	0.12	5	0.02	0.08	3	0.03	10	0.06	620	0.4	24	4.0	7.0	1.0	3.5	—	22
20	67	0.24	15	0.08	0.03	14	0.10	3	0.13	1155	0.3	47	8.2	11.0	2.1	8.1	—	—
21	160	0.52	23	0.04	0.40	19	0.06	64	0.60	2753	1.0	38	10.0	5.3	5.1	6.4	—	39
22	110	0.40	20	0.04	0.31	18	—	82	0.55	2933	2.7	40	7.0	3.0	4.0	3.3	—	—
23	—					—	—	—	—	2685	0.9	46	14.5	—	4.7	—	—	—
24	160	0.02	14	2.62	0.12	45	2.00	38	0.18	3519	0.2	169	35.0	12.2	14.6	5.5	347	—
25	300	0.30	50	0.37	0.40	—	—	76	0.26	5507	0.6	271	55.0	23.8	7.7	7.4	401	6
26	220	0.24	10	0.88	0.54	9	1.36	103	0.23	4408	0.2	100	15.0	4.0	7.1	0.1	352	4
27	140	0.15	5	0.61	0.69	6	1.93	132	0.31	5306	0.8	93	17.0	4.0	9.9	0.1	403	22
28	440	0.16	33	0.41	0.45	11	2.10	147	0.20	3056	0.6	55	9.0	4.0	4.9	0.5	104	7
29	181	0.18	12	0.78	0.48	6	1.62	90	0.08	3099	0.3	59	9.9	5.9	9.1	1.7	90	9
30	—	0.05	—												—	—	—	—
31	630	—	9	—	—	89	—	—	0.02	11311	5.5	204	29.0	—	46.3	0.2	498	—
32	440	0.58	10	1.15	0.49	10	0.42	103	0.17	2077	0.3	57	5.0	3.0	5.5	0.2	68	1
33	490	1.12	14	0.72	0.50	2	0.25	93	0.64	1996	0.3	46	4.1	12.8	4.4	0.8	70	1
34	25	0.14	31	0.04	0.13	22	—	13	—	793	—	53	7.8	—	1.6	6.7	—	—

Entry Number	Feed Name Description	International Feed Number[a]	Dry Matter (%)	MEn (kcal/kg)		Protein (%)	Ether Extract (%)	Linoleic Acid (%)	Crude Fiber (%)	Calcium (%)	Total Phosphorus (%)	Nonphytate Phosphorus (%)	Potassium (%)	Chlorine (%)
35	grain	4-03-120	90	2898	(1317)	11.6	3.5	—	6.1	0.03	0.30	0.14	0.43	—
	OATS *Avena sativa*													
36	grain	4-03-309	89	2550	(1159)	11.4	4.2	1.47	10.8	0.06	0.27	0.12	0.45	0.11
37	grain, pacific coast	4-07-999	91	2610	(1186)	9.0	5.0	—	11.0	0.08	0.30	—	0.37	0.12
38	hulls	1-03-281	92	400	(182)	4.6	1.4	—	28.7	0.13	0.10	—	0.53	0.10
	PEA *Pisum* spp													
39	seeds	5-03-600	90	2570	(1168)	23.8	1.3	—	5.5	0.11	0.42	—	1.02	0.06
	PEANUT *Arachis hypogaea*													
40	kernels, meal mechanically extracted (peanut meal) (expeller)	5-03-649	90	2500	(1136)	39.8	7.3	1.43	13.0	0.16	0.56	—	1.13	0.03
41	kernels, meal solvent extracted (peanut meal)	5-03-650	92	2200	(1000)	50.7	1.2	0.24	11.9	0.20	0.63	0.36	1.19	0.03
	POULTRY													
42	by-product, meal rendered (viscera with feet and heads)	5-03-798	93	2670	(1214)	58.0	13.0	2.54	2.0	3.00	1.70	—	0.30	0.54
43	feathers, meal hydrolyzed	5-03-795	93	2360	(1073)	86.4	3.3	—	1.0	0.33	0.55	—	0.31	0.28
	RICE *Oryza sativa*													
44	bran with germ (rice bran)	4-03-928	91	2100	(955)	12.9	13.0	3.57	11.4	0.07	1.50	0.21	1.73	0.07
45	grain, polished and broken (Brewers rice)	4-03-932	89	2990	(1359)	8.7	0.7	—	9.8	0.08	—	—	0.00	0.08
46	polishings	4-03-943	90	3090	(1405)	12.2	11.0	3.58	4.1	0.05	1.31	0.14	1.06	0.11
	RYE *Secale cereale*													
47	grain	4-04-047	88	2626	(1194)	12.1	1.5	—	2.2	0.06	0.32	0.08	0.46	0.03
	SAFFLOWER *Carthamus tinctorius*													
48	seeds, meal solvent extracted	5-04-110	92	1193	(542)	23.4	1.4	—	30.0	0.34	0.75	—	0.76	—
49	seeds without hulls, meal solvent extracted	5-07-959	92	1921	(873)	43.0	1.3	—	13.5	0.35	1.29	0.40	1.10	0.16
	SESAME *Sesamum indicum*													
50	seeds, meal mechanically extracted (expeller)	5-04-220	93	2210	(1005)	43.8	8.6	1.90	9.7	1.99	1.37	0.26	1.20	0.06
	SORGHUM *Sorghum bicolor*													
51	grain, 8-10% protein	4-20-893	87	3288	(1495)	8.8	2.9	1.13	2.3	0.04	0.30	—	0.35	—
52	grain, more than 10% protein	4-20-894	88	3212	(1460)	11.0	2.1	0.82	2.3	0.04	0.32	—	0.33	—
	SOYBEAN *Glycine max*													
53	flour by-product (soybean mill feed)	4-04-594	89	720	(327)	13.3	1.6	—	33.0	0.37	0.19	—	1.50	—
54	protein concentrate, more than 70% protein	5-08-038	93	3500	(1591)	84.1	0.4	—	0.2	0.02	0.80	0.32	0.18	0.02
55	seeds, heat processed	5-04-597	90	3300	(1500)	37.0	18.0	8.46	5.5	0.25	0.58	—	1.61	0.03
56	seeds, meal solvent extracted	5-04-604	89	2230	(1014)	44.0	0.8	0.40	7.3	0.29	0.65	0.27	2.00	0.05
57	seeds without hulls, meal solvent extracted	5-04-612	90	2440	(1109)	48.5	1.0	0.40	3.9	0.27	0.62	0.24	2.02	0.05
	SUNFLOWER, COMMON *Helianthus annuus*													
58	seeds, meal solvent extracted	5-09-340	90	1543	(701)	23.3	1.1	0.60	31.6	0.21	0.93	0.14	0.96	—
59	seeds without hulls, meal solvent extracted	5-04-739	93	2320	(1055)	45.4	2.9	1.59	12.2	0.37	1.00	—	1.00	0.10
	TRITICALE *Triticale hexaploide*													
60	grain	4-20-362	90	3163	(1438)	15.8	1.5	—	4.0	0.05	0.30	0.11	0.36	—
	WHEAT *Triticum aestivum*													
61	bran	4-05-190	89	1300	(591)	15.7	3.0	1.70	11.0	0.14	1.15	0.34	1.19	0.06
62	flour by-product, less than 4% fiber (wheat red dog)	4-05-203	88	2568	(1167)	15.3	3.3	—	2.6	0.04	0.49	—	0.51	0.14
63	flour by-product, less than 9.5% fiber (wheat middlings)	4-05-205	88	1800	(818)	16.0	3.0	1.87	7.5	0.12	0.90	0.23	0.99	0.03
64	flour by-product, less than 7% fiber (wheat shorts)	4-05-201	88	2162	(983)	16.5	4.6	—	6.8	0.09	0.81	—	0.93	0.07
65	grain, hard red winter	4-05-268	87	2800	(1273)	14.1	1.9	0.59	2.4	0.05	0.37	0.11	0.45	0.05
66	grain, soft white winter	4-05-337	89	3120	(1418)	10.2	1.8	—	2.4	0.05	0.31	—	0.40	0.08
	WHEY *Bos taurus*													
67	dehydrated	4-01-182	93	1900	(864)	12.0	0.8	0.01	0.2	0.97	0.76	—	1.05	0.07
68	low lactose, dehydrated (dried whey product)	4-01-186	91	2090	(950)	15.5	1.0	0.01	0.3	1.95	0.98	—	3.00	2.10
	YEAST, BREWERS *Saccharomyces cerevisiae*													
69	dehydrated	7-05-527	93	1990	(905)	44.4	1.0	—	2.7	0.12	1.40	—	1.70	0.12
	YEAST, TORULA *Torulopsis utilis*													
70	dehydrated	7-05-534	93	2160	(982)	47.2	2.5	0.05	2.4	0.58	1.67	—	1.88	0.02

[a]First digit is class of feed: 1, dry forages and roughages; 2, pasture, range plants, and forages fed green; 3, silages; 4, energy feeds; 5, protein supplements; 6, minerals; 7, vitamins; 8, additives; the other five digits are the International Feed Number.

Entry Number	Iron (mg/kg)	Magnesium (%)	Manganese (mg/kg)	Sodium (%)	Sulfur (%)	Copper (mg/kg)	Selenium (mg/kg)	Zinc (mg/kg)	Biotin (mg/kg)	Choline (mg/kg)	Folic Acid (Folacin) (mg/kg)	Niacin (mg/kg)	Pantothenic Acid (mg/kg)	Vitamin B6 (Pyridoxine) (mg/kg)	Riboflavin (mg/kg)	Thiamin (mg/kg)	Vitamin B12 (μg/kg)	Vitamin E (mg/kg)
35	71	0.16	—	—	—	—	—	—	—	440	—	23	11.0	—	3.8	7.3	—	—
36	70	0.16	43	0.08	0.21	8	0.30	17	0.11	946	0.3	12	7.8	1.0	1.1	6.0	—	20
37	73	0.17	38	0.06	0.20	—	0.07	—	0.11	959	0.3	14	13.0	1.3	1.1	—	—	20
38	100	0.08	14	0.04	0.14	3	—	0.1	—	284	1.0	7	3.0	2.2	1.5	0.6	—	—
39	50	0.13	—	0.04	—	—	—	30	0.18	642	0.4	34	10.0	1.0	2.3	7.5	—	3
40	156	0.33	25	0.07	0.29	15	0.28	20	0.76	1655	0.4	166	47.0	10.0	5.2	7.1	—	3
41	142	0.04	29	0.07	0.30	15	—	20	0.39	2396	0.4	170	53.0	10.0	11.0	5.7	—	3
42	440	0.22	11	0.40	0.51	14	0.75	120	0.30	5952	1.0	40	12.3	4.4	11.0	1.0	310	2
43	76	0.20	21	0.71	1.50	7	0.84	54	0.44	891	0.2	27	10.0	3.0	2.1	0.1	78	—
44	190	0.95	324	0.07	0.18	13	0.40	30	0.42	1135	2.2	293	23.0	14.0	2.5	22.5	—	60
45	—	0.11	18	0.07	0.06	—	0.27	17	0.08	800	0.2	46	8.0	—	0.7	1.4	—	14
46	160	0.65	12	0.10	0.17	3	—	26	0.61	1237	0.2	520	47.0	—	1.8	19.8	—	90
47	60	0.12	58	0.02	0.15	7	0.38	31	0.06	419	0.6	19	8.0	2.6	1.6	3.6	—	15
48	495	0.35	18	0.05	0.13	10	—	41	1.43	820	0.5	11	33.9	—	2.3	—	—	1
49	484	1.02	39	0.04	0.20	9	—	33	1.67	3248	1.6	22	39.1	11.3	2.4	4.5	—	1
50	93	0.77	48	0.04	0.43	—	—	100	0.34	1536	—	30	6.0	12.5	3.6	2.8	—	—
51	—	0.15	15	0.01	0.08	—	—	—	0.26	668	0.2	41	12.4	5.2	1.3	3.9	—	7
52	—	0.12	—	0.01	0.11	—	—	—	—	—	—	—	—	—	1.1	—	—	—
53	—	0.12	29	0.25	0.06	—	—	—	0.22	640	0.3	24	13.0	2.2	3.5	2.2	—	—
54	130	0.01	1	0.07	0.71	7	0.10	23	0.3	2	2.5	6	4.2	5.4	1.2	0.2	—	—
55	80	0.28	30	0.03	0.22	16	0.11	16	0.27	2860	4.2	22	11.0	10.8	2.6	11.0	—	40
56	120	0.27	29	0.04	0.43	22	0.10	27	0.32	2794	1.3	29	16.0	6.0	2.9	4.5	—	2
57	—	—	43	0.03	—	15	0.10	45	0.32	2731	3.6	22	15.0	5.0	2.9	3.2	—	3
58	—	0.68	—	—	0.30	—	—	—	—	3791	—	264	29.9	11.1	3.0	3.0	—	—
59	30	0.75	23	2.00	—	4	—	—	1.45	2894	—	220	24.0	16.0	4.7	3.1	—	11
60	44	—	43	—	0.15	8	—	32	—	462	—	—	—	—	0.4	—	—	—
61	170	0.52	113	0.05	0.22	14	0.85	133	0.48	1880	1.2	186	31.0	7.0	4.6	8.0	—	14
62	46	0.16	55	0.04	0.24	6	0.30	65	0.11	1534	0.8	42	13.3	4.6	2.2	22.8	—	33
63	40	0.16	118	0.12	0.26	18	0.80	150	0.37	1439	0.8	98	13.0	9.0	2.2	16.5	—	40
64	73	0.25	117	0.02	0.20	12	0.43	109	—	1813	1.7	107	22.3	7.2	4.2	19.1	—	54
65	50	0.17	32	0.04	0.12	6	0.20	31	0.11	1090	0.4	48	9.9	3.4	1.4	4.5	—	13
66	40	0.10	24	0.04	0.12	7	0.06	28	0.11	1002	0.4	57	11.0	4.0	1.2	4.3	—	13
67	130	0.13	6	0.48	1.04	46	0.08	3	0.34	1369	0.8	10	44.0	4.0	27.1	4.1	23	0.2
68	238	0.25	8	1.50	1.05	7	0.10	7	0.64	4392	1.4	19	69.0	4.0	45.8	5.7	23	—
69	120	0.23	5	0.07	0.38	33	1.00	39	1.05	3984	9.9	448	109.0	42.8	37.0	91.8	1	2
70	90	0.13	13	0.01	0.34	14	1.00	99	1.39	2881	22.4	500	73.0	36.3	47.7	6.2	4	—

Author's note: ME is metabolizable energy. The "n" means 0-nitrogen (there is no more nitrogen being accumulated than is being lost). For simplification, the calories listed in parenthesis can be considered the same as those for human food although kilocalories is the precise scientific term for measurement. Calories are per 1.1 lbs. of feed, whereas kilocalories are per 2.2 lbs. of feed.

*Nutrient Requirements of Poultry, 8th revised edition, copyright 1984, National Academy of Sciences.

Table 6-6. Bushel Weights for Various Grains.

	lb./bushel	kg./hectoliter
Barley	36-48	46-62
Corn	46-56	59-72
Oats	22-40	28-52
Rye	49-56	63-72
Sorghum (milo)	51-57	66-74
Wheat	45-63	58-81

will makeup the remaining 75 percent of the mixture with a final preferred protein content. (Fig. 6-3).

☐ If a 15.0 percent protein level is desired in the final product, this means there is 15.0 pounds of protein per 100 pounds of mixture. If you want the mixture to definitely include 20 pounds of wheat in each 100 pounds of mixture, this would be 20.0 percent wheat in each 100 pounds of mix. The wheat in each 100 pounds of mix would supply 2.04 pounds of crude protein (10.2 × 20.0 percent).

☐ The remainder of the 15.0 pounds of crude protein needed per 100 pounds of mixture must then come from the 75.0 pounds of corn and soybean supplement. (The remainder would be 15.0 pounds—2.04 pounds = 12.96 pounds).

☐ Now to determine what combination of the 75.0 pounds of corn and soybean supplement will provide the remaining 12.96 pounds of protein needed, you must first calculate what percentage of protein will be needed in the corn and soybean concentrate to provide the total 12.96 pounds of

protein in the 75.0 pounds of feed: 12.96 ÷ 75 × 100 = 17.28 percent protein needed.

☐ Now use the square method previously outlined in Fig. 6-2, except the second step. The conversion in the last step would be for 75 pounds because the wheat and vitamin-trace minerals have already taken up 25% of the mixture.

The final ration would look like this:

Ground corn................ 57.43%
Ground wheat............... 20.00%
Soybean supplement......... 17.57%
Vitamin-trace minerals........ 5.00%
total 100.00%

To check, multiply the known protein content of each ingredient by the amount of the ingredient used:

Ground corn =   8.8 × 57.43 = 5.05
Ground wheat = 10.2 × 20.00 = 2.04
Soybean sup =   45.0 × 17.57 = 7.91
protein 15.00%

There is no protein in the vitamin-trace minerals so these are not included in the protein total.

A calculator will sure come in handy for quick figuring. It sounds more complicated than it really is. Once the basics are learned, it should all come back to you once the square is drawn.

210

Chapter 7

Home Remedies
for Pullets and Hens

Good egg production depends not only on good feed but on good management. Good management includes watching for signs which indicates disease, parasites or bad habits. If any of these gain a foothold, they are always more difficult to correct or remedy.

Part of a handler's daily routine should include inspection of the flock. This does not have to take long. Just glancing over each bird as they walk around will tell a handler if everything is normal in the way they act. Most chickens that are sick or parasitic will sit around a lot with their feathers ruffled out about them as if trying to keep warm. Other signs might include a decline in feed or water.

Always make it a habit to consciously listen to your chickens. Many handlers will go about tending to their flock's needs daily without really listening to them. Respiratory problems can readily be heard when only a few chickens are sick. A handler must be ready to act quickly. Many of the more common dreaded diseases will cause labored breathing, coughing, and sneezing. Any birds found gasping,

wheezing, coughing or sneezing, should be isolated from the rest of the flock and then observed further to determine the problem.

Make the isolation quarters as warm and comfortable as possible. During cold weather, birds in isolation will be unable to stay warm enough without the rest of the flock's body heat. A small lamp can be placed in a small enclosure to keep the sick chicken comfortable. Even a small dog house will do for isolation quarters.

When a diagnosis is made, the handler can treat the whole flock even if they show no prominent symptoms. The chickens in isolation should be treated away from the rest of the flock. When daily tending is done, always tend to the chickens which aren't sick first so a disease is not transferred. Wear separate boots into isolation pens and wash your hands between tending the sick and nonsick chickens. Keep feed scoops, feeders, waterers, and feed separate, too.

If it's a highly contagious disease, it's best to destroy the sick birds at once so there is no chance of infecting other birds on the farm. Incinerating is the best method, but burned carcasses should be kept from wild animals to prevent them from spreading disease.

Further observations when tending the flock daily include looking at their hind ends. A mass of dirty, fouled feathers around the vent means diarrhea is present. Look to see how many others have dirty rears. Compare the symptom of diarrhea with any other symptoms the flock may display. Diarrhea might simply mean the chickens have had to drink water containing bacteria or algae. It might indicate the presence of worms or disease if other symptoms are found.

Sanitizing and disinfecting the drinking water will bring about a speedy recovery when the diarrhea is caused from unsanitary drinking water.

Blinking and glassy-eyed chickens should also be looked for during daily tending. The watering of the eyes can usually be spotted more easily than mucous coming from the nostrils. Mucous from the nostrils will usually show up as dirt caked around the beak's nostrils from dirt adhering to the mucous substance.

Follow all medication directions and precautions carefully and exactly. Wash hands after handling any medication or vaccination solutions. Observe withdrawal times printed on labels. This is the time that elapses between the last dose and the time the birds are butchered or their eggs gathered and eaten. Time is needed to prevent residues of the medication in your meat and eggs.

Most handlers seem to be of only two types. Either they are overly concerned about problems which arise in their flock, or, they could care less. The ideal handler temperament would be midway between the two. When handlers give in to the many anxieties (that can crop up almost constantly while caring for a flock) they are prone to overlook the most important details or problems in exchange for many small ones. These handlers must differentiate between the real and the minor problems to be of service to his flock.

Minor problems are those that can be taken care of by management practices. These include bumblefoot, breastbone blisters, lice control,

periodic worming, and broody hens.

Major problems are unexpected crises that can cause mortality or economic loss. These include cannibalism, frosted combs, egg binding, egg eating, feather pulling, injuries, and disease symptoms.

AMMONIA BURNS (KERATOCONJUNCTIVITIS)

Floor-raised chickens with builtup litter are more prone to ammonia burns of the eyes. Birds will first be seen moving about slowly because of impaired vision. They will be found blinking their eyes. The eyes will be watering and the face will be swelled. On further examination, the shape of the eye will appear to look squinty or lopsided instead of round (Fig. 7-1).

The cause the problem is excessive ammonia gases in the litter. As the chickens scratch around, their eyes and mucous membranes are almost in constant contact with the ammonia in the litter. The cornea becomes ulcerated and the mucous membranes can also be damaged, leading to blindness and respiratory infections.

Old, wet litter should be replaced with good, dry litter and ventilation should be improved to keep litter dry. Feed a Vitamin A supplement (or cod-liver oil) to help heal damage done to the eyes.

AVIAN TB (TUBERCULOSIS)

The organism that causes avian TB is similar to the one that causes TB in humans. It is a slow-spreading disease usually affecting birds over one year of age. A few birds at a time will first lose weight. They will appear unthrifty and their combs and wattles will shrivel and turn pale. Later, birds will have diarrhea and will die. The birds might also have become lame.

The organism is spread through the droppings of infected birds. It can be spread by other animals including rodents. There will be yellowish colored tumorlike lesions in the liver, intestines, and other organs of the body (Fig. 7-2).

There is no known treatment for the disease. Birds should be disposed of by incinerating. Swine, rabbits, sheep, and sometimes cattle can become infected so premises should be disinfected thoroughly and animals kept apart. Further precau-

Fig. 7-1. Ammonia burns from litter cause the eyes to appear lopsided (courtesy of L. Dwight Schwartz, D.V.M., Senior Pathologist, Michigan State University).

tions include keeping poultry litter, feed, and any poultry remains away from swine. Rodents must be kept in check.

BEAK TRIMMING

Egg eating or cannibalism requires trimming the beaks of older chickens. If done with nail clippers, only part of the top beak can successfully be cut off. Cutting the lower beak will cause severe bleeding unless cauterized.

Only about one-quarter of the upper beak is removed with nail clippers. Do not cut past the lighter white area. If bleeding does occur, dredge the end of beak in some thick cobwebs or apply

Fig. 7-2. An Avian TB chicken liver showing characteristic yellowish colored tumor-like lesions (courtesy of L. Dwight Schwartz, D.V.M., Senior Pathologist, Michigan State University).

very firm pressure over the end of the beak until bleeding stops.

The idea of trimming the beak is so there is a slight space between the upper and lower mandible. Then if birds are engaging in feathering pulling, the feathers will thereby slip out from the beak when grabbed. In egg eating, the slight tenderness of a newly clipped beak will really be felt if the chicken attempts to peck open an egg.

Some hens have such a curbed beak that it will be difficult to clip enough of the top of the beak off so both mandibles do not touch in the front center. In this case, a handler can question whether the eggs or the hen are more important. If the hen is a very bad egg eater, a handler can chance cutting more of the beak until the edge of the top of the beak is blunt and not pointed anymore. A pointed beak will more readily break into an egg.

My rule of thumb for a bad egg eater is as follows. If the chicken hasn't screamed, enough of the beak has not come off yet because I want the end of the beak to be tender. Electric beak trimming will afford a more drastic trimming of the beak, with no danger of the bird bleeding to death.

The following information on beak trimming is reprinted with the permission of Lyon Electric Company, Inc.:

Older Bird Beak Trimming

Started birds and layer beak trimming at an older age is usually done on regular beak supports. Selection of the blade used in relation to the birds age is important. The older the bird the heavier the blade should be. As a general rule of thumb, the K blade will perform satisfactorily on birds up to six to seven weeks old. Use the H blade on birds six to eleven weeks old and the S blade for birds 12 weeks and older. When beaks are trimmed on birds up to 12 weeks of age, a variety of methods have been used. Generally, two-thirds of the upper beak is removed but no closer than one-eighth inch to the nostril (Fig. 7-4). If the lower beak is trimmed it should protrude beyond the upper beak one-eighth of an inch. When only the upper beak is removed the lower beak will continue to grow and can become quite long. While this may not be a disadvantage in some cases, it can, if not trimmed become a weapon to use on other birds. Beak trimming of birds over 12 weeks is generally accomplished by removing two-thirds to three-fourths of the upper beak again determined by the birds age and maintaining a distance of up to one-eighth inch from the nostril. The lower beak is cut one-eighth of an inch longer than the upper beak.

On the methods just described, the trimming of the upper and lower beak is done separately. Some poultrymen prefer and report success in trimming both beaks in one operation if the bird is not too old. For this method, the bird is held in the left hand and grasp the neck near the head with the right hand. With the thumb on the back of the head, use the forefinger on the throat to draw back the lower beak and tongue so the lower beak will be cut less than the upper (see Fig. 7-4). This gives a brief choking action, but it is necessary to withdraw the tongue for enough to avoid burning it. Approximately three-fourths of the upper beak and one-fourth of the lower beak is removed.

When trimming older bird beaks, be sure to hold the head square with the blade and operate the foot pedal or power unit so the cauterizing blade cuts through the beak at a constant rate. Avoid burning the tongue. Bleeding can occur if the trimming is done too fast or if the blade is not clean and at proper temperature. Use only the amount of heat necessary to stop bleeding and keep the beak against the blade long enough to cauterize properly.

Fig. 7-3. Part of upper beak to remove on an older bird (courtesy of Lyon Electric Company, Inc.).

Fig. 7-4. Both beaks can be removed if the bird is not too old (courtesy of Lyon Electric Company, Inc.).

Effects of Excessive Heat in Beak Trimming

The costliest error in beak trimming is the use of excessive or prolonged heat, especially when doing severe beak trimming. The heated blade is primarily to cut and sear the surface to stop bleeding. The application of too much heat could result in a ball like growth on the beak that is tender. This can be painful to the bird when eating and drinking and cause the bird to be lost. Never use more heat than necessary to do the job. Some birds are bleeders, and some bleeding is better than unnecessary burning.

BUMBLEFOOT

Bumblefoot is an abscess on the bottom of the foot. It usually occurs in older and heavier birds and breeds. The chicken will usually be found lame because of the tender swelling on the bottom of the foot. Sometimes an open wound will be found. If allowed to remain in this condition, the entire leg may become involved.

The hard core swelling or pus in the swelling must be cut out or lanced. Pressure should be applied to control the bleeding. Thoroughly clean the remaining hole and apply an iodine tincture. The remaining hole can also be packed with an am-moniated mercurial or sulfathiazole ointment.

Prevent bumblefoot by supplying low roosts for heavy birds. Make sure no sharp objects or nails are present where birds can injure their feet. The force of heavy birds jumping from high roosts can eventually cause the bottom of the foot pad to be injured.

CAGED-LAYER FATIGUE (OSTEOMALACIA)

Layer fatigue is a syndrome that shows up as rickets in adult caged layers. In older layers, the cause is usually a phosphorous or Vitamin D_3 deficiency, plus a lack of exercise. The syndrome is found more in hens that are caged singly. If two hens are caged together, they get more exercise just walking about each other and competing for feed. Feed a phosphorus and Vitamin D_3 supplement.

In younger layers under 30 weeks of age, the cause will usually be from a calcium deficiency (especially during high production). If enough calcium is not available, the calcium will be drawn from the bones and the hen will become crippled.

Many times oyster shells are not made available to caged hens because of the single feeder that is used with layer cages. Caged layers are then unable to attain the amount of calcium they need. Layers should always have their ration in the feeders top dressed with oyster shells. Do not add extra calcium to the mixed ration because the hens will be forced to eat, and they will consume too much calcium which will cause bad shells.

Hens will show a speedier recovery if allowed to remain on the floor awhile and especially if the cause is from a lack of exercise. Because caged hens are more difficult to inspect for abnormalities when they walk, it's a good idea to occasionally place a few of them out on the floor if they seem to want to sit too much.

CANNIBALISM

Cannibalism can start any time. A handler might have no problems with cannibalism all through chickhood. Then one day he might come across a pullet who is bleeding near the vent or the top of the wing. He might even find a dead chicken, sometimes with the entire entrails removed from

215

the rear vent area. The beginning of egg laying and vices such as feather pulling can cause cannibalism.

Feather pullers will be seen any time while raising. An observant handler will spot them during daily tending. Many will first be seen purposely bending their heads down, (usually) looking at the vent feathers, then grabbing them and pulling. These vent fluff feathers are easier to pull out and feather pullers know this. Some may go after tail feathers. All feather pullers should be severely debeaked so feathers cannot be grabbed. If allowed to continue, others will join the vice. When feathers are removed, blood usually comes from the hole where the feather was attached. This blood is then pecked at by everyone, and cannibalism results.

When birds are beginning to lay, the first eggs passing through the vent will sometimes cause the vent to tear slightly, causing some blood to appear. This is readily spotted by the other hens who then begin to peck at the blood. The pecking can continue until the entire rear end is pecked out and the entrails pulled out and eaten.

Occasionally a predator might gain access to a few of the chickens and only injure them enough to cause them to bleed. The rest of the flock will then pick on the injured birds.

If you know cannibalism is somewhere in your flock, the culprits can be found by watching the chickens. Sometimes the culprits will not do a thing unless the handler is not in sight. You might even have to spy on them through a small hole in the building wall.

You'll find the problem is actually only caused by a few, or maybe just one, hen in the entire flock. Once she is found and either eliminated or has had her beak clipped, the problem is rectified.

If cannibalism is a result of egg production beginning, a handler can only try to spot bleeding vents. Sometimes chickens being pecked on will be found trying to hide from the others. Always look for and inspect hens (or roosters) who seem as though they are trying to hide under nests or feeders.

Chickens that are pecked on should have their wounds sprayed with a blue wound dressing and allowed to heal a few days before being placed back into flock. To find out if there are chronic troublemakers, spray the backs of those seen pecking vents with the blue methyl violet antiseptic spray or gentian violet. In this way you can tell who is doing it more often.

There are ways to help prevent cannibalism in older chickens. A handler can keep the building darkened when laying is about to begin. Not dark but only darkened.

Excessive wheat can sometimes cause chickens to turn cannibalistic. If you're feeding quite a bit of wheat in the scratch feed, try omitting the wheat for a couple of days. This sometimes works.

Chickens can become bored and begin to peck when there is not much to do or a ration is not interesting. Do not crowd birds. Provide plenty of roosts, feeders, and waterers. Feed an assorted ration that appears different in consistency, texture, and various grains. A good scratch feed, available grit, oyster shells, and, a mash or crumble ration will keep the birds' interest in feed. If cannibalism is a problem, treating the birds daily for a while with a wet mash or hot potatoes can turn their interest around.

Handlers will find most cannibalism will occur with white feathered breeds. This is because blood and bits of feed show up more, readily than on dark-feathered chickens. Also see Sodium Deficiency symptom in Table 3-8.

CORYZA (ROUP, COLD)

Coryza is an infection of the upper respiratory tract that involves the sinuses, nostrils, and windpipe. It most commonly affects chickens 14 weeks of age and older. It is spread from bird to bird, with recovered birds acting as carriers.

Spreading is through the feed and water. The bacteria cannot live outside the body and will die at a 72 degree Fahrenheit (22.22 degree C.) temperature if exposed for four days.

Symptoms include a swelled face and difficult breathing. Eyes may water if the symptoms are long standing (Fig. 7-5). There will be an offensive-smelling discharge stuck to the nostrils that will usually have dirt adhered to it (Fig. 7-6). Birds will

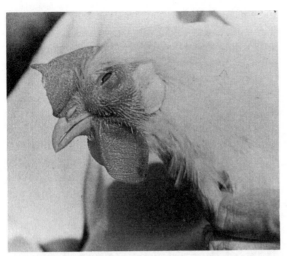

Fig. 7-5. A long-standing case of Infectious Coryza showing swelled face and watery eyes (courtesy of L. Dwight Schwartz, D.V.M., Senior Pathologist, Michigan State University).

consume less feed and water and reduce egg production. There is sometimes diarrhea. Young, growing chickens will become stunted in growth.

The course of the disease might be a few days to as many as three months. Mortality is usually about 20 percent of the flock or less.

Treat with Agribon (sulfadimethoxine) or sodium sulfathiazole. If unavailable or results are not seen, use sulfamerazine, sulfamethazine, or Gallimycin (erythromycin). The sulfa drugs are not FDA approved for pullets over 16 weeks of age or for chickens that produce eggs for human consumption. Observe all warnings and withdrawal times on labels.

Most outbreaks first occur because of a handler mixing other flocks in with his. Once an outbreak occurs, future flocks should be given the coryza vaccine. It is expensive so it's better to prevent outbreaks from occurring through good management practices.

Small flocks can further be treated by washing the crusts formations from eyes and nostrils with a sterile boric acid solution. Dry thoroughly and apply Argyrol (10 percent solution) directly into the nostrils of the birds for a nonirritating antiseptic. Keep birds as warm as possible.

EGG BINDING (IMPACTED OVIDUCT)

Binding does not happen too often. If it is found early, treatment will be needed to save the hen. If a hen is found to be straining and her abdomen is large and distended, the oviduct is blocked. This is caused by a weakness of the oviduct muscles or when it becomes twisted and the eggs cannot move down the tract. The fluid part of the obstructed eggs is reabsorbed and the solid parts of the eggs are then left to accumulate and block the oviduct. If not treated, the hen usually will die.

Lubricate the vent with petroleum jelly. Then gently manipulate the abdomen where a hardness can be felt from the obstruction. If the eggs will not move down, use a syringe filled with mineral oil to lubricate the tract. Holding the hen with the vent facing up, very slowly release the oil into the vent. Hold the hen in this position for at least five minutes so oil can work it's way down the tract. Then turn hen right side up and gently manipulate the egg mass out toward the vent area.

EGG EATING

If the flock is not watched, severe egg eating will develop. Severe can mean most of the flock engage in the vice of eating eggs. Even just one egg eater will do away with a half a dozen of eggs or more per day! Because this bad habit will be picked up by others, it must be noticed and cured as quickly as the handler can be made aware of the problem.

Fig. 7-6. In Infectious Coryza, discharge from the nostrils will cause dirt to adhere around the nostrils and beak.

This is where production records come in handy. As soon as a substantial drop in regular production is noticed, the handler can scrutinize the entire flock.

Egg eaters are adept at their habit. They will peek into open nests and devour the eggs totally so that not one piece of shell or yolk can be found as evidence. When the habit is just beginning, the inexperienced egg eaters will sometimes be found with yolk smeared over their beak and head. As the habit goes on, even this will not be evidenced. A handler must look for clues.

Because egg eating is usually started with eggs the hens find on the floor, every effort must be made to prevent hens from laying floor eggs. The best procedure to discourage this is to not provide comfortable inviting corners and cubby holes. Keep equipment out in the open so little nooks are not unintentionally made. Keep nests and feeders either low enough or high enough so that hens are discouraged from nesting under them. Remove all litter for a few days until chickens use the nests continually instead of the floor.

Advanced egg eaters can be seen walking along perches attached to nests purposely looking for eggs to eat. This is why curtains should be placed over nest openings. Don't worry, layers will push the curtains aside to enter and lay eggs.

A handler can lay, not throw, an egg in the center of the pen to find out how bad the problem is. If many go after the egg and actually eat it . . it's bad.

When egg eating is a problem, the building should be darkened by using 15- or 25-watt bulbs during supplemented lighting. Windows should be draped with burlap bags so bright sunlight does not filter into the building. Most Vitamin D from the sunlight is screened out when the rays go through objects such as windows. If a handler is worried about sunlight procuring the chickens' health, cod-liver oil can be fed in the waterers to replace any vitamins that may be lost. The use of colony nests should help clear up egg eating problems, also.

ENTERITIS

Enteritis is not a disease in itself, but rather a symptom of an infection or parasites that irritate the digestive tract. The irritation will cause diarrhea or bleeding that will be found in the droppings. Coccidiosis, worms and bacteria, usually salmonella type bacteria, are the usual causes.

When simple enteritis breaks out, try sanitizing the water first with potassium permanganate or vinegar. The potassium permanganate solution is made by dissolving 1 small 300 mg. tablet in a quart of very hot water. It dissolves very slowly so make this stock solution a few hours ahead. Then place a couple teaspoons of this solution into each 2 gallons drinking water. Vinegar will work fast. Place about 1/4 cup of vinegar into each gallon of drinking water the first day. The second and third day about 1/4 cup of vinegar to every 2 gallons of water is used. Simple enteritis is usually cleared up in a couple days.

If infection does persists, try to identify the cause. Drugs can be used such as nitrofurans, enteric sulfa drugs, neomycin, penicillin-streptomycin, and bacitracin. Do not add disinfectants to drinking water when medicating as it will affect the action of the drugs.

Continue to keep waterers disinfected so the problem does not occur again. Keep areas around waterers dry.

FOWL POX

There are two forms of lesions produced with Fowl Pox: dry form and wet form. The dry form involves raised wartlike lesions on the unfeathered part of the chicken such as the vent, legs, comb and wattles (Fig. 7-7). Lesions of the wet form are contained in the mouth, upper throat, sinuses, and nasal passages.

Mosquitoes are the primary source of infection although Fowl Pox is also passed in the air. Each lesion represents a bite from an infective mosquito. Mosquitoes become infected from biting infected birds. This slow-spreading viral disease is said to be one of the oldest poultry diseases found, and it is distributed worldwide.

As lesions are formed, they dry and form scabs that eventually fall off and leave bleeding areas. Other symptoms will be an unthriftiness, retarded

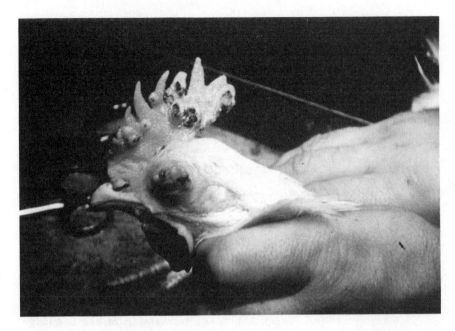

Fig. 7-7. Wartlike lesions on the unfeathered parts of a chicken with Fowl Pox (courtesy of L. Dwight Schwartz, D.V.M., Senior Pathologist, Michigan State University).

growth, any a drop in production.

Treatment consists of vaccinating with fowl pox vaccine. Small-flock owners can treat lesions with silver nitrate. An antibiotic should be used in the drinking water for about three days. Argyrol can be placed in the nostrils of chickens who have the wet form of the pox, make sure the bird's head is held back long enough to allow the antiseptic to reach lesions in the throat.

Prevention can be had by vaccinating birds at one day of age and again at nine weeks of age. If pullets are purchased, they should be vaccinated at 10 to 12 weeks of age.

LACERATIONS

Chickens can occasionally get hurt and cut on sharp objects such as metal feeders and nails. The wounds should be sprayed with blue methyl violet antiseptic. Small cuts that are not bleeding pro-fusely will dry quickly and the birds can be placed back into the flock almost immediately. Very open wounds where the skin is missing will require that the bird be placed in isolation until the wound is healed. Then just before placing the bird back in with the rest of flock, spray the wound again. By using the above method, some very large open wounds will scab over and heal quickly without an infection appearing.

LARYNGOTRACHEITIS

This is a highly contagious viral disease that causes labored breathing, with blood in the throat, sinuses, and mouth. Watery eyes will be the first symptom

Fig. 7-8. A bird afflicted with Laryngotracheitis gasps for air because of blocked air passages (courtesy of L. Dwight Schwartz, D.V.M., Senior Pathologist, Michigan State University).

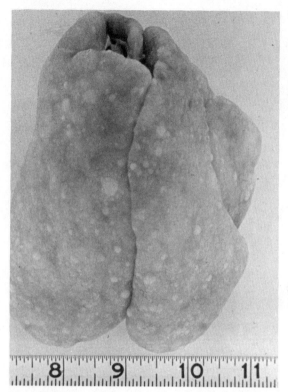

Fig. 7-9. Lymphoid Leukosis is commonly called "Big Liver Disease" because of the tumorous enlarged liver (courtesy of L. Dwight Schwartz, D.V.M., Senior Pathologist, Michigan State University).

noticed, along with a severe drop in egg production. Birds affected will be seen sitting quite motionless and occasionally stretching neck and head out, with mouth open, in order to try to get air through the blocked air passages (Fig. 7-9). There will be coughing and sneezing and shaking the head to try to free air passages.

Spreading is from bird to bird, infected buildings, and infected carcasses. The primary spread is by man as the infection is carried on clothing, shoes, and vehicle tires. Recovered chickens can remain to be carriers for two years. Most birds which die, do so because of blockage in the trachea, which restricts breathing.

Treatment consists of strict quarantine measures. Vaccinate all flock birds, incinerate dead birds, and administer antibiotics. Clean out nasal

passages and place small amount of Argyrol in nostrils. Be careful not to choke birds from the liquid as it passes down the windpipe.

Use eye or nose drop methods to vaccinate 6-week-old birds for prevention. The vaccination is not always 100 percent successful, but it is an excellent tool to be used during outbreaks or when the disease threatens the area.

LYMPHOID LEUKOSIS (BIG LIVER DISEASE)

This cancerlike contagion is similar to Marek's disease. The incubation period takes 16 weeks for symptoms to be seen.

Egg production will stop, and there will be weakness, an enlarged abdomen, and emaciation (with shrunken and pale combs). Later stages will produce a greenish diarrhea. On opening the bird, tumors can be found on the bursa of Fabricius, spleen, kidney and liver causing the liver to enlarge (Fig. 7-9). Other organs might also be affected.

Spreading is by carrier birds, direct contact with affected birds, egg passage, and contaminated buildings and premises.

There is no treatment. Mortality should reach a peak at about three weeks. Do not use birds as breeders to secure hatching eggs. The disease must be distinguished from Marek's, TB, pullorum, Newcastle, avian encephalomyelitis, arthritis, tumors, botulism and cataracts. Prevention depends on good and sanitary management practices.

MITES, BED BUGS, AND TICKS

All poultry can be infested with these pests. Some are bloodsuckers and some burrow under skin and scales. Some live on feathers and some are found in the air passages and organs. The most common are listed here.

Mites. The Common Chicken Mite also called the Red Mite is only about one-thirty-fifth (1 mm) long. It is gray and has eight legs. When engorged with blood, the mite will appear to be a red to black color. It lives in cracks and crevices of the poultry house and only visits the birds at night to feed. Setting hens may be bothered with the mites during the day. An examination to find the mites on the birds should be done at night. Mite masses, excrement, mite eggs and silver-colored skin casts will be found in cracks and crevices in the building walls, ceilings, floors and roosts. Eggs are not usually found on the birds. The mites can remain dormant in an empty poultry house for a half of a year.

Northern Fowl Mites, also called Feather Mites, spend their entire life cycles on the chickens, and they bother them constantly (Fig. 7-10).

Common on wild birds in the United States and Canada, these mites are slightly smaller than the red mites and appear only as dust like particles that move when disturbed. They will bite and irritate handlers occasionally. Thousands of mites will eventually kill a chicken because of the loss of blood.

Infested chickens will drop egg production to 20 percent. Heavily infested roosters will not mate properly. Mite infested chickens have a dull look to their feathers, with soiled and scabbed feathers and skin. Food intake goes down and weight is rapidly lost. The combs will become very pale and dry looking.

The Northern Fowl Mite is one-twenty-sixth of an inch long and is usually dark red to black although this may vary. It can take only 10 weeks for a chicken to harbor 20,000 mites!

The Scaly Leg Mite burrows under the scales of the feet and legs and deposits eggs. Eggs hatch in about five days into larvae then into nymphs and further into adults. The complete life cycle takes only two weeks. The one-one-hundredth of an inch adult can only be seen when magnified.

Older hens can become so infested as to lose toes. Legs and feet become crooked and this causes lameness. The scales of the legs and feet are raised and can become detached easily.

Control of this mite is done by dipping the birds' feet and legs into kerosene, motor oil, or fuel oil. Be careful not to get the oil on the feathers or skin. Dipping will smother the pests by not allowing air to enter in under the scales. One treatment is usually all that's needed. Repeat in one month for heavy infestations.

Bed Bugs. These infest both poultry and humans. Adult bugs are reddish-brown and about one-quarter of an inch long. They visit the chickens at night to feed and suck blood. They can bother a setting hen enough to cause her to leave the nest and she might not return to hatch the eggs.

These pests can survive for a long time without feeding. They like warm temperatures so they are not a problem in cold buildings. The pests may not be noticed until the handler begins itching and

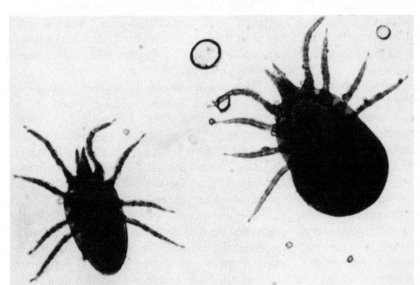

Fig. 7-10. A greatly enlarged view of the Northern Fowl Mite (courtesy of L. Dwight Schwartz, D.V.M., Senior Pathologist, Michigan State University).

develops welts. The bugs appear as flat, oval, wingless insects except when full of blood.

Ticks. Fowl Ticks are also called the chicken tick or blue bug. Adults are flat thin-bodied and oval. They are one-quarter to one-half of an inch long. Only young larvae remain on poultry for a week. Feeding usually takes place in the dark. These pests can live for two years without feeding!

Infested chickens will lose weight, become unthrifty, and produce fewer eggs. The chickens may appear with drooped wings, pale combs and wattles, and a shakiness when standing. Control of all these pests is similar to the control used for ridding the birds of lice.

Because lice and northern fowl mites are on the chickens all the time, dusting the birds is the main goal. The common chicken mites, bed bugs, and fowl ticks must be mainly controlled by dusting the litter and building. Sevin (carbaryl) is the usual insecticide to use for treatment. Period dusting will assure the pests do not multiply to great proportions.

NEWCASTLE DISEASE (PNEUMOENCEPHALITIS)

This use to be one of the most dreaded poultry diseases. Many flocks of commercial and home flocks were destroyed because of this rapidly spreading and contagious respiratory disease. Exotic birds were the main source of infection prevalent in the United States in the early 1970s.

Strict management to prevent the disease from being transmitted on contaminated clothing, shoes, tires, feed bags, poultry crates and equipment will aid to further keep this disease in check everywhere. It is another fine reason for not letting visitors into your poultry pens and yards.

The symptoms appear suddenly and spread quickly through the flock. Birds appear chilled with feathers ruffled, there is a watery discharge from the nostrils, gasping for air, a hoarse chirp and facial swelling in chicks, wheezing sounds, paralysis, twisted necks, trembling and overall discomfort. There is high mortality in young birds. Adult birds will show a noticeable decrease in feed and water consumption and a substantial drop in egg production.

This disease must run it's coarse, about two weeks, but egg production will not begin again for about six weeks. There is no specific treatment. Antibiotics can be administered to prevent a secondary bacterial infection. Increasing the temperature of the building or brooding area will help to make the birds more comfortable.

The disease is passed in the egg but is of no importance because the embryos die before hatching. A vaccine can be given at 10 days of age and repeated at three months of age when using combined Newcastle-Bronchitis vaccine. The usual technique is the eye-drop method. A drinking-water method is available, but will not vaccinate as well. Most 4-H and show chickens are required to be vaccinated by the Newcastle-Bronchitis vaccine.

PARATYPHOID (SALMONELLOSIS)

This can be of significance to the public's health because all animals, reptiles, and man are susceptible. The salmonellae in man is associated with food-poisoning bacteria. It is a blood poisoning disease of chicks that causes symptoms similar to pullorum. There is dullness, chilling, weakness, increased thirst, diarrhea, pasted vents, chirping, and joint swellings.

Adult birds will exhibit diarrhea, emaciation, retained yolk sacs, dehydration, enteritis and a swollen liver, which is pale yellow and contains vary-colored spots. Sometimes the infection will localize in the eye or the synovial membranes.

The organism can be spread through incubators, chick boxes, buildings, feed, water, rodents, animals, flies, and wild birds. Contaminated poultry and animal by-products used in feeds are another source of infection. All types of birds can become infected. Mortality is usually from 5 to 20 percent. Do not use birds that have had paratyphoid for a breeder flock.

Medicate with Nitrofuran drugs, sulfadimethoxine, sufamethazine, or sulfamerazine. Injectable spectinomycin or gentamycin can be used also. Further prevention involves not mixing various age birds or species together in a flock.

Fig. 7-11. To administer any method of vaccine or medication yourself, fold down the wings and place the chicken between your legs so that your hands are free.

Fig. 7-12. A pullet receiving an eye drop type of vaccine.

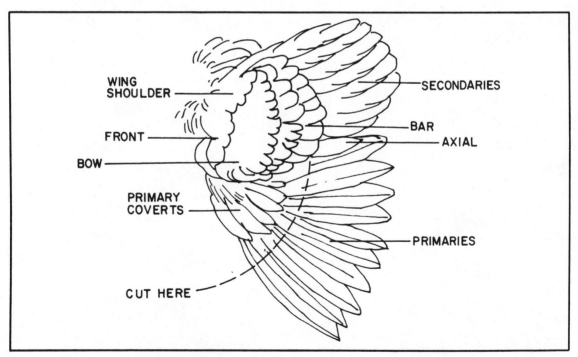

Fig. 7-13. The dotted line indicates where the primary feathers are cut off of one wing in order to prevent flying.

VACCINATING

For handlers interested in a suggested schedule for vaccination, see Table 4-2. If a handler must administer eye and nose drop vaccines himself, it will be easiest if the bird is held between the legs when the vaccine is given (Figs. 7-11 and 7-12). This is also a good way to steady the bird when giving shots or working on the bird's face such as cleaning out nostrils.

WING CLIPPING

Wing clipping involves cutting one row of feathers off one wing. This causes the bird to become unbalanced when flying is attempted. It's usually done to lightweight breeds to prevent flying.

Hold the bird between your legs and stretch one wing out for clipping. It's best to clip the same side wings on all birds. This way if one gets away from you, it will be quicker to tell which one was not clipped among the clipped birds.

Use ordinary scissors and cut off the last row of feathers on one wing only. This will be the largest-looking feathers called the primaries. See Fig. 7-13. One clipping will last a full season.

Chapter 8

Roosters

From the beginning of poultry domestication, with the first jungle fowl in India, there have always been roosters around for practical reasons of reproduction. This does not imply a need to keep them in today's flocks unless breeding is a goal. There are probably as many reasons thought up by handlers for keeping roosters as there are reasons to keep hens.

Something special must have been seen in those first jungle fowl as they scampered uninhibited through forest, plains, and hills. It could not have been beauty, for other birds possessed much more radiant colors. It could not have been for their meat and eggs because the fowl were no bigger than today's bantams and the hens laid only 1 or 2 dozen eggs all year.

Perhaps it was the rooster's spirit that brought the jungle fowl into domestication. Cock fighting was very popular in these Eastern countries even then. Today, there are actually no well-founded excuses to support the keeping of roosters in an adult flock of hens, other than for breeding purposes.

But, we all have our weaknesses.

MEAT

Meat production use to be considered the main reason to keep roosters, but today's broilers have pretty well taken care of this excuse to raise roosters past the age of eight weeks old.

Some 70 years ago, almost every farm kept straight-run flocks using the pullets for eggs and the cockerels for meat. An occasional specimen was kept to breed hens for reproduction because hatcheries were only coming into focus. It was considered a necessity to keep roosters.

Occasionally, today's handlers might desire to butcher and cook only fresh chicken. In this case, a few extra general-purpose heavy breed roosters in the flock will be well spoken for. This is one advantage the general-purpose heavies have over cornish rock cross broilers. The cost would be outstanding if a broiler was fed for five or six months. Roosters cost more to keep than hens because they consume more feed.

FERTILE EGGS

The breeding of hens will naturally necessitate the need for roosters, but unless you're goal is to hatch and sell chicks on a large scale there is no need to keep large quantities of roosters. If the hens are conditioned by feeding a good breeder ration, one good rooster will provide plenty of good fertile eggs from 15 to 20 hens.

The hobby aspect of raising and producing fancy and very good strains of chickens usually requires a couple of roosters for each small flock of each separate breed. Rare, fancy, and good strains of chickens are costly and laborous to produce. The loss of just one rooster can mean the end of breeding one particular strain forever. As insurance, most will keep more roosters than actually needed.

NOSTALGIA AND SHOW

There's a wonderfully nostalgic feeling one gets peering at a partially sunlit horizon while listening to a rooster's crowing as it echoes loudly, then faintly, through a morning of complete tranquility. For a short while we are inspired as we wonder admirably over this creature's enthusiasium and spirit so early in the morning.

Nothing else can take the place of a real country morning that includes the rooster's hearty crowing. For many people, country living would not be complete without a colorful rooster proudly strutting in the barnyard. The characteristics and beauty of chickens has caused many handlers to raise chickens for other than food production.

CROWING

The crowing a rooster creates can be a problem under some circumstances, and especially if there are neighbors who live in hearing range of the crowing. Many people, unfortunately, do complain to handlers about the crowing they hear from a handler's roosters. It seems we can never move far enough away from such people. It can make you wonder why these people move to the country in the first place. In agricultural areas, livestock are bound to be seen, smelled, and heard.

Crowing can begin anytime of the day or night. It is not something reserved for morning. It does not even need to be a bit lighted for roosters to crow. Good crowers can be heard at midnight, 1 A.M., 2 A.M., etc., in a completely darkened building.

Perhaps something wakes them or they're just eager to start the day. I can't really say, for I've never mustered up enough courage to go out and see why they crow so early. As long as the chickens aren't squawking, I can resist the temptation to peek in on them to find out what's going on. If crowing bothers a handler, he's either raising the wrong type of livestock or has kept way too many roosters.

I've heard of roosters being surgically decrowed, but I believe this is as cruel as debarking a dog.

EGG EATING

Egg-eating roosters are not uncommon. Some begin the habit when hens start or they might begin on their own. Floor eggs are always a concern because this is where egg eating habits begin. The same precautions must be taken with roosters as with hens who eat eggs.

Debeaking roosters can cause a problem for breeding purposes. The space left between the mandibles of debeaked roosters can prevent proper mating as the beak is used to steady the roosters. A large space will cause the hen's feathers to slip out from between the rooster's beak as he proceeds to grab hold of her head.

FIGHTING

Roosters are territorial. If another rooster, who does not belong, enters, he will immediately try to show the outsider who's boss. Most fights do not last long unless the roosters are fighting cocks bred for continual stamina and endurance.

When "outsiders" are brought together, there might be some blood drawn and the fighting might intermittently occur for a few hours. Usually neither bird will be hurt badly enough to warrant concern over any fighting.

The time to be concerned is after the fighting

has ceased. Blood resulting from battle wounds can attract the hens enough to begin picking at them. Overpowered roosters can be killed by hens in this manner.

Even if the roosters have been raised side by side in see-through pens, there's bound to be a ruffling of feathers when either one steps into the other's territory. It's much better to introduce the old flock roosters into pens containing only the roosters you want to add to the flock. In this way, because there are no hens to "protect," territorial rights are lessened and battle wounds can heal before roosters are then placed with the hens a few days later.

Occasional fighting between flock roosters begins in the spring and persists off and on throughout the summer. Most fights have to do with breeding "rights." Many times a rooster will immediately attack any other rooster who attempts breeding the hens.

Roosters can be particular as some will attack only certain roosters or only roosters mating certain hens in the flock. This can be a cause of infertile hatching eggs, especially if too many roosters are in the flock.

NONFERTILITY

A handler might believe his roosters are no good if he constantly gets poor hatches. Natural nonfertility is rare even with old roosters. The usual cause is overweight birds who inefficiently breed. Other causes are an incorrect breeder ration or parasites. Feeding a ration for egg production is one thing, and feeding hens and breeder roosters for the production of chicks is another. You not only want the eggs to hatch, but you want good-quality, healthy chicks to hatch. Supplemental vitamins, including Vitamin E for the roosters, will help attain this.

Having too many roosters in a pen of hens can cause many infertile eggs. Hens will hide behind feeders, under nests, and occasionally in nests in order to avoid being bred.

Too many roosters also stir up fights and attacks that in general upsets normal breeding. Roosters will attack other roosters who attempt to breed hens by initially knocking them off before the actual mating takes place.

Because roosters can be particular, some hens are mated continually while some are not bothered much at all. This will cause many nonfertile eggs from some hens. If just a few different pens are showing bad hatches, and all other causes can be eliminated, it could simply be boredom with the hens. Remove the roosters and place them back into the pens with the hens only one day per week. Once mated, a hen's eggs will continue to be fertilized in her body for almost three weeks.

PROTECTIVE INSTINCTS

The same quality of protectiveness admired in roosters can also become a problem. Roosters will alert hens to danger by standing tall and vocally signaling. It seems their "duty" outdoors is to stand guard while hens are busy foraging. Their short low cackle is immediately responded to by the hens who quickly look up from the ground to see what the danger seems to be.

Some roosters are more protective than others and will attack their handler if they even think one of their hens is being hurt. Some will only attack if a flock hen is picked up by the handler. Some protect only the hens in their pen while others will jump at partitions in an effort to protect hens in the next pen. Then there are some compliant roosters who only display excitability when their handler picks up their hens.

I just love the hens who call my bluff. These are the ones who scream at you should you dare to come near them. Their hopeful idea is that the rooster will get you before you get them!

The protective instinct is lessened when many roosters are kept in a flock. Contrary, the older the rooster the more protective he can become. A rooster that never bothered a handler for one or two years might suddenly not want him to handle any of his hens.

Most roosters that attack for the first time cannot be trusted not to attack again no matter what their punishment. Some will avoid attacking often and some stubborn ones attack very often. An old rooster's sharp spurs can be sawed off.

A different coat, hat, or boots worn into a pen

Fig. 8-1. Head of a Single Comb Brown Leghorn rooster (Artist, George E. Howard, Secretary of National Poultry and Pigeon Association, USDA circa 1896).

can startle a rooster enough to attack. The same circumstance can arise when a stranger enters a pen.

If you must keep older roosters, safeguard yourself when entering pens by wearing long pants and sleeves. Always be ready to protect your face when bending down in a pen. Carry a baseball bat with you. Most people impulsively react to a sudden attack by a rooster by kicking out at them. When you're also making sure the kick won't kill the bird, you can stretch and tear ligaments in your leg by the jolt caused by abruptly stopping the swing of the leg. It happens so fast you're totally unprepared to react with caution when using parts of your body to avoid attack. If the thought of using the baseball bat in hand is already etched in your mind, you will automatically use the bat instead of your leg.

Many handlers, I would assume, will laugh at this subject. If they had to try and take care of their flock with a stiff brace worn around their leg

because of torn knee ligaments, they would most likely consider it a relevant and highly indispensible topic.

FROZEN COMBS AND DUBBING

Single-comb roosters (Fig. 8-1) sometimes have their tall, erect combs frostbitten in very cold weather because of the limited circulation in the comb and because it is far from the heat produced from the top of the rooster's head. Hens with large combs usually have no problem because their comb will fall over to the side of their head (Fig. 8-2) where it has contact with the warm surface. Rose comb and pea comb breeds do not have much frost bite because the combs are much shorter.

After the edge (or sometimes almost half) of the comb has been frostbitten, there's not much which can be done to save the looks of the comb. A handler can only try to make the experience more comfortable for the bird by rubbing petroleum jelly into the comb. If it's first found bleeding, an antiseptic such as gentian violet or Argyrol should be put on and allowed to dry before the ointment is put on.

Frozen combs and wattles can be avoided by

Fig. 8-2. Head of Single Comb Brown Leghorn hen (Artist, George E. Howard, Secretary of National Poultry and Pigeon Association, USDA circa 1896).

228

dubbing them. This means to cut off the parts with shears. Game chickens are also dubbed for show purposes. If sex can be determined, day old cockerels can be dubbed. Perform the operation on a warm day or excessive bleeding might occur.

Using sharp scissors to decomb baby chicks, cut the comb off clean and evenly—leaving a line only where comb was. After cutting, lay a clean feather atop the cut surface or sprinkle a little flour, fine mash or, cobwebs over cut to prevent excessive bleeding. Afterwards, an astringent should be ap-plied before releasing finger pressure around the comb area. An electric cautery will avoid excessive bleeding.

Dull scissors, tin snips, or special rounded dub-bing shears are used for older birds when dubbing. A clamp should be applied to the combs of older birds before cutting, and released when blood has clotted. Keep dubbed birds away from others until complete healing has taken place. It will take a cou-ple weeks before the comb looks scab free and smooth.

Chapter 9

The Parts of a Chicken

The chicken has various colored feathers on the outside of it's body to insulate and protect it from the elements (Fig. 9-1). The inside of a chicken's body is unlike other animals who chew their food in their mouth and then await digestion in the stomach. Birds chew their food in their gizzard *after* leaving their stomach, as most digestion does not take place in the chicken's stomach.

As for that "incredible, eatable egg," there are some people who might be turned off to eggs if they knew the actual process to produce eggs in the reproductive tract of a chicken. To fully understand the process is to fully understand the fundamentals of the chicken.

To most consumers of eggs and poultry meat, this information might seem unnecessary to them. To a handler, knowledge of the various organs within the chicken's body will help any handler who butchers his chickens or attempts to examine the parts for symptoms of disease.

DIGESTIVE SYSTEM

Beginning from the mouth of the chicken on down the neck, through the body and ending under the tail, the parts will be discussed in the order in which they are situated throughout in the digestive system (Fig. 9-2).

Tongue. A chicken's tongue is shaped like a narrow, pointed arrow or heart. The tongue is used to manipulate food from the front of the mouth toward the back (in the absence of teeth and lips). The tongue is considered to be an organ.

Esophagus. Feed is first lubricated in the tubelike esophagus which leads from the mouth.

Crop. Feed and grit is delivered and held in storage within the thin pouch that forms the crop about midway in the esophagus.

Proventriculus. This is the actual stomach of a chicken, although most digestion does not take place here. It is a small, widened area only about two inches long at the end of the esophagus before entrance into the gizzard.

Gizzard. The gizzard is actually a pouch surrounded by large, thick muscles that crush food as it enters. The presence of grit mixed with the feed in a gizzard provides extra cutting and grinding ac-

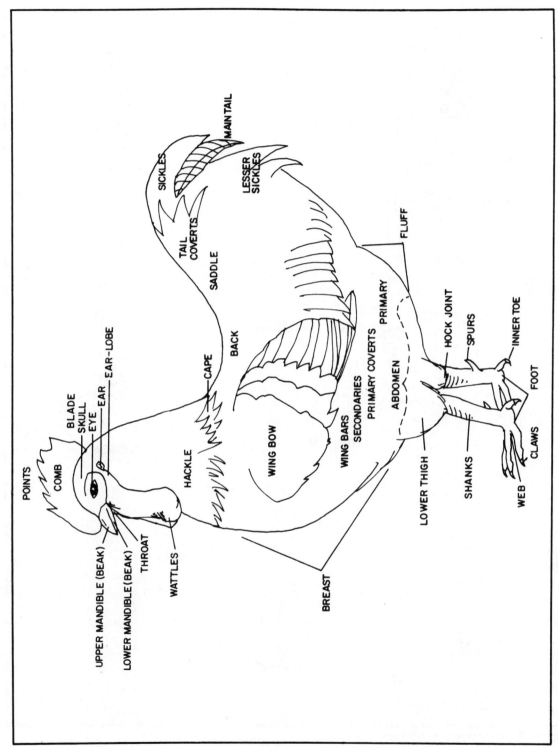

Fig. 9-1. The exterior parts of a chicken.

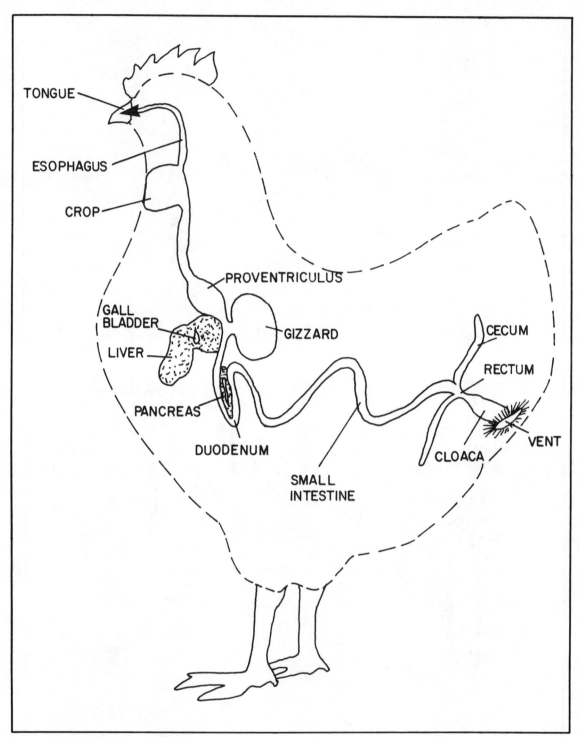

Fig. 9-2. Digestive organs of a chicken.

tion to break down large grains for further and quicker digestion elsewhere. The gizzard pouch is removed from the muscle during final dressing after butchering.

Pancreas and Duodenum. Following the gizzard is the pancreas, a long, thin, flat red liver type of membrane that secretes juice used to neutralize acid secretions and break down proteins, fats, and starches. The pancreas of calves and lambs is used for food and is called sweetbreads, but the pancreas of chickens is too small to have much food value and is not used for food. The duodenum is the intestine that encircles the pancreas.

Liver. Bile is separated from the blood in the liver.

Gallbladder. This is a small type duct filled with the green bile fluid. It is attached to the liver and is pinched off carefully when the giblets are cleaned after butchering.

Small Intestine. This is the area of the digestive system used to absorb the nutrients the chicken eats. Protein is broken down here to form amino acids. This intestine forms an irregular circle with tissue and larger veins connecting and holding the shape. From these intersecting veins, the nutrients are quickly absorbed and carried out

through the body.

Cecum. These are two blind pouches about 4 to 5 inches long and are only attached at one end near the bottom of the small intestine and the beginning of the large intestine (rectum). Most digestion is already performed before reaching this area so their function is neglible.

Rectum. This is the large intestine in the bird. It's length is about 3 inches long and it serves to direct fecal waste toward the cloaca.

Cloaca. The cloaca is where urine is discharged to be excreted with the fecal matter, which is then called droppings. In hens, the reproductive system interconnects here, also.

Vent. This is the opening through which both droppings and eggs are passed out of the body.

REPRODUCTIVE SYSTEM

The actual reproductive system of the hen contains two main parts—the ovary (Fig. 9-3) and the oviduct (Fig. 9-4). Hens contain both a left and right ovary and oviduct but only the left ovary and oviduct are used to develop eggs. The right ovary and oviduct do not function and remain dormant.

Ovary. This is a cluster of round developing yellow yolks attached to the middle of the back

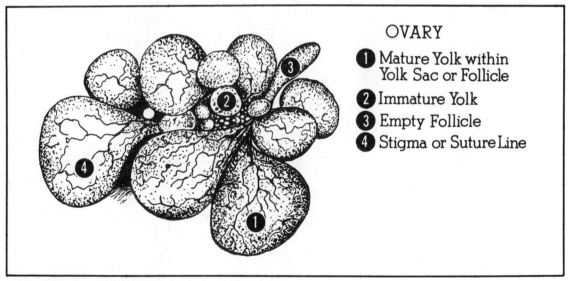

OVARY
1 Mature Yolk within Yolk Sac or Follicle
2 Immature Yolk
3 Empty Follicle
4 Stigma or Suture Line

Fig. 9-3. Cluster of developing egg yolks in a hen's ovary.

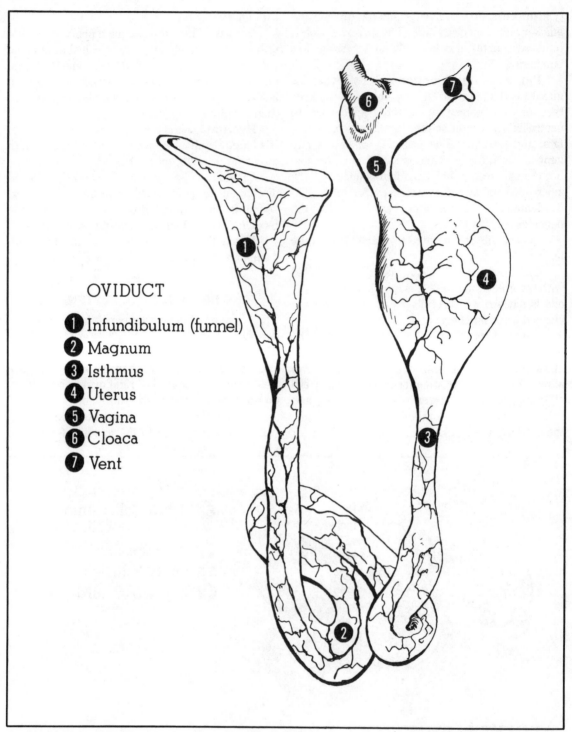

OVIDUCT

1 Infundibulum (funnel)
2 Magnum
3 Isthmus
4 Uterus
5 Vagina
6 Cloaca
7 Vent

Fig. 9-4. A hen's oviduct in which the egg travels and develops.

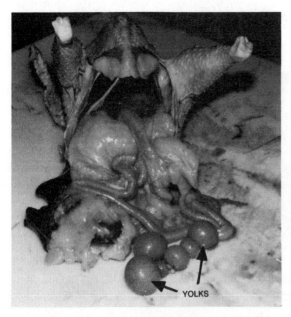

Fig. 9-5. An older, butchered hen showing much fat around organs and various size egg yolks that can be used for cooking purposes if a handler does not want to waste them.

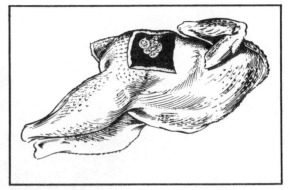

Fig. 9-6. The position of the ovary in the carcass of a hen.

(Figs. 9-5 and 9-6). Even chicks have a small but fully formed ovary with 3,600 to 4,000 microscopic future yolk sacs.

Oviduct. This is a tubelike organ, about 25 to 27 inches long, that collects the tiny yolk sacs when ovulation occurs 30 minutes after an egg is laid. The organ performs five functions before the actual egg is laid.

Infundibulum (funnel). This is the first part of the oviduct, and it is about 3 to 4 inches long. It is here where the small yolk begins *its* journey down the oviduct. Fertilization also takes place here if sperm are available.

Magnum. It takes the yolk 15 minutes to move from the funnel to the beginning of the 15-inch-long magnum. It takes the yolk about three hours to complete the journey through the magnum. Three of the four layers of the white are formed here. Almost all the white's protein is secreted here, also.

Isthmus. This part of the oviduct is about 4 inches long and takes the developing egg about 1 1/4 hours to pass through. Water, mineral salts, and two shell membranes are added here.

Uterus. This wider part of the oviduct is 4 inches long. The egg remains here for about 21 hours. The fourth white layer and minerals pass through the shell membranes by pressure and the shell and it's pigment are added here. The water and solids content of the white becomes equally distributed in the layers of white.

Vagina. This is a 2-inch area in which the egg moves through.

Cloaca. The fully formed egg enters here before actually being laid.

Vent. This is the opening from which the egg is finally laid 26 hours after the previous egg is laid. It is also the same opening from which the bird excretes droppings. *Vent* means a small opening that permits escape, relieves, or unburdens, at the rate of 70 pounds of manure yearly.

Chapter 10

The Egg

Man has found chicken eggs to be a wonderful source of nutritious food and an excellent subject for laboratory research. When a handler is knowledgeable about the egg's structure and its components, he will be able to remedy problems when defective eggs are found.

No matter what shell color the egg has the nutrients are the same. They are formed and produced the same way and their structure and components are the same. A double or triple yolker is actually an abnormal egg.

EGG PARTS

The egg's structure and components protect the developing chick embryo of a fertilized egg. A complete diet is contained within the egg to feed the developing embryo while it is being incubated. The egg is considered to be one of the most nutritious and versatiled foods. It contains about 77 calories.

Yolk (Ovum). The yolk consists of five parts: The germinal disc (blasdoderm), latebra, a light yolk layer, dark yolk layer, and the yolk membrane (vitelline). See Fig. 10-1.

The white germinal disc lies on one side of the yolk. This is where an embryo begins to develop. A tubelike structure extends from the germ to the center of the yolk. The yolk feeds the developing embryo by way of the latebra.

The yolk comprises 31 percent of the weight of an egg. Yolks contain practically all of the known essential vitamins, except Vitamin C. These are iron, phosphorus, sulphur, copper, potassium, sodium, magnesium, calcium, chlorine and manganese. The yolk contains 17.5 percent of the total protein.

White (Albumen). The white also consists of five parts: The chalaziferous, chalazae (kah-lay-za), the inner thin layer, the outer thin layer and the firm or thick layer.

The chalazaes are the two white, twisted cordlike structures that come out from each side of the yolk. They serve to keep the yolk positioned in the center of the egg so the yolk does not bounce around and break. The white serves to protect a

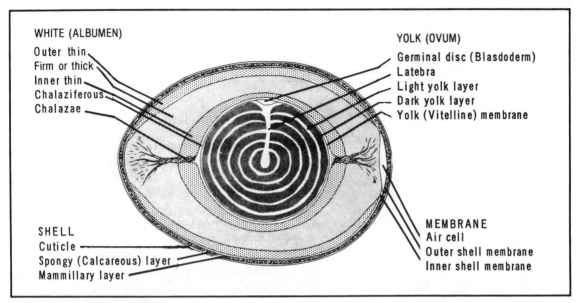

WHITE (ALBUMEN)
Outer thin
Firm or thick
Inner thin
Chalaziferous
Chalazae

YOLK (OVUM)
Germinal disc (Blasdoderm)
Latebra
Light yolk layer
Dark yolk layer
Yolk (Vitelline) membrane

SHELL
Cuticle
Spongy (Calcareous) layer
Mammillary layer

MEMBRANE
Air cell
Outer shell membrane
Inner shell membrane

Fig. 10-1. The parts of an egg.

developing embryo. It also feeds the embryo along with the yolk.

The white makes up about 58 percent of the egg's weight. It is composed mostly of proteins, although it does contain B vitamins, especially Riboflavin, that gives the white a greenish tint. The difference in a thick or thin white is due to the amount of mucin, a protein substance, which the egg contains.

Shell Membranes. These cover the air cell and are divided into two layers of tough fibrous membranes composed chiefly of protein. Both layers are only about twenty-four, ten-thousandths of an inch thick.

When the egg is first laid, there is no air cell. As the warm egg cools, the contraction causes these membranes to pull away from the inside of the egg and forms the *air cell.* Because of the naturally larger surface area in the large end of the egg, the air cell is usually formed here. Odd-shaped eggs or rough handling can cause the air cell to end up elsewhere in the egg.

Shell. The shell is actually composed of three layers and constitutes about 11 percent of the egg's total weight. Just below the *cuticle,* the protective *bloom,* is the *spongy layer.* Below this is the *mam-*

millary or *inner layer.* The pores of the egg go through all 3 layers and serve to connect them (Fig. 10-2). The cuticle has a chemical composition similar to the shell membrane. When the egg is laid, the liquid cuticle covers the egg and fills the pores to protect the egg from contamination and moisture loss.

The shell is about 95 percent calcium. Tons of this calcium are disposed of yearly from households.

HOW TO CANDLE AND WHY

Small-scale raisers who want to market or hatch their own eggs should become familiar with candling methods. Most commercial eggs are graded under the federal-state egg grading service conducted under cooperative agreements between the USDA and one or more cooperating parties within each state where the service is available. The program is supported by the applicant fees.

Some states allow the marketing of graded eggs to retail outlets, on a small scale, if the cases of eggs contain the person's name who did the grading. The individual state department of agriculture must be contacted for pertinent regulations.

Because eggs are not considered processed, they can usually be sold on farm premises requiring no regulations other than the eggs be fresh and wholesome. Meat that is butchered is considered processed and is not allowed to be sold off the farm.

Hand candling is used very little in commercial grading today. Automated equipment and mass scanning devices have replaced manual candling. A candler device must first be made or purchased. A simple candler can be made with a shoe box or metal index box by cutting a 1-inch circle in the top (Fig. 10-3) and inserting a flashlight. A metal index box can have an electrical cord run through a hole in the side, with a lightbulb socket attached.

Compact egg testers can be purchased (Fig. 10-4). Some are wandlike (Fig. 10-5) and can be run over the tops of eggs in cartons or egg trays without removing the eggs. Most are equipped with a low-heat bulb so eggs do not get heated while candling. This can cause sweating to occur on refrigerated eggs. Eggs to be candled and coming from a very cool environment should be tempered in the room to be used for candling with as moderate a temperature as necessary to avoid sweating.

A wand candler can be made by shaping a cone out of cardboard. Place a 1-inch hole in the pointed end and tape the cone securely to the end of a flashlight.

Once your candler is all set up and the eggs are ready, you can begin to candle. Whatever room is used must be devoid of any and all light for proper candling. A small, windowless room with the door closed is excellent.

Simply place the large end of the egg over the hole of a box-type candler (Fig. 10-6). Wand candlers are placed over the large end of the egg without picking them up. Rotating the egg will bring more of the contents of the egg into view.

By practicing candling on different colors of eggs, ages of eggs, and various stages of incubated eggs, a handler will eventually become adept at

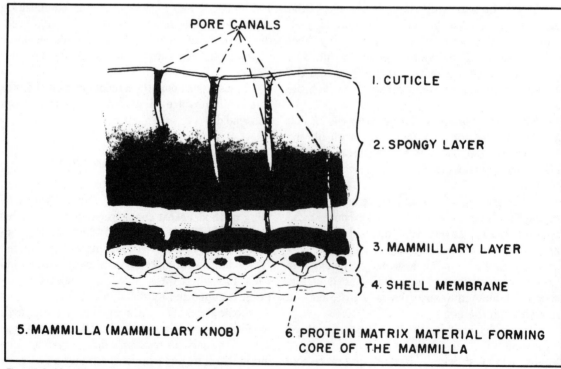

Fig. 10-2. Magnified radial section of an egg shell.

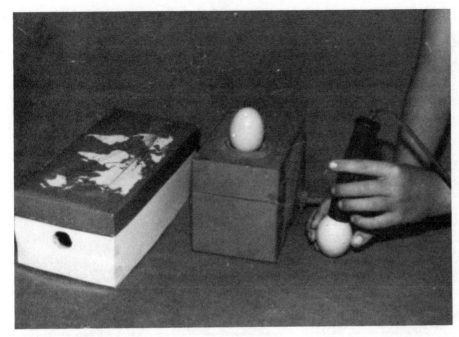

Fig. 10-3. A homemade, shoe-box candler, a metal index-box candler, and a wand candler positioned over an egg.

identifying quality of his eating eggs and incubation stages within eggs.

Abnormalities of eggs can be identified by candling. These include the following:

Double-Yolked Eggs. These result when two yolks are released about the same time or when one yolk is lost into the body cavity for a day and picked up by the funnel when the next day's yolk is released.

Yolkless Eggs. These are usually formed around a bit of tissue that has come off of the ovary or oviduct. This tissue stimulates the secreting glands of the oviduct and a yolkless egg results.

Double Eggs. This is an egg within an egg. An egg goes backwards up the oviduct and the next day's egg is picked up and added to the first egg, with a shell forming around both.

Blood Spots. Red spots of blood in an egg are

Fig. 10-4. A compact adjustable egg candler (courtesy of Lyon Electric Company, Inc.).

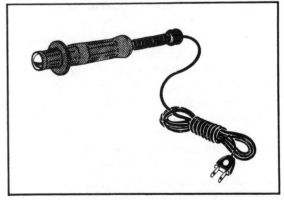

Fig. 10-5. This Cool-Lite tester is automatic, turning "on" when picked up and "off" when laid down (courtesy of Lyon Electric Company, Inc.).

Fig. 10-6. Large end of egg positioned over candler light for candling.

caused by the rupture of one or more small blood vessels in the yolk follicle during ovulation.

Meat Spots. These are either blood spots that have changed to a brownish color from chemical action or are the result of tissue picked up from the reproductive organs during the egg's passage through the oviduct. Frightening the hens is also said to cause meat spots.

Abnormalities that are seen without candling are:

Soft-shelled Eggs. These eggs are usually prematurely laid eggs that have not had sufficient time in the uterus to acquire shell deposits.

Thin-Shelled Eggs. Deficiencies in the hen's diet, including calcium, heredity or disease can cause thin-shelled eggs.

Glassy and Chalky Shelled Eggs. Malfunctions of the hen's uterus cause these conditions. Glassy eggs are less porous, but still won't hatch even though they keep their quality for eating use.

Off-Colored Yolks. Substances in feed affect the yolk color and flavor of eggs.

I once had a hen lay a flat, square egg! The egg evidently broke somehow, being pressed into a square shape when the first shell membranes were being formed. Then the egg continued through the hen's uterus and continued to be covered with shell material until eventually laid. Surprises like this can really make a day more interesting.

EGG BREAKOUT TEST

The first quality standards for individual eggs were developed in 1925. In the early days of the federal-state grading service for poultry and eggs, the work consisted largely of examining eggs and poultry purchased by the U.S. Navy in order to determine compliance with procurement specifications. Grading and inspection service of this type gradually was extended to other government agencies and private institutions that purchased eggs and poultry products.

Research workers and breeders experimented for years on a more objective way of determining interior quality based on the measurement of the height of the thick white correlated with the weight of the egg. Statistical analysis of the quality variation found in eggs from flock of uniform age, managed under similar conditions, showed that a small sample of eggs randomly selected from these flocks each week was highly accurate in reflecting the average quality of the lot.

Based on the extensive research and the statistical analyses, USDA implemented a quality control program in 1959 that involved egg breakout tests. This program made possible the marketing of high-quality eggs from the controlled flocks under the fresh fancy AA label or identification. A program to market grade A eggs under the quality control program was also made available (with less stringent requirements than the fresh fancy or AA program).

A small sample of eggs was randomly selected from flocks under the programs. These eggs were then broken out and the height of the thick white measured with a micrometer (Fig. 10-7) and the reading correlated with the weight of the eggs. This resulted in a Haugh unit figure used to determine the quality of the egg. The higher the Haugh unit the higher the quality of the egg.

While the programs were excellent marketing tools for high-quality eggs, their use was very limited. The fresh fancy quality program practically ceased and the grade A program was not used. Special handling was required for these programs, and additional equipment and facilities were required beyond those for the regular voluntary programs. The use of these programs was restricted

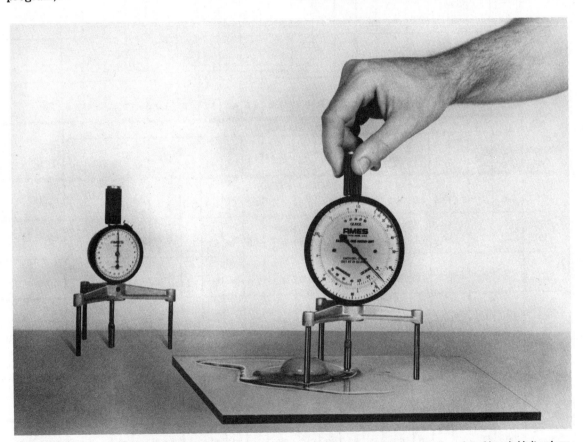

Fig. 10-7. Micrometer (left) comes furnished with a calculator to convert the millimeter readings into Haugh Unit values, as well as USDA and Van Wagenen chart scores. Model positioned over broke out egg on right enables a handler to set egg weight and then read Haugh Units directly (courtesy of B.C. Ames Co.).

Table 10-1. Haugh Unit Conversion Chart.

HAUGH UNITS (MILLIMETERS)

Egg Weight	55	56	57	58	59	60	61	62	63	64	65	66	67	68	69	70	71	72	73	74	Egg Weight
18	2.8	2.9		3.0	3.1	3.2	3.3	3.4	3.5	3.6	3.7	3.8	3.9	4.0	4.1	4.2 4.3	4.4	4.5	4.6	4.7	18
19	2.9	3.0	3.1	3.2		3.3	3.4	3.5	3.6	3.7	3.8	3.9 4.0	4.1	4.2	4.3	4.4	4.5	4.6	4.7	4.8 4.9	19
20	3.0	3.1	3.2	3.3	3.4	3.5	3.6	3.7	3.8	3.9	4.0	4.1	4.2	4.3	4.4	4.5	4.6 4.7	4.8	4.9	5.0	20
21	3.2	3.3		3.4	3.5	3.6	3.7	3.8	3.9	4.0	4.1	4.2	4.3	4.4	4.5	4.6 4.7	4.8	4.9	5.0	5.1 5.2	21
22	3.3	3.4	3.5		3.6	3.7	3.8	3.9	4.0	4.1	4.2	4.3	4.4	4.5	4.6	4.7 4.8	4.9	5.0	5.1	5.2 5.3	22
23	3.4	3.5	3.6	3.7	3.8	3.9	4.0	4.1		4.2	4.3 4.4	4.5	4.6	4.7	4.8	4.9	5.0	5.1	5.2 5.3	5.4	23
24	3.5	3.6	3.7	3.8	3.9	4.0	4.1	4.2	4.3	4.4	4.5	4.6	4.7	4.8	4.9	5.0	5.1	5.2 5.3	5.4	5.5	24

HAUGH UNITS (MILLIMETERS)

Egg Weight	55	56	57	58	59	60	61	62	63	64	65	66	67	68	69	70	71	72	73	74	Egg Weight
25	3.6	3.7	3.8	3.9	4.0	4.1	4.2	4.3	4.4	4.5	4.6	4.7	4.8	4.9	5.0	5.1	5.2 5.3	5.4	5.5	5.6	25
26	3.8	3.9		4.0	4.1	4.2	4.3	4.4	4.5	4.6	4.7	4.8	4.9	5.0	5.1	5.2 5.3	5.4	5.5	5.6	5.7 5.8	26
27	3.9	4.0	4.1		4.2	4.3	4.4	4.5	4.6	4.7	4.8	4.9	5.0	5.1	5.2	5.3 5.4	5.5	5.6	5.7	5.8 5.9	27
28	4.0	4.1	4.2	4.3		4.4	4.5	4.6	4.7	4.8	4.9	5.0	5.1	5.2	5.3	5.4 5.5	5.6	5.7	5.8	5.9 6.0	28
29	4.1	4.2	4.3	4.4		4.5	4.6	4.7	4.8	4.9	5.0	5.1	5.2	5.3	5.4 5.5	5.6	5.7	5.8	5.9	6.0 6.1	29
30	4.2	4.3	4.4		4.5	4.6	4.7	4.8	4.9	5.0	5.1	5.2	5.3	5.4	5.5	5.6 5.7	5.8	5.9	6.0	6.1 6.2	30

Egg Weight	55	56	57	58	59	60	61	62	63	64	65	66	67	68	69	70	71	72	73	74	Egg Weight

HAUGH UNITS

75	76	77	78	79	80	81	82	83	84	85	86	87	88	89	90	91	92	93	94	95	Egg Weight ▼
										(MILLIMETERS)											
4.8 4.9	5.0	5.1	5.2 5.3	5.4	5.5 5.6	5.7	5.8 5.9	6.0	6.1 6.2	6.3	6.4 6.5	6.6 6.7	6.8 6.9	7.0	7.1 7.2	7.3 7.4	7.5 7.6	7.7 7.8	7.9 8.0	8.1 8.2	18
5.0	5.1	5.2 5.3	5.4	5.5 5.6	5.7	5.8 5.9	6.0	6.1 6.2	6.3	6.4 6.5	6.6 6.7	6.8	6.9 7.0	7.1 7.2	7.3 7.4	7.5 7.6	7.7	7.8 7.9	8.0 8.1	8.2 8.3	19
5.1 5.2	5.3	5.4	5.5 5.6	5.7	5.8 5.9	6.0	6.1	6.2 6.3	6.4 6.5	6.6	6.7 6.8	6.9 7.0	7.1	7.2 7.3	7.4 7.5	7.6 7.7	7.8 7.9	8.0 8.1	8.2 8.3	8.4 8.5	20
5.3	5.4	5.5	5.6 5.7	5.8	5.9 6.0	6.1	6.2 6.3	6.4	6.5 6.6	6.7	6.8 6.9	7.0 7.1	7.2	7.3 7.4	7.5 7.6	7.7 7.8	7.9 8.0	8.1 8.2	8.3 8.4	8.5 8.6	21
5.4	5.5	5.6 5.7	5.8	5.9	6.0 6.1	6.2	6.3 6.4	6.5	6.6 6.7	6.8 6.9	7.0	7.1 7.2	7.3 7.4	7.5 7.6	7.7 7.8	7.9	8.0 8.1	8.2 8.3	8.4 8.5	8.6 8.7	22
5.5	5.6	5.7 5.8	5.9	6.0 6.1	6.2	6.3 6.4	6.5	6.6 6.7	6.8	6.9 7.0	7.1	7.2 7.3	7.4 7.5	7.6 7.7	7.8 7.9	8.0 8.1	8.2 8.3	8.4	8.5 8.6	8.7 8.8	23
5.6	5.7 5.8	5.9	6.0	6.1 6.2	6.3	6.4 6.5	6.6	6.7 6.8	6.9	7.0 7.1	7.2 7.3	7.4	7.5 7.6	7.7 7.8	7.9 8.0	8.1 8.2	8.3 8.4	8.5 8.6	8.7 8.8	8.9 9.0	24

75	76	77	78	79	80	81	82	83	84	85	86	87	88	89	90	91	92	93	94	95	Egg Weight ▼
										(MILLIMETERS)											
5.7 5.8	5.9	6.0	6.1 6.2	6.3	6.4 6.5	6.6	6.7	6.8 6.9	7.0	7.1 7.2	7.3 7.4	7.5 7.6	7.7	7.8 7.9	8.0 8.1	8.2 8.3	8.4 8.5	8.6 8.7	8.8 8.9	9.0 9.1	25
5.9	6.0	6.1	6.2 6.3	6.4	6.5 6.6	6.7	6.8 6.9	7.0	7.1	7.2 7.3	7.4 7.5	7.6 7.7	7.8	7.9 8.0	8.1 8.2	8.3 8.4	8.5 8.6	8.7 8.8	8.9 9.0	9.1 9.2	26
6.0	6.1	6.2	6.3 6.4	6.5	6.6 6.7	6.8	6.9 7.0	7.1	7.2 7.3	7.4	7.5 7.6	7.7 7.8	7.9	8.0 8.1	8.2 8.3	8.4 8.5	8.6 8.7	8.8 8.9	9.0 9.1	9.2 9.3	27
6.1	6.2	6.3 6.4	6.5	6.6	6.7 6.8	6.9	7.0 7.1	7.2	7.3 7.4	7.5	7.6 7.7	7.8 7.9	8.0 8.1	8.2	8.3 8.4	8.5 8.6	8.7 8.8	8.9 9.0	9.1 9.2	9.3 9.4	28
6.2	6.3	6.4 6.5	6.6	6.7	6.8 6.9	7.0	7.1 7.2	7.3	7.4 7.5	7.6	7.7 7.8	7.9 8.0	8.1 8.2	8.3	8.4 8.5	8.6 8.7	8.8 8.9	9.0 9.1	9.2 9.3	9.4 9.5	29
6.3	6.4	6.5	6.6 6.7	6.8	6.9 7.0	7.1	7.2 7.3	7.4	7.5 7.6	7.7	7.8 7.9	8.0 8.1	8.2 8.3	8.4	8.5 8.6	8.7 8.8	8.9 9.0	9.1 9.2	9.3 9.4	9.5 9.6	30

75	76	77	78	79	80	81	82	83	84	85	86	87	88	89	90	91	92	93	94	95	Egg Weight

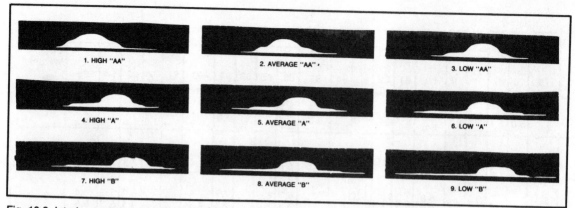

Fig. 10-8. Interior quality of eggs that meet the specifications of the U.S. Standards for Quality of Individual Shell Eggs with respect to white and yolk quality. Scores 1, 2, and 3 represent the appearance of broken-out eggs of high, average, and low AA quality; 4, 5, and 6 represent high, average, and low A quality; and 7, 8, and 9, high, average, and low B quality.

by their cost and the fact that producers and packers did not receive premiums for the product sufficient to justify the costs. Thus the programs were eliminated in 1981.

The breakout method of determining interior quality is a way to fine-tune knowledge with comparisons made with the candled appearance. To be of top quality, eggs must have a high percentage of thick white (Fig. 10-8). A lack of this factor can be attributed to breeding and disease of the chickens, and to improper care of the egg after production.

Shell color and thickness, egg size, quality and quantity of thick white, quantity of eggs produced, and, to some extent, freedom from blood spots are hereditary factors that can be bred into the egg-laying flock. The baby chicks or pullets for the initial flock or flock replacement should be procured from a source that can give reasonable assurance that these factors have been carefully considered in the breeding program. If the strain and breed you have does not measure up when egg breakout tests and candling are compared, you might want to switch to another strain or breed, or think twice about breeding your present flock.

To further measure an egg's quality, in regards to measuring the height of the white as well as yolk and white condition, the following equipment should be used.

□ A micrometer mounted on a tripod, such as illustrated in Fig. 10-7, is satisfactory to measure the height of the thick white. It should be graduated to read in tenths of a millimeter. Another type of instrument for measuring the height of the thick white is also available. It is similar except that there is a provision made for setting the weight of the egg on a graduated dial on the face of the instrument. The instrument is so graduated to get the direct Haugh unit reading (Fig. 10-7, right).

A Haugh unit conversion chart (Table 10-1) is used to establish Haugh unit readings for broken-out eggs.

Application of this chart is simple. After the egg weight is determined and the white is measured, locate the micrometer reading in the proper weight column. The Haugh unit reading is found directly above or below the properly located micrometer reading in the column marked "Haugh Units."

□ A flat glass surface, approximately 12 or 18 inches or larger, should be placed on a frame that can be leveled. A mirror of approximately the same size as the glass is needed for observing the under side of the egg. The frame should be set on a table of such height that the dial of the micrometer will be at eye level when you are using it.

□ A standard individual egg scale is used to

244

indicate the weight in ounces per dozen for each egg.

☐ A breaking knife is very convenient for opening the eggs. Special breaking knives can be obtained from a supply house dealing in egg-breaking equipment.

☐ A squeegee is handy to move the broken egg from the glass surface to a suitable container.

Because top-quality eggs must have normal shells, select good-shelled eggs when obtaining the sample of examination. The eggs should be cooled or tempered to a uniform temperature. It is generally agreed that eggs should be cooled at the farm to 60 degrees Fahrenheit (15.55 degrees C.) or below.

Care must be taken in using the breaking knife so that the thick white is not ruptured. Consistent results can best be obtained by using a breaking knife. Blunt edges, such as a table edge, can cause the shell to splinter, with the possibility of puncturing the thick white. The egg should be held as near the glass as possible and the contents should be emptied very gently from the shell.

In some eggs, the envelope of thick white is rather firmly attached to the shell membrane in the small end of the egg. When this is noted, rupture of the thick white can generally be prevented by slowly raising the half shell. White heights should not be measured when the thick white can be ruptured or when the yolk membrane is ruptured for any cause.

The surface on which the egg contents are placed must be level. One egg at a time should be broken because it is important to measure the white height immediately after breaking. A delay of a few minutes can make difference in the Haugh unit reading.

The micrometer must be checked before using. Set it on the glass and turn the measuring rod down until it touches the surface of the glass on which the broken-out egg will be placed. To be sure that the rod is actually touching the surface of the glass, push the edge of a thin sheet of paper against the intersection of the rod and the glass. The face of the micrometer is then turned so that the indicator will read zero. The procedure should be repeated from time to time during the breaking operation to be sure that the micrometer is properly adjusted.

When determining white quality with a micrometer, select a flat area in the surface of the widest expanse of the thick white for measurement.

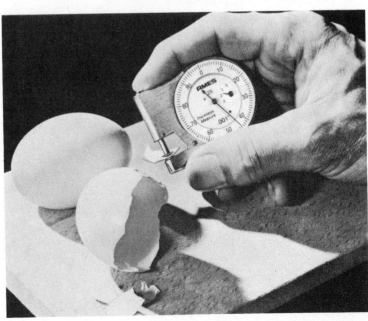

Fig. 10-9. An egg-shell thickness measure with a piece of shell placed between contacts will allow a handler to know when shell thickness is becoming marginal to avoid costly egg breakage. Model shown reads in 1001-inch graduations with a 1312-inch range (courtesy of B.C. Ames Co.).

Eggs with very high whites will not have a flat surface, and in such cases a point about halfway between the yolk and the edge of the widest expanse of thick white should be selected. Care should be taken to avoid measuring areas over an air bubble or chalaza. The measuring rod should be rolled down slowly until it makes contact with the surface of the white and should be raised and cleaned before placing over the next egg to be measured.

Further testing of egg quality can be done with an egg shell thickness measure (Fig. 10-9). A piece of the egg's shell is simply placed between the contacts of the thickness measure. Rounded contacts allow measuring on the curved surface of the shell. The dial shows actual thickness in thousandths of an inch. A metric dial can be purchased instead to read out in hundredths of a millimeter. Most of this type of equipment is furnished with complete instructions for use.

Knowing the exact quality of eggs a flock is laying, will help you determine the very best strain to raise when very high quality eggs are desired. In some areas, a premium price will be paid for eggs advertised as such.

Sources

B.C. Ames Co.
131 Lexington Street
Waltham, MA 02254

Egg scales, micrometers and egg shell thickness gauges.

Brower Manufacturing Company, Inc.
640 South 5th Street
P.O. Box 251
Quincy, IL 62306

Incubators, feeders, waterers, brooders, racks, nests and miscellaneous poultry equipment.

Crow Poultry and Supply Co.
Windsor, MO 65360

Incubators, brooders, feeders, waterers, bands, traps, pharmaceuticals, vaccines and miscellaneous.

Hockman's Inc.
Box 7187Z
San Diego, CA 92107-0187

Pickers, egg washers, candlers, debeakers, feeders, waterers, brooders, incubators, nests, and mills.

Hoffam
Gratz, PA 17030

Feeders, waterers, nests, brooders, incubators, crates and miscellaneous.

Kuhl Corporation
Kuhl Road
P.O.Box 26
Flemington, NJ 08822

Feeders, waterers, nests, brooders, incubators, egg equipment, and butchering supplies.

Leslie-Locke
(Customer Service)
Atlanta, GA 30339

Wind turbines.

Lyon Electric Company, Inc.
3425 Hancock Street
P.O. Box 81303
San Diego, CA 92138

Debeakers, candlers, thermometers and hygrometers.

Marsh Manufacturing Inc.
14232 Brookhurst Street
Garden Grove, CA 92643

Incubators, brooders, and miscellaneous.

Nasco
901 Janesville Ave.
Fort Atkinson WI 53538

Nasco West
1524 Princeton Ave.
Modesto, CA 95352

Shovels, scoops, mills, incubators, brooders, feeders, waterers, nests, butchering, egg equipment, and miscellaneous.

National Band and Tag Company
P.O Box 430
721 York Street
Newport KY 41072

Manufacturers of tags, bands, punches, and applicators.

Omaha Vaccine Co.
P.O. Box 7228
3030 "L" Street
Omaha, NE 68107

Pharmaceuticals, tinctures, syringes, vitamins and insecticides.

Rocky Top General Store
P.O. Box 1006
Harriman, TN 37748

Incubators, brooders, feeders, waterers, pharmaceuticals, vaccines, egg equipment and miscellaneous.

Shenandoah Manufacturing Co., Inc.
P.O. Box 839
Harrisonburg, VA 22801

Brooders, feeders, and nests.

Sidney Shoemaker
P.O.Box 331
Mt. Gilead, OH 43338

Incubators, brooders, pharmaceuticals, vaccines, feeders, waterers, bands, butchering equipment, traps, cage supplies and miscellaneous.

Stromberg's
50 Lake Route
Pine River, MN 56474

Incubators, brooders, bands, traps, and miscellaneous.

Veterinary and Poultry Supply, Inc.
P.O. Box 454
Goshen, IN 46526
&

Michigan Branch
330 E. 40th St.
Holland, MI 49423

Pharmaceuticals, vaccines, syringes, insecticides, tinctures, feed additives, and vitamins.

Warner Corporation
North Manchester, IN 46962

Brooders, feeders, waterers, and miscellaneous.

Glossary

air cell—The collection of air, usually in the large end of an egg, formed as a newly laid egg cools and contracts.

albumen—More commonly called egg white.

Aves—Name given to all birds that are warm-blooded, reproduced from eggs, have body feathers, wings, and a toothless bill.

axial feather—The short feather which separates the secondary and primary feathers of the wing.

bantam—A small version, usually one-fourth to one-fifth the weight, of a standard-size chicken, with some a breed of their own.

bareback—A chicken that has feathers missing from the back because of poor feathering qualities.

battery—Boxlike compartments arranged together to brood or grow out chickens.

beard—On chickens, a protruding group of feathers on the upper throat of some breeds combined with muffs.

bedding—The litter material used under the feet of chickens to provide dryness, comfort, and scratching material.

belling—The procedure of tapping two eggs together to detect hairline cracks by sound.

bleeder loop—Metal instrument which simultaneously lances the chicken's skin and holds a small drop of blood in the adjacent loop for blood testing.

blind check—Fine, hairlike cracks in the shell of an egg.

bloom—Slang for the protective cuticle substance that covers the shell of an unwashed egg.

body check—A crack in the shell of an egg that still has it's shell membranes intact so the contents do not leak.

booster—A feed or mixture fed to chickens to promote or aid laying.

brassiness—Abnormal yellowish coloring in the feathers of chickens, particularly white varieties, caused by overexposure to the sun, diet, or heredity.

breaking up—The act of bringing a broody hen

out of her state of broodiness.

breed—An established group of chickens that have the same characteristics and, when bred, produce the same.

broiler—A young chicken, usually under 13 weeks of age, of either sex, that is tender-meated, with soft, pliable, smooth-textured skin and flexible breastbone cartilage.

brood—The offspring of chickens, hatched at one time and cared for together. Also, the procedure used to protect and keep chicks warm until they no longer need supplemental heat.

brooder—Structure used to artificially heat baby chicks without a hen.

brood hen—A mother hen setting on eggs in order to hatch them.

broodies—Name given to hens that want to become mothers.

brooding coop—A pen or box used to confine a mother hen and her chicks.

broody—A hen and her condition when she is ready to set on a clutch of eggs in order to hatch them.

broody coop—A pen, box, cage, or crate used to break up broody hens.

by-products—A material leftover in the process of producing one thing.

candling—The procedure of using light on eggs to see through it's shell and observe the contents.

capon—A male chicken, usually under 8 months of age, that is unsexed because of having been castrated surgically to keep him tender-meated with soft, pliable, smooth-textured skin.

chalazaes—The two white, twisted cordlike structures that come out from each side of an egg's yolk and help keep the yolk positioned in the center of the egg.

cauterize—To burn or sear to destroy dead tissue when beak trimming to avoid infection.

chick box—A heavy-duty ventilated cardboard box used to ship baby chicks through the mail.

cloaca—Part of the digestive system of a chicken where urine is discharged to be excreted with the fecal matter, which is then called droppings.

clucking—The sound made by a brooding hen or a mother hen when calling her chicks.

clucks—Broody hens.

clutch—More commonly, a nest of eggs, but also a brood of chicks.

cock—A male chicken one year of age or older with coarse skin, hardened breastbone tip, and tough, darkened meat.

cockerel—A male chicken less than one year of age.

colony—A type of nest or cage used by many chickens at the same time.

comb—The nonfeathered flesh on top of the head of chickens that stands out from the head of all males and most females.

concentrates—A reduced volume of protein intensified in the percentage of strength.

confinement rearing—The practice of keeping chickens housed or penned constantly without access to the outdoors.

copulatory organ—The organ inspected at hatching time when vent sexing is done.

coverts—The small feathers on the wing that cover the base of the quills of the primary feathers or on the tail that covers the base of the main tail feather quills.

crop—A saclike structure at the beginning of a chicken's digestive tract near the base of the neck. It temporarily stores and softens food for further digestion.

cross—Offspring of two or more breeds or varieties of a breed that are mated.

crumbles—A type of feed that is the result of taking ground feed and processing it into small granules that small chicks can easily fit into their mouth and assimilate in their digestive tract.

culling—Eliminating undesirable chickens from a flock or brood in order to achieve a better quality flock.

cuticle—The clear substance that covers the shell of an egg as it's laid in order to fill in the shell's pores and protect the contents.

down—The first covering on the body of chicks is soft and fluffy; it is later shed and replaced by feathers. Also, the fluffy portion of feathers near their base called the undercolor.

drawing—The process of removing the viscera from chickens during butchering.

dressed—The cleaning and drawing of a butchered chicken.

dropped eggs—Eggs indiscriminately laid out in the open by inexperienced pullets.

dropping pit—A shallow hole provided under roosts or laying cages where droppings are allowed to accumulate and then are cleaned out.

droppings—Combined feces and urine eliminated by chickens. Manure.

dubbed—The close trimming of the comb, wattles and ear lobes of chickens to prevent frozen combs or for show purposes. Both standard and bantam Old English Game and Modern Game chickens are dubbed for show.

dumpy—Description of young chickens or adult chickens that appear sickly and who sit huddled with heads tucked in toward body with feathers usually ruffled out as if cold.

dusting—The process chickens go through as they stretch and flap wings, tossing dirt and sand over their body to eliminate parasites and soothe their skin. Also, a method used by handlers to powder chickens or pens with an insecticide.

ears—The small openings at the top of a chicken's ear-lobes on each side of it's head and covered by a small wisp of bristly feathers.

earlobes—The bare skin directly below the ears that is either white or colored.

egg breed—Pertains to the type chickens bred exclusively for the production of eggs.

egg tooth—Small whiteish nail-like substance on tip of upper and lower mandible of newly hatched chicks which soloughhs off by the fourth day, used as an aid to chip open eggshell during hatching.

embryo—The early stage of development of a chick inside an egg.

fancy breed—When purchasing, usually pertains to a breed of chicken not commonly found or bred extensively today, although the breed may have been very commonly bred and raised a long time ago.

feather—The individual shaft, partly hollow, from which thin, soft barbs extend to form a flat surface, many of which make up the protective covering on a chicken.

feathered out—The plumage condition of young chicks when feathers have completely replaced their lost down.

fleshing—The small amount of fat in combination with a meaty carcass suitable for butchering.

flights—The long primary feathers on the wing, sometimes manually clipped to prevent flying.

flight coverts—The short, wide, double row of feathers that cover the base of the flight (primary) feathers of the wing.

flighty—Chickens that scamper about and flutter their wings in a nervous manner.

flock—A single group of chickens.

fluff—The group of soft feathers that grow on the underside of the abdomen, thighs, vent and keelbone area. Also, the soft downy unwebbed feather barbs growing at the base of the feathers.

fowl—Usually refers to a full-grown chicken to be used as food.

free choice—Method of feeding grain, mash, grit, and oyster shells so chickens consume the amount they want, when they want, as it is kept in front of them constantly.

fryer—A broiler.

funnel—The first part of a hen's oviduct that takes the yolk down into the reproductive tract for the process of forming the egg. Fertilization takes place here also if sperms are present.

general purpose—breed, variety, cross, or type of chicken that has potential meat and egg production qualities.

germ—The small white structure that lies on one side of an egg yolk. This is where embryos begin to develop.

gizzard—Large muscle situated about midway in the chicken's body and connected to the digestive tract. Helps assimilate digestion by crushing food into small particles.

grit—Small stones, sand, and gravel swallowed by chickens to be used in the gizzard to help break feed into smaller particles.

grower feed—The second type of feed given to chickens when growing them. It contains a lower percentage of protein then the first (starter) feed.

hackle—The long feathers on the neck of chickens.

heavy breed—Standard-size chicks or adult chickens that grow enough meat on their carcass to make them worthwhile for butchering purposes.

hen—A female chicken one year of age or older when exhibiting for show. Otherwise, a female chicken that has reached full sexual maturity.

hen-feathered—A male chicken that has oval shaped (female) feathers rather than pointed (male) feathers on the saddle, wing bows, sickles, and hackle.

hock—The joint that separates the lower thigh (drumstick) and the shank.

holding coop—A cage or pan that is off the ground and used to hold and keep chickens during their fasting period before butchering.

hybrid—Mainly refers to any chicken that is the result of a cross between two or more breeds or varieties.

hygrometer—An instrument that measures humidity in the air of a room or incubator.

incubator—An enclosed container that is artificially heated and humidified for hatching eggs.

insemination—Mainly refers to the artificial injection of semen into a hen, usually done manually with the aid of a straw device.

isthmus—A part of the oviduct in a hen where water, mineral salts, and two shell membranes are added to a developing egg.

keel—That part of a chicken's body which lies over the breastbone.

keel-bone—The long bone protruding from the breast. Also called the breastbone or sternum.

killing cone—Metal funnel used to hold a chicken's head downward, with it's body confined, to restrain it's movement during the killing process of butchering.

latent heat—In ventilation, refers to the usable heat produced by chickens. It cannot be used to heat the air.

layer—A female chicken that is sexually mature enough to lay eggs.

layer feed—Any feed in crumble, pellet, or mash form that has been formulated and balanced for use by chickens that are to produce eggs.

lesser sickles—The long, curved feathers in the tail of a male chicken but excluding the main pair on top.

litter—The bedding material used under the feet of chickens to absorb moisture and provide dryness, comfort, and scratching material.

lopped comb—The single comb of some female breeds that falls over to one side of the head.

main tail feathers—The stiff, uncurved feathers of the tail that make up the main base of the tail.

mandible—Either part of a chicken's beak.

mash—Any feed ground into a fine, almost powdery texture.

micrometer—An instrument used to measure the height of an egg's white as well as the yolk and white condition to ascertain it's quality as an eating egg.

micro switch—Also called a snap switch, used in combination with wafers to regulate the temperature in most small incubators and brooders.

molting—The normal yearly shedding of old feathers before new ones grow in as nature's assurances of a good protective covering against the elements.

mucin—The protein substance whose amount determines the thickness of the white of an egg.

muffs—Found only in breeds that also have a beard and appearing as clumps of feathers protruding from below the eyes and from the beard, over the ear lobes.

multipurpose breed—Same as general-purpose breed.

nostrils—The two openings found on the upper mandible (beak) used for breathing.

ovary—The cluster of small, round, developing,

yellow yolks attached to the middle of a female chicken's back at the beginning of the reproductive tract. Both a left and right ovary and oviduct are present, but only the left is used (the right remains dormant).

oviduct—The tubelike organ of the reproductive tract, about 25 to 27 inches long, that collects the tiny yolk sacs when ovulation occurs.

pea comb—A low comb that comprises three raised rows of very small pea-shaped edges as found on the Cornish breed.

pecking order—The status of each individual chicken within a flock of chickens. Where they stand in relation to acceptance and importance to the others in the flock.

pedigree—A recorded or known line of descent of a breed of chickens.

pellet feed—Feed that has been heat-treated, moistened, and pressed through die molds to achieve a product resembling the form of large rice or small bullets.

pin feathers—Undeveloped or very small feathers that have only just grown out from the skin.

pinion—The section of a chicken's wing past the outer joint. Also, the procedure for removing the outer wing joint to prevent flying.

plumage—The feathers that cover the chicken.

poultry—Any domestic bird that is reproduced, raised and used for their meat, eggs, and feathers.

primaries—Also called flight feathers, the long, outer, stiff feathers of the wing hidden by the secondaries when the wing is normally folded in next to the body.

primary coverts—Short wide feathers that cover the base of the long primary (flight) feathers.

pubic bones—The two small pointed-spaced bones that protrude below the vent.

pullet—A female chicken less than one year old when exhibited at a show. Otherwise, a female that has not reached full sexual maturity.

purebred—Any chicken of a breed with distinguished characteristics maintained by reproduction of the same.

quill—The stiff, hollow base of a feather near the chicken's body. The outer end is called the shaft.

relative humidity—The percentage of moisture in the air as compared with the amount the air could contain at the same temperature.

roaster—A chicken of either sex, usually three to four months of age, that is tender-meated, with soft, pliable, smooth-textured skin and breastbone cartilage that is somewhat less flexible than that of a broiler or fryer.

rooster—Name given to a male chicken when no particular age is concerned. Also, a mature male with coarse skin and tough meat.

roosting—The placement of a chicken on a perch, roost, tree branch, etc., while it is at rest or sleeping.

rose comb—Consists of a solid mass of rounded points, broader in the front and tapering to a pointed spike, that is more pronounced in some breeds.

ruffled feathers—Usually sick, chilled, or stressed chickens that sit around with heads drawn in toward body, with feathers fluffed out about them.

saddle—The rear of back in a male chicken covered by long, pointed, sweeping feathers.

scalding—A process using very hot water to soften and relax the muscles that hold the feathers, for easier plucking.

scales—Thin, clam-shaped growths similar in substance to nails, that overlap each other, shingle-style, completely covering a chicken's shanks and the tops of the toes.

scratch—Chicken feed consisting of various whole and cracked grains. Also, the digging of litter and dirt by chickens.

secondaries—The long, stiff feathers that grow next to the outer primary feathers.

sensible heat—In ventilation, refers to the usable heat given off by a chicken's body and respiration that can be used to heat their environment.

sexed—Refers to chickens that have been examined, and in the process, have had their sex determined.

sex feathers—The hackle, back, saddle, sickles,

and wing-bow feathers of a male chicken that are pointed on the end as compared to the rounded feathers of females.

sex-link—Chick sex can be determined at hatching time by the color or rate of feathering.

shaft—The continuation of the quill of a feather that goes down the middle, from which the individual barbs are attached.

shank—The portion of the leg covered with scales below the hock joint, excluding the foot and toes.

shoulder—The part of the chicken's body where the wing is attached.

sickles—The curved pair of long feathers in the middle of a male's tail on top that are the main sickles. Also, the long curved feathers that hang over the side of the tail called the lesser sickles.

single comb—A fairly thin formation, resembling a half oval with 5 or 6 graduated defined points. Stands erect in males and, depending on breed, erect or looped in females.

slip—A chicken that was unsuccessfully caponized and is then neither a cockerel nor a capon.

slipped wing—A defect of a chicken's wing where primaries do not fold in normally under secondaries or where the feathers overlap in the wrong direction.

sodium silicate—Solution used to preserve eggs by water glass method.

spurs—The stiff, slightly curved protrusions on the inner rear side of the male's shanks that grow larger as the bird ages and can be rounded or very pointed. Occasionally found on females.

stack brooder—Any box type of brooder that can be set on top of each other independently or by the use of a rack.

stags—Infrequently used to refer to cockerels that have achieved pronounced spur and comb development.

standard breed—Any breed other than a bantam.

started pullet—A female chicken raised to 6 to 8 weeks of age.

starter feed—The first feed given to chicks consists of a higher protein content than later feeds. Can be mash or crumbles.

stern—The area in the rear of a chicken that extends from the two pointed pubic bones down to the rear of the breastbone (keel-bone).

stewer—A mature female chicken, more than 10 months of age, with meat less tender than a rooster and with a nonflexible breastbone tip.

stock—Group of chickens from a related strain.

straight run—A brood of chickens that have not been sexed and therefore contain both pullets and cockerels.

strain—Descendants of the same ancestors.

strawberry comb—Similar to a rose comb, but more of an egg shape and lacking the pointed spike in rear.

stub—Show talk for a short piece of a feather on the legs, feet or toes, of a clean-legged breed.

supplement—Anything added to feed or water to make up for a lack or deficiency.

sweetened litter—Bedding that has had the ammonia fumes from urine reduced by the addition of lime.

tail coverts—The curved, pointed feathers that cover the base of the main tail feathers of the male and the oval feathers that surround the main tail in females.

thighs—Includes the lower thigh (drumstick) and the upper thigh, which is the feathered parts of the legs between the hock joints and the body.

throat—The front of the upper neck of the chicken.

throwbacks—Reversion to an ancestral characteristic or breed type.

top-dressing—The actual application or the material placed over the surface of litter or feed.

trance—The mental concentration a brood hen exhibits as she incubates a clutch of eggs.

trapnest—A nest that contains a device to let hens enter but not exit.

tremulous air cell—An air cell in an egg that moves freely toward the top whatever direction the egg is rotated. Usually caused by rough handling.

trio—A group of chickens that contains two females and one male.

undercolor—The color of the soft, downy fluff

portion of feathers that are hidden by the larger webbed portion of the feather as they lie over each other.

uropygium—The bulge from which the tail feathers grow.

uropygial gland—The gland located at the base of the tail feathers which secretes oil and is used by chickens to groom and preen their feathers.

uterus—Part of a hen's oviduct where the shell and it's pigment are added to complete the formation of the egg.

vaccine—Preparation introduced into a chicken's body to produce immunity of a specific disease.

vagina—A 2-inch area of the hen's reproductive tract in which the egg moves through.

variety—Pertains to an established group of chickens which contain different characteristics within a breed.

vent—The opening from which an egg is laid and from where droppings are excreted.

V-shaped comb—Two small projections resembling horns, as in the Polish chickens.

wafer—A thin, flat disk (usually two are attached) to form a 3-inch double disk, constructed of tempered brass and filled with ether. Used to maintain the temperature in smaller incubators and brooders.

water glass—Method to preserve eggs with sodium silicate.

wattles—The thin, soft, fleshy growths on each side of the beak and on the upper part of the throat. Usually larger and longer in males and either of a red or purple color—depending on breed.

web, feather—The outer portion of the feather that is smooth and not fluffy.

web, foot—The small portion of stretched skin growing between the toes.

web, wing—The skin that stretches between the joints of the wing.

welded wire—Fencing material that is spot welded where each wire crosses over each other.

whitewash—Solution made with lime and painted over the interior walls and ceiling of a chicken building in order to brighten, whiten, and disinfect.

wing bay—The triangular portion near the end of a folded wing that comprises the secondaries.

wing bow—The area of feathers, near the shoulder, that cover the bar portion. Also, a mark of color on the bend.

wing clipping—The cutting off of the primaries of one wing to prevent flying.

wing coverts—Two rows of short, wide feathers that cover the base of the flight (primary) feathers.

wing fronts—Small portion of feathers near the shoulder in front of the wing bow.

wing points—The very ends of the primary and secondary feathers.

woven wire—Wire that is weaved to form a fencing without welds.

Further Reading

American Standard of Perfection, American Poultry Association, Inc., Troy, New York. Complete description of all recognized breeds and varieties of domestic poultry. The 1983 edition contains well over 450 color photographs. Although it has mainly black-and-white, and has fewer photographs, I prefer the 1980 edition. It has a complete index that is much easier to use when looking up birds. The 1980 edition also contains a section on the standard color for baby chicks that has been left out of the new edition.

Backyard Poultry, Rt. 1, Box 7, Waterloo, WI 53594. A magazine containing helpful hints on raising poultry.

Bantam Standard, by American Bantam Association, Box 610, North Amherst, MA 01059. Strictly on bantam breeds of poultry. Many black and white photos.

Broiler Raising in Canada, Information Services, Agriculture Canada, Ottawa K1A 0C7. Ask for publication no. 1509. Very good tips on raising broilers.

Egg-Grading Manual, Handbook No. 75 for sale by the Superintendent of Documents, U.S. Government Printing Office, Washington, D.C. 20402. For those wishing to know more about marketing and grading eggs.

Egg Production Tests results currently done by the following: Ms. Patricia A. Dugan, Ag. Test Supervisor, Dept. of Animal Science, College of Life Science and Agriculture, University of N.H., Durham, NH 03824. Dr. Grady Martin, North Carolina Random Sample Laying Test, Scott Hall, N.C. State University School of Agriculture, Box 5307, Raleigh, NC 27650. Mr. Alan H. Bentley, Livestock and Poultry Products Division, Food Production and Inspection Branch, Agriculture Canada, Ottawa, Ontario K1A-0C5.

External Parasites of Texas Poultry, Texas Agricultural Extension Service, Texas A & M

University System, College Station, TX 77843. Pub. B-1088. A good little pamphlet with many black-and-white photographs of parasites that effect poultry in many areas of the country.

Feather Fancier, R.R. 5, Forest, Ontario, Canada NON 1J0. Monthly newspaper featuring history of birds. Basic and advanced articles on rearing and breeding, stock and show advertising.

Hen House Herald, P.O. Box 1011, Council Bluffs, Iowa 51502. Mailed monthly, news and views of poultry, small and exotic animals and fowl, ads for shows, swap meets and ads.

Manual of Poultry Diseases, Texas Agricultural Extension Service, Texas A & M University System, College Station TX 77843. Pub. B-1031. A good, inexpensive pamphlet pertaining to vaccinating, parasites, and disease.

Merck Veterinary Manual, published by Merck and Co., Inc., Rahway, NJ 07065. Contains a special section on treating poultry for disease and parasites.

National Poultry Improvement Plan, USDA, APHIS-VS, Room 828, FCB #1, Hyattsville, MD 20782. For Directory of Participants Handling Egg-Type and Meat-Type Chickens ask for pub. APHIS 91-41. For Directory of Participants Handling Exhibition Poultry ask for pub. APHIS 91-42. For anyone who wants to check on hatcheries in the plan meeting a "U.S. Pullorum-Typhoid Clean" classification. The publications will tell breeds and capacities hatched. Not all hatcheries listed sell retail.

Nutrient Requirements of Poultry, Eighth Revised Ed., National Academy Press, 2101 Constitution Ave. N.W., Washington, D.C. 20418. By the National Research Council, Committee on Animal Nutrition, National Academy of Sciences. Highly regarded, semitechnical information on the nutritional requirements, signs of deficiencies, growth rates, and feed and water requirements of different classes of poultry, with metric conversion table.

Poultry Grading Manual, Handbook No. 31 for sale by the Superintendent of Documents, U.S. Government Printing Office, Washington, D.C. 20402. For anyone needing further information on grading and marketing poultry products.

Poultry Health Handbook, 2nd Ed. by L. Dwight Schwartz, D.V.M. published by College of Agriculture, Pennsylvania State University, Box 6000, University Park, PA 16802. Presently out of print, but a revised edition might be printed. A very good book, in layman language, on poultry diseases, parasites, sanitation, and vaccinations.

Poultry Management Reference Manual, College of Agriculture, Pennsylvania State University, Box 6000, University Park, PA 16802. Arranged in table form for easy reference to hatching, brooding, laying, and eggs.

Poultry Press, Box 947, York, PA 17405. Monthly newspaper containing news and photos of shows across the country, poultry clubs, classifieds and timely tips and advice.

Poultry Times, P.O. Box 1338, Gainesville, GA 30501. A bi-weekly newspaper with a commercial slant, but very interesting and helpful articles and photos any handler might like to read and use.

Index

shears, debeaker and dubbing, 40
shelter requirements for chickens, 112
space requirements for chickens, 112
spurs, 254
stern, 254
synovitis, infectious, 96

T

tapeworms, 107
temperatures, brooding, 29

ticks, mites, and bed bugs, 220
toe clipping as a marking system, 103
toe clipping, manual, 102

V

vaccinating, 103, 224
vaccination schedule, 105
vent, 158, 255
ventilation needs, 124
vitamins, 199
vitamins, sources of, 81

W

wafers, 44
water additives, 89
water glass, 255
water requirements, drinking, 88
waterers, 45, 134
wattles, 255
wing clipping, 224
wings, how to band, 69
worms, 104
worms, cecal, 106
worms, thread, 104

Edited by Steven Bolt

OTHER POPULAR TAB BOOKS OF INTEREST

TAB TAB BOOKS Inc.

Blue Ridge Summit, Pa. 17214

Send for FREE TAB Catalog describing over 750 current titles in print.